REACHING JUDGMENT AT NUREMBERG

REACHING JUDGMENT AT NUREMBERG

BRADLEY F. SMITH

Basic Books, Inc., Publishers   New York

The author gratefully acknowledges permission to reprint an excerpt from "Birds and Fishes" by Robinson Jeffers, from his book *The Beginning and the End and Other Poems.* Copyright © 1963 by Steuben Glass. Reprinted by permission of Random House, Inc.

Library of Congress Cataloging in Publication Data

Smith, Bradley F
    Reaching judgment at Nuremberg.

    Bibliography: p. 335
    Includes index.
    1.   Nuremberg Trial of Major German War Criminals, 1945–1946. I. Title.
D804.G42S64   341.6′9   76-26715
ISBN: 0-465-06839-1

To Helen

CONTENTS

Contents

ACKNOWLEDGMENTS

THE PREPARATION of this volume owes a great debt to historians and archivists at many institutions who gave of their time and assistance, especially Agnes F. Peterson, Hoover Institution, Stanford University; Marilla Guptil, John Mendelsohn, Edward Reese, William Cunliffe, Robert Wolfe (Chief, Modern Military Branch), and Patricia Dowling (Diplomatic Branch), National Archives; James Miller and James Hastings, Federal Record Center, Suitland, Maryland; Donald Schewe, Franklin D. Roosevelt Library; Harry Clark and Philip D. Lagerquist, Harry S. Truman Library; Jon Kepler, Dwight D. Eisenhower Library; David Crosson and Gene Gressley, University of Wyoming; Edward Lyon and Carolyn A. Davis, Syracuse University; D. C. Watt, University of London; Mary K. Hembree, Thomas Marvin, and John Martin, Justice Department. I also owe a special debt of gratitude to John Mendelsohn at the National Archives who made the original suggestion to investigate the Biddle documents housed at Syracuse University.

A number of generous individuals read earlier versions of the manuscript, in whole or in part, including Rudolph Binion, Agnes Peterson, Richard Purvis, John Mendelsohn, Bruce Richardson, Carole Norton, and Helen Jackson. To them I want to express a special note of thanks. John Mendelsohn and Agnes Peterson also provided invaluable assistance on the illustrations, while Martin Kessler and Jed Horowitz smoothed editorial waves and ripples.

The Mabel McLeod Lewis Memorial Fund of Stanford University provided a basic grant that supported much of the research. The Hoover Institution kindly allowed me to make use of a travel grant for another project to examine some materials necessary for this one.

To all who helped in any way, may I repeat my thanks and stress that, although the kindness was yours, the responsibility for the final product is surely mine.

"No, no!" said the Queen.

"Sentence first—verdict afterwards."

"Stuff and Nonsense!" said Alice.

PREFACE

Time may prove you right and me wrong.
                                        Justice Robert Jackson

Time will not be concerned with our opinions—right or wrong.
                                        General William Donovan [1]

ON NOVEMBER 20, 1945, Sir Geoffrey Lawrence of Great Britain opened the first of 403 public sessions of the trial of major Nazi war criminals before the International Military Tribunal in Nuremberg, Germany. By the time Sir Geoffrey closed the last session, on October 1, 1946, one hundred witnesses had been heard, thousands of documents had been submitted, and affidavits bearing hundreds of thousands of signatures had been brought before the Tribunal. The ten-month trial saw three men acquitted, seven men sentenced to prison, and twelve men condemmed to death by hanging, including one who had been tried in absentia. Three Nazi organizations were declared to have been criminal. As the statistics accumulated and the evidence leading to verdicts and sentences was slowly gathered, most of the world became sufficiently aware of the proceedings to add the phrase "Nuremberg trial" to its vocabulary. By the end it was clear that, at least for our epoch, the city of Nuremberg would primarily be associated not with Wagner's opera *Die Meistersinger von Nürnberg,* nor with Hitler's massive Nazi party rallies, but with what all of us took to be *the* trial of war criminals.

The American public's attention did not stay riveted on the trial throughout its whole course. The years 1945–46 marked the transition from war to peace and filled the lives of most Americans with complex problems and new interests. The trial had to compete not only with the beginning of the "cold war," but also with the first new American automobiles manufactured in four years. The trial could not win such a contest, especially since the Nuremberg procedural system guaranteed that many of the sessions would be dull and repetitious. Public interest peaked at the beginning and the end of the proceedings, but in between it was excited only occasionally by a particularly dramatic witness or a horrifying document.

There was no comparable loss of interest among American lawyers, however. Throughout the trial, and for nearly four years after its conclusion, a lively and, at times, bitter controversy over Nuremberg stirred the legal profession. Some of the most prominent and respected figures in American law had participated in the trial: former Attorney General Francis Biddle was on the bench; Justice Robert H. Jackson, of the Supreme Court, was the chief U.S. prosecutor; Professor Quincy Wright, one of the country's foremost authorities on international law, served as adviser to the American members of the Tribunal. These men, as well as other members of the Nuremberg staff, and specialists who did not participate in the trial but supported its principles, vigorously defended Nuremberg on the rostrum and in the legal journals. Yet there was also sharp criticism of the trial from the American legal fraternity—not only hushed murmurs of dissent, such as the widely circulated, and apparently accurate, rumors that members of the Supreme Court were critical of the trial and Justice Jackson's role in it, but detailed technical critiques by renowned authorities such as Professor Hans Kelsen of Berkeley. The legal journals rang with Nuremberg controversies: were "launching aggressive war" and commission of "Crimes Against Humanity" actually criminal acts punishable at law, or merely sonorous phrases used by the victors to cloak their purge of the vanquished; could a trial resolve such enormous atrocities, without doing violence to the basic principles of Western law; indeed, was Nuremberg actually a trial or merely a vigilante revenge dressed up in ex post facto law?

Despite the initial vigor of these controversies, the early 1950s saw a gradual decline of interest in the Nuremberg trial. Once it slipped from public view, the legal discussions also abated, and were ultimately relegated to footnotes and bibliographies.

During the fifteen to twenty years following 1946, the trial enjoyed brief revivals of popular and legal interest. An issue or individual associated with Nuremberg appeared now and then in the news; the United Nations periodically debated whether to codify "Nuremberg law"; Justice Jackson died in 1954; every few years Martin Bormann, who had been sentenced to death in absentia, would allegedly be spotted in some corner of the world. Occasionally some enterprising publisher or television producer would release a Nuremberg epic that, in turn, would set off a brief flurry of Nuremberg reminiscences.

But in the late 1960s concern over war crimes trials became deadly serious once more. For the United States was then tortured by the Vietnam conflict, and the old "Nuremberg questions" about criminal responsibility and the waging of aggressive war were immediately relevant. Analogies between American conduct in Vietnam and that of the defendants at Nuremberg were heatedly debated, and the legal journals were replete with the themes of the late 1940s. But this time it was also being asked whether the Nuremberg trial itself did not constitute a precedent for judging U.S. policy in Southeast Asia. Bertrand Russell's Stockholm trial condemned American policy and "convicted" U.S. leaders of war crimes, but it seems to have been too propagandistic to affect American public opinion seriously. The real sore point in the American war crimes debate over Vietnam was apparently not Stockholm, but Nuremberg: there was an uneasy feeling that American leaders might be found guilty if the law used to judge the leaders of Nazi Germany a quarter century before were applied to ourselves.[2] This concern, unfortunately, did not lead to a serious reexamination of the actual Nuremberg charges or the rulings of the Tribunal; before the Vietnam issue progressed in that direction, it began to fade from public attention. Shortly thereafter the legal journals again became silent, leaving behind the question whether Nuremberg had led anywhere at all.

While popular and legal interest in Nuremberg rose and fell in tune with its newsworthiness and with world events, historians' concern for the trial followed a completely different course. In the years immediately following World War II, the trial was greeted as a veritable documentary bonanza by historians interested in Nazi Germany and the diplomacy of the 1930s. Nuremberg was a source from which they could mine an enormous number of documents without confronting the classifications and restrictions with which nervous governments customarily protect official records of the recent past. Consequently, nearly every account of the Nazi years written through the late 1950s owed a major debt to the documents made public by the Nuremberg trial. Then a reaction set in as historians began to have second thoughts about these documents and what they purported to prove.[3] Such criticisms were paralleled by the opening to research of a great wealth of new materials from the holdings of the Allied governments and the hoard of captured Nazi records that had not been used in war crimes trials. That this documentary treasure should have increased doubts about the reliability of Nuremberg documentation was at least ironic, because the trial and the publicity surrounding its documentary evidence had played a significant role in encouraging the Allied governments to make more material available. Nonetheless, by the 1960s, except for the momentary flurry of interest occasioned by the discovery of a stray document in the prosecution files, the trial evidence ceased to play a pivotal role in historical study. Twenty years after the end of the trial, professional historians had relegated Nuremberg to oblivion.

Only now are historians gradually coming to realize what part of the public had sensed all along, namely, that Nuremberg was not only a source of historical material but was a vital and absorbing aspect of contemporary history.[4] A moment's reflection suggests that many of the significant forces that shaped the European and American transition from war to peace and then to cold war appeared in microcosm during the trial. The changes that World War II and its aftermath produced in American values and policy show up in striking clarity at Nuremberg. Perhaps the trial deserves our attention even more because it was a crucial episode in modern man's effort to grapple with the responsibility of leaders for unleashing war and causing mass atrocities.

Yet Nuremberg's significance is not the only reason historians are now starting to look upon it as history. Much of the documentation essential to appraising the background and backstage processes of the trial is only now becoming accessible. Though not as comprehensive as one might wish, the currently available documentation is sufficient to answer many outstanding questions and place the trial in a new perspective. Previous studies have necessarily had to content themselves with summarizing the published transcript and Judgment or generalizing rather grandly about legal principles and Allied intentions. This is the first study that penetrates behind the public trial sessions by utilizing heretofore classified documents of the U.S. and British governments and records from inside the Tribunal's secret deliberations. Since this book enters new territory, it is only fair that the reader should have a preview of the sights to be seen and some of the benefits to be gained from the journey.

The U.S. and British documents show clearly that there never was a fixed or well-defined Nuremberg plan or policy. The Allies stumbled and compromised their way into the business of a major trial of war criminals, and neither the government leaders nor the prosecutors clearly grasped the uncertainties inherent in the enterprise. There was much talk of the need for a trial, together with an admonition about possible hazards, but few expected that it would open a Pandora's box so wide that the proceedings would threaten to pass beyond the control of the governments. So the Allied leaders and prosecutors plunged ahead, piling uncertainty upon complexity until the case became so confused that clarity and order could be imposed only from on high—which is to say that the Nuremberg judges, not the government leaders or prosecutors, ultimately had to produce the necessary order in the case so that they could write a general opinion and render a series of verdicts.

The judges struggled long to find legally defensible solutions to the riddles posed by charges such as conspiracy and aggressive war and by accusations alleging Nazi organizations to be criminal. The resulting general opinion, or Judgment, corrected many of the gravest weaknesses and most threatening dangers inherent in the Allies' decision to prosecute their defeated enemies. When the Tribunal turned to consider individual defendants, it was again frequently divided, many of its verdicts and sentences being determined by close votes and strained compromises. In this volume it is now possible to see how the Nuremberg Court actually sealed the fate of the twenty-one defendants. For example, Albert Speer poses a leitmotiv question in his recently published prison diaries, namely, why was he sent to Spandau prison for twenty years.[5] If he means why did the judges sentence him to twenty years rather than acquit him, sentence him to death, or give him some other penalty, he, and the reader, may readily find the answer by turning to pages 218–223 below. There, Speer will discover that the British and French judges sympathized with him so strongly that they wanted to impose only a token sentence. But the Soviet judges wanted him hanged, and although the American senior judge, Francis Biddle, was favorably impressed by Speer's personality, he, too, initially wanted Speer executed. Albert Speer escaped the gallows and went to Spandau for twenty years because the French and British judges agreed to compromise on a longer term of imprisonment, thereby persuading Biddle to drop his demand for execution and accept a moderate prison sentence instead.

Since similar information is contained herein on all the defendants, from Hermann Goering to Franz von Papen, many of the questions and mysteries that have hung over Nuremberg for thirty years should be laid to rest. Although this is an exposé of considerable historical importance, it should be placed in a broader and more significant context. The Nuremberg judges functioned more like a traditional court and had a far more important impact on the Nuremberg case and subsequent events than has been recognized heretofore.

What follows, then, is their story—the development of the Nuremberg trial as seen from the bench. It is important because much of it is based on new material that chronicles the decisive role played by the judges. It is also a complex story, filled with government policy decisions and tangled legal controversies. But beyond that, it is a most human story of eight men who had to answer grave questions, and who did so in a manner that gives the rest of us greater cause to hope than to fear.

REACHING JUDGMENT AT NUREMBERG

CHAPTER 1

The Setting

I am quite happy without a lawyer.

Rudolf Hess.[1]

To ASSESS the judgment in a trial, we must first know who is doing the judging, who is being judged, and what are the charges and the system of law in use. Satisfactory answers to these questions will be difficult to obtain in even the simplest trial. For a giant proceeding like the International Military Tribunal at Nuremberg, there will be formidable obstacles to any answers. But if what can be dealt with fairly simply is summarized, we may then be able to trace the more complicated aspects back to their roots.

Since there was no jury at Nuremberg, the Court both presided over the trial and made the Judgment. The members of the Court were technically known as "members of the Tribunal," not judges, although the latter term will be used here for the sake of convenience. There were eight "members": a senior and an alternate from each of the four victorious Allied Powers in the European war. The American senior member, Francis Biddle, whose role in the trial will be a central feature of this narrative, was a respected representative of Philadelphia society, the wartime attorney general of the United States, and a familiar figure in New Deal circles. John Parker, Biddle's alternate, was a less well-known federal judge from North Carolina, who had once been considered for a seat on the Supreme Court. Parker felt that his primary duty at Nuremberg was

3

to ensure that the trial was conducted in a manner that would be acceptable to the members of the American Bar.[2] The senior British member, Sir Geoffrey Lawrence (later Lord Oaksey), who struck the Americans as a ruddy and cheerful embodiment of John Bull, was at his best in dealing with the day-to-day events in the courtroom. The British alternate, Norman Birkett, on the other hand, had been one of England's greatest trial lawyers prior to his elevation to the bench, and turned out to be a gifted legal draftsman. The French alternate, Robert Falco, a member of the French appeals court, showed himself to be an able jurist both in court and during deliberations. Donnedieu de Vabres, the senior French judge, was a professor of law at the Sorbonne, and, although he got along well with his colleagues, he often seemed to them to be an unworldly and perhaps irrelevant academician.[3] In strong contrast, the Soviet alternate, Lieutenant Colonel A. F. Volchkov, bore all the marks of a hard-line party man, uncompromising and often at a loss about what to do in the unfamiliar Western legal system. His senior Soviet colleague, Major General I. T. Nikitchenko, was almost the antithesis, for he was intelligent, understood the Western system, and possessed a quick sense of humor. Nikitchenko often disagreed with Western legal practice and strongly championed Soviet interests, but his good sense and bonhomie were a major asset to the Court.[4]

The agreements by which the Four Powers established the Tribunal imposed little in the way of procedural rules on the Court, but they did make provision for the election of a president of the Tribunal prior to the opening of the trial. The British Government assumed that Biddle wanted to be president and made elaborate preparations in an effort to head him off. The British were right in their estimate that Biddle keenly desired the presidency, but he himself had concluded, on reflection, that the Americans might be playing too dominant a role in the trial.[5] The United States had been the chief advocate of a war crimes judicial process, and, since the trial was held in the American zone of Germany, most of the facilities and personnel were also American. Biddle's hesitations were strongly reinforced by Justice Robert Jackson, the American chief prosecutor, whose influence and power epitomized the strong American presence at the trial. When Jackson urged Biddle to obtain French support and select Britain's Sir Geoffrey Lawrence as president of the Tribunal, Biddle yielded and agreed to do so.[6] In October 1945, when the Tribunal met for the first time in Berlin, the British, who expected to face a fight over the presidency, discovered that only the Soviet Union supported Biddle; the French, as well as Biddle himself, advocated making Sir Geoffrey Tribunal president.

Geoffrey Lawrence was an easygoing, affable man, who, as president, was somewhat hesitant to take aggressive control of his fellow judges or of the trial. His great strengths were a gift for compromise, regardless of doctrine or theory, and a personal charm that smoothed over most of the conflicts and bad feelings inevitable in such a long and important trial. To Lawrence must go major credit for the Tribunal's singular ability, in spite of many factors pointing toward conflict and trouble, to function smoothly from the first day to the last. There were, to be sure, resentments and problems. Biddle could not help but feel disappointed that he had not been chosen president. Birkett, though careful not to reveal it to others, was deeply hurt that first he had been asked to be the senior British member and then had been passed over and made alternate to Lawrence.[7] The British and American judges were frequently disturbed by the mysterious reactions of their counterparts from France and the Soviet Union, who tended to see legal issues and procedures very differently from the Anglo-Americans. The representatives of the three Western countries were also often at a loss to explain what animated the Soviets or to predict how they might act in a given situation. Nevertheless, for ten months these eight strong-willed men continued to get along together and to enjoy each other's company, both in court and out. In the end, they transcended every momentary conflict and got the job done. Such cooperation, coinciding as it did with the start of the cold war, was a truly remarkable achievement.

While Lawrence and the rest of the Court wrestled with the formidable problems facing them, they were at least spared direct confrontation with the demands of the several governments. The agreements establishing the Tribunal were silent on whether the members were to be independent of, or were to act as spokesmen for, their respective countries. The assumption of both the British and the American governments seems to have been that their judges would enjoy customary judicial independence. The existing documentary evidence suggests that the Anglo-American judges did in fact act free of government direction. Both of the American judges were fiercely independent men. Biddle particularly relished a chance to show that he was no one's servant, and there are indications that Washington had no desire to tangle with either of its representatives. In the middle of the trial, when the U.S. War Department became concerned about a ruling by the Tribunal that might affect the large number of SS and police prisoners held by the American Army, Assistant Secretary of War Howard C. Peterson did not try to approach the American judges but appealed instead to the chief U.S. prosecutor, Robert Jackson. Even Jackson, however, could not offer the War Department much comfort on this issue, for, as he reported to Peterson, his "confidential information" suggested that the British and American judges were inclined to rule against the prosecution.[8] In the end, the Tribunal did not sustain many of the prosecution's charges, including the one at issue here, but the important point in this connection is that the judges were so independent that the War Department did not have the slightest glimmer of their views, and Jackson himself was forced to depend on hint and rumor to gauge their position. This did not mean that there was no understanding or communication, aside from official relations, between the American judges and the American prosecutors during the trial. Biddle and Jackson had known each other for a long time, and on occasion harmless communication between them was automatic. When Julius Streicher, the infamous "Jew baiter," in testifying on how he had become an anti-Semite, remarked that he had met many Jews "in the Democratic Party," Biddle noted that his fellow Democrat, "Bob" Jackson, had looked up to the bench and smiled at him.[9] Such incidents show that there was no wall between the bench and the prosecution, but that is true in every court. The American judges and prosecutors met socially; furthermore, Biddle and Parker were not cut off from the influence of the American Bar. They had legal advisers in Nuremberg and in addition obtained the opinions of American legal specialists through the mail. Like most political figures, Biddle also used a newspaper clipping service to keep abreast of American public opinion on the trial.[10] These very arrangements for obtaining legal advice and press information show that Biddle, on the one hand, was in the mainstream of American legal and governmental practice and, on the other, had no intention of being a mere agent of Washington policy makers. During the deliberations of the Tribunal, both Biddle and Parker demonstrated their freedom by repeatedly voting against positions taken by the American prosecution.

As regards the British members of the Tribunal, the documentary material currently available reveals only two marginal incidents involving direction from the home government. Prior to the opening session in Berlin, in October, Birkett and Lawrence were briefed by officials from the Foreign Office on some organizational questions, including that of the presidency of the Court.[11] And in December, 1945, one representative from the Foreign Office and one from the British occupation forces met with Birkett to discuss a Tribunal ruling that would affect the massive number of SS and Gestapo prisoners in Allied custody.[12] Aside from these two incidents, the record is silent. This, when coupled with the general personality and character of the two British judges, makes it virtually certain that they were not receiving significant direction from London. During the deliberations, they did identify more consistently with the positions taken by the prosecution than did the American judges, but they also strove to maintain greater social and personal distance from the British prosecution team.[13]

The meager materials now available that have any bearing on the actions of the French judges show that, at one point in the deliberations, Donnedieu de Vabres frankly admitted that he had been officially notified of his government's wishes regarding a point before the Tribunal (it, too, referred to the problem of criminal organizations).[14] Given the sparseness of the documentation, it would be extremely imprudent to conclude from this incident that Donnedieu de Vabres and Robert Falco were regularly controlled from Paris. Their behavior during the deliberations is the safest guide: their arguments and votes were so independent that they frequently disagreed with the prosecution, with the other judges, and almost as often with each other.

Obviously the position of the Soviet members of the Tribunal represents a special problem. Their behavior at times made them seem like automatons who, as most Western observers assumed, were in Nuremberg merely to follow Stalin's orders. They vigorously defended the Soviet line, but on occasion, it must be noted, the Americans, and especially the British, supported their respective countries' interests just as strongly. The Soviets, particularly Volchkov, took a consistently hard line, voting to condemn all defendants on all counts and to sentence every possible defendant to death by hanging. More often than not, however, they found at least one Western member to support them in their rigid stands. They filed strong dissenting opinions on a number of verdicts and on the life sentence given to Rudolf Hess. But the Soviet decision to dissent publicly was made late in the trial, and Francis Biddle was deterred from making a similar public dissent (in the case of Admiral Karl Doenitz) only by a last-minute compromise. Although the Soviet representatives may have received closer direction than their Western counterparts, they were not radically different in their performance from the other judges. As long as the public sessions of the trial lasted, the general instructions the Russians apparently received were adequate to deal with the infrequent issues that arose for decision. When the deliberations on the Judgment began, however, maneuver and compromise were at a premium and no instructions were adequate to cope with the situation. Nikitchenko adjusted to circumstances very quickly and showed himself to be as accomplished a horse trader as his Western colleagues. In one deliberative session, Biddle and Nikitchenko wanted to sentence Hjalmar Schacht to life imprisonment, while Lawrence and Donnedieu de Vabres held out for a light prison sentence. The deadlock was so complete that a recess had to be called. When it ended, Nikitchenko sidled up to Biddle as they walked back to the deliberation room and asked "how far down" Biddle thought they would have to go in order to pick up another vote for a stiff sentence.[15] Through a series of bizarre developments, Schacht was ultimately acquitted, but Nikitchenko's attitude and actions in this case were not those of a robot mechanically carrying out orders. All in all, it is reasonable to conclude that, although there were different degrees of independence granted to the Tribunal members, and although the individual judges made different use of their prerogatives, the defendants faced a court surprisingly free from outside control.

Before we can go much further in analyzing the Court or the actions of the judges, we must first briefly introduce the defendants and then proceed to the far more complicated task of examining the charges and the legal foundations of the trial. Paradoxically, the most important consideration regarding the defendants was not who was in the dock but who was not. Five persons were glaringly absent from the trial of Nazi leaders—Adolf Hitler, Heinrich Himmler, Josef Goebbels, Martin Bormann, and the head of the Krupp combine. The first four had been the most powerful figures in the twilight of the Third Reich, but Himmler and Goebbels were definitely dead, Hitler was likely so, and Bormann was missing and quite possibly dead. With regard to the fifth, the prosecution blundered badly in naming the elderly Gustav Krupp as a defendant. Krupp was mentally incompetent, which ultimately led the Tribunal to rule that he should not be tried in absentia; his case was therefore separated from that of the other defendants. Trials in absentia were authorized by the Allied Agreement that had established the Tribunal, and although the provision was not used for Krupp, it was invoked by the prosecution in the case of Bormann. With a logic perhaps more comprehensible to lawyers than to the laity, the judges decided that, since Bormann's presence, and very existence, could not be established, it would be proper to try him in absentia.

Consequently, the trial of the top Nazi leaders proceeded with no representative of German heavy industry in the dock, while the absentia proceedings against Bormann were little more than a mock trial. With Hitler and Himmler missing, and Bormann present in name only, there was the unavoidable impression that most of the actual defendants were secondary figures. Hermann Goering, somewhat slimmer, and freed from his drug habit, was the only one present who had been a top leader during the regime's balmiest days and had held on to a measure of authority until nearly its end. But even Goering's claim to primacy was partially a sham kept alive by both the defense and the prosecution. The prosecutors wanted to convict a top Nazi, and Goering wanted to present himself as the strongest defender of the Third Reich and as Hitler's loyal paladin; both sides wanted to hide the fact that from 1941 on Goering's career had centered in narcotics and theatrical charades on his Karinhall estate. The Reich Marshal had roused himself only in the last days of the war to make fumbling gestures in favor of a negotiated settlement—gestures that led Hitler to order his immediate arrest.

Still, Goering could point back to a far more significant career than that of the only other prominent Nazi to survive the debacle, Rudolf Hess. Hess had been secretary of the Nazi party and Hitler's confidant until 1941, when he made a bizarre flight to Scotland, ostensibly in pursuit of peace. After four years in British custody, Hess was taken back to Nuremberg, although it was obvious that he was only marginally competent to stand trial. Hess's blatant mental disorder—one of the defense counsel referred to the "burnt out craters in Hess's face" [16]—cast an aura of irrationality over the whole trial.

Joachim von Ribbentrop, the former foreign minister, had always been somewhat of a comic figure in diplomatic circles, alternately cringing before Hitler and then swaggering as if he, too, were a man of strength and resolution. In court, he was awash with self-pity, maintaining that he had known nothing about Hitler's foreign policy, which was only a partial exaggeration, but one that did little to enhance his significance or veracity in the eyes of the Court.

Most of the other defendants who had held political office were those who had fallen prey to Hitler's favorite method for disposal of people with slight value in the central leadership of the state and the Nazi party. Such men were sent off to become local administrators (Gauleiter), governors, "protectors," and the like in the conquered territories. After having spent months and years in frustrating competition with the thousands of officials who scrambled for Hitler's favor, these failures in the struggle for influence were given a measure of authority and power in the provinces. The price of power, however, was high, for they were the ones who had actually to apply the murderous racial and ruinous economic policies that emanated from Berlin. Alfred Rosenberg, the notoriously woolly headed publicist and "philosopher" of the Nazi movement, strove for years to influence Hitler's policies, but in the end he was sent to scorch Russia and prepare it for Nazi settlement. Hans Frank, Hitler's lawyer, who proclaimed himself the spokesman for Nazi law, was dispatched to Poland to preside over a program of mass murder and exploitation. Old Konstantin von Neurath, foreign minister from 1933 to 1938, was not even a Nazi party member, but still he was made protector of some of the occupied Czech territories and became the hangman of Prague. Seyss-Inquart had an extended career in the conquered territories, first in his native Austria, then as Frank's assistant in Poland, and finally as Nazi commissioner in the Netherlands. After ten years as minister of the interior, Wilhelm Frick's turn came in 1943, when he was sent to Prague as protector after Neurath had resigned the title and the deputy protector, Reinhard Heydrich of the SS, had been assassinated. Baldur von Schirach, the longtime head of the Hitler Youth, received a more pleasant form of exile from the center of power in Berlin when he was made Gauleiter in Vienna in 1940. Franz von Papen made a career of distant exile after his resignation as vice-chancellor in 1934. Not a member of the Nazi party, Papen escaped being a murderous accessory by going first to Vienna as ambassador and then spending the war in the relatively harmless post of German envoy to Turkey.

These political officeholders were joined in the dock at Nuremberg by four military and naval officers. Admiral Erich Raeder had commanded the German Navy until 1943, when he was replaced by the chief of the German submarine fleet, Admiral Karl Doenitz. The latter had the added distinction of having been chosen by Hitler to be his successor as chief of the Nazi regime in its dying days. Field Marshal Wilhelm Keitel, as chief of the High Command of the armed forces, had held the top German military post during World War II. General Alfred Jodl had served as his chief of operations in the Military High Command.

The remaining defendants included a pair of well-known men who had lost influence and power fairly early in the Nazi era and a larger group of figures who had enjoyed little public attention but held a substantial measure of power right to the end. Julius Streicher, one of the earliest Nazis, was Gauleiter of Nuremberg and a notoriously rabid anti-Semitic journalist and pornographer, whose antics finally compelled Hitler to drop him from his Nazi party posts in 1940. Another early political casualty, Hjalmar Schacht, was the prewar head of the Reichsbank and minister of economics who held on to the title of minister without portfolio until 1943. Schacht was not a member of the Nazi party but a patrician financier who would have been horrified to find himself coupled with Streicher in this narrative, or anywhere else. But his career was analogous to Streicher's, for he was prominent in Hitler's regime until 1938–39, when he passed out of public life, except for an occasional ceremonial appearance. His successor as Reichsbank president and economics minister was Walter Funk, a man of insignificant appearance and moderate gifts who held on to a measure of authority over the economy until the end of the regime. Whatever economic authority was lost by Funk passed largely to two other defendants, Fritz Sauckel and Albert Speer. Sauckel was an old Nazi, a rough-hewn laboring man and party leader in Thuringia, who during World War II had been appointed chief of the German labor program. This post gave him responsibility for recruiting, or forcing, labor from the conquered territories to go to Germany and toil in industry and agriculture. From 1942 on, the man who established the industrial labor quotas that Sauckel had to fill was the minister of armaments, Hitler's favorite architect, Albert Speer.

Funk, Sauckel, and Speer used a large measure of force and compulsion in their economic operations during the war. From 1942 on, as Himmler's deputy, Ernst Kaltenbrunner held in his hand the instruments of repression on which his colleagues relied. A huge, morose man, both lawyer and policeman, Kaltenbrunner was ill through much of the trial. But with Himmler and Heydrich dead and many of the secondary SS chiefs dead or in hiding, the prosecution sought to place the responsibility for the mad SS-Gestapo kingdom on Kaltenbrunner's shoulders.

The names of two other persons also appear in the indictment: Robert Ley, who had headed the German labor service, but managed to commit suicide before the trial began and Hans Fritzsche, a middle-level official in the Propaganda Ministry who, though tried with the other defendants at Nuremberg, obviously had possessed little power during the Nazi years. Fritzsche had, in fact, been added to the list of defendants only because Goebbels was dead and Fritzsche happened to be one of the few officials captured by Soviet troops. The Russian Government wanted at least a sprinkling of their prisoners among the defendants, but Fritzsche was a poor choice; he did not even belong to the rank of secondary leaders, and from the start of the trial his acquittal seemed highly likely.

At first glance it may appear impossible to determine the common characteristics of these men that led the Allied governments to consider them the "major Nazi war criminals" of World War II. But if one allows for the lack of controlling focus, owing to the absence of Hitler and Himmler, one sees that the group does have a certain unity. The defendants were there as representatives of the organizations and episodes of the Third Reich that the Allies found most reprehensible and deserving of punishment. The representative and collective nature of the defendants must be stressed, for, in addition to the individuals before the Court, the Allied prosecutors asked the Tribunal to declare that six Nazi German organizations had been "criminal." These included the most familiar Nazi paramilitary formations, the brown-shirted SA (Storm Troopers) and the notorious black-shirted SS. Himmler's police apparatus was also represented; the prosecution sought to have the Gestapo and the SD (originally the SS's security service) branded as a single criminal organization. The Allied prosecution also wanted to reach all those holding positions of authority in the Nazi party down to the local level by having the Nazi's "Leadership Corps" ruled a criminal organization. The members of the government were made liable by a declaration that all members of the Reich Cabinet since 1933 had been members of a criminal group. Finally, the prosecution listed those who had held high planning and operational posts in the German military in the prewar and wartime periods, and asked that this composite, labeled the "General Staff and High Command of the Armed Forces," should likewise be proclaimed criminal.

The prosecution asserted that there were individual "representatives" of each of these organizations included among the defendants in the dock. This was correct with regard to the large number of former members of the Cabinet and the "Leadership Corps" of the Nazi party; Kaltenbrunner was there to stand for the SS and, together with Goering (for a short period), the Gestapo-SD. The representation of the General Staff and High Command, however, was somewhat confused. Although the list of posts used to denote "membership" in the group included those long held by Jodl, Keitel, and Raeder, it had been so drawn up that Doenitz could not be considered a member until he took command of the navy in 1943. More significantly, among the defendants the only representative of the SA who had ever played an important role in the organization was Hermann Goering, and he had not held such a post since 1923!

Thus, the indictment charged that both organizations and individuals were on trial. Most of the defendants were present, but Bormann was not. Most of the organizations had existed as actual units during the Third Reich, but the General Staff and High Command had not. The leadership of most of the organizations was represented by at least one defendant in the dock, but the chiefs of the SA were not. These anomalies, plus the individual-organization trial plan itself, should provide ample warning that the charges in the indictment and the legal foundations of the trial were unusual and remain difficult to understand.

The indictment contained four charges, but, like most features of the trial, it is probably wisest not to attempt to run at the charges in direct numerical order. Count Three was actually the most clearly defined charge and the easiest to summarize. Under Count Three, the indictment charged eighteen of the defendants with violations of the traditional laws of war because they had committed such acts as mistreatment of prisoners of war, murder, and devastation not justified by military necessity. The third count simply added together the sections of the Hague Rules of Land Warfare and the Geneva Convention that interdicted certain wartime actions against military and naval forces as well as against civilians and civilian property. Questions could be raised about who was and who was not covered by the Hague and Geneva rules, and it is also possible to argue that complete victory may free the victor from obligations under the rules. But such considerations need not concern us here. Count Three by and large, charged violations of the traditional laws and rules of warfare, and, of the eighteen defendants prosecuted under this count, only Hess and Fritzsche were found not guilty.[17]

But total war and mass ideological movements have greatly extended the scope, form, and havoc of war in the twentieth century. Many of the victims of World War II could make no claim for protection on the basis of codified rules such as those of Geneva or The Hague, for those agreements had not been prepared for a world of gas chambers and atomic weapons. Those who had slaughtered civilians to terrorize a government or break the popular will of the opposition were not clearly chargeable under Count Three. The Nazi persecutors and exterminators did not violate most of the traditional rules of warfare—a conclusion that was simply impossible for the battered peoples of Europe to accept in 1945. Thus, Count Four, "Crimes Against Humanity," was employed by the prosecution to reform the rules of warfare in order to correspond to the realities of the twentieth century. It charged as crimes murder, extermination, and "persecution on political, racial or religious grounds," whether committed "before or during the war," just so long as such acts were undertaken or executed in connection with other acts "under the jurisdiction of the Tribunal." Thus, religious persecution was punishable if committed in conjunction with a war crime as specified in Count Three (or in conjunction with the actions covered by Counts One and Two, which will be considered shortly). Count Four is the logical consequence of total war, but it contains the seeds of serious legal controversy. By adding the phrase "before or during the war," Count Four made it possible at Nuremberg to prosecute actions that had taken place in pre-1939 Nazi Germany and in the territories of Czechoslovakia and Austria "peacefully" occupied in 1938. It thus permitted the prosecution of prewar "war criminals." The core of the criticism of Count Four is the obvious fact that there was no code of law or international agreement in existence in 1933, 1939, or even 1944 that made it illegal to persecute religions or to exterminate populations. That is, if one considers only statutory law, the prosecution of prewar and wartime acts under Count Four was an exercise in ex post facto prosecution, declaring an act to be a crime and punishing it as such *after* it had been committed. By implication, Count Four sought to prosecute functionaries of the state as well as those who formulated state policy. A wayward general might shoot hostages or wantonly burn a town and be prosecuted under Count Three, while the leadership of the government or those holding ultimate sovereignty could go untouched. But it is difficult, if not impossible, to imagine that mass deportations or exterminations could be carried out except on orders from the highest state authorities. The prosecution of policy makers and heads of government or state was such a delicate and weighty problem that it had long been carefully skirted by diplomats and international lawyers. But Count Four (as well as Counts One and Two) was clearly intended to make such individuals prosecutable. Thus, the critics argued that Count Four was in reality new law, both in whom it charged and what it charged.

Those who drafted the Nuremberg indictment defended Count Four against such criticisms by pointing to the murderous farce that the exemption of policy makers and sovereigns had made out of international law. To prosecute a lieutenant for shooting a handful of hostages while exempting the head of state or government from responsibility for ordering such an act was clearly preposterous. Modern war was no longer a gentlemanly contest; it was—here the Nuremberg fathers paradoxically echoed Hitler—a struggle of masses and ideologies, without rule or limit. Those who wrote the Nuremberg indictment, however, went on to argue that only by imposing responsibility on government leaders, responsibility backed by the force of punitive international law, could peaceful human life be possible. Furthermore, they contended that such a conclusion was not an innovation either in modern law or in modern thought. Law was not simply produced by treaties and statutes, especially in international relations; it took shape through the customary usage and belief of the "civilized" people of the world. By 1945, mass murder of civilians had thereby evolved into an international crime; the Allied Powers had repeatedly warned the Axis leaders that such actions were criminal and would be punished. The only innovation was procedural; international public conscience had defined the crime, and Count Four was therefore not an application of ex post facto law.

This short summary should adequately clarify the basis for Count Four, so that it is not necessary to pursue the matter further. The Tribunal itself did not delve very deeply into the legal basis of the count, and, of the seventeen defendants charged under it, only Hess and Fritzsche were acquitted. Those readers who may wish to further investigate the legal implications may find some leads in the bibliography at the end of this volume; on the other hand, the timid will find more than enough challenge with Counts One and Two.[18]

The second count of the indictment, headed "Crimes Against Peace," was so important, and its wording so singular, that it seems best to quote it in full:

All the defendants with divers other persons during a period of years preceding 8 May 1945 participated in the planning, preparation, initiation, and waging of wars of aggression which were also wars in violation of international treaties, agreements and assurances.[19]

The key phrase in Count Two, "crimes against peace," was as much an innovation in international law as was the phrase "crimes against humanity" in Count Four. Count Two, even more explicitly than Count Four, aimed directly at the highest authorities in the state, for it was surely they who had planned and executed the decisions for war. But what was most singular about Count Two was that it contained two coequal elements, namely, "wars of aggression" and "wars in violation of international treaties, agreements, and assurances." By means of this dual section, the indictment skirted a troublesome problem in international law—there was no definition of aggressive war. Throughout the trial, the Court was faced with a pair of unpleasant alternatives; it could attempt to define aggressive war, or it could restrict "crimes against peace" to violations of agreements and treaties. The Tribunal generally chose the latter alternative, but this did not provide a complete escape from the legal thicket, for there still remained the troublesome question whether international treaties contained or implied criminal sanctions. That is, did any of these treaties specify penalties or declare who should be held criminally liable in the event of violations? The inevitable answer is that no treaty contained such provisions, not only because their formulations would be complex and questionable in international law, but because the people who drew up the agreements assumed that they would be the most likely candidates for violating them. There are obvious limits to the innovative self-sacrifice one can expect from statesmen.

But the fathers of the Nuremberg trial, the formulators of the American plan and the signatories of the Treaty of London, were not prepared to admit that Count Two was a pure innovation. Again, they resorted to the argument that international law, like common law, grows through changes in attitude and custom; by 1939, the peoples of the civilized world had come to believe that the launching of aggressive war was a crime not only morally wrong, but one that warranted the most severe punishment. While granting that bilateral agreements, such as the Nazi-Soviet Nonaggression Pact of 1939, did not contain lists of penalties for violations, or even imply the existence of such penalties, the champions of Count Two argued the necessity of going beyond such specific agreements to gauge the climate of the time. Ever since the turn of the century, a growing legal movement, conforming to public opinion, had sought limitations on the harshness of war, through the Hague Rules, and controls over the outbreak and spread of war, through such agreements as the Covenant of the League of Nations (1919) and the Kellogg-Briand Pact (1928) both of which denounced the use of war as an instrument of national policy. Additionally, regional understandings were made, such as the Havana Resolution signed in 1928 by the Pan-American states. The Havana agreement did not define aggression, but it declared aggressive war to be "an international crime against the human species."

Germany had adhered to several such agreements: it had joined the League of Nations in 1926 and signed the Kellogg-Briand Pact in 1928 (though it had left the League in 1933 and, of course, never had to adhere to the Havana declaration). Yet the prosecution asked the Tribunal to agree not merely that Germany had signed and then violated the League Covenant and the Kellogg-Briand Pact, but that its leaders were criminally punishable because they had participated in the growing trend of international agreements that implicitly made aggressive war and treaty violations illegal. Thus, when the Nazis secretly tore up the Nazi-Soviet Pact and launched a massive invasion into the Soviet Union in 1941, they should have known from the general development of international agreement that public opinion and the Allied governments would hold their conduct to be criminal. Obviously, this was a complex, wide-ranging argument. It asked the Tribunal to validate a series of assertions about contemporary history and society. That the Tribunal found this charge much more troubling than Counts Three and Four is indicated in the extended discussion of Count Two found in the final Judgment and in the decision to acquit four of the sixteen defendants charged under this count.

Formidable as Count Two may seem, it is a model of simplicity and directness when compared with the issues raised by Count One.

The first count in the indictment charged all twenty-two defendants with participation in a common plan, or conspiracy, to prepare and execute the substantive crimes enumerated in Counts Two, Three, and Four. To quote the indictment:

All the defendants, with divers other persons, during a period of years preceding 8 May 1945, participated as leaders, organizers, instigators, or accomplices in the formulation or execution of a common plan or conspiracy to commit, or which involved the commission of, Crimes against Peace, War Crimes, and Crimes against Humanity. . . .[20]

Conspiracy is an old and well-established concept in Anglo-American law; the defining characteristic of the crime is an agreement or understanding between two or more persons to commit a criminal act. Proof of individual guilt rests on a demonstration that the defendant knowingly and voluntarily participated in a plan to commit a recognized crime. There has been an increasing recognition in modern Anglo-American legal practice that prosecution of conspiracy is subject to great abuse, for proof of knowledge is nearly always difficult and may run dangerously close to the prosecution of unpopular opinions and ideas. More recent trials, such as that of the Chicago Seven, have demonstrated anew the difficulties and hazards of conspiracy prosecution. These dangers have led to the development of unusually precise evidentiary rules in Anglo-American conspiracy law; nevertheless, even in countries where conspiracy law has been long established, it is still a highly debatable form of prosecution.

In the realm of international law, the risks are infinitely greater. Many legal systems, including those of continental Europe, do not recognize the crime of conspiracy and, therefore, have none of the safeguards surrounding the offense in British and American law. The legal systems of France, Germany, the Soviet Union, and the other continental countries whose nationals participated in the Nuremberg trial, do have laws directed against certain types of criminal combinations or group activities. What they do not have are provisions for adding any sort of conspiracy charge to the prosecution of a criminal act that involves more than one person. Since the Nuremberg trial rested on joint action by four powers, two of which were continental states, the inclusion of a conspiracy count posed monumental difficulties, not the least of which was the unfamiliarity of

German defendants with the conspiracy system. As a partial compromise, the indictment referred both to a conspiracy and to "a common plan," the latter term being more familiar to continental jurists because of its use in prosecuting collective or group crime. But this addition did not fully meet the problem that confronted continental lawyers. The novelty for them was the addition of a second level of criminality—the planning, or conspiratorial, level—on top of a series of substantive crimes such as the mistreatment of prisoners, the wanton destruction of property, and others which could themselves be prosecuted and judged.

Thus, without exploring more subtle issues raised by the wording of Count One—the use of such terms as "divers other persons," the vague dating placing the conspiracy, or common plan, in "a period of years preceding 8 May 1945"—we can see how Count One raised extremely difficult problems. Nevertheless, as assistant American prosecutor Sidney Alderman's introductory remarks to the Tribunal show, the prosecution attached great importance to Count One. According to Alderman, "the conspiracy case under Count One, and the aggressive war phase of the entire case is really, we think, the heart of the case." [21] During the Court's final deliberations, this opinion was echoed exactly by Judge Norman Birkett when he pleaded with his colleagues not to weaken the conspiracy element in the Judgment, for, if they did, he feared that the "heart" of the case would be lost. [22] In the end, Count One divided the Tribunal more deeply and more bitterly than any other aspect of the trial, and the final verdicts reflected the depth of the divisions. Of the twenty-two defendants charged under Count One, only eight were found guilty, and all of these were also convicted of "planning" aggressive war under Count Two.

Obviously, the indictment presented the Tribunal with many legal challenges and ultimately forced it to make important compromises. The statutory basis of the trial, the London Charter, and the events that occurred during the trial itself also produced much head shaking among the eight men on the bench. Before we can hope to assess the relative importance of these many factors, we must consider how the Allied governments came to present the Tribunal with such a series of formidable problems. To do this, we must briefly trace the important developments in war crimes policy that evolved during World War II.

CHAPTER 2

The Road to Nuremberg

Can anybody give me an example in the history of the world where you have found an organization guilty? Has any court ever convicted an organization?

Henry Morgenthau, Jr.[1]

THE TURNING POINT of the European war may well have come with the battles of Moscow in 1941 and of Stalingrad and El Alamein in late 1942, but the turning point in Washington's wartime mood did not occur until the late summer of 1944. By then the Allies enjoyed nearly complete control of the air over Germany, and had badly beaten the fleet of U-boats in the Atlantic. In that same summer, the Soviet Army rolled relentlessly forward in the East and, in the West, the Allied forces consolidated their landing in Normandy and began pushing toward the Rhine. German defeat seemed inevitable. In Washington, predictions of Germany's impending collapse were so rife that Secretary of War Stimson thought the buoyant mood might seriously hurt war production and the supply of military manpower.[2] But he also felt that preparations had to be made to cope with a sudden German collapse. The War Department had not planned adequately prior to Mussolini's precipitous fall in 1943 and, as a result, had suffered many political headaches; so, while warning publicly against overoptimism, Stimson was now determined to prevent similar planning mistakes regarding the fall of Germany.

The governments in exile that spoke for the territories under German occupation had even stronger reasons to believe, in mid-1944, that the Allies needed to do some serious planning in regard to postwar Germany. With the Nazis retreating, these governments not only wanted to know what the Allied powers intended to do with liberated Europe, they also wanted the Germans warned in no uncertain terms that they should not unleash a final wave of death and destruction. In their view, what was urgently needed was a clear war crimes policy that would threaten German malefactors with dire consequences if they ordered more atrocities.⁰ And Jewish groups, who by this time possessed detailed information on the mass extermination of the European Jews, urged the Allies to try every possible device, from bombing Auschwitz to announcing a war crimes policy, in an effort to save the hapless victims still in Nazi hands.[4]

The cry by the smaller Allied governments and the Jewish organizations for a deterrent war crimes policy had, of course, been raised before 1944. From the beginning of the war, several ominous, if vague, declarations of impending retribution, like the St. James Declaration of 1942 and the declaration of the Big Three foreign ministers at Moscow in 1943, had been proclaimed. In addition, by the fall of 1942 the Western Powers had agreed to the formation of the United Nations War Crimes Commission (UNWCC), which began to compile lists of accused war criminals a year later. The Russians did not join the UNWCC, but as their army advanced it gave a more specific unilateral warning about the fate that awaited Nazi offenders. By the end of 1943, in the large and well-publicized Kharkov trials of German officials and Soviet collaborators, the Russians demonstrated that these threats had not been hollow. The British and American governments, however, were reluctant to issue specific warnings, and they opposed initiating any action until after the war was over. This attitude prevailed partly because neither the United States nor Britain had experienced the horrifying reality of a Nazi occupation, and partly because there was a degree of skepticism regarding war crimes reports, based on the exaggerated tales of German atrocities in Belgium which the Anglo-Americans themselves had circulated during World War I. Resistance to war crimes publicity, however, was strongest among military chiefs in Washington and London, who feared that too much threatening publicity might set off enemy reprisals against Allied prisoners of war. So deep was their apprehension that, when the advancing armies began war crimes trials in Sicily in 1943, the two Allied governments quickly intervened and ordered them stopped. By 1944, the U.S. Army refused to segregate suspected German war criminals in POW camps, and the British Government followed the same practice.[5]

Considering the views of the War Department, as well as the State Department's customary coolness to what it regarded as outside meddling, it seems highly unlikely that the United States would have been moved by pressure from the smaller Allied governments or from Jewish groups to adopt a clear policy on German war criminals in the late summer of 1944. But in late August another, very formidable force raised the war crimes issue. It was the always energetic, and sometimes aggressive, secretary of the treasury, Henry Morgenthau, Jr.

During 1943–44, Morgenthau had become increasingly disturbed as detailed reports of the Nazis' mass extermination of European Jews began to filter into Washington. Not only was he deeply upset by the horrors themselves, but he was also angered by the lackadaisical attitude taken by the U.S. Government. The State Department's reluctance to embark on extraordinary measures to aid the victims so outraged him that he undertook a personal campaign to force official Washington into action.[6] Morgenthau, through his position and his long personal friendship with Franklin D. Roosevelt, possessed great political influence.

Morgenthau's feelings about the holocaust reinforced his views on plans for postwar Germany. The atrocities committed by Germany, after twice plunging the world into war within a quarter of a century, had, he felt, canceled any right to lenient treatment. With the view that only the strictest postwar control could bring peace to the world, Morgenthau went to Europe in August 1944, ostensibly to examine the financial situation. While in Britain, one of the numerous Treasury representatives assigned to the American armed forces—men whose very existence irritated the army—showed Morgenthau a copy of army directives for the treatment of occupied Germany.[7] The directives, one of the products of Stimson's demand for precautionary planning, dealt primarily with administration of German territory in the period immediately after conquest or occupation. But to Morgenthau the emphasis on reconstruction was a shocking indication that the army intended to "mollycoddle" the Germans, to treat their economy and society in a way that implied Germany was merely another country liberated by the Allies and not a defeated belligerent.

Once back in Washington, Morgenthau launched a vigorous campaign to replace the army's directives with a tough plan of occupation. Together with Treasury officials, he began to bombard the War and State departments with questions and complaints about postwar planning for Germany. Using the directives and the army planning handbook as ammunition, Morgenthau went straight to Roosevelt to challenge the German policies of Secretaries Stimson and Hull. At the same time that he voiced criticisms, he left a memorandum in which he quoted passages from the handbook to show that the army intended to be easy on the Germans.[9] Deeply disturbed, Roosevelt, who was, as he said later, "in a tough mood" on Germany, [9] fired off a memorandum to Stimson stating that "this handbook is pretty bad" [10] and demanding that a tougher policy be developed on postwar Germany. At this point, Roosevelt was definitely in Morgenthau's pocket on the German question, for, despite his claim that he had made the discoveries in the War Department's handbook on his own, the passages he sent to Stimson were appropriated from Morgenthau's memo.[11]

Roosevelt's support of Morgenthau left the War and State departments in a tight corner. Both Hull and Stimson, already submerged with a plethora of wartime problems, were advanced in years and in poor health. Glad of an opportunity to come to terms with Morgenthau, the two secretaries readily agreed to join him and Roosevelt's close aide Harry Hopkins in a committee to advise the President on German occupation policy.[12] As soon as the committee took shape, Morgenthau pressed the attack. The Treasury Department prepared the now famous "Morgenthau plan," which called for a policy of "pasturization" aimed at reducing Germany's capacity to make war in the future. The scheme, however, went beyond deindustrialization, envisioning an all-embracing denazification and demilitarization system and the internment of masses of state and Nazi party personnel. The Treasury memorandums proposed that labor teams be created, made up of Nazi party leaders, government officials, and soldiers, for use as labor reparations in the Allied lands ravaged by war and Nazi occupation. Massive deportation of Nazis to remote corners of the globe was also suggested, and in one Treasury conference a serious discussion took place on the thorny problem of how to deal with SS offspring under the age of six! [13] Morgenthau and his supporters had no patience with involved war crimes procedures. They accepted the Allied pledge that lower level war criminals would be sent back to the areas of their crimes to be dealt with there. But for major war criminals, the high officials of the Nazi party and state, the Treasury had a very simple proposal: a list of the criminals to be given to the advance Allied military forces, who would use the list to identify and immediately shoot captured prisoners.[14]

While the Morgenthau plan drew coolness and caution from the State Department, Secretary of War Stimson offered severe criticism of the whole treasury scheme from the moment of its inception. Though 77 years old at the time, and slowed by heart trouble, Stimson was a formidable antagonist. Despite his Republicanism, his long and distinguished governmental career gave him an almost transcendent political prestige even among New Deal Democrats. He had been secretary of war under President Taft, a colonel in France during World War I, governor of the Philippines in the early 1920s, and secretary of state under President Hoover. Roosevelt had recognized that Stimson would best be able to give the military vigorous leadership during the war, while simultaneously protecting the War Department from political sniping at home. As secretary of war from 1941 on, Stimson had indeed fulfilled Roosevelt's hopes by strongly defending the War Department's domain. But the very breadth of Stimson's political experience meant that his thinking and activity would extend far beyond the confines of the War Department. He had long been interested in international cooperation and was especially concerned with strengthening and advancing the cause of international legality. It was Stimson who, as secretary of state in 1931, verbally blistered the Japanese for their advance into Manchuria; the official American policy refusing to recognize the resulting Japanese state of Manchukuo was labeled the "Stimson doctrine."

The War Department's opposition to the Morgenthau plan went beyond criticism of its simplistic economic ideas. Morgenthau was penetrating directly into Stimson's realm with schemes based on arbitrary power politics. Repeatedly, Stimson approached Roosevelt and Morgenthau to point out the plan's obvious pitfalls. Germany could not be deindustrialized without bringing injury to Europe's economy and the threat of starvation to millions of Germans. The weapon of "economic repression" was dangerous, Stimson wrote to Morgenthau, because such methods "do not prevent war; they tend to breed war." [15] Stimson also strongly objected to the proposed summary execution of the Nazi leaders. Some form of judicial process had to be used instead, for, as he told Roosevelt, "the very punishment of these men in a dignified manner consistent with the advance of civilization, will have the greater effect upon posterity. . . . I am disposed to believe that at least as to the chief Nazi officials, we should participate in an international Tribunal constituted to try them." [16] While stressing that he was "unalterably opposed" to much of Morgenthau's economic and political program, Stimson tried to convince the president that he was not in favor of "soft treatment." The only point of disagreement concerned "a matter of method entirely," he wrote, for "we are all trying to devise protection against recurrence by Germany of her attempts to dominate the world." [17]

Stimson's strong stand in favor of a judicial process made it essential for the War Department to come up with a proposal that would offer prospects of controlling Germany without using economic repression, deportation, and summary execution. The rudiments of such a plan were contained in the original army directives for Germany. Among other provisions, the directives had called for the seizure and detention of the top Nazi leaders and all other persons who might constitute security risks. Two days after Roosevelt's note to Stimson indicating that the occupation program for Germany was too soft, Stimson telephoned Assistant Secretary of War John J. McCloy to talk about possible stronger measures that might be used against war criminals. "Swift punishment" should be meted out to the top leaders, Stimson said; then the process of prosecution would move down the chain of command, beginning with the internment of the whole Gestapo. [18] But Stimson also wanted to encourage the German people to prosecute their own villains, especially the group he referred to as the "Stormtroopers," by which he presumably meant both the SA and the SS. [19] These ideas were rather vague, but Stimson was clearly thinking in terms of trials and some form of group punishment. By September 5, 1944, his thoughts had taken a somewhat clearer form. Writing to Roosevelt and Morgenthau, he produced a straightforward summary of his views:

It is primarily by the thorough apprehension, investigation and trial of all the Nazi leaders and instruments of the Nazi system of terrorism such as the Gestapo, with punishment delivered as promptly, swiftly, and severely as possible, that we can demonstrate the abhorrence which the world has for such a system and bring home to the German people our determination to extirpate it and all its fruits forever. [20]

This was a good thrust in the struggle with Morgenthau, but the idea of combining a trial with collective punishment still lacked a clear form and a definite procedure. The Stimson approach opened up the unpleasant possibility that the United States might become involved in an endless series of trials if Germany were to be effectively purged.

Despite the wartime crusading enthusiasm in Washington, a permanent presence on the European continent was the last thing desired by Roosevelt and his top officials. To many of them, the most appealing aspect of Morgenthau's proposal was that it was a policy of "smash and run." [21] The U.S. Government wanted to establish a righteous world, but only if it could be done swiftly.

The responsibility for developing a War Department plan that would permanently control Germany by means of quick and simple judicial action fell to Assistant Secretary McCloy. The task of actually designing such a plan then bounced down McCloy's chain of command until it finally came to rest in a catchall office of G-1 personnel entitled the "Special Projects Branch." Because of its obvious concern with the fate of American POWs in German hands, the personnel office had long been considering how to modify the mounting pressure for war crimes trials so as not to induce the Germans to reprisals. [22] The head of the Special Projects Branch, a New York lawyer named (Colonel) Murray C. Bernays, was aware of the strong pressure from Jewish groups for a public statement of war crimes policy that might act as a deterrent to the Nazi killings. But, like many people in Washington, Bernays had trouble keeping his eye on wartime atrocities. Whenever he touched the question, his focus seems to have moved inexorably away from the wartime exterminations and back to the Nazis' prewar persecutions within Germany. This predilection for emphasizing the relatively moderate persecutions of the 1930s at a time when mass murder was still continuing is difficult to explain. As late as 1949, when the panorama of the wartime holocaust was visible to all, Bernays, whose father was Jewish, made the incredible assertion that most of the anti-Jewish atrocities had been committed "before the war." [23] By 1944 he must have seen reports of the exterminations, but they apparently did not penetrate his consciousness any more than they did that of most others in Washington. Ingrained doubts about atrocity stories, an inability to grasp the reality of the holocaust, and the seeming futility of any effort to stop it, all played a part in this failure to comprehend reports of Auschwitz and other camps. It should be noted that one explanation of Bernays's strange focus is that Washington was alive with both Jewish and non-Jewish refugees from prewar Germany who served as executive officials and advisers to the U.S. Government. Quite naturally, they tended to direct official attention toward prewar Nazi actions, the circumstances of which they knew all too well.

That Bernays, like most of his colleagues, had a limited view of German atrocities fitted him perfectly for the task at hand. His primary assignment was not to develop a plan to stop atrocities, but to formulate a system that would defer action until after the war was over, thus sparing American personnel from reprisal. Of equal importance was the discovery of a clear and relatively simple formula that would give the War Department an effective answer to the Morgenthau plan.

Bernays struggled with these problems throughout the first part of September, then, on the 15th, he produced a memorandum of six pages entitled "Trial of European War Criminals." [24] This short paper is the most important single source for the ideas that shaped the subsequent prosecutions at Nuremberg. It may, indeed, be one of the most significant documents in modern international law. Bernays began by summarizing the obstacles that stood in the way of a traditional prosecution; particularly, the large number of prospective defendants and the inherent difficulty of prosecuting prewar Nazi actions as if they were war crimes. Great stress was laid on the demand of the smaller Allied governments that the prewar crimes be so categorized, that their perpetrators be punished so that survivors of the persecutions would feel satisfied that justice had been done. To prosecute only a fraction of the Nazi actions in the belief that most of the perpetrators were repeaters, would simply not appease all the persecuted groups and nationalities. The crimes and criminals had to be collectivized in order to restore some sense of order and justice. [25]

This was one of the main reasons Bernays totally rejected Morgenthau's idea of summary executions; a few quiet liquidations would not satisfy anyone. Furthermore, the Morgenthau plan would violate American judicial ideals, and it would not cope with the thousands of second-rank Nazi culprits. In his memorandum, therefore, Bernays boldly suggested a judicial plan that promised not only to solve all the existing problems but, in addition, to make the German leaders responsible for the actions of their subordinates, and to demonstrate to the German people the dangers of racism and totalitarianism. In Bernays's scheme, the Nazi party and the German Government organizations, such as the Gestapo, the SA, and the SS, would be charged before an international court with having conspired to commit murder, terrorism, and so forth in violation of the laws of war. Only individual defendants would be tried by such an international court, but each defendant would be representative of an organization accused of being part of the criminal conspiracy. When a representative defendant was convicted and sentenced by the court, then every other member of his organization would be judged to have been a criminal conspirator and would be liable to arrest, summary trial, and punishment by the Allied authorities. Since the prosecution in the international court would presumably contend that the conspiracy dated from the earliest days of the Nazi regime, all customary time limitations applicable to war crimes would disappear, and prewar crimes could be included in the conspiracy charge. The whole war crimes problem would thereby be reduced to a few simple elements: the swift judicial procedure would satisfy the participatory demands of the most diverse groups of victims and also provide the Allied occupation authorities with a flexible instrument to cleanse Germany of its war-making potential. The plan did not grant the members of Nazi organizations the customary protections of due process, but that did not seem to be a very pressing criticism at the time. Compared with the Morgenthau plan, any judicial proceeding appeared to be moderate and humane. Similarly, reliance on the peculiarly Anglo-American concept of conspiracy did not look like a serious flaw in the fall of 1944, because the War Department was not concerned to make a blueprint for an actual trial; all it needed was a postwar judicial proposal that would satisfy the spokesmen for the tormented victims and at the same time thwart the efforts of Henry Morgenthau. By September 15, 1944, Bernays was satisfied that he had produced just that, and the memorandum on the "Trial of European War Criminals" began to move up through War Department channels.[26]

We need not examine every way station that the plan touched en route. Suffice it to say that by mid-October it had reached the office of the secretary of war, where it received a sympathetic hearing from both McCloy and Secretary Stimson. The events of September and early October had made the arrival of the Bernays plan particularly timely. In early September, the secretary of the treasury's plans for postwar Germany had seemingly been approved by Roosevelt. When the president invited Morgenthau at that time to join him in Quebec for a meeting with Winston Churchill, the secretary of the treasury took a copy of the plan along with him. Churchill, deeply aware of the postwar financial plight that awaited Britain, was understandably solicitous of Morgenthau's economic views. Morgenthau also received unexpected assistance from a member of Churchill's party, Lord Chancellor Simon, who had brought along his own plan for executing the top Nazi leaders without trial. Toward the end of the Quebec conference, both Roosevelt and Churchill hastily signed copies of Morgenthau's plan for the "pasturization" of the German economy and the combined Simon-Morgenthau plan for the summary execution of Nazi leaders.

It has long been known that the actions of Roosevelt and Morgenthau at Quebec took place without the agreement or knowledge of even the most powerful members of the American Cabinet, such as Hull and Stimson. What has not been known until now is that on the war crimes issue Churchill and Simon also operated arbitrarily and independently of their government. As early as June 1942, Foreign Secretary Anthony Eden had prepared a Cabinet paper calling for a political rather than a judicial disposition of the top Nazi leaders, but no Cabinet action resulted.[27] Then, in November 1942, the British ambassador in Moscow sounded out Molotov on the Soviet attitude toward summary execution. Molotov's response was very cautious but did stress the need for "appropriate formalities" because Stalin was afraid that unless there was a trial he, Roosevelt, and Churchill would be accused of having killed Hitler and company out of a desire for personal revenge.[28]

Not until November 1943 did the British Cabinet get around to formally considering summary execution, but opinion was so sharply divided that no decision was possible. In February 1944, the Cabinet tried once more, and this time it did tone down a Churchill plan for immediate execution of the Nazi leaders, by replacing it with a proposal to put such "world outlaws" in strict confinement. Churchill took this Cabinet suggestion with him to the Cairo meeting, and, according to British records, Roosevelt "showed interest" in the idea.[29] But, in fact, the Americans did not consider it promising enough to follow up, and on the British side both the prime minister and the Foreign Office were still inclined toward summary execution. In the early spring of 1944, the Cabinet charged the Foreign Office with the responsibility of preparing a general paper for the Cabinet on the major war criminals issue, and both the Foreign Office and the PID (the Political Intelligence Department of the British War Office) prepared lists of between fifty and a hundred names of leading Nazis who should be executed immediately after capture. [30] Eden had advocated "political disposition" of the Nazi leaders for nearly two years, but when the moment came to take the lead in pushing through an execution procedure he became hesitant and squeamish. Sir William Malkin, the Foreign Office legal adviser, completed a draft proposal for the Cabinet and a number of Foreign Office officials added their supporting arguments in attached minutes. At the end of these minutes, however, Eden wrote:

I confess to having read no more than [the] above minutes. But I have such complete confidence in Sir W. Malkin in all things and may I confess it, so little taste for this subject that I am prepared to agree to all that is proposed here. A. E. May 26 [1944]. [31]

With such a weak champion, it is easy to understand why summary execution again failed to obtain Cabinet approval during the general discussion in June. [32]

Churchill, however, would not let the issue be dropped, and in August he wrote to Major General Sir Hastings Ismay, chief of staff to the minister of defence, urging that publication of a list of fifty to a hundred leaders scheduled for summary execution would be the best means of opening up a "gulf" between the Nazi leadership and the German population. [33] Still, when the Cabinet met on September 4, the new formulation of the summary execution plan that had been prepared by Lord Simon and two of his colleagues was not laid before it. The Cabinet was only told that Simon's paper had been given to the prime minister, but no Cabinet action was asked for or taken. [34] The Foreign Office did not see Simon's paper until September 18, after the prime minister had returned from Quebec, [35] and there was obvious Foreign Office concern over the offhand manner in which the affair had been conducted. [36] By the 27th, Churchill himself had become "a little anxious" because of the perennial fear that any public policy announcement might lead to retaliation against British POWs. [37] By the October 4 Cabinet meeting, the prime minister asked that no action be taken on the question and that events be allowed "to take their course" until the position of the United States and the Soviet Union was clarified.[38] With that, British major war crimes policy sank into such a limbo that it would not begin to recover for six months.

When Morgenthau returned to Washington from the Quebec conference, he did not, unlike Churchill and Simon in London, encounter a winding down of the problem. Instead, he was accorded a rather chilly reception by Stimson and Hull, the latter being especially incensed by Morgenthau's sortie into top-level foreign policy. With the secretaries of state and war united in opposition to the secretary of the treasury, a new round in the Cabinet conflict over postwar plans for Germany seemed inevitable. But this battle of titans never came off, because Morgenthau's powerful political position was undercut before the struggle could be fairly joined.

Word of Morgenthau's plan and the agreements made at Quebec was leaked to the press, probably from a source inside the State Department, and a storm of public protest washed over the Administration, nearly drowning Henry Morgenthau, Jr.[39] The treasury secretary's difficulties were compounded by Josef Goebbels, the Nazi propaganda minister, who seized upon these reports to stir up popular German resistance by painting a picture of the dire fate and mass misery which the Morgenthau plan would mean for a defeated Germany. Better to fight to the death, he screamed. Thus, when the Allied advance began to slow down in late September and early October, much of the American press attributed it to a German resistance stiffened by the menace of the Morgenthau plan. Morgenthau was rendered so completely harmless that Stimson came to his defense, stating in a public letter that the War Department did not attribute blame to the secretary of the treasury for the strong German resistance or the increased Allied casualties.[40] Roosevelt, on the other hand, made every effort to dissociate himself from Morgenthau's ideas. On one occasion, he admitted that a "serious mistake" had been made at Quebec but, marshalling all his disingenuous charm, he also claimed not to remember ever having signed the Morgenthau memo.[41]

With the Morgenthau forces swept from the field, no obstacle stood in the way of a War Department plan for war criminals. Colonel Bernays was ordered to report, with an oral summary of his ideas, to the secretary of war's office on October 24. Stimson, who had made part of his legal reputation in an antitrust conspiracy case, was so impressed that, three days later, he sent Bernays's memorandum on "The Trial of European War Criminals," together with a strong letter of support for it, to the Navy Department and to Secretary Hull.[42] During the subsequent months, while Morgenthau's influence was at its nadir, numerous War Department conferences were held, many with representatives of the Navy, State, and Justice departments attending. The legal foundations of the Bernays plan were also explored in the offices of the Judge Advocate General, the legal section of the State Department, and the specialists in the Justice Department.

These deliberations, however, were soon complicated by another war crimes problem. A number of the smaller Allied states sponsored a proposal urging the United Nations to declare that the launching of the war itself was a crime for which the Nazi leaders should be punished. The British Foreign Office flatly rejected the idea as having no basis in existing international law, and many top State Department officials agreed.[43] But behind the scenes, Stimson wanted the proposal to receive serious study. He had sponsored nonrecognition of Japanese conquests in 1931; now he had the opportunity to establish a legal basis for collective control of aggression. On November 27, at the bottom of a letter to Hull, Stimson penned a handwritten note that read, "I regard this matter as so important, that I request an opportunity for the expression of my personal views by the Sec'y. or in his absence the Acting Secy. H. L. S."[44] With Stimson championing both the aggressive war proposal and Bernays's war criminal plan, the two were certain to become intertwined.

By late December, the Yalta meeting of the Big Three was imminent, and some war crimes policy had to be agreed to in the event the question should arise during the conference. The discussion on war crimes rapidly rose to the cabinet level of the U.S. Government, and the War Department circulated to the State and Justice departments a modified version of the Bernays plan, with aggressive war included as one of the crimes charged against the Nazi leaders. The champions of this composite proposal believed that it represented far more than a mere alternative to the ideas put forth by Morgenthau, providing as it did for the traditional device of a trial to deal with the Nazi leaders. But this traditional trial, paradoxically, would be a long step forward in developing an international law to control future aggressors. The attitude of Colonel William Chanler, deputy director of the Civil Affairs Branch, a member of Stimson's law firm and a personal friend in civilian life, was typical of much War Department opinion. "Duelling was finally stopped," he wrote in a letter of December 20, 1944, "by making it a common crime and debunking the aura of honor and chivalry which surrounded it. Let's try and do the same with war as an instrument of National Policy." [45]

Since the War Department was so eager to try to control war by means of a trial, it seems only fitting that it was the Justice Department which raised most of the objections to the trial plan. In a memorandum of December 29, Assistant Attorney General Herbert Wechsler urged that the provisions charging the Nazis for prewar acts and acts against German nationals, as well as for launching the war, should all be dropped from the plan because they would constitute an ex post facto prosecution. Wechsler also noted that conspiracy was a peculiarly Anglo-American concept and suggested that a more limited form of "common plan" be used instead. Other shortcomings of the proposal, in Wechsler's view, were the prosecution of organizations and the fact that the plan called upon an international court to do too much on too many issues. [46] Wechsler's superior, Attorney General Francis Biddle, seems to have shared many of his doubts. A memorandum from the attorney general, dated January 5, 1945, stressed that acts committed before the outbreak of war should not be prosecuted and expressed serious doubt about any charges aimed at an aggressive war conspiracy. The attorney general's note also expressed concern over the prosecution of organizations and suggested that in lieu of this approach "very many courts" be used to prosecute subordinate criminals. [47]

What makes the reservations of the assistant attorney general so significant is that he later served as legal adviser to the American judges during most of the Nuremberg trial. Of even greater consequence, of course, is the fact that Attorney General Biddle, who had such doubts about the modified Bernays plan, was to become the senior American member at the Nuremberg Tribunal. Obviously, the doubts that Wechsler and Biddle harbored about conspiracy and the prosecution of group crime would play a major role in the shaping of the Nuremberg Judgment in the fall of 1946.

Equally significant and far more perplexing is the fact that Biddle underwent a temporary change of heart between January 5, 1945, when he dictated his criticism of the War Department plan, and

January 21, when he approved a modified summary of the same proposal. Time pressures on Biddle were, of course, great though his department did manage to produce some modifications in the War Department plan. But a system had to be developed quickly to guide the President at Yalta, and, with Morgenthau fallen into disgrace, the War Department had put forward the only well-developed proposal. As happened repeatedly with American wartime policy making, the War Department had the initiative. By January 1945, even Roosevelt was speaking in that department's war crimes idiom. On January 3, in a note to the secretary of state, his remarks on planning regarding major war criminals seemed to assume that there would be a trial, for he wrote: "The charges should include an indictment for waging aggressive and unprovoked warfare in violation of the Kellogg Pact. Perhaps these and other charges might be joined in a conspiracy indictment." [48] Franklin Roosevelt had made a long journey since Quebec, and a seasoned New Deal politician like Francis Biddle recognized that it was pointless to run head on against the direction the President was taking, especially in wartime.

With Stimson and the State Department now united, and Roosevelt expressing sympathy for Stimson's position, there was virtually no chance that the War Department plan would be rejected. Furthermore, in the course of January, the most glaring Nazi atrocity against American troops occurred—the massacre of a group of American POWs by an SS detachment at Malmedy, in Belgium, during the Battle of the Bulge. It was a rather modest atrocity, as Nazi horrors went, but it stung the government in Washington. It had been committed by an SS combat detachment, which, from all appearances, seemed to be acting pursuant to higher orders. Until this incident, even Stimson seemed to have had reservations about including all the military SS (the *Waffen* SS) in the prosecution of criminal organizations. Malmedy swept away all such hesitation. [49] Henceforth, the War Department wanted the whole SS prosecuted, and serious questions began to be raised about the responsibility of the German Army high command for the use of such troops and for the methods they employed.

In the full flood of horror and anger surrounding Malmedy, Francis Biddle joined Secretaries Hull and Stimson in signing a modified summary of the War Department plan, entitled "Memorandum for the President: Trial and Punishment of Nazi War Criminals." [50] It called for an Allied court to try the German leaders and their organizations for the commission of "atrocious crimes" and for joint participation in a "broad criminal enterprise" to commit those crimes. The charges to be covered by the "broad criminal enterprise" were: acts committed before the outbreak of the war; those committed against German nationals; and, especially, "the waging of an illegal war of aggression." [51] With the three Cabinet members finally in agreement, the issue seemed settled, and in late January 1945 Roosevelt took the memorandum with him to Yalta. But at the Yalta conference, under the pressure of other controversies, the war criminal question did not come up for discussion by the Big Three. So, when the president returned to Washington in February, official American policy on the major war criminals was still in limbo. The president had indicated sympathy for the War Department approach but he had not officially approved the secretaries' memorandum or even initialed it.

In the weeks after Yalta, numerous vital issues affecting the war in Europe and Asia demanded action. And the start of the president's fourth term was marked with complex new difficulties in the areas of peacemaking and postwar adjustment. As these problems increased, Roosevelt's stamina faltered, for he was gravely ill. In March, he made one last effort to resolve the war crimes problem with the Allies by sending his speech writer, Judge Sam Rosenman, to hammer out a common formula with the British in London. Rosenman, who was in Europe on another mission, was an old friend of Bernays and strongly sympathized with the War Department approach. [52] But neither he nor anyone else had Roosevelt's written agreement to the War Department plan.

Between October and Rosenman's arrival in March, the British position on what course to follow regarding the major war criminals had undergone little change. In mid-October, Churchill had journeyed to Moscow and in the course of that visit heard Stalin's opinion that a trial of the major Nazis was absolutely essential. Stalin's strong rejection of summary execution further inclined Churchill not to press for an Allied, or even a Cabinet, decision. [53] Both the lord chancellor and the British attorney general, Donald Somervell, were still opposed to a trial, but along with all the top British officials, they were content to follow a policy of wait and see. Nothing official on the subject had been heard from Washington since the Quebec conference, but informal talks with State Department specialists apparently led the Foreign Office to believe that the U.S. Government was still opposed to a trial.[54] On one occasion, the Foreign Office did receive a hint from the ambassador in Washington, Lord Halifax, that Stimson favored a trial, but it was not until January 1945 that London began to get vague indications that a major policy fight over the treatment of war criminals was taking place in Washington and that the advocates of trial seemed to be gaining the upper hand.[55]

The British were thus caught completely unaware when Rosenman descended on London with the trial plan that Hull, Biddle, and Stimson had prepared for the president in January. After some shuffling and confusion, the British arranged for him to meet with a number of top officials; discussions occurred with Simon, and Rosenman also spent a weekend with the prime minister. The Rosenman-Churchill meeting seems to have had no serious consequences, but Lord Simon tried to cope with Rosenman by trotting out the old summary execution plan that had been used at Quebec. Rosenman, however, flatly rejected the idea of execution without trial and observed that Stimson was strongly opposed to it as well.[56] No mention was made of Roosevelt's position, nor were questions raised about what had happened to his opinions since Quebec. Still, Simon saw the handwriting on the wall—the U.S. Cabinet and Stalin were both against summary execution, and the Lord Chancellor's pet scheme was therefore doomed. In its place he worked out a proposal involving a double compromise. The British would accept the American plan to prosecute criminal organizations as a device to get at the "intermediate level" of criminals, those who had played a significant role in any of the organizations. For the major criminals, Simon proposed that the Allies prepare what he called a "document of arraignment" setting out a detailed record of their crimes. They would be given a brief opportunity to refute the charges therein, and, if they failed to do so effectively, they would be disposed of by a political decision of the Allied governments. Simon implied that this meant execution but did not exclude the possibility of lengthy confinement.[57]

While Rosenman and his advisers considered the proposal, Simon hurried to the Cabinet to obtain approval for what he had done. Instead of support, however, he met virtually unanimous opposition, for the Cabinet concluded that he had managed to blend together the worst features of the judicial and political alternatives. The Cabinet's "general view" was that a full trial for the Nazi leaders "was out of the question." [58] It ordered Simon to inform Rosenman that the British Government had rejected his document of arraignment proposal and also instructed Simon and the Foreign Office to prepare messages for Washington explaining why the British government opposed a trial. [59]

In the meantime, Rosenman, totally unaware of the divisions in the British camp, was troubled by Simon's document of arraignment suggestion. Desperate, he cabled the State Department asking for instructions from the Cabinet on what approach he should take; but the reply that came on April 11 from Edward Stettinius, who had replaced Hull as secretary of state, stated merely that it would not be possible to coordinate the views of the War, State, and Justice departments "until tomorrow." [60] But, for Rosenman's mission, tomorrow and the instructions never came, for on the 12th he was informed that the British Government had disavowed the Simon plan, and from Washington he received the even more crushing news that Roosevelt had just died in Warm Springs, Georgia.

The discussions in London collapsed, and Rosenman hurried back to Washington for the funeral. The capital was in a state of shock, and the programs that had not received official presidential approval, among them that for war crimes, seemed to be in trouble. But Harry S. Truman took charge as president much more rapidly and firmly than most observers had expected. On April 17, Judge Rosenman cabled the American staff in London that he had talked with the new president, whom he found "definitely opposed to political disposition of [the] top criminals," though probably willing to make some concessions on trial procedure. [61] This was the crucial turn in the road that led to Nuremberg. Truman had accepted the three secretaries' January memorandum on war criminals as the established policy of the U.S. Government, and he was not prepared to move very far from its provisions. There were to be no more debates in Washington over war criminal procedure or the use of a trial; Truman, a former judge, had made up his mind and that was that.

In late April and early May, the new president's firmness on this and other issues became more visible; it also became clear that the war against Germany would soon end, with the United States left holding a commanding military and economic position in Western Europe. The U.S. Government, consequently, was ready to act with determination and confidence, if not bravado, on all outstanding questions.

In early May, Rosenman was sent to the United Nations Conference in San Francisco, charged with the responsibility of convincing the British, Russians, and French to accept the U.S. war crimes trial plan. He was strengthened in this formidable task by dramatic signs of the American Government's resolve.[62] On April 29, Justice Robert H. Jackson of the Supreme Court agreed to head the European war crimes prosecution effort, and on May 2 Truman officially appointed Jackson to the post of "Chief of Counsel for the Prosecution of Axis Criminality." [63] The impressive title of the post and the appointment of so prominent a judicial figure to fill it gave clear warning that the United States would not dally any longer. Behind the scenes, the preparations made by the U.S. staff showed equal determination. For weeks, an American interagency team, again featuring Colonel Bernays, had been shaping the American plan into an executive agreement, to be presented to the other powers in San Francisco. When Jackson became chief prosecutor, but before his appointment was publicly announced, this executive agreement was substantially redrafted by Bernays, Colonel Cutter from the War Department, Assistant Attorney General Wechsler, and Justice Jackson himself.[64] Although its essential elements were finished by April 30, the document continued to be corrected and retyped right up to the time it was handed to the Allied representatives in San Francisco.

Once again, the British Government had not made equally effective use of the time that had elapsed since Roosevelt's death. Though warned by John J. McCloy during a visit to London in mid-April that Stimson was committed to a trial, [65] and also alerted by the British Embassy of the existence of a rising tide of American opinion demanding immediate measures with regard to war criminals, the London government decided to move slowly and cautiously.[66] Even when word reached London that Truman had decided there must be a trial, the initial reaction of Lord Simon was to press efforts to bring the United States over to the summary execution alternative.[67] But the onward rush of events caught up with the British Government. On May 2, Anthony Eden, who was leading the British delegation in San Francisco, cabled an urgent message asking for Cabinet instructions on a war crimes meeting that the foreign ministers of the Big Three were holding on the following day. The British Cabinet discussed the cable on May 3 and agreed that, if the United States and the USSR had decided definitely in favor of a trial, there was no point to continued British opposition. With Hitler and Mussolini already dead, some Cabinet members concluded that a conspiracy and criminal organization trial might be made to produce a simple and effective procedure. Therefore, the Cabinet decided to accept the idea in principle, while putting the onus for "producing a workable procedure" on the Americans, before "finally committing" the British Government "to an agreement." [68] What no one in London seems to have suspected was that the Americans already had a polished trial plan in their pocket.

On May 3, Rosenman showed the draft executive agreement to Molotov and Eden in a special meeting arranged by Secretary of State Stettinius. Eden managed to keep a straight face and indicated that Britain was prepared to abandon its opposition to a trial if, as Rosenman reported to Truman, the "Russians join with us in favoring a trial." [69] Since the Soviets had always wanted a trial, and again reiterated this desire in San Francisco, the Americans took Eden's remark to be Britain's formal, public capitulation on the trial question. In American eyes, the only issue remaining was to get agreement from the other powers on the plan to prosecute aggressive war and other crimes as part of the charges to be brought against criminal organizations.

The foreign ministers did not concern themselves with the latter question, but they did agree to allow immediate discussion of the American executive agreement by specialists from the Three Powers, together with a French representative. [70] The first probing session between the legal specialists of the four Allied states occurred on May 5. Rosenman, backed by Assistant Secretary of War McCloy (Jackson did not go to San Francisco), tried to achieve an expeditious decision, but, as should have been anticipated, numerous questions were raised that set off rounds of rewording and redrafting. Surprisingly, the criminal conspiracy idea did not call forth sharp protest from the continental representatives. The main controversies were over inclusion of the "crime" of "launching an aggressive war" and the implementation of the charges against criminal organizations. The Americans agreed to much rewording throughout the paper and also tried to meet two practical but far-reaching objections. The proposal contained in the American executive agreement called for a Tribunal composed of one judge from each of the Four Powers, with a voting procedure that required three votes for conviction. Both the British and the Soviets objected to this procedure, and the United States consequently agreed to add the following sentence: "In the event that the Tribunal is in disagreement as to its judgment, the accused may be brought to trial before a second Tribunal." [71] In the course of redrafting, this passage was later removed, but in the actual deliberations of the Nuremberg Tribunal the Soviet senior judge again raised questions about voting procedure. Though troublesome and time-consuming, this kind of question could seemingly be dealt with directly. More significant was the repeated Soviet probing on major issues, which in one instance led to the inclusion of a new concluding sentence to the draft agreement:

The signatories agree that the Control Council for Germany shall establish policies and procedures governing (a) the return of persons in Germany charged with criminal offenses to the scene of their crimes in accordance with the Moscow Declaration and (b) the surrender of persons within Germany who are in the custody of any of the signatories who are demanded for prosecution by any party to this Agreement. [72]

This was a very strong formulation of the promises that Roosevelt had given to Stalin at Yalta regarding the extradition of war criminals and Soviet nationals. Controversy over this question has reverberated right down to the current popularity of Solzhenitsyn's *Gulag Archipelago*. In this instance, the passage in question was toned down in later drafts, but its inclusion in the San Francisco paper indicated that complete agreement would be difficult to obtain, if for no other reason than that implications of the war crimes question touched on other vital aspects of relations between the Great Powers.

Rosenman, however, seems to have thought that the core of the trouble in San Francisco was that the specialists dallied and the foreign ministers were too preoccupied to give their governments' assent to the final plan. On May 10, Rosenman put McCloy in charge of the discussions and hurriedly departed for Washington, informing the other delegations that he would return as soon as they received authority to sign. [73] Although some perfunctory conversations occurred after May 10, when Rosenman left, the slim chance that a final agreement could be worked out in San Francisco evaporated. Once again the focal point of the war crimes question shifted to Washington, but there was no longer any confusion about who was personally responsible. Jackson had taken charge, and he easily beat back a final effort by Henry Morgenthau to overthrow the trial plan. Jackson also persuaded the military authorities to delay most of their proceedings against lesser war criminals and to coordinate their activities with his own.[74] A top-echelon prosecution staff was quickly assembled by Jackson, with Sidney Alderman, general counsel for the Southern Railway, as deputy prosecutor, and a staff including General William Donovan, Director of the Office of Strategic Services (OSS), the wartime central intelligence service, former Assistant Attorney General Francis Shea, and Colonel Bernays, who was transferred from the War Department. This group began to plan the structure of the American prosecution organization and to make preparations for the collection of evidence. Liaison agreements for document collection were made with the State Department and with the OSS. In addition, Donovan promised to provide the prosecution staff with large numbers of OSS support personnel.[75]

With such extensive plans and influential support, Jackson was not about to accept the indecisive results that had emerged from the San Francisco conference as final. Like Rosenman, he seems to have believed that the root of the trouble was the slowness and inefficiency of Allied diplomacy, and that the answer to the problem was to exert more pressure. Following Jackson's lead, the State Department ordered the U.S. embassies in London, Paris, and Moscow to urge the Allied governments to accept the American plan and appoint chiefs of counsel comparable to Jackson. London was prodded by visits from a series of special emissaries, including Joseph E. Davies and Jackson himself.[76]

The British somewhat resented the pressure and publicity surrounding Jackson's appointment. "We shall be in for a rough passage," wrote a member of the Foreign Office in May, "if we do anything short of accepting the U.S. proposal."[77] Still eager to limit "the rather large ideas" of the Americans, the Foreign Office wanted to restrict the number of defendants, simplify the procedure, and if possible hold the Allied negotiations in London rather than Washington.[78] The British Government, however, had made its basic decision, and it was hesitant to change chiefly because its end-of-the-war political crisis had brought in a caretaker Cabinet that was cautious about decision making. A special Cabinet committee did recommend, in principle, acceptance of the American plan on May 18, and British officials used every possible occasion to assure the Americans that their government, having abandoned its summary execution policy, was prepared to cooperate with the Americans in proceeding as rapidly as possible.[79]

When Jackson arrived in London on May 28, he thus found the British in a most conciliatory mood. While awaiting formal Cabinet approval, British officials were ready to proceed on the assumption that the new Attorney General David Maxwell Fyfe would be appointed to a position of negotiator-prosecutor comparable to that held by Jackson, as he indeed was appointed on May 29. Similarly, the British were prepared to continue discussions on the assumption that the caretaker Cabinet would give its approval to the American draft, which it did on May 30.[80] How far the British position had shifted was revealed by a remark Maxwell Fyfe made to Jackson. The British attorney general had concluded, on reflection, that a trial would have a distinct advantage, for, if the British Government were going to keep armed forces in Germany to control that country, "we must have the support of public opinion." Britain was "therefore as anxious as the United States to have indisputable proof of the [atrocities of the] Nazi regime."[81] On his part, Jackson showed himself highly pleased by the British attitude (the hospitality at Claridge's seems to have dazzled every American wartime visitor to London) and he made every effort to be as moderate and reasonable as possible. He was apparently inclined to limit the prosecution of criminal organizations to the SS and the Gestapo and echoed the opinion of his deputy, General Donovan, that some of the Nazi leaders of "weak and low character" might provide evidence against their colleagues and thereby bring the trial to a quick conclusion.[82]

The first meetings between Jackson and the British thus ended on a most optimistic note, and no sooner had the justice left London than the British formally announced their acceptance, in principle, of the American proposal, and invited the other powers to meet in London on June 25 to conclude a final agreement. After a short delay, the French and Soviets also announced their readiness to meet in London; however, there was much confusion over the appointment of the respective chiefs of counsel of the three governments. The British appointment of Maxwell Fyfe (later the Earl of Kilmuir) had to be changed in the middle of the London negotiations because the Conservatives lost the general election. Lord Shawcross of the Labor party assumed the position of chief of the British War Crimes Executive, while Maxwell Fyfe became his deputy. The French first selected Professor Donnedieu de Vabres (later appointed the senior French judge at Nuremberg), but quickly changed their minds and sent Judge Robert Falco to negotiate in London (he reappeared at Nuremberg, too, but as France's alternate Tribunal member). The Soviets sent General I. T. Nikitchenko as their chief negotiator in London, and he also became a Nuremberg judge. Thus, many of the men on the Nuremberg bench, or closely associated with it, had played roles in formulating the laws on which the trial was based. In addition to the three judges just mentioned, it should be remembered that both Herbert Wechsler and Francis Biddle had helped to develop the basic American plan.

Despite these peculiarities, if not judicial indelicacies, the United States had, through overwhelming pressure, achieved its goal by mid-June. The other three Powers had agreed to hold a trial and to accept the American San Francisco draft as the basis for discussions in London. But the means used to obtain agreement meant that the Allied representatives went to London with more questions than answers. As the U.S. ambassador in Paris, Jefferson Caffery, reported on June 19, just one week before the conference opened:

While there still appears to be confusion in the minds of the French as to the exact functions of the representatives which they have appointed to meet with Justice Jackson and the British and Soviet representatives, it is believed that this can best be explained to them at the London Conference.[83]

The Soviets also seemed to be confused about the U.S. proposal, for they had views of their own about dealing with war criminals. On May 28, 1945, during a meeting in the Kremlin between Stalin and Truman's special emissary, Harry Hopkins, the question arose of what should be done with German General Staff officers. Stalin noted that by the term "staff officers" he meant not only those with formal military staff training, but all German officers who had done general staff work. That meant around 25,000 people. Stalin went on to suggest that these men should all be kept under arrest, "possibly for ten or twenty years." Hopkins raised no objections to this proposal but observed that the U.S. wished to try the General Staff as a criminal organization, to which Stalin made the droll response, he thought it "a very good idea if it were legally possible." [84] For Stalin to raise questions about legal propriety should have given the

U.S. pause in its cheerful rush forward toward a war crimes trial.

A conversation between Secretary of State Stettinius and the Soviet minister in Washington, Nikolai V. Novikov, on June 14, should have provided further indication that there might be trouble ahead. Novikov did not know that the Soviet government had agreed to participate in the London war crimes conference and continued to voice his doubts, despite Stettinius's repeated assurances that the Soviets would participate. With less than two weeks remaining before the opening of the conference, the Americans had clearly moved too far and too fast. Novikov, in his doubt and confusion, continued bringing up the two considerations that the Soviet government had told him needed to be raised about the American plan. Specifically, he asked how the Allies could prosecute the Gestapo and SS when the Big Three at Yalta had condemned them and ordered them dissolved—to the Soviets, that condemnation was final and any subsequent proceeeding would be meaningless and perhaps blasphemous. Secondly, in Soviet language the chiefs of counsel, whom the Americans thought of as independent prosecutors, had become a "Committee of Inquiry" [85]—a phrase that sounded a bit ominous even to Stettinius. But the secretary of state swept ahead, dismissing Novikov's queries as "matters of detail," and threw in yet another American contribution to the general confusion. He told Novikov that, in the month since the discussions in San Francisco, the U.S. Government had prepared a new and refined version of the original proposal because, in the secretary's words, the United States "regarded it as a rather basic document in future International Law."

Actually, Jackson's staff and the War Department had done a great deal of revising and redrafting in the post–San Francisco period, but they had completed their labors by mid-May. The American Government had sat on the final revision for nearly a month while it pressed the Allied governments for agreement, in principle, to the original proposal. Apparently only in the conversation with Novikov did Stettinius wonder out loud whether the Americans could "advance matters" by letting their Allies see the current proposal. Novikov, with masterful understatement, replied that such a step would be "helpful," and with an assurance from Stettinius that copies of the revised proposal would be sent to the French, British, and Soviet embassies, the Russian finally was allowed to escape from the State Department. [86] The American effort to inform their allies of revisions was so belated, however, that the new proposal, handed to the British Embassy in Washington, did not pass through the Foreign Office registry in London until July 3—two weeks after the American negotiating team arrived in London.[87]

Two days following the Novikov-Stettinius talks, new indication reached the State Department that Soviet war crimes attitudes might be complex. The British ambassador in Moscow, Clark Kerr, had discussed the issue with Molotov on June 13, and a report of their conversation was relayed from London to Washington on the 16th. Molotov had told Kerr that the Soviets were prepared to accept the American proposal made in San Francisco (he of course did not know that it had subsequently been revised), with "some minor amendments." Molotov, however, also said that "the cases of Paulus and other German generals in the Russians' hands" might need to be discussed and consideration given to the help that "certain of these" had provided to the Soviet Union.[88]

Paulus had been commander of the German forces that had surrendered at Stalingrad; he had, along with other high-ranking German officers, agreed to cooperate with the Soviet authorities after his capture, and had made a number of appeals to the Germans who were still fighting, urging them to surrender or to overthrow the Hitler government. The Western powers had long been nervous about Soviet intentions regarding the "Free German Committee" that the Russians had formed from among the cooperative German prisoners and a nucleus of refugee German communists. Any mention of Paulus and "cooperative German officers" should have sounded warning bells in Washington. War crimes was not a simple issue but one that might easily interact with other sensitive points rapidly emerging between East and West.

The danger signs, though, were all ignored. The British had been compelled to make a quick public reversal, the French were floundering in helpless confusion, and the Soviets—from Stalin's remark about "legality" to Molotov's observations on Paulus—were showing that war crimes prosecution could be as difficult as any one of the Great Powers chose to make it. The Americans, however, held the initiative, and they chose to continue full speed ahead.

CHAPTER 3

The London Conference
and the Nuremberg
Indictment

If you are determined to execute a man in
any case, there is no occasion for a trial; the
world yields no respect to courts that are
merely organized to convict.

Robert H. Jackson [1]

THE LARGE and well-equipped American staff arrived in London on June 20, 1945. It had come to negotiate an agreement quickly and to prepare the documentary materials necessary for a trial. Despite the serious errors made in preparatory diplomacy, the American delegation had many solid assets. They came to a gray, shattered Europe in that summer of 1945, a Europe that anxiously felt the necessity and urgency of a new start. The Americans, with their enthusiasm, money, and equipment, seemed capable of coping with every problem, from smashed railroads to war crimes.

Europeans stood knee-deep in the horror and wreckage left by six years of war and twelve years of Nazism. No one doubted that Nazi Germany had started the war. Millions were dead, and the memory of a savage Nazi occupation was still a bitter reality from central Russia to the Atlantic. Each day's newspaper revealed new chapters in bestiality out of concentration camps and death factories, such as Auschwitz and Treblinka. Nazi Germany had too drastically proven its power and ruthlessness. Scores had to be settled and a groundwork barring revival of such power had to be laid.

The mood in the U.S. Government and in the American delegation in London harmonized closely with that prevailing among the peoples of Europe. Although the Americans had been spared most of the war's horror, they were eager to move quickly and to innovate where necessary. President Truman himself, in a letter to General Evangeline Booth of the Salvation Army, agreed that strong, and perhaps unprecedented measures were necessary to deal with war criminals. Due to their "barbaric practices," Truman asserted, "we have a stern duty to teach the German people the hard lesson that they must change their ways before they can be received back into the family of peaceful civilized nations." [2] This self-righteous tone may sound embarrassing today, but it conformed perfectly to the times and caused no popular resentment against the United States in 1945. It was the timidity and concern for legal technicalities on the part of the other Allied governments that aroused public opinion.

The American difficulty was not innovation, but a tendency, as old as the republic, to believe that our particular innovation was going to be good for everyone and would receive instantaneous approval. At most times, such expressions are somewhat muted by isolationist sentiment and the efforts of professionals in the State Department. But during World War II, these restraints were greatly weakened. Amateur negotiating teams, such as Jackson's, tended to embody the national characteristics undilutedly; and, with little experience in diplomacy, they plunged forward recklessly. Jackson was not subordinate to the State Department, since he had been given a special assignment by the president. The justice reported only to Truman. It was left to Jackson to decide what, if any, information should be sent to the State Department. Jackson's staff members had little inclination to move slowly; most of them were young reserve military officers caught up in the great upswing of confidence that accompanied the American victory in Europe. They saw this assignment as the adventurous climax of their military service and were neither awed by the ruins of the European civilization that surrounded them nor attracted by the prospect of long drawn-out deliberations.[3]

Yet, even when allowance is made for these circumstances, the intensity of the American delegation's belief that it could produce an agreement smoothly and quickly remains astonishing. In early June, Jackson reportedly told one of his assistants that he expected to conclude an agreement within a week.[4] On June 25, the day *before* the negotiations began, the justice was so optimistic after a brief conversation with the chief French representative that he cabled directly to the White House to say that the "prospects of agreement on [the] protocol are good. Will you advise me whether, if it is agreeable, I am authorized to sign. . . . Think it very desirable to be in a position to close matter if possible." [5] A few days later, he received the desired authorization, but by then negotiations were in full swing and he was unpleasantly aware that there was little prospect for a quick settlement.

The British bore little responsibility for Jackson's disillusionment, because they placed only minor obstacles in the way of the American rush to an agreement. There were some touches of resentment at American high-handedness, and there was also some uneasiness about how a trial procedure reconciling Soviet and Western legal systems might be developed.[6] But, like their American counterparts, the British also revealed an amazing ignorance about the systematic nature of Nazi atrocities. On one occasion, for example, Maxwell Fyfe announced his perception, as if revealing a heretofore unsuspected truth, that Maidenek concentration camp "could only have been run with the approval of the German government." [7] What hampered the British team, even more than their ignorance of Nazism, was their muddled picture of what was contained in the American prosecution plan. First of all, opinion was divided on whether the Americans planned one trial or perhaps three or four.[8] British confusion on this point is readily understandable because, on June 9, Jackson's deputy, General Donovan, told the British that he envisioned "a series of trials by the same court on the same indictment" of groups of Nazi defendants.[9] Maxwell Fyfe seems to have believed that all other considerations were to be subordinated to that of convicting Goering of a capital crime because, in his opinion, the conviction of Goering as ranking Nazi leader would discredit the whole regime.[10]

The British also had trouble understanding what the Americans planned to do with the conspiracy and criminal organization prosecution, and whether the main focus of the trial was to be on war crimes or on aggressive war. After long discussions, they decided to try to keep the Americans focused on a Nazi "conspiracy to dominate Europe" theme as the best way of limiting the number of defendants and the quantity of necessary evidence.[11] The British did an enormous amount of work sifting through biographical data on the Nazi leaders that had been compiled by the Foreign Office—data that were far more accurate and up to date than those the Americans would subsequently use.[12] Out of this process came a compact list of ten defendants—Goering, Hess, Ribbentrop, Ley, Keitel, Streicher, Kaltenbrunner, Rosenberg, Frank, and Frick. With this list the British hoped to convince the Americans that one trial based on the "conspiracy to dominate Europe" theme was both possible and desirable.[13]

By the time Jackson and his party arrived in London, anxious to nail down British support for their revised executive agreement, Maxwell Fyfe and his aides had already completed much of their own preparatory work. Extensive Anglo-American talks, therefore, began immediately, even though the French and Soviet delegations had not yet arrived. Since Jackson's team was so obviously delighted by British cooperativeness,[14] the British quickly took the initiative by trying out their prospective defendant list. Jackson had been so worried about obtaining Allied agreement for the basic trial system that he had allotted no time for picking the defendants. Caught unaware, the Americans could do little but voice their agreement that the list should not be "overloaded," while leaving open the possibility that more names could be subsequently added.

Throughout the talks with the British, Jackson showed himself cooperative, although his comments and opinions about the Soviet Union were mixed. He stated that he did not want the trial held in the Soviet zone of Germany, and he also stressed that, if the Soviet delegation did not arrive on time, he proposed "a public announcement of the adjournment of the Four Power discussions" that would put the blame squarely on the Russians.[15] Yet, on another occasion, the justice remarked that it was essential *not* to alienate the French and the Russians by presuming that the Anglo-Americans were "the only champions of justice in the world." [16] The British continued to be impressed by Jackson throughout the talks, and in general the Anglo-Americans were so pleased with each other's reasonableness and the prospects for a quick agreement that they decided to go ahead and set up subcommittees to begin drafting an indictment and planning the organization of the actual trial.

The situation looked rather different to the French and Soviet representatives when they arrived on June 24 and 25. The continental delegates needed time to take stock of the situation, but when they did so they discovered that their Anglo-American allies had not only come to an understanding on a number of general points but were well on the way to organizing the actual trial. The weak French Government was not in a position to object too strongly, but the powerful Soviets were, and they had good reason to feel slighted. The conduct of the Anglo–Americans was perfectly suited to awaken Soviet suspicions, leading to a Russian conviction that it was best to slow down the tempo of operations. The American decision to submit the revised proposal that Stettinius had mentioned to Novikov, rather than the one used at San Francisco, gave the Soviets a perfect means to stop the Anglo-American steamroller. Jackson tried to get things moving in the first conference session on June 26, but the Soviets and the French complained that they had received the revised draft of the executive agreement only the day before.[17] The obvious unreasonableness of the American demand for quick action under these circumstances forced Jackson to take a more hesitant and conciliatory approach. By day's end it was agreed that the delegations would read the American proposals and then make any recommendations or revisions they thought necessary. Although the pace of the session had been slow, Jackson and his staff seem to have attributed this to the need to proceed in three languages and were relatively well satisfied with the results. But again they misread the signals, apparently thinking that, once the Soviets and French had studied the plan, they would agree as readily as the British had done.

Within a few days these hopes were shattered, and criticisms and suggestions rained down on the American plan. The Soviets were concerned over the content of some of the crimes mentioned in the draft and over the procedures set forth to prosecute them. The main Soviet criticism focused on the concept of prosecuting organizations. Nikitchenko quickly brought up the same objections that Novikov had raised with Stettinius: How could a mere Tribunal presume to rule on a question such as the criminality of the SS, which had already been dealt with by the Big Three? How could an organization such as the Gestapo be prosecuted when it had already been dissolved by the Allied authorities and no longer existed? Going further, Nikitchenko challenged the whole notion of organizational crime. In this he was quickly seconded by the French and ultimately, the British, whose second thoughts about the legality of prosecuting criminal organizations were accompanied by increasingly apprehensive doubts about American plans to prosecute German prewar economic leaders.[18] The British feared that attacks on German companies might raise questions or accusations embarrassing to Anglo-American firms.

The revised American draft also came in for heavy criticism on the ground that the crimes enumerated therein were ex post facto. It was an especially telling argument, for the draft employed unusually direct language in asserting that acts such as launching wars were literally criminal. It also included a paragraph defining international law as the sum of treaties, the laws of nations, and the values developed by "the dictates of public conscience." [19] This notion did not bother the Soviets particularly, but it troubled the more cautious British and precise French.

The question of ex post facto prosecution and the criminal organization controversy were mere skirmishes, however, when compared with the furor that erupted over the suggestion of prosecuting conspiracy. On this issue, lines were quickly drawn—the continental countries, France and Russia, versus the British and the Americans. During much of the discussion, the Russians and French seemed unable to grasp all the implications of the concept; when they finally did grasp it, they were genuinely shocked. The French viewed it entirely as a barbarous legal anachronism unworthy of modern law, while the Soviets seem to have shaken their heads in wonderment—a reaction, some cynics may believe, prompted by envy. But the main point of the Soviet attack on conspiracy was that it was too vague and so unfamiliar to the French and themselves, as well as to the Germans, that it would lead to endless confusion. In this contention they were clearly right, but the Americans had gone too far to scrap the plan; every Soviet and French objection was met by American rewording and compromise in an effort to cast the idea in more familiar and acceptable language. Periodically, in the middle of these lengthy discussions, the French would become nervous and the Russians impatient, until one or the other would return to the idea that the whole conspiracy basis be abandoned.[20]

All of these problems and criticisms tumbled into the hands of Justice Jackson, who was not in a strong position to cope with them. The best way for the Americans to convince their fellow allies to go along with them was to assert that prosecution would be easy and that they had the situation under control. Behind the scenes, however, Jackson's staff was giving little indication of smooth or effortless efficiency. Of necessity, it had been assembled quickly and included a heterogeneous collection of people. With little time to adjust their personality differences, they were required to produce immediately an organization for negotiation and prosecution. Many of the staff were young military lawyers with little trial experience, less administrative background, and no familiarity with the intricacies of international relations. Their knowledge of Nazi Germany was generally meager, although this deficiency was partly offset by their use of a sizable contingent of German political refugees as advisers.

The complex situation called for a chief with unusual administrative and diplomatic ability. Robert Jackson was a brilliant trial attorney and a legal stylist of unusual power. His performance as solicitor general, attorney general, and member of the Supreme Court had earned him the respect of Felix Frankfurter and other legal giants. But Jackson was not a gifted administrator and frequently showed himself to be short-tempered and combative, especially when under pressure. Perhaps no man could have preserved his dignity as a Supreme Court justice while at the same time functioning as an aggressive administrator and referee. As it was, Jackson neither asserted strong central direction nor resolved the bitter personal feuds and conflicts that riddled his organization. This weak leadership continued throughout both the negotiations and the trial itself.

There were troubles not only in negotiation but also in the logistics of gathering evidence. Centers for the collection of evidence had been established in Washington, London, and Paris, and elaborate systems to translate materials had also been developed. In addition, what seemed a veritable army of American investigators equipped with typewriters and mimeograph machines, was scurrying throughout England and the continent, apparently assembling an overwhelming case for the prosecution. This formidable appearance certainly helped the Americans convince their colleagues that, if they would only agree to the American plan, the case was as good as won. Actually, the document collection system had one serious flaw—it simply was not producing the necessary documents.

On June 30, Jackson wrote to the assistant secretary of war that, although the flow of evidence from the continent was well organized, it did not provide "proof for the larger case," for Nazi planning and for the existence of a conspiracy.[21] Jackson concluded that this vital proof would have to come from the holdings of the American and other Allied governments' archives, especially those of the British—a vain hope, indeed, by late June 1945. Colonel Bernays, who had been brought from Washington to serve as an adviser during the negotiations, was given the responsibility for document collection in London. By early July, Bernays's discouragement bordered on despair; the material obtained from the OSS was largely useless and the interrogations of enemy captives had also produced little. In a letter to a friend in the War Department he wrote that to prepare the case properly "a minor miracle" would be necessary. "We have repeatedly won the case with glorious brave talk in conference," he observed, "but the actual proof could be listed on a very few 3 x 5 filing cards written on one side." [22] Bernays was not prepared to give up, though. By August, as the flow of captured documents increased and the London staff obtained a better picture of what was at hand, his confidence and that of most of the rest of the staff picked up. Even then, it never remotely equaled the beaming surety that the Americans radiated in public.

Jackson would have needed iron nerves, indeed, to calmly handle Allied demands for radical changes while the Americans sat on an empty evidentiary box. He did manage to maintain a fairly effective public image of calmness during the negotiations, but his view of the situation and the prospects for agreement vacillated wildly. He was optimistic just before negotiations began, [23] and after the first day of discussions he notified Rosenman that there was "general agreement by all parties in substance." [24] Three days later, he wired his Washington staff that the Soviets were raising objections regarding the provisions on criminal organizations. On July 4, he sent a cable to Secretary of State James Byrnes (who had just replaced Stettinius), in which, commenting on the possibilities of agreement, he concluded that it was "too early to be sure we will get it but [the situation is] by no means hopeless." [25] By July 12, he was still optimistic and informed the White House that he had "little doubt that on matters of substance we will prevail." [26] Yet, six days later, in the third week of negotiation, he notified McCloy that the "Russian situation is most discouraging" and revealed that he was preparing an alternate proposal to be used "as a last resort" before "breaking up." [27] The very next day he cabled the Washington staff that it "now looks probable that we will have [an] agreement for international trials which will embody [the] substance of our plan." [28] Also on July 19, Jackson cabled Byrnes, "I am hopeful that agreement regarding major criminals will soon be ready for signature." [29] On the 20th, however, he cabled Byrnes that only "something approaching an ultimatum" would work with the Russians. [30]

With due allowance for the stresses he faced and the ups and downs of negotiations that his messages partially reflect, it is clear that Jackson was hardly in control of the situation. The unfamiliar attitudes and methods of the other delegations seemed genuinely to surprise him, and the readiness of the Soviets and French to go back over controversial ground again and again made him nearly frantic. He seems to have harbored strong suspicions of the Soviets before the negotiations started, and these attitudes were apparently stiffened by conversations with American military officers on the continent, who made numerous complaints about what they held to be Soviet obstructionism. [31] By the third week of July, at the latest, Jackson was so convinced that the Soviets were difficult and dangerous that he began considering breaking off negotiations and prosecuting just those war criminals in U.S. custody. [32]

It should be noted that Soviet behavior at London was often baffling and that Nikitchenko was a tough negotiator. Jackson was genuinely concerned that the defendants should get something resembling due process; clearly, the Soviets did not share this concern. Jackson also discerned that one of the essential war crimes issues would divide East and West, and he saw it much more perceptively and sooner than most of official Washington. He cabled Byrnes on July 6 that the United States should prepare some response to Soviet requests for exchange of war criminals because, in Jackson's view, many of these demands would be "purely political" and there would be little chance for a fair trial. [33] On this issue, Jackson's hardline anti-Soviet appraisal was accurate, but on other issues he was far too eager to sweep aside Russian suggestions.

The Soviets were surely right in viewing the American war crimes proposals as both extremely complicated and controversial. It is difficult to pinpoint a single Soviet criticism or suggestion that did not have serious substance. More fundamentally, though, the other three delegations, unlike Jackson's group, did not have a free hand in the negotiations because they were directly subordinate to their respective foreign ministries. Every significant suggestion or revision had to pass through the bureaucratic maze to obtain government approval. The Foreign Office records show that this was not always easy, even for the British team. How much more difficult, then, it must have been for the French and the Soviets. Yet, Jackson was in no mood to delay and in no position to make fundamental compromises. The Americans had begun too early and gone too far to abandon the basic plan in mid-July, and much of Jackson's staff, especially the author of the plan, Colonel Bernays, tended to look at any substantive alteration as a betrayal of the proposal and of American ideals. Instead of agreeing on a set of specific charges and abandoning the conspiracy and criminal organization approach, the Americans looked elsewhere for a solution to their problems.

First, they demanded a dramatic increase in the number of defendants. But this panicked the British, who envisioned a monstrous trial with three to four hundred defendants.[34] Privately, the Americans came up with an even more extreme answer to their critics. By mid-July, they had prepared a new draft agreement that, though containing the same charges as the original plan (war crimes, aggressive was, conspiracy, and so forth) and permitting the prosecution of criminal organizations, additionally provided that, instead of a Four Power trial, each of the Allies would prosecute and try the war criminals they held.[35] This scheme had less prospect for success than the original plan for it contained many of the troublesome legal features that had bothered the French and Soviets and offered no compromises in other areas. But Jackson had become so disillusioned with the continental Allies that he had lost his enthusiasm for any joint prosecution. His patience with the Soviets was wearing ever thinner. Even though he knew that the Russians were reluctant to choose a site for the trial, he stressed the need for immediate agreement on holding the trial in the American zone, at Nuremberg. When the Soviet delegation agreed to join the others on an inspection trip to the Bavarian city, then backed out at the last moment, Jackson's patience snapped. He seemed obsessed with the idea that, if adequate physical preparations were to be made for any trial, an immediate site decision was essential. While escorting the French and British to Nuremberg—which was, by the way, the best trial site available because of its confinement facilities as well as because of its historical significance—Jackson pondered how to produce a showdown with the Soviets.[36]

His first idea was to arrange a secret agreement with the French and the British, and then confront the Soviets with an ultimatum that either they accept or be dropped from the Allied team. This wild idea was shelved after reconsideration and Jackson flew off to see whether McCloy and Byrnes might arrange a solution at the Big Three meeting that was about to open in Potsdam.[37] Jackson's preference at this stage was to make a "reasonable" effort to reach agreement with the Soviets, but, if that failed, to adopt the alternate plan whereby the United States would prosecute the prisoners in its own custody.[38] Byrnes indicated sympathy for Jackson's problems and approach, but stressed that the president had delegated the task solely to the justice and therefore the State Department would not interfere.[39]

But the question of a war crimes trial did arise at Potsdam, and the international trial idea was aided, and probably ultimately decided, by the deliberations of the Big Three. The British had grown increasingly concerned over Jackson's anti-Soviet attitude and tended to place the blame for the deadlock in London on Jackson, not on Nikitchenko. The British had also learned of Jackson's inclination to wreck the London talks and strike off alone and were anxious to use the opportunity of the Potsdam meeting to prevent this.[40] They were hampered by the confusion surrounding the British general election, which turned Churchill out and made Clement Attlee prime minister of a Labor government. This change, coming in the middle of the conference, seemed to weaken British influence, but it did not prevent Attlee from achieving the main goal sought by the British war crimes negotiators. The prime minister elicited a pledge from Truman that the United States remained committed to a Four Power trial; this took the sting out of Jackson's threats and, in the words of one member of the Foreign Office, would surely give "Justice Jackson more patience." [41] The British had long held that the main obstacle to agreement was Jackson's threatening manner and suspicion of the Soviets. Truman's pledge would tame Jackson and prepare the way to get things in London moving again.[42]

The final push was not provided by the British, however, but by Byrnes, who wanted to aid Jackson. It was not difficult to bring up the topic at Potsdam, for Marshal Stalin was eager to talk about war crimes and, better, war criminals. He pressed the others to issue a public statement specifying the names of the Nazi leaders who would be placed on trial. The British and American representatives did not want to go over the heads of the London negotiators by specifying the names of particular defendants, and Byrnes tried to jog the Russians into being more cooperative in London. In the midst of the discussion, he pointedly told Stalin that "if the Marshal could instruct his representatives to try to reach agreement it would be well." [43] All that the enigmatic Stalin said in reply was "that is another question," and continued to demand that the Big Three decide on a list of names.[44] In the end, however, he agreed to a compromise proposal whereby the Allies "should" make public a list of major Nazi defendants by September 15. Allied unity was thereby preserved, and, in addition, the London negotiators had until mid-September to come up with their own comprehensive list.[45]

In London, however, Justice Jackson was considering ever more extreme measures to provoke a breakdown of negotiations and avoid the distasteful "difficulty of working with the Russians in a trial." [46] But now the Soviets were bent on producing a quick agreement. No extant evidence links this Soviet attitude of conciliation to Jackson's desire to force a showdown; in fact, there is no indication that the Russians knew of the turmoil inside the American camp. It is probable that the discussions at Potsdam and the commitment to the September deadline prompted instructions to the Soviet delegation in London that an agreement should be quickly arranged. Such a conclusion need not imply that the Soviets had been stalling to exert political pressure—although the switch regarding the inspection visit to Nuremberg is at least peculiar. The slowness of the Soviet negotiators may be traceable again to the confusing and complex American proposal and to a lack of clear instructions that may have made Nikitchenko extremely cautious.

In any event, to Jackson's team, poised to issue the Soviets an ultimatum, Nikitchenko's sudden willingness to agree must have seemed well-nigh miraculous. In the last fifteen minutes of a short negotiating session on August 2, Nikitchenko blandly announced that the Soviet Union accepted the latest American redrafting of the paragraph charging the existence of a Nazi "common plan and conspiracy." He also agreed—as Molotov had implied at Potsdam—that the trial be held at Nuremberg, stating in conclusion that the Russians would be ready to sign a final agreement within three days.[47] What Jackson had struggled for six weeks to accomplish was unceremoniously dropped into his lap in a quarter of an hour, and the London negotiations were over.

On August 8, with due solemnity, the leaders of the four delegations signed two short documents entitled "The Agreement" and the

"Charter of the International Military Tribunal." The Soviet Union had wisely suggested that the understandings between the Allies should be summarized in an "agreement" separate from the Charter that would serve as the legal foundation of the trial. The two-page agreement contained a qualified pledge that the Allies would return lesser war criminals "to the scene of their crimes." Jackson's doubts about remanding everyone whom the Soviets might brand a war criminal had resulted in the deletion of the clause inserted at San Francisco promising to turn over anyone "demanded" by one of the powers.[48]

The seven-page "Charter of the International Military Tribunal" retained the major points originally put forth by the Americans, but it also showed the effects of much patching and compromise. The Charter was composed of seven major subsections, beginning with one entitled the "Constitution of the International Military Tribunal" and closing anticlimactically with a mundane one-sentence passage on "Expenses." The first subsection concerned some of the procedures to be followed by the Court and contained one extremely important clause, I 4(c), which stated that all decisions should be taken by majority vote, with the Tribunal president having the power to break all ties except those regarding convictions and sentences. These would require "affirmative votes of at least three members of the Tribunal." Probably unwittingly, the inclusion of this clause guaranteed that, if the prosecution failed to make a strong case against a particular defendant, extensive bargaining and maneuvering would be required on the bench to obtain three votes first for a verdict and then, if the finding were guilty, to set sentence.

By far the most significant section of the Charter was the one entitled "Jurisdiction and General Principles." It contained under its subsection, Article VI, the list of crimes that the Tribunal could judge. Here, French and Soviet recommendations had left significant marks, and much of the conspiracy and criminal organization prosecution had been pushed into the background. The introductory passage did include the statement that the Tribunal was empowered to try and judge persons either "as individuals or as members of organizations," but conspiracy was not listed as a separate offense. Instead, there were merely three prosecutable offenses: "Crimes Against Peace," "War Crimes," and "Crimes Against Humanity." The title of the first of these charges had apparently been originated by the Soviet alternate delegate, A. L. Trainin, while the term "Crimes Against Humanity" seems to have been suggested to Jackson by the English legal specialist Hersch Lauterpacht.[49] Some of the American conspiracy idea showed up under Count One, Crimes Against Peace, which were defined in part as the "planning, preparation, initiation or waging of a war of aggression . . . or participation in a common plan or conspiracy for the accomplishment of any of the foregoing." Similar "common plan or conspiracy" clauses, however, were not included under Counts Two and Three (War Crimes and Crimes Against Humanity). At the very end of Article VI, a sentence was added that achieved the ultimate in confusing compromise:

Leaders, organizers, instigators and accomplices participating in the formulation or execution of a common plan or conspiracy to commit any of the foregoing crimes are responsible for all the acts performed by any persons in execution of such plan.

A quick glance might lead one to conclude that this sentence was intended to delineate a fourth prosecutable crime, that is, conspiracy. But on closer examination, such impression is difficult to sustain. The crimes enumerated in Article VI had identifying numbers from 6(a), for Crimes Against Peace, to 6(c), for Crimes Against Humanity, but the final sentence alluding to conspiracy–common plan (the Charter's phrase), had no number. This omission suggests that it was not intended to be the basis for a separate count in an indictment. In addition, since "participation in a common plan or conspiracy" was specifically included in the description of Crimes Against Peace but omitted from that for War Crimes and Crimes Against Humanity, the conclusion is implicit that the three offenses were to be handled differently—which is incompatible with the view that the conspiracy–common plan sentence at the end of Article VI was intended to apply equally to all three charges. Finally, a careful reading of this sentence shows that the stress was placed on the criminal liability of a conspirator for the acts of everyone else involved in the execution of the plan. Criminal liability for the related acts of others, in addition to liability for the conspirator's own involvement, is an implied element in conspiracy charges under Anglo-American law. But to have it spelled out this way in Article VI suggests that the main intention of the Article's last sentence was to emphasize that the major

Nazi war criminals were personally responsible for all the horrors and atrocities that had flowed from their planning and preparation.

One might, of course, brush aside these considerations, as those framing the indictment ultimately did, in hopes that the Tribunal would sustain a conspiracy charge relating not only to Crimes Against Peace but also to War Crimes and Crimes Against Humanity. However, when the Tribunal came to weigh the charges in the indictment, the only place it could turn to for legal guidance was the untidy language of Article VI, and when it did so, conspiracy charges related to War Crimes and Crimes Against Humanity were unsupportable. The compromises made in London thus seriously weakened the American plan and made a straightforward prosecution based on a wide-ranging conspiracy charge impossible.

The definition of "War Crimes" in Article VI contained few controversial elements, being largely an enumeration of traditional crimes of war, such as murder, wanton destruction of cities, and the like. But the description of the innovative offense "Crimes Against Humanity" was both complex and confusing. After listing a series of acts such as "enslavement" and "extermination," paragraph 6 (c) went on to state that these were Crimes Against Humanity if they were committed "in execution of, or in connection with, any crimes within the jurisdiction of the Tribunal, whether or not in violation of the domestic law of the country where perpetrated." Serious punctuation difficulties arose during the wording of this subparagraph, [50] but the most important point concerning the definition is that Crimes Against Humanity were strictly limited regarding time. Because the Anglo-Americans were, frankly, reluctant to make prewar domestic acts of the German Government offenses against international law, Crimes Against Humanity were connected to other alleged illegal acts falling within the jurisdiction of the Tribunal, that is, acts which occurred after war began or after a conspiracy—common plan had been made to launch aggressive war. Consequently, unless the Court held that a conspiracy had existed, nothing that the German Government had done, persecution, torture, or whatever, was a Crime Against Humanity if it took place before September 1, 1939. Only a finding that a conspiracy had existed before that date could establish the basis for ruling that Crimes Against Humanity had been committed in Austria, Czechoslovakia, or Germany itself.

Further difficulty was produced by the provisions relative to criminal organizations. The language employed in Article IX of the Charter was especially tortured:

At the trial of any individual member of any group or organization the Tribunal may declare (in connection with any act of which the individual may be convicted) that the group or organization of which the individual was a member was a criminal organization.

Presumably, this meant that the indictment would charge a series of organizations with criminality. If the Tribunal convicted an individual defendant, it might also designate any of the listed organizations of which he was a member as "criminal." So, for example, if Field Marshal Keitel made aggressive war plans and was a member of the High Command of the armed forces, then the Tribunal might designate the High Command a "criminal organization." But the Charter did not explain how close the association had to be between the defendant and the particular organization, nor did it specify whether the acts in question had to have been performed in his official capacity. Obviously, the serious difficulties and dangers inherent in prosecuting organizations, and especially the effort to link defendants with organizations, had not been smoothly resolved by Article IX. Many of these problems had surfaced in the London discussions but had generally been evaded by cloudy language. Like the conspiracy issue, then, they were left for the Tribunal to resolve.

The Charter also contained a number of compromises on the role of the prosecution and the procedures to be followed by the Tribunal. The prosecutors, working as a "committee," to use the Soviet phrase, would do such things as approve the list of defendants, but each prosecuting nation would be largely independent in the actual conduct of the case. With wide latitude granted to the individual prosecutors, coordination would be difficult and, in the end, the task of pulling the separate parts together would again fall to the Tribunal. Fortunately, however, the Charter gave the Court wide powers; it could interrogate defendants, use simplified rules, and screen evidence to determine relevancy. In an effort to make the proceedings fast-moving and brief, the Charter imposed few restrictions on the Court. The great emphasis that the Charter placed on the Tribunal's power to limit irrelevant evidence was intended to prevent "political" speeches by the defendants or accusations that the Allies had committed war crimes.[51] Except as a mitigating factor, the Tribunal was forbidden to entertain pleas based on the defense of superior orders; this defense had been denied in the original American draft and was banned in all subsequent revisions.[52] The Court's powers regarding criminal organizations were also restricted. It could decide whether an organization was criminal, but it had no power to determine the fate of the individual organization members except the twenty-two defendants before it. The task of dealing with the mass organizational membership was left to the Allied occupational authorities. The Tribunal's overriding task was to render individual verdicts and sentences, rule on the organizations, and provide an explanation of the "reasons" for its judgment.

Originally, the Americans had conceived of a case so tightly organized and so interlaced with criminal charges that the Tribunal would have little to do but accept the prosecution's presentations, wait out the defense, and then render judgment based on the simple guidelines in the American plan. But the compromises and revisions contained in the London Charter had changed all that. No matter how the indictment was written or how the prosecution developed the case, the Tribunal would still have to make important legal decisions. The basis of the Court's judgment had to be the Charter, and its murkiness, especially on conspiracy and criminal organizations, meant that the Tribunal would have to deliberate, interpret, and make judgment like a real court.

The complications that would face the Tribunal, however, were not caused solely by the Charter. In order to go to trial, there had to be an indictment, and, if it was in a clear and convincing form, some difficulties could be minimized. Such an instrument needed a list of the charges against the individual defendants and organizations, complete with an evidentiary summary to indicate that there was reason for trial. But even though an Anglo-American subcommittee began work on drafting an indictment in June, Four Power agreement on the indictment did not come until two months after the end of negotiations on the Charter. For, as with the Charter negotiations, a series of unforeseen complications arose that led to long delays and bitter controversies.

The British and American indictment committees made a brief effort to come up with a list of defendants in June, just before the Charter negotiations began. On June 21, the British casually submitted their list of ten prospective defendants headed by Goering. As we have seen, this list was the result of extended discussions and represented a compromise between those who wanted a token list of five or six and those who sought to get large numbers, ranging from fifty to one hundred. Their final list was prepared with great care and included major representatives from each area of the Nazi system that was targeted in the original American plan.[53] All ten of those on the British list were indicted; eight were ultimately condemned to death; only Hess escaped with a life sentence, while Ley committed suicide before the trial opened. But the British submitted their list in such an offhanded way that the Americans took it to be the product of little more than tea-shop chatter or an after-dinner conversation.

Such lack of system, obviously, would never do, so the Americans hurriedly set about making their own list. Bernays and one of his aides spent June 22 developing the American roster of defendants. Significantly, they first listed the five Nazi German organizations that they most wanted to have declared criminal: the "Leadership Corps" of the Nazi party, the Reich Cabinet, the General Staff and High Command of the armed forces, the SS, and the Gestapo. In the actual trial, the prosecution asked that six organizations be declared criminal, the sixth being the SA (the Stormtroopers or "Brownshirts"). Bernays began choosing individual defendants by deciding which German leaders best represented the five organizations he had cited. His initial list included forty-six names, but when duplications occasioned by multiple memberships and marginal individuals were eliminated, the number was cut first to twenty-six and then to sixteen. Of these sixteen, all ended up in the dock at Nuremberg except Ley and Hitler, the latter appearing as a gratuitous contribution from the land of the dead. Yet the names missing from Bernays's list of June 22 are as interesting as those included. Fritzsche and Raeder were not included because they were Soviet prisoners and in June the Americans had no idea that they were in captivity. Documentary material as to the importance of Sauckel, Jodl, and Bormann in the later stages of the regime had not yet been collated. Conversely, Schirach, Papen, and Neurath seem to have been omitted, in part, because the indictment staff was as yet unclear on how to deal with the early phases of the Nazi regime. Of course, the list also was marked by simple inconsistencies, because Schacht, an early dropout from a position of prominence, was included while Papen and Neurath, also early dropouts, were not. A singular feature of the American list was that it lacked the name of any leading industrialist; only Funk, Speer, and Schacht were there as representatives of the economy.[54]

As would have been true of any list, the sixteen names chosen by Bernays did not satisfy everyone. The British noted with surprise that Schirach was missing, and they also raised questions about the inclusion of Admiral Doenitz, because the British Admiralty believed that the German Navy had "behaved on the whole pretty well." [55] This stand was highly ironic for during the final deliberations it was the British judges who demanded that Doenitz, who was indicted and tried, be convicted, while one of the American judges held out for acquittal.

Far more important than the factors affecting the inclusion or exclusion of particular names was the method employed in the general preparation of the defendant list. The names were chosen before an indictment had been prepared and even before the Charter establishing the law on which some of them would be tried had been negotiated. They were primarily selected not because of their personal actions, cruelty, or notoriety, but because they fitted into the American plan for prosecuting organizations. Frequently, the prosecution of organizations at Nuremberg has been treated as if it were an afterthought, but, in fact, it was the heart of the American trial plan. The individual defendants were merely the performers through whom the main drama was played out.

The development of the list of sixteen defendants and some general discussions on drafting were the only things accomplished on the indictment during late June. In mid-July, the British proposed an indictment plan based on eight counts, two on general conspiracy, four on specific "aggressive acts," and two on breaches of the Hague Convention. The whole British draft, including a tentative list of defendants, covered only two and a half pages. Its brevity accorded with the British desire to avoid an elaborate trial by using simplified charges and "specimen selections" of evidence. Originally, they had wanted no trial at all, by late June they were talking about a sharply limited trial, and even by mid-July they were still advocating the prosecution of very few defendants on simple charges.[56] The Americans took the short indictment plan under advisement—apparently to appease the British—but, in fact, by early August the U.S. team seems to have overcome most of its doubt about pulling the case together and was pointing toward a large trial, with multiple charges and a large number of defendants. This confidence had nothing to do with the Charter negotiations that were still stumbling along on the edge of deadlock but arose from the improvement in the American evidentiary system, which was now producing results.

Many of the more dramatic documents later used in the trial were in American hands by early August, including the Hossbach notes of Hitler's meeting with his top aides in November 1937 and the so-called "Schmundt file" chronicling German actions against Czechoslovakia in 1938.[57] Serious gaps still remained, and on occasion there was shocking ignorance. Although in June Bernays had prepared the list of defendants predicated in part on plans to prosecute the General Staff as one of the criminal organizations, on July 2 he ordered one of his assistants to gather additional information on the subject because he said that he felt "very vague indeed about what the German General Staff really is and consists of." [58] Well might he have been uneasy, because the "Great General Staff" had been abolished after World War I and, although there were General Staff officers in Hitler's *Wehrmacht* (armed forces), they were hardly in control of military policy decisions.

Yet, despite such occasional pursuit of phantoms, the prosecution proved increasingly successful in its efforts to collect necessary documentation. By July 20 Bernays was able to circulate a five-page memorandum outlining the categories into which evidence should be assembled to support the probable trial charges. The four categories were: the "Nazi master plan" (aggressive war conspiracy); "preparatory measures" (preparations for aggression); "occupation of neighboring German areas"; and "military conquest" (acts of aggression and war crimes, covering the period 1939–45).[59] These four general points, with their numerous subheadings, corresponded quite closely to the organization that the Americans later used in the preparation of their case at Nuremberg. Once the documentary collection system began to work well the Americans could bide their time on drafting an indictment, since every day's findings strengthened the U.S. contention that a large and complex trial was feasible. As a more confident Justice Jackson reported to Washington in the course of July, "We are proving [the] responsibility of [the] top authorities for criminality and common plan to utilize terrorism, exterminations, etc. by better evidence than we had expected." [60]

Only when the negotiations on the Charter showed promise of imminent success did the Americans turn much of their effort toward the prospective defendants and the indictment. On August 4, they released a massive annotated list of one hundred top Nazis, including a biographical sketch of each person and his organizational affiliations. In the next few days, a pair of short indictment drafts and a long draft of the aggressive war case were prepared by the American team and transmitted to Jackson.[61] On August 9, the day after the Charter was signed, the Americans gave an explanation of their documentary system to Allied representatives. The Soviets were especially impressed by the "scientific and efficient" organization, and all the prosecutors pressed the Americans for permission to use their collection. But even when the U.S. prosecutors agreed to throw open the doors to all, they did not still the complaints and disagreements. The British wanted to simplify the evidence, take stock of what existed, pick the defendants, and go to trial immediately. The Americans, on the other hand, contended that what they wanted was not merely to convict a handful of defendants but to spread the net as widely as possible and even suggested preparing an indictment with a list of a hundred or so co-conspirators. The French and the Russians bounced back and forth, now seeming to favor the American idea for a big trial, now supporting the British insistence on a short and simple process.[62]

On August 13, the Soviets suggested a plan that offered a way out. Instead of collectively haggling about the case as a whole, the Soviets recommended that it be divided into four parts. They would handle the war crimes and crimes against humanity that had occurred in Eastern Europe, and the French would cover similar crimes that had taken place in the West. The British would prepare the case for crimes against peace, and the Americans would deal with conspiracy and criminal organizations. This suggestion was accepted by the Western Powers, which stressed, during the discussion, that the division applied only to trial preparation. In fact, the four prosecution teams seized on the idea with great enthusiasm, and it not only served to delineate responsibility for preparing evidence, but became the blueprint for the actual presentations at Nuremberg.[63]

Much of the confusion during the Court proceedings, as well as the decisive role ultimately played by the Tribunal, can be traced to this agreement of August 13. In a memorandum of August 14, Jackson reported the agreement to his staff and stated that the other powers had agreed that the Americans should prepare a case covering criminal organizations and the "common plan or conspiracy" to commit Crimes Against Peace and "any of the other crimes," that is, War Crimes and Crimes Against Humanity.[64] The American prosecution team regarded this as Allied approval of its proposal for a large case and rejection of the restricted case favored by the British. It further assumed that next an indictment would be drafted that would charge not only conspiracy to commit Crimes Against Peace but conspiracy to commit War Crimes and Crimes Against Humanity as well. The London Charter, which had been signed less than a week before, did not clearly authorize the last two charges of conspiracy, and a case developed in this way could be subject to serious challenge by the defense. But, considering that the Americans had the documents, the personnel, and the enthusiasm, it was inevitable that they would push the conspiracy and criminal organization case to the fullest, using every conceivable substantive crime as evidence for the existence of a conspiracy. Their presentation would inevitably cover much of the same ground from the conspiracy side that the other three prosecutors covered in arguing more substantive charges. The Tribunal would have to listen to the whole story twice, and the expeditious trial called for by the London Charter was bound to evaporate.

All these implications of the August 13 agreement were realized: there was a big trial, multiple conspiracy charges were included in the indictment, and the Court faced prosecution presentations that repeatedly ran over the same material. The three factors, however, combined to enhance the importance of the Tribunal, because it alone was in a position to resolve the resulting procedural and legal problems.

The agreement of August 13 was the decisive event in the preparation of the indictment. Most subsequent developments were anticlimactic, except for a series of incidents and conflicts that, as Jackson remarked to President Truman, could "make you laugh or cry," depending on your point of view.[65] In the third week of August, at a time when most of the surviving top Nazis were in American custody, the Four Powers held meetings to prepare the definitive list of defendants. It was agreed by all concerned that they might as well consider Hitler to be dead, and his name was removed from consideration. The French and the Russians then agreed to include the other fifteen names from the list that the Americans had originally prepared in June. The two continental delegations, however, in-

sisted on the addition of nine more names; specifically, Krupp, Raeder, Schirach, Sauckel, Jodl, Bormann, Papen, Neurath, and Fritzsche. The British were anxious to keep the defendant list as short as
possible, but ultimately the Anglo-Americans accepted the nine additions, and the list of twenty-four defendants who were to appear in
the dock at Nuremberg became final.[66] In the actual trial, the prosecution did not fare very well with the nine defendants whom the
French and Soviets had added. Bormann was sentenced to death in
absentia, but there were only two other death sentences (Jodl and
Sauckel). Papen and Fritzsche were acquitted, Krupp was never
prosecuted, and the three remaining defendants, Raeder, Schirach,
and Neurath, received prison sentences. By contrast, of the fifteen
on the initial American list, one was acquitted (Schacht), one, as
previously mentioned, committed suicide (Ley), three received
prison sentences (Speer, Funk, and Doenitz) and the other ten were
hanged.

Complications resulting from the Soviet and French additions did
not have to wait until the trial, for in August there were already
problems and surprises. On August 24, Jackson sent a list of twenty-
two names to the State Department, together with a note informing
Byrnes that it was the final defendant list. Four days later, he cabled
the State Department again with the news that he had "just learn[ed
that the] Russians have Raeder and Fritzsche in their custody" and
asked, rather sheepishly, that these two names be added, the resulting roster of twenty-four names being regarded as final.[67] In the
message to Byrnes, one defendant's name was listed as "Alfred
Krupp." [68] The State Department sent a confirming telegram back
to Jackson, correcting the name to read "Baron Alfried Krupp," [69]
whereupon Jackson, on August 27, sent still another telegram to
Byrnes, telling him to change the Krupp name from "Alfried" to
"Gustav." [70] The French and the Russians had wanted a Krupp on
the list, but the Krupps were in the American occupation zone and
the U.S. forces had apparently not discriminated carefully enough
between the various Krupps. In the confusion and scramble to develop the final defendant roster, the Americans removed Alfried,
the operating head of the Krupp firm, from the list and in his place
included that of his senile and mentally incompetent father, Gustav.

Once the defendant list had been agreed to, and with no inkling of
the problems represented by the name Gustav Krupp, the chief
Allied prosecutors seemed to lose a sense of urgency. The American

staff in London continued to work on a draft indictment and a defendant summary (which one of them described as being "5 inches thick").[71] Jackson, however, took a number of European trips during this period, including one to Rome, where he received a dossier from the Vatican on Nazi persecution of the Catholic Church. Finally, in mid-September, against the wishes of the British, he moved his headquarters to Nuremberg, where he could supervise the physical arrangements for the trial directly.[72] During this same interval, the Soviets withdrew Nikitchenko and the French removed Falco as their chief negotiators without hurrying to appoint replacements. The British retained the best general direction of any of the delegations, although Lord Shawcross was only nominally in charge and the day-to-day decisions were made by Maxwell Fyfe.

By September 17–18, the remaining members of the four delegations finally struggled to a "general impression" of agreement for the indictment provisions on Counts One and Two, that is, conspiracy and Crimes Against Peace.[73] On September 20, Colonel Telford Taylor for the United States and André Gros for France made some recommendations for altering the draft indictment that Roberts of Great Britain had prepared. The French suggestions were "only of a minor character"; the revisions proposed by the Americans were also in Taylor's words, "changes more in arrangement than in substance." The four delegations present in London, therefore, believed that on September 20 they were on the edge of final agreement.[74] But, when the texts were sent to Nuremberg, members of the American staff raised many objections, and Colonel Robert Storey, chief of the documents division, recommended to Jackson that "the entire indictment be reconsidered"[75] The justice apparently needed little urging and began to redraft the document himself. On September 23 the British learned about Jackson's rewriting.[76] Maxwell Fyfe was apparently so disgusted with this latest instance of American arbitrariness that he simply dumped the problem in the laps of the Americans, telling them that when the United States finally produced a definitive proposal the British would consider it, but not before.[77] Again, the American drafting team worked out a new form of Count One, this time blending together the London and Jackson versions. The draft was approved by Jackson on September 26, whereupon the British, who were quietly seething, agreed to send a two-man delegation to reconsider Counts One and Two in Nuremberg. Calm good manners triumphed and the British delegation in

Nuremberg accepted the bulk of the American changes and then returned to London to wrap up the rest of the indictment agreement.[78] With marvelous bad timing, the French chose this moment to recommend that the whole indictment be redrafted, but Maxwell Fyfe and the American Sidney Alderman wearily swept such a monstrous idea aside and on October 1 struggled for yet another "in principle" agreement on the whole indictment.[79]

But the opéra bouffe was still not over. On October 2 came a telephone call from Jackson in Nuremberg, demanding that the German General Staff, which had earlier been dropped, be put back on the list of accused organizations. The British, who had opposed this idea earlier, bitterly protested against the change. The harried Alderman, meanwhile, managed to obtain French and Soviet support for a formula defining the higher ranks of German staff and operational officers as the "General Staff and High Command." By a vote of three to one this entity was added to the list of accused organizations.[80] The British Cabinet withheld its assent to the addition until October 9, but six organizations (SA, SS, Gestapo-SD, Reich Cabinet, "Leadership Corps" of the Nazi party, and General Staff and High Command of the armed forces) were nonetheless added to the indictment.[81]

On the night of October 3, yet another telephone call came from Nuremberg. This time Jackson made the amazing demand that two or three more industrialists be added to the list of defendants. There is no indication that the justice had become aware of the joker in the name Gustav Krupp; he seems merely to have felt that the industrialists should be more generously represented in the dock. The next day, Alderman dutifully tried to obtain agreement to amend the list of defendants as Jackson wanted, and to add a handful of his own favorite Nazis as well. But the other delegations, who had run out of patience, swiftly and firmly combined to defeat the American demand three to one.[82] This vote was a final, fitting climax to the bizarre proceedings, for it represented a Soviet rejection of a suggestion by the world's largest capitalist power that more industrialists be included as defendants. The indictment battle was, at last, really over, and on October 6 the document was signed and authenticated by the four chief prosecutors.

The indictment and the list of defendants that the prosecution took into the trial was fraught with pitfalls. Some individuals and some organizations had been added to the defendant list with little thought or preparation. Even before the indictment was signed, members of the prosecution staff began to have second thoughts about some of the defendants. No case had been prepared against Fritzsche because the Soviets had tossed him into the hopper so late; and as for Neurath, as early as October 4, one of the American prosecutors, after reviewing the evidence, recommended that the case against him be dropped.[83] But no action was taken to deal with the Neurath case or to shore up other weak points.

The major difficulty was the lack of central direction in preparing the indictment and the case for the prosecution. Negotiations went on, committees were formed, and the chief prosecutors met periodically; but the Americans were wary of too close an association with their allies, and the meetings had little effect. Of course there were other pressing matters, such as the preparation of the trial documents and the physical arrangements in Nuremberg, but, without firm leadership at the top, signs of meandering negotiation in the indictment were inevitable. While Jackson bears a major share of responsibility for this situation, none of the delegations was characterized by strong and level-headed leadership during this critical period.

The most glaring example of carelessness came after the text of the indictment had been given to the press, twelve days after it was signed by the prosecutors. The Soviet prosecutor abruptly demanded that the passage in the indictment originally included by the Soviet Union charging the Nazis with murdering 925 Polish officers in Katyn, near Smolensk, should be changed to read that the Nazis had killed "11,000 Polish officers." The Soviet effort to blame the Nazis for the Katyn massacre would probably have backfired in any event, because much of the evidence that subsequently surfaced at the trial indicated that it was the Russians, not the Germans, who had done the killing. But for the Soviets to have publicly changed their minds and increased the number of victims by over 1000 percent while the world press looked on was the perfect way to produce a propaganda disaster.

Yet it is not altogether fair to stress the failings of the indictment and the Charter, or even to emphasize that bad seeds planted there would produce worse blossoms during the trial. The negotiations had been a prodigious undertaking, with few precedents to guide the participants. No one, for example, had foreseen the complications that would be caused by the American plan. Yet all Four Powers genuinely believed that preventing excesses was as important as creating a smoothly running machine. The British tried from the very beginning to modify the ambitious plans of their Allies; the Soviets and the French sought to limit the possible dangers of conspiracy and criminal organization prosecution; the Americans were determined to avoid anything resembling a Soviet purge trial. These precautionary attitudes, coupled with the enormous problems and the short time available, guaranteed that the result would not be simple and tidy.

Surely, through all of this the Allies were drawn together as much by a desire for revenge and a hatred for things Nazi and German as by a determination to punish criminal acts. Realistic appraisals of the hazards of their endeavor were not lacking. As early as June 30, John M. Troutbeck, a Counsellor in the Foreign Office German Department, prepared a memorandum on the dangers inherent in a conspiracy prosecution. Troutbeck warned that "criminal conspiracy" would become a common phrase in future international relations, and that states would use it to justify all manner of policies.[84] A month later, the historical adviser to the Foreign Office, E. L. Woodward, expressed doubts from a historical perspective about the prosecution of the Nazis for planning an aggressive war. "There was indeed no plot," Woodward wrote; ". . . the other Great Powers knew in 1937 that German military preparations were on a scale to make Germany stronger. . . . It is therefore unreal—and it will seem unreal to historians—to speak of a German 'plot' or 'conspiracy' [merely because the Powers were ready] to condone all German breaches of faith and to make agreements with the German Government." Noting that "it is notoriously difficult to prove 'intentions' from diplomatic documents," Woodward felt that it would be best to ignore foreign policy accusations and concentrate on Nazi war crimes and atrocities.[85]

In the end, the doubts of Troutbeck, Woodward, and others were overridden by the actions of the Allied governments; but these acts were not done blindly, nor were they motivated solely by bitterness and hatred. Together with the pressures of public outrage, there was also a sense of high moral purpose—the Great Powers would this time seize the opportunity to ensure peace by prosecuting crimes under international law.

On August 21, 1945, in the middle of the struggle over the indictment, Jackson wrote to Stimson to thank him for an earlier letter.

Stimson's letter, Jackson wrote, had helped sustain him through the long days of difficult negotiations in London. The words that encouraged Jackson are a reminder that more was involved in London than bungling and human weakness and hatred. Thirteen years after his condemnation of Japanese aggression in Manchuria, this is what Stimson wrote:

I am particularly gratified to see the battle for which we fought in 1932 in a fair way to be won. 'Truly the world do move.' [86]

CHAPTER 4

The Trial

I am satisfied the defendants received a fair trial.

Harry S. Truman [1]

ON SEPTEMBER 12, Francis Biddle and Judge John Parker were designated as senior and alternate American Tribunal members by President Truman. No sooner had they been selected than the American prosecutors began urging them to leave immediately for Germany. Parker, however, was reluctant to fly, and, since the British were slow in naming their judges, the Americans saw no reason to hurry. The American party departed from New York aboard the *Queen Elizabeth* on October 2 for a leisurely journey to Europe.[2]

The sea voyage gave the judges and their aides, headed by professors Quincy Wright of Chicago and Herbert Wechsler of Columbia, an excellent opportunity to weigh the major legal problems posed by the trial. Long conferences were held on October 2 and 4, and the most important considerations raised in these discussions were then summarized in an eight-page memorandum prepared to assist the American judges once the Tribunal assembled. The overriding conclusion that emerged in this memorandum was that, despite the Charter, a host of legal problems confronted the Tribunal. The Court needed to establish its own organization and set rules and procedures as quickly as possible. More important, it had to begin to

Where judgment was reached—the Nuremberg judges assembled in closed session (from left to right: Norman Birkett, Sir Geoffrey Lawrence, Lieutenant Colonel A.F. Volchkov, Major General I.T. Nikitchenko, John Parker, Francis Biddle, Robert Falco, and H. Donnedieu de Vabres). What went on in this chamber—how the judges actually voted and arrived at their verdict—was unknown until now.

Judge Francis Biddle—his recently discovered personal diaries shed important new light on the trial. NATIONAL ARCHIVES

Justice Robert Jackson, the chief United States prosecutor, listening to summary speeches. Jackson's general strategy became a key issue with many of the judges. UNITED PRESS INTERNATIONAL

DOENITZ
10 Years

RAEDER
Life

von SCHIRACH
20 Years

SAUCKEL
To Hang

JODL
To Hang

GOERING
To Hang

von RIBBENT
To Hang

The defendants—and their final fate. (Rudolf Hess, who received a sentence of life imprisonment, is the only defendant not visible. He is hidden behind Goering.) WIDE WORLD PHOTOS

The defense attorneys discussing the proceedings (from left to right: Dr. Hans Marx, for Julius Streicher; Dr. Otto Stahmer, for Hermann Goering: Dr. Fritz Sauter, for Joachim von Ribbentrop; and Dr. Gunther von Rohrscheidt, for Rudolf Hess). WIDE WORLD PHOTOS

A "light" moment—defendants break into laughter as evidence is introduced. (In front row of prisoners' box, left to right: Hermann Goering, Rudolf Hess, Joachim von Ribbentrop, and Field Marshal Wilhelm Keitel. In back row, left to right: Grand Admiral Karl Doenitz, Grand Admiral Erich Raeder, and Baldur von Schirach.)

Albert Speer at the trial. His twenty-year sentence was a compromise which none of the judges had favored initially.

Julius Streicher, the "Nazi Jew-baiter," entering the court. His personal appearance and general demeanor in court weighed heavily against him.

Dr. Hjalmar Schacht, the German financier, and Hans Fritzsche, the Nazi propagandist, listening nonchalantly during the Nuremberg proceedings. Both were acquitted. Their demeanor in court weighed heavily in their favor. UNITED PRESS INTERNATIONAL

wrestle with a series of substantive problems, especially three that should now be familiar to us: the criminality of aggressive war, the problem of criminal organizations, and the denial of superior orders as a legitimate defense. The memorandum faced these issues squarely. With the criminal organization idea, for example, it discussed the use of collective punishment as questionable under the best of circumstances, but even more so in a trial predicated on the premise that individuals were criminally responsible under international law. Although the memorandum did not directly consider the problem of conspiracy, it raised the point that designating an organization criminal could have legal and moral force only if membership had been voluntary and criminal aims and activities had penetrated through the whole system and operation of the organization. The dilemma of whether criminal charges for "aggressive war" were ex post facto played an important role in the memorandum. Biddle's notes, made after the meeting of October 3, show that this issue was discussed sharply and frankly. Quincy Wright had said that both the procedure and the prospective punishment might be ex post facto, and Biddle seems to have agreed. The only way out which Biddle saw was to beg the question by having the Tribunal state it was bound by the London Charter and therefore unable to examine the legitimacy of the document on which it itself rested.[3]

Even before arriving in Europe, therefore, the American members of the Tribunal had confronted some of Nuremberg's main legal difficulties. They knew that there were serious pitfalls in the general situation and grave legal problems in the Charter itself. Biddle's answer was the practical one of avoiding every unnecessary excursion into general international law, while trying to minimize the less pleasant effects of the Charter itself. But he worriedly ended his note on the October 3 meeting by observing that merely to follow the Charter provisions on branding organizations criminal could have the unpleasant result of giving the Soviets, or anyone else, authority to shoot merely on proof of membership, unless the consequences of membership were specified.[4]

Biddle's approach of sticking to the Charter and tempering it where necessary was probably the most important decision made by any member of the Nuremberg bench. We know little about how the French and Soviet judges initially viewed the case; as regards the British Tribunal members, we know that at the start they were concerned more with smoothing out Soviet-American conflicts than with delineating possible legal approaches to the trial.[5] In the course of the proceedings, however, judges from the other countries gradually reached the same conclusion as Biddle, or at least adapted themselves to his approach. The final opinion, or Judgment, tracked the Charter almost exactly, with rare excursions into broader international law when the Charter provision proved especially intractable. This does not mean that the Americans, or the other judges, were free of bias or were capable of rising above the overwhelming public demand that the Nazi leaders be made to pay for their evil deeds. None of the eight judges seems to have had the slightest doubt that the defendants were men who deserved severe punishment, but this attitude, paradoxical as it may sound, was not a decisive factor. As Biddle and Parker realized early, their central problem as Tribunal members was to try to reach a publicly acceptable verdict while upholding a charter with a shaky basis in international law. They wanted to leave this situation with legal reputations and the judicial process intact. In short, not just the judges' biases against the defendants, but their attitude toward legal process and the situation's complexities were the decisive factors.

There was going to be a trial at Nuremberg and either the prosecution or the defense, if able accurately to estimate the situation facing the Tribunal, would be in fair position to score heavily. Presentations that were keyed solely to the Charter, providing the Tribunal with acceptable explanations for how to get around its less palatable features, particularly those on criminal organizations, would have a good chance of succeeding. There was, no doubt, little prospect of victory for the defense, but eloquent appeals to international law would surely be of no help at all. The Tribunal knew the legal problems and did not need them described in detail; what it wanted was an answer to difficulties, short of the unthinkable option of quashing the proceedings and freeing all the defendants. By October 1945, the period of negotiation and of total domination by the prosecution was over—now the Tribunal's needs and views would predominate.

Under the terms of the London Charter, the Tribunal was to hold its opening session in Berlin. The American members of the Court arrived in the ruins of the German capital early in the second week of October, after an episode in which the Air Transport Service took them to Paris instead of Berlin.[6] Once in the right city, the Americans spent the first few days getting acquainted with their Tribunal colleagues. Biddle found the appearance of the French judges comical, thought the British inept, and in his notes quickly began to refer to Nikitchenko as "Nick." [7] The selection of Lord Justice Lawrence as president did nothing to dampen Biddle's self-confidence, and in his notes he confided that since Lawrence depended on him so heavily he would still "run the show." [8]

From the start, both the Tribunal and the prosecution were very concerned about the IBM system of simultaneous translation that would be used for the first time in an international proceeding. The members of the Court were uneasy about how this system would operate and whether it would provide an accurate record of oral testimony. Jackson was even more worried, for, if the system failed, it might produce a comic spectacle, and Jackson significantly remarked that what he feared most during the trial was "not the hatred of the defendants, but ridicule." [9]

Such utterances suggest that Jackson's responsibilities were still lying heavily upon him and that he was not well situated to gauge the mood of the Tribunal. Although he correctly advised the Court not to hold a closed session with only the prosecutors present, he later agreed to meet privately with Biddle, Parker, their advisers Wechsler and Wright, and the legal specialist for the American Occupation Authorities, Charles Fahy. In this session, Jackson argued strongly that the Court should not set up its own administrative machinery but should depend on the prosecution organization. Biddle countered just as strongly that the Court needed its own administration to preserve its independence and impartiality. Jackson refused to yield, contending that this was not an ordinary trial, and that some of the niceties had been eliminated when Nikitchenko switched from negotiator-prosecutor to judge. This was a serious gaffe, for Biddle must have been somewhat sensitive to the fact that he, too, had played a part in the formulative stages of the war crimes planning and was consequently especially determined to establish the traditional features of judicial impartiality. [10]

This was the first argument between a chief prosecutor and a Tribunal member, and the prosecutor clearly lost it. Both in Berlin and in Nuremberg, the Tribunal demonstrated that it rejected Jackson's contention that it should acknowledge its tainted ancestry by cohabitating with the prosecution. The Court set rules of procedure, established its own secretariat, and began to grapple with the practical problems associated with the trial. When the British prosecution authorities unilaterally decided on a form to be used by members of organizations in petitioning the Tribunal, the Court sharply chastised the British for infringing on its prerogatives and demanded the withdrawal of the offending form.[11] Jackson soon found himself forced to shift ground as the Tribunal took command. He had initially laid stress on the readiness of the prosecution to make evidentiary materials available to the defense, but, as the Court pressed him to agree to access procedures, he backed away from the implication that he might be obligated to assist the defense. While denying any desire to be a "raw prosecutor," Jackson emphasized that prosecution was his only job, and that the Court would have to resolve the questions concerning evidence for the defense. By so doing, Jackson underscored what the American members of the Tribunal had originally sought to achieve, the restriction of the prosecution to its customary role so that the Court would not appear to be discolored by partisanship.[12]

With this line of demarcation established, the first test of the system came in the second and third week of November, when the Court was forced to deal with pretrial petitions on behalf of Hess, Streicher, and Krupp. Though interesting, the hearings on Streicher and Hess need not detain us, for no serious division occurred on either man. Streicher was ruled competent, while hearings on Hess, which took up the first few days of the Court proceedings, ended with Hess's dramatic announcement that his amnesia had been feigned and that he was ready to stand trial. The Court does not seem to have put much stock in Hess's statements; it believed him to be a crank of diminished capacity who was nonetheless legally sane and capable of standing trial. With that, the Hess problem was resolved.[13]

The Krupp affair was far more serious, for by mid-November it was obvious to all that Gustav Krupp was a senile old man whose mind could control neither his thoughts nor his bladder. Once his condition was recognized, his participation in the trial became out of the question and none of the members of the Tribunal, including the Soviet representatives, favored putting him in the dock. Although the Tribunal had agreed to try Bormann in absentia, neither it nor the prosecution gave serious consideration to such a trial for Krupp. The Tribunal only had to face the distasteful reality of one absentia trial because the American prosecution came up with an even more unusual suggestion in regard to Krupp. It asked that the indictment be amended so that Alfried Krupp's name could be substituted for that of his father. This would have meant a short delay in opening the trial, which was scheduled for November 20. The French and Soviet prosecutors, after temporarily leaning toward an absentia trial for the elder Krupp, now swung around to support Jackson's plan for substitution.[14] But the British adamantly opposed the idea. Lord Shawcross found the suggestion outrageous and denounced it in open court saying, "This is a Court of Justice, not a game in which you can play a substitute if one member of a team falls sick." [15] The unity of the prosecution was thereby shattered, and the harmony of views between the prosecutors and judges of the individual countries did not fare much better. When the French prosecutor, Charles Dubost, argued in favor of substitution, the French senior judge, Donnedieu de Vabres, queried: "You said just now that it was your opinion that the name of Krupp the son should be substituted for that of Krupp the father. Did you really mean the word 'substitute'?" [16] Even Jackson had a difficult time with the judges, and the questions that Biddle slipped to Tribunal president Lawrence forced Jackson so much onto the defensive that he pleaded with the Tribunal to put a Krupp in the dock or the whole case "against the German armament makers" would collapse. In the end, the American chief prosecutor made the incredible suggestion that perhaps the young Krupp would voluntarily "step into the shoes" of his father.[17]

In the closed deliberations on the motion to amend the indictment, the Tribunal members from Britain, France, and the United States were united in their opposition to the substitution scheme. Birkett and Parker were clearly shocked by the idea, and Biddle also rejected Jackson's "amazing" suggestion. Only the Soviets failed to share their colleagues' legal scruples and supported substitution. Nikitchenko was absent during most of the discussion and voting, but his alternate, Volchkov, argued vigorously that Alfried Krupp be added to the defendant list, and he employed every possible procedural maneuver to obtain a favorable vote or force a delay in the Tribunal's ruling. Finally, the members from the other three nations joined together and, in a series of tightly drafted motions, rejected the prosecution petition to amend the indictment, as well as all Volchkov's requests for delays, and ruled that Gustav Krupp's case should be separated so that he would not be tried in his incompetent condition. When the voting ended, Nikitchenko, who was present during the final discussion, declared that, although he was very displeased with the results, he would waive Russia's right under the Charter and would not file a public dissent.[18]

The significance of the hearings on the Krupps can hardly be overestimated, not only for Allied postwar policy toward the German economy as well as for the future of the Krupp firm, but also for the Nuremberg trial itself. The all-powerful prosecution machine did not fall apart over the Krupp case, but Lord Shawcross's public dissent, as well as the bitter discussions that had occurred in private, showed that prosecution unity could no longer be taken for granted. The Tribunal had demonstrated to the defense and to itself that it could stand up against strong prosecution pressure. Behind the scenes, the Tribunal had weathered its first serious internal disagreement; the Soviet waiver of the right to dissent suggested that discussion and compromise could be made to work in the deliberative chamber.

Parenthetically, the Krupp hearings may also have planted seeds of doubt about Robert Jackson in the mind of Francis Biddle. The two men had worked together in the past with no obvious signs of friction, and during the trial there would be occasions when they could deal with each other in considerate, perhaps even friendly, ways. But in the course of the proceedings Biddle was repelled by what he saw as Jackson's doctrinaire attitude and his periodic loss of self-control. Whether or not the Krupp affair was crucial, Biddle clearly had doubts about Jackson from the earliest days. By the time the Court opened its formal session on November 20, the entire American prosecution had a tarnished image, and Jackson and his aides were in need of dramatic initial victories.

Jackson opened the case of the prosecution with a long, moving address focused on general issues rather than on the misdeeds of the individual "broken men" before the Court. Conspiracy and the actions of the six accused organizations, particularly the "Leadership Corps" of the Nazi party, were the main points for Jackson, and he called upon the Tribunal to strike a blow for peace by condemning the Nazi war machine and its leaders. But, the issue of the trial transcended even this, Jackson told the Court, for he wished to make clear that, if the law was to serve a useful purpose, "it must condemn aggression by any other nations, including those which sit here now in judgment." [19] The Tribunal's mission, Jackson stated in conclusion, was to satisfy civilization's appeal to put "the forces of international law, its precepts, its prohibitions and, most of all, its sanctions, on the side of peace, so that men and women of good will, in all countries, may have 'leave to live by no man's leave, underneath the law.' " [20]

It was a masterful performance, worthy of Jackson's reputation as a first-rate trial lawyer; in one stroke the prosecution's image had been restored, and much of the damage from pretrial squabbling repaired. By emphasizing the need to make a precedent for the legal control of aggression, Jackson not only appealed to the heartfelt desire of the postwar population but also provided the Tribunal with a high purpose that would justify overlooking some irregularities in the case. To establish a stable peace, courts, especially the Nuremberg Tribunal, would have to play a significant role in making it clear to warmongers that they could be severely punished.

Jackson's assertion that the same law applied to all was, in part, hypocritical, for neither the prosecution nor the Tribunal would allow the defendants to cite Allied misdeeds as justification for their own acts. Only Germans were on trial, and no consideration of Allied actions was to be permitted. Despite this qualification, Jackson's contention that it was an issue of general law that applied must have been welcomed by the Tribunal. Although they had only this trial and these German defendants to worry about, the judges were surely troubled by the resemblance of the proceedings to actions under a bill of attainder, that is, a law passed to make possible the prosecution of specific individuals. Jackson's speech implied that the Allied governments held the principles of the London Charter to be generally applicable—a very doubtful assumption, but one which publicly declared that the Tribunal was not proceeding under a bill of attainder. It was not the Tribunal's job to determine how the Allies would subsequently fulfill Jackson's pledge; its concern was only that the current proceedings should not be cast in the form of a prettified vendetta.

On the heels of Jackson's eloquent address, a small army of American prosecutors, armed with bundles of captured documents, trooped to the rostrum to relate the details of the Nazi conspiracy. A barrage of facts and charges thundered down on the heads of the Tribunal, the defendants, and their counsel. The accusations were the predictable ones: the Nazis had carefully planned to take over Germany and to use it as a base from which to attack the rest of Europe and then, by calculated savagery, to seize the assets of the continent for themselves. But, if the prosecution's accusations were easily foreseeable, the scope and significant detail of the captured documents were not, and these caused a sensation. The American documentary collection system which began so disappointingly in June, had worked efficiently from August to November. Even though only 40 percent of the U.S. documents were logged by November 7, the result of the effort obviously stunned both the defense and the Tribunal.[21] There were numerous documents from the highest levels of the Reich government, such as Hitler's matter-of-fact explanation to the top Reich officials in 1937 of the alternate ways to destroy Czechoslovakia and seize Austria, or the plans for looting Russia, made in 1941, which sounded like the arrangements for a murderous Easter-egg hunt. There seemed to be no end to the documents that the Americans had in their possession, and each new revelation contained more terrifying facts and more brutal language than the one before.

Jackson's opening idealistic tone and the subsequent documentary avalanche left an impression on the Tribunal that the rest of the proceedings would not eradicate. No defense could have nullified the effect of the initial rush by the American prosecution, but the German defense attorneys were in an especially poor position to put up more than token resistance. The Allied authorities had not tried to find outstanding defense attorneys but had assembled a respectable group of approved counsel. A defendant might choose one of these lawyers, or request court approval for one of his own choice. However, the attorneys, like all postwar Germans, were suffering from the shock of defeat and the destruction and desolation that surrounded them. Generally chosen because they were anti-Nazis or had at least been cool to Hitler's regime, the German defense attorneys in the main considered the defendants to be the source of their own, and their nation's, misfortune.[22] They were as shocked, and often as angered, by the revelations of cynical brutality as were the Court and the public. They also faced severe practical disadvantages. They had few assistants and lacked the resources (as well as the authority, which the prosecution did possess), to garner evidence from among the ruins. Moreover, they had been given little time to prepare a defense, they had to confront novel charges, and they had to conjecture on the scope of the evidence held by the prosecution, at least until the trial opened. The rules and procedures employed in the trial were a blend of Anglo-American and continental law, which presented additional problems for the defense. Of course, some elements of the procedure were also new to the prosecution but they had established the system and, thus, had time both to reflect upon, and adjust to, its innovations. The emphasis on documentary evidence rather than testimony by witnesses resembled continental usage more than Anglo-American, but it hurt the defense because of the great wealth of documents held by the American prosecution. And when, in the course of the trial, attention focused on oral testimony, the defense was again in difficulty because of continental unfamiliarity with procedure of cross-examination.

Generally, the adversary approach to trial so familiar to Anglo-Americans was extremely difficult for continental attorneys to grasp. Unrestrained combat between prosecution and defense, with the Tribunal as referee, was not their idea of the way to attain a judicious conclusion. They were accustomed to a system based on more understanding between defense, prosecution, and the bench; at Nuremberg, however, the defense and prosecution were mortal combatants, and the German attorneys could not escape the impression that they were considered auxiliaries of the damned. Some of the prosecutors, and many of the Allied soldiers on duty in Nuremberg, were hostile not only to the defendants, but to Germans in general. It was the heyday of rules against fraternization between victor and vanquished, and, in personal relations as well as in regard to the facilities provided, the defense attorneys were constantly reminded that they were second-class citizens, if citizens at all.[90] Perhaps these factors ultimately encouraged the German lawyers to identify themselves more closely with their clients and to work harder in their defense, but in the early days of the trial the hostile atmosphere clearly cowed them.

The initial successes of Jackson and the American team, however, did not produce a rout of the defense, because the prosecution, characteristically, overplayed its hand. The prosecutors were so eager to exploit their documentary materials that they tried to have the Court accept in evidence a flood of English-language document translations without providing copies in German, French, and Russian. The defense protested that it was left completely at the mercy of the prosecution, with no means to evaluate or contest the materials before the prosecutors presented them to the Court. The Germans' complaints were seconded by the French and Soviet members of the Tribunal, who were as much in the dark as the defense. Indeed, the

Americans proceeded so independently that even the British prosecutors were not given copies of the documents.[24] The U.S. prosecutors assured the Court that every effort was being made to provide multilingual copies of documents to the Tribunal and the defense prior to their presentation in Court, but they claimed that the obstacles to translation were insurmountable. While the Court was considering what to do about the situation, the American prosecutors blundered again and released to the press copies of documents that they intended to submit to the Court in the future. Both Biddle and Lawrence were visibly angered by these press releases, which they saw as clear signs that the prosecution was more interested in headline hunting than in the Court's orders to put primary emphasis on providing multilingual documents. The Tribunal responded with stiff orders on the necessity of multilingual exhibits and also provided a solution of genius to the translation problem. It directed that, to be accepted in evidence, every prosecution document had to be read out in open court. The document would then automatically pass through the IBM four-language translation system and become available in English, German, French, and Russian. By this decision the Court not only solved a technical problem, but also seriously disabled the prosecution plan of attack. The American prosecution wanted to exploit its documentary assets to the fullest, hoping to bury the opposition and the Court in such a wealth of material that the Nazis' all-embracing master plan would be proved incontrovertibly. But once the prosecutors were required to read every single passage into the record, the amount of material that could be used was severely restricted.[25] Much of the documentary treasure trove had to be discarded, and the lengthy prosecution readings that resulted from the Court's order were boring and, often, anticlimactic.

The prosecution never totally recovered from this setback. Some vigorous presentations were subsequently made, but they bore the marks of improvisation and never equaled the force and vigor of the first American efforts. Shorn of its documentary wealth, the prosecution's lack of coordination showed up more clearly, and the Court was made to suffer through countless mistakes in prosecution planning. The sequence of presentations during the first month was enough, in itself, to confuse the most alert observer. For example, the chief English prosecutor, Lord Shawcross, had important functions to perform in London, so he gave his opening address in the middle of the American presentation. Then the Americans added another day's evidence on their case relating to Count I (Conspiracy) followed by the British again, with a presentation concentrating on Count II (Crimes Against Peace). Thereupon, the Americans came back to present another week of Count I evidence that related to Counts Three and Four (War Crimes and Crimes Against Humanity). This kind of presentational leapfrog occurred repeatedly during the trial, since the interests of all four prosecuting nations had to be satisfied and then mistakes in presentations corrected. As the trial wore on, it became painfully apparent to everyone that, in the words of one of the British prosecutors, the Americans had "poached considerably" in areas reserved for the other prosecutors.[26] The same points were made over and over and the same document passages were repeatedly read into the record. Only particular subjects, such as the economic preparations for the attack on the Soviet Union, received triple treatment, but nearly every significant incident that had taken place during the Nazi years was gone over at least twice.

The American and British prosecutors were also somewhat hobbled by their ignorance of continental law, and the effectiveness of all the prosecutors was restricted by their unfamiliarity with German history and German institutions. The majority of those making the presentations to the Court did not even read or comprehend the German language, and there was no way that advisers could completely protect them from grotesque incidents and unintentionally comic effects. Repeatedly, the prosecutors confused the offices of the Nazi party with those of the German Government, and they also frequently floundered helplessly with German terms or situations that called for references to German documents. In a characteristic incident, the American deputy prosecutor, Sidney Alderman, solemnly informed the Court on November 29, 1945, that "we are fortunate in having General Jodl's handwritten diary in German script which I can't read." [27] Such incidents were surpassed only by the prosecution's occasional attempts at folk humor. In the most celebrated incident, a nervous American prosecutor began his presentation by stating to the Court that his knees had not knocked so hard "since I asked my wonderful little wife to marry me." [28] This statement caused the rather straitlaced Birkett to note in his diary that "the shocking taste is really almost unbelievable," while in his evidentiary record Francis Biddle managed to capsulize his reaction to the incident in one word—"Jesus!" [29]

By mid-December, the prosecutors had made so many serious blunders that one of the defense counsel remarked dryly, "If they keep it up it may be possible to get the Gestapo declared not guilty." [30] In fairness to the members of the prosecution, however, it should be noted that there were also serious instances of ignorance on the part of the Tribunal. In a court session of December 10, Lord Lawrence asked one of the prosecutors to whom he was referring with the term "Reich Marshal." Since Reich Marshal Hermann Goering was the chief defendant, the question was not altogether comforting. [31] But the Tribunal was usually more discreet about its ignorance; more important, it was there to learn, while the prosecutors were supposed to be doing the teaching.

The prosecution presentations lasted from November 21, 1945, until mid-March 1946, and the poor organization and repetition progressively increased the Tribunal's irritation level. The French and Soviet prosecutors, who stood at the end of the line, and who held few new documents in their hands, also had the greatest difficulty with the procedural system. Not surprisingly, they also ran into the most difficulty with the Court. From mid-January 1946, Biddle's notes are filled with complaints about the slowness of the French prosecutors, especially Dubost, who seemed to know little about his documents, thereby driving the Tribunal members to distraction. [32] The impatient Birkett, reaching the edge of despair, complained that after listening to the Americans cover the material in too great detail he was compelled by the French "to sit in suffering silence, whilst the maddening, toneless, insipid, flat depressing voice drones on in endless words which have quite lost all meaning." [33]

The main responsibility for this state of affairs did not lie with the French and the Russians; after the first American documentary rush, the shock value of paper evidence had simply worn off. Documentary material that would have seemed unique in any other trial appeared repetitive and of marginal significance at Nuremberg. By the third month of the trial, the Tribunal literally pushed aside endless sheaves of economic statistics and other financial records. On January 30, the unfortunate Dubost referred Lawrence to a particular document that had been presented to the Court a few days previously. The president made no effort to find the item in question, remarking merely that the prosecution had submitted so many documents that if all of them were "on the Bench before us you would not be able to see us." [34] Yet according to Birkett and Biddle, Lawrence himself had contributed to the difficulty by being too easygoing and lax in his control of the presentations. [35] They wanted him to assert himself more vigorously, but the most Lawrence would do was to intervene occasionally with a wry comment, urging speed and the avoidance of some of the repetition. When the defense presentations began, the Court paid a stiff price for this relaxed attitude of the bench.

The basic cause of the redundancy and boredom lay in the American presentation system. Jackson was convinced that the main weight should be carried by documents rather than the testimony of witnesses. He beat down the opposition among his own staff and sold the idea to the chief prosecutors of the other three powers. The format was unusual for those accustomed to an Anglo-American court, but Jackson argued that it was essential to exploit the rich documentary finds in order to build an incontrovertible historical record. The British enthusiastically supported the idea, not only because they hoped thereby to prevent disclosure of some of their own documentary sources, such as the admiralty records, but also because they hoped it would produce a short and speedy trial. [36] The French and Soviet prosecutors also found the suggestion congenial, for they saw the advantages of tapping American documentary resources, and they were more familiar with the documentary approach. On the eve of the opening of the trial, Jackson shifted ground somewhat and decided to use a few witnesses "to try out the defense" and "to introduce a little drama into the case." But by this time, the British had become even more opposed than the Americans, to the use of witnesses, fearing that it might prolong the trial and also raise issues helpful to the defense. [37] However impressive the arguments of Jackson and the British, the documentary approach showed itself admirably suited to produce a very dull trial. The press corps was the first group to show signs of boredom; the number of reporters quickly thinned and newspaper coverage of the trial decreased. The repetitiousness also quickly overcame the participants. Of the chief prosecutors, Lord Shawcross was virtually never in Nuremberg, and the other prosecutors were regularly in court only when their national group was making a presentation. Ultimately, Jackson disappeared from the courtroom for weeks at a time, and the defendants often dozed during the proceedings. The notes of Birkett and Biddle are replete with references to the contented repose of the accused, and even the Tribunal staff was not immune. At one point, a minor scandal had to be dealt with in a closed-door session because a French Tribunal aide seated next to the bench had snored so loudly that he had interfered with the proceedings.[38]

After the first weeks, only living witnesses could break through the haze and bring the courtroom back to life. Even though the prosecution did not use its witnesses very deftly, the occasional personal accounts clearly caught the interest of the courtroom spectators and the Tribunal. While the prosecution generally failed to personalize its case, the defense had little choice but to depend on witnesses. With few usable documents available, the defense attorneys put their clients on the stand and hoped for the best. Paradoxically, even though the humanity of some of these persons was highly suspect, this approach succeeded in humanizing the case. The judges obviously related to the living defendants, and gave numerous indications during the deliberations that they had studied them with great care. Tribunal members commented on the appearance, speech, and character of particular defendants—to the advantage of some and to the disadvantage of others.[39] But the defendants were all appraised as human beings, while the judges rarely spoke of the prosecution's case in personal terms.

Along with the prosecution's failure to use witnesses effectively went another weakness, resulting from the American plan. The anguished cry of the Gestapo and SS camp victims, those who had been tortured psychologically and physically, was not heard clearly at Nuremberg. Here and there such a voice *was* raised, and the Tribunal and the courtroom would seem to be frozen in horror. But witnesses to the great atrocities were used very sparingly and those who did appear were seldom questioned in a way that brought their suffering and torment to life. Planning of aggressive war was the big issue for the Americans, and they emphasized only those war crimes that suggested the existence of a conspiratorial plan or could be related to war planning. What the American team simply would not recognize was that, despite some reason for skepticism about atrocities in 1944, the central fact of 1945–46 was massive Nazi programs of human torture and extermination. The public outrage and European postwar demand for revenge was not focused on an abstract argument about Nazi aggressive plans in 1937 or a devious plot against German trade unions in 1933; it was centered on the slaughter of Allied civilians, on the ruthless treatment of POWs, and, especially, on the systematic horror of the exterminations. Yet, atrocities found little place in the American presentation and even less in the British case on Crimes Against Peace. By the time the Russian and French turns came, the pattern of the trial had been set and their emphasis on economics did little to enliven it. Whenever one of the killers or the victims appeared, the atmosphere quickly changed.[40] SS Gruppenführer Otto Ohlendorf, one of the leaders of the extermination teams in Russia, was put on the stand by the Americans and his matter-of-fact description of the mass killings obviously chilled the Court. But no one on the prosecution side seems to have drawn the requisite lesson, and atrocity testimony continued to be used sparingly. So complete was the de-emphasis on atrocities that later in the trial the defense made the incredible decision to put Rudolf Hoess, commandant of Auschwitz extermination camp, on the stand to support its contention that the mass killings had been carried out in secret and were not part of a general conspiracy. That Hoess, who was in Allied custody, had not been used as a prosecution witness is surprising enough, but that the defense could have so completely misjudged public opinion and believed that Hoess's cold-blooded chronicle of mass suffering and death would be an asset to the defense indicates the degree to which the American prosecution's fixation with conspiracy had come to dominate the whole trial.[41]

This conspiracy fixation, however, did not rule the feelings of the Judges either during the court proceedings or during deliberation. They showed a strong emotional response to the atrocities from the first film of the concentration camps down to the often jumbled testimony of the few victims called as witnesses by the Soviets and the French.[42] The trial Judgment also showed that the Tribunal placed heavy emphasis on War Crimes and Crimes Against Humanity. Of the eighteen defendants charged under both these counts, only two were acquitted, and, of the sixteen convicted, two were given prison terms, two were given life imprisonment, and twelve were hanged.

The prosecution's failure to shift its approach and adjust to the mood of the Court was due chiefly to the same old problem of a deficiency in overall direction. The Americans initially took the lead, but only with the avowed intention of dominating the trial while leaving scraps for the other prosecutors. Yet, their leadership slackened as the trial dragged on. Jackson blew hot and cold and frequently seemed to have lost interest in the case; he had minimal respect for the French and made no effort to disguise his distrust and dislike of the Russians.[43] Consequently, it was very difficult for the prosecution to take the measure of the bench and adjust its approaches accordingly. This was true not only in regard to atrocities, but also in regard to the legal difficulties that remained unresolved by the Charter and the indictment. The prosecution did not even specify the date at which the Germans had begun their alleged aggressive war planning. Instead, a jumble of evidence was presented, including notes from Hitler's staff conferences, statistics on rearmament, and various meandering assertions from *Mein Kampf*. But, without a specific date, it was left to the Court to choose a year and then decide which defendants were privy to the planning. Similarly, in regard to the grand conspiracy, the prosecution was peculiarly reluctant to specify who was a party to it, when the conspiracy had begun, and whether its criminal objectives had changed over time. Much evidence was presented suggesting that the prosecution wanted a declaration from the Tribunal stating that the conspiracy went as far back as the early 1920s, but the prosecution would not pick a definite beginning date or specify who was in the conspiracy at any given time.

The prosecution's reticence added to the burdens of the Tribunal and compounded the problems of the defense even more. As the conclusion of the prosecution's presentation neared, the defense became increasingly nervous about the vagueness of certain allegations, especially those applied to the prosecution's request that the six organizations be designated criminal. The defense wanted clarification of the allegations regarding organizational membership and the periods of time for which the groups were alleged to have been criminal. Some members of the Tribunal had long been plagued by doubts regarding the organizations, and nothing that the prosecution did during its time at the rostrum had substantially changed this. In early December, the Tribunal created a subcommittee consisting of Birkett and Parker to study the problem, and Birkett teetered on the fringe of judicial ethics by discussing the question with representatives of the Foreign Office and the British occupation authorities in Germany.[44] On December 12, the Tribunal held a hearing with the prosecutors, and in this session Jackson clung stubbornly to the idea that proof of individual criminal knowledge was not a necessary element to establish organizational criminality. If some members committed criminal acts, Jackson argued, that would be sufficient to hold all liable—presumably including "charwomen," Biddle acidly remarked in his notebook.[45]

The Tribunal was not satisfied by Jackson's answers and, in a closed session on January 5, the judges instructed Birkett to draft a letter to the prosecutors, setting out the questions that troubled the Tribunal. Seven days later, in another closed session, the Tribunal members began to discuss this draft and, by a vote of three to one, decided that they did not have authority to fix sentences for individual members of organizations declared to have been criminal, nor did they have jurisdiction over the courts that the occupying powers might use to try such individuals. In taking such a stand, the majority was not only reflecting the relevant clauses of the London Charter, but was trying again to limit its legal and jurisdictional responsibility as much as possible. However, the senior French member, Donnedieu de Vabres, was so concerned about potential injustices inherent in organization prosecution that he refused to agree that the Court should limit its authority even to the present case and voted against the motion placing individual sentences and the conduct of the occupation courts outside the reach of the Tribunal.[46]

This proceeding was secret, but the letter to the prosecution that was read out from the bench on January 14, 1946, contained questions that should have alerted anyone to the grave uncertainties harbored by the Tribunal. While disclaiming any desire to interfere with the prosecution's conduct of its case, the Tribunal noted that under Article IX of the Charter it was required to set procedures for persons who wished to petition the Tribunal regarding the possible designation of an organization as criminal. Before establishing such procedures, the Tribunal needed to know the intentions of the prosecution on a number of matters. Specifically, it asked the prosecutors what tests of criminality they proposed to apply to organizations and their members. Did membership have to be voluntary? And did members need to have knowledge of the criminal purposes of the organizations for the Tribunal to designate the organization criminal? In addition, the Court wanted the prosecution to set the exact time period of the alleged criminality of each organization and to decide whether any subgroups should be made exempt. Finally, it called for a factual summary of the criminal nature of each organization and an explanation of how this criminality was connected to the acts of individual defendants.[47]

Jackson immediately took charge of preparing the prosecution's reply, and almost as quickly ran into serious difficulty. Suggestions on how best to proceed flooded him from the American and British prosecution staffs, and even from the American occupation authorities in Germany.[48] Unfortunately, these opinions were sharply divided both on the approach and on how many concessions to make in order to satisfy the Tribunal. Jackson understood the serious concern of the judges, but he was under heavy pressure to yield nothing and to demand that the Tribunal give a blanket declaration of criminality without imposing qualifications or limitations. The British showed little inclination to deal realistically with the problem or to give ground to the Tribunal, [49] but the strongest advocate of no compromise was the American assistant secretary of war, Howard Peterson, who was disturbed by the prospect of prosecuting members of organizations that the Tribunal declared to have been criminal. In early February, Peterson requested not only that the prosecution ask the Tribunal for a blanket declaration of criminality for all the organizations, but also for preset sentences according to the ranks of the members of each organization. What he apparently had in mind was that the Tribunal would give each rank a specific sentence: for example, all higher-ranking SS leaders would get a penalty of, say, twenty years; medium-ranking leaders, a sentence of ten years, and so on down the line. Such a procedure surely would have eased Peterson's worries over whether he had enough personnel to carry out real trials; with crimes and sentences fixed in advance, all that would have been required in subsequent proceedings was the establishment of identity and rank of the individual. Everything else would have been done administratively.[50]

When Jackson failed to heed Peterson's suggestions in preparing his address to the Court, the assistant secretary wrote a long letter to the justice vigorously protesting the idea of making any concessions to the Tribunal. A cabled summary of Peterson's complaints reached Jackson on February 18, while he was in the midst of preparing his speech. By this point, the assistant secretary had given up his demand for fixed sentences, but he was still obsessed by the fear that "impossibly long individual trials" would result if criminal organization members were allowed grounds on which they might defend themselves in subsequent proceedings. Knowledge of criminality should not have to be proved in subsequent trials, Peterson believed; the only defenses that he wanted to allow were "mistaken identity" or compulsion to join or remain a member. Even then, Peterson was not ready to allow what he called fear of "political or economic retaliation" as a legitimate form of defense based on compulsion. The assistant secretary's concern in all this had nothing to do with the judicial situation or even with the possible criminality of the organizations and their members. All he saw were hundreds of thousands of persons in U.S. Army custody and too few men and too little money to carry out a large number of real trials. The army problem was administrative, and Peterson wanted the Court to provide him with the basis for an administrative solution.[51] Jackson replied to Peterson in a most conciliatory way on February 26, but emphasized that from all indications there was little prospect that the Tribunal would give a general declaration of criminality for all the organizations. He cited various practical indicators of why compromise was necessary and then stressed his conviction that the British and American Tribunal members wanted "to do their full duty in finding [the] organizations criminal [but] they do not want to be put in [a] position of making a sweeping declaration which will be pointed to by those in control of great areas of Europe as authorizing a new reign of terror." [52] Jackson also clearly showed that his own suspicions of the Soviets had placed him in a peculiar predicament, for he added; "I am not in a position to say that there is no merit in that fear." [53] The justice stressed that he sympathized with the army's problem, but felt that compromises would have to be made in order to get anything from the Tribunal, in his opinion, what he proposed to say to the Court was "likely to be about [the] best we can do." [54]

This was cold comfort for Peterson, but he actually had little need to worry, for a nearly simultaneous message from General Lucius Clay, the American member of the Allied Control Council for Germany, provided an answer to the problem. After citing the difficulties that might arise in prosecuting criminal organization members on the basis of a circumscribed Tribunal ruling, Clay, with a cheerful adaptability that might have pleased the earlier police authorities in Germany, told Peterson that "whatever [the] Tribunal's decision we will be in a position through [a] proposed Denazification law [making the same organizations criminal] to handle the members not selected by the Chief of Counsel or Deputy for separate criminal trials." [55] In other words, if the Tribunal did not give the army the law, the army would make its own law and still dispose of the criminal organization members, by administrative means, if it wished to. Clay was as good as his word; on March 5, the new denazification law was approved, and, as the general subsequently reported to Peterson, under this law "we have the means of coping with the mass of membership cases, whatever may be the decision of the Tribunal with respect to the organizations." [56] With such determination and legal versatility, the army had no need to trouble the Tribunal or Jackson any further.

The justice's preparatory problems, however, were still far from over. On February 20, the Soviet chief prosecutor, General R. A. Rudenko, gave formal notice that the Russians opposed any concession on the organizations. The Soviets, who had been extremely cool to the organization prosecution idea at the London Conference, had become its principal proponents in Nuremberg. Rudenko informed Jackson that, in the Soviet view, the Tribunal had no authority to give directions to Allied occupation courts that would try organization members. If the Tribunal tried to make distinctions between the subgroups of any organization, the Russians would consider it a form of interference with the prerogatives of the occupation courts and thus attempt to make a "highly important limitation [in the] national sovereignty" (underscored in original) of the Soviet Union. Furthermore, Rudenko declared, the Tribunal had already received enough evidence and, therefore, defense witnesses should not even be heard on the organizations. In the Russian view, none of the members should be exempted from the declaration of criminality and not one inch should be conceded to the doubts expressed by the Tribunal. [57]

Jackson met this situation forcefully and effectively. He told the Soviets and the other prosecutors that concessions would have to be made; the Court had given clear warning that, if something was not done, the whole organization case might be lost. If the other prosecutors wished to dissent, or hold their positions in open court, fair enough, but the United States was going to give ground. [58] The role of a strong compromiser is extremely difficult, but it is doubly so when the same man has to compromise what he himself has wrought. Jackson carried it off with vigor, and it was surely one of his most impressive hours as leader of the prosecution.

After two weeks of careful preparation, the justice addressed the Tribunal on February 28. He defended the idea of prosecuting criminal organizations by arguing that these six groups had been the instruments of power in the Nazi system. It was necessary to strike at them not only to clean the slate of evil within Germany, but also to smooth the way for the occupation by neutralizing the most dangerous Nazis. Yet Jackson swallowed his own misgivings and assured the Court that there was little likelihood that members would be subject to wholesale prosecution or persecution by the occupation authorities. Turning to the tasks facing the Tribunal, Jackson agreed that "ordinary legal principles" put the burden of proof on the prosecution, and he brought forth five criteria to be used in determining organization criminality. An organization had to be an identifiable group with a general purpose; its membership must have been predominantly voluntary; the aims of the organization must have been criminal under the terms of the London Charter; the membership must have been aware "in general" of the group's criminal aims, and some members of the organization had to be currently on trial and convicted for an offense "on the basis of which the organization" might be declared criminal.[59]

Jackson had gone a long way to ease the Tribunal's task, abandoning some of the earlier extreme claims made by the prosecution; now voluntary membership had to be established, and some general knowledge by members of the aims and purposes of the organization had to be proven. But Jackson's speech still failed to clarify fully the relationship between individual defendants and organization prosecution, and the precise periods during which the prosecution alleged that the organizations were criminal remained uncertain. The indictment indicated that the SA, the SS, and the "Leadership Corps" of the Nazi party should be held liable from the earliest days of the party, while the state organizations—the Gestapo, the Reich Cabinet, and the General Staff—were prosecutable from 1933. Although Jackson did not repudiate these time periods, he did grant that the Tribunal had the "power to condition its declaration so as to cover a lesser period of time than that set forth in the Indictment." [60] This appeared to be a broad hint that, if the Tribunal retained its doubts about organization prosecution, it would be better to declare all the organizations criminal for restricted time periods rather than to sever certain subgroups from responsibility, or quash the charges. This preference was made even clearer by the announcement that the prosecution was prepared to exclude only a handful of subgroups—the staffs of the lowest Nazi party leaders (*Ortsgruppen-*, or town, *Zellen-*, or neighborhood, and *Blockleiter*, or street groups), various honorary reserve and guard units of the SA, and the clerical and janitorial employees of the Gestapo.[61]

The rationale behind some of these exclusions is rather difficult to grasp even today. The prosecution asserted that the organizations were illegal because of the criminal camaraderie of their members and the illegal functions performed by them. Therefore, since the SA reserves were not full members, their exclusion made sense; and since Gestapo janitors did not have criminal functions and were not part of anything approximating an order or fellowship, their exclusion also made sense. Conversely, SS members who were also janitors remained liable because the prosecution held that they were not just employees but part of a blood brotherhood. The decision to exclude the staffs of the lower party officials is really perplexing, because these people, to the extent that they were not merely clerks (in fact, the Blockleiter frequently had no staff), were more analogous to lower-level SS members than to Gestapo menials. Consequently, although the prosecution intended these exclusions to be final, and Jackson emphasized that in the prosecution's opinion no more precise definition of the groups was necessary, there were no clear criteria to explain why some subgroups should be severed and others retained. On balance, however, this was a modest blemish in Jackson's performance, for he had succeeded in answering most of the questions raised by the Tribunal and had seemingly put the criminal organization case back on its feet.

At recess, the Tribunal members expressed their satisfaction with Jackson's address; they apparently felt he had lifted many of the legal burdens from their shoulders. Biddle shared the general enthusiasm but noted that some questions remained, particularly whether or not more subgroups, or "classes," of members should be excluded.[62] During the afternoon session of February 28 and the morning session of March 1, the other prosecutors and a group of defense attorneys amplified and commented on Jackson's remarks. The supplementary statements by the prosecution added little that was new, but the defense attorneys pounded at the sensitive issues—the dangers of collective guilt; the difficulties of linking some organizations, such as the SA, with individual defendants; and the enormous practical problems inherent in coping with the hundreds of thousands of organizational members who wished to make statements for the defense.

Toward the end of the session on March 1, Jackson came back to deal with the defense arguments and to answer the Tribunal's questions. In response to defense pleas that the organization members might be dishonored by a general declaration of criminality, Jackson remarked acidly that for such men no more dishonor was possible.[63] He also held his ground under the questioning of the French judge, Donnedieu de Vabres, who raised the possibility that the Tribunal should try to limit the punishment that could be imposed by subsequent occupation courts. Jackson flatly rejected this suggestion, agreeing with the Soviet prosecutor that under the terms of the London Charter the Tribunal was limited to making a simple declaration of criminality and nothing more.[64] When it was pointed out to him that Article XI of the Charter referred to punishment imposed on an organization member "by the Tribunal," Jackson still refused to accept the idea that the Tribunal could restrict the action of future courts. With the openness that was his most engaging characteristic, he merely remarked: "Frankly, the wording of this article has bothered me as to just what it does mean," [65] but in any event he was sure that it did not support Donnedieu de Vabres's plea for general restrictive powers. Similarly, when Biddle pressed him on the dangers inherent in declaring organizations criminal in view of the Allied Control Council for Germany's adoption of law (#10) which listed penalties up to and including death for mere membership in such organizations, Jackson remarked: "I am frank enough to say I would not have drafted it in the language [in which] it is drafted." [66] Pressed by Biddle as to the reasons why only Gestapo clerks and janitors were excluded and not lower-level functionaries of all groups, Jackson reached new heights in openness. "One of the difficulties with the Court," he remarked, "is that it tries to be logical, and ought to be logical perhaps. [But] I have always thought that was the great merit of the jury system, that juries do not have to be, and in prosecuting we do not have to be." [67] The justice went on to argue that most of the Tribunal's apprehension was unfounded, for

the United States is not interested in coming over here 3,500 miles to prosecute clerks and stenographers and janitors. That is not the class of crimes, even if they did have some knowledge that we are after, because that is not the class of offender that affects the peace of the world.[68]

Again, a splendid statement, but the Tribunal was still left with the question of why not, then, omit all the lower-level employees.

By his good-natured frankness, Jackson had managed to pass through a difficult hour with the Tribunal, while making minimal concessions to the defense. The British deputy prosecutor, Maxwell Fyfe, in his turn, seemed initially to fare as well as, or even better than, Jackson. In reply to the Tribunal's suggestion that it would have to be proved that members knew of their organizations' criminal purposes, he noted that it was "only too true" that the participants had "made a habit of sticking their heads in the sand and endeavoring to abstain from acquiring knowledge of things that were unpleasant." [69] But this kind of behavior must constitute no defense at all, he maintained, and the Tribunal should consider only one question: "Ought a person in that position reasonably to have known of the commission of the crimes?" [70] This was a tight, firm answer, keyed perfectly to the feelings and legal needs of the Tribunal; but, when the questioning turned to specific organizations, Maxwell Fyfe's reasonableness quickly disappeared. Biddle asked him: "Would you say that a member of the SA who had joined, let us say, in 1921, and resigned the next year [that is, seventeen years before World War II] was guilty of conspiring to wage aggressive war and guilty of War Crimes?" Without a pause, Maxwell Fyfe replied yes, and, when Biddle asked whether this would apply also to an SA member who joined the organization after its leadership had been wiped out in the Blood Purge of June 30, 1934, Maxwell Fyfe again replied yes, that such a man was still guilty because the SA survived as a "symbol." [71] Immediately after this exchange, the Soviet chief prosecutor, Rudenko, faced these same questions on the SA and provided essentially the same whimsical answers as Maxwell Fyfe.

On the following day, March 2, a group of defense counsel underwent their turn at probing examinations by Tribunal members. Dr. Egon Kubuschok argued that the Reich Cabinet, which he represented, was too small a group to warrant prosecution as a criminal organization—an argument that obviously impressed the Tribunal, for the Judgment cited it as one of the major reasons for not holding the Cabinet criminal. [72] Other defense attorneys stressed that the crucial test for all the organizations should be whether the members knew of the criminal intent of their leaders, adding that such knowledge was impossible to prove because the Führer and his aides had kept their plans hidden. Biddle considered this a serious argument and duly jotted it down in his notes. [73] In the defense presentations, which were about to begin, nearly every defendant maintained that he had not known about Hitler's criminal plans. Such pleas of ignorance seemed absurd and offensive to many observers, as they strike one today, but knowledge of an organization's criminal purposes had been made a crucial issue by the prosecution and the Tribunal, and it was perfectly reasonable that the defense would try to make it a key element for the individual defendants.

After two and a half days of speeches and questioning, the open hearing on criminal organizations was finally brought to a close on March 2. Justice Jackson's eloquence had not resolved all the Tribunal's doubts, and the defense had managed to make some telling points. It needs to be stressed, however, that the driving force in this hearing was not the defense but the Tribunal itself. This was to be the only open discussion of legal questions that would occur during the trial, and it shows us numerous issues that were troubling Tribunal members. Both the defense and the prosecution made vigorous responses to the Tribunal's specific questions, but neither side drew any broader conclusions. The Tribunal had shown that it wanted help in navigating the legal shallows of the Charter; it did not consider the moral indignation of the prosecution nor the vague references of principle by the defense to be of much assistance in coping with the practical problems before it. Neither party in the trial seems to have grasped that, if the Tribunal had this kind of trouble on criminal organizations, it probably had similar concern on other issues, such as conspiracy and aggressive war planning. The obvious lesson that should have been drawn from the criminal organization hearings was that the defense and prosecution should produce approaches to those issues that would incline the Tribunal to favor their respective positions. Granted, the Court neither gave them such advice nor offered a formal opportunity to present such arguments. But the temper of the Court was obvious, and no opportunity should have been lost to provide directive hints to the Bench. Instead of doing this, however, the prosecution used the following days to provide more supplemental details and then rested its case on March 5.

During the transition from prosecution to defense, which occurred between March 2 and March 13, the Tribunal carried on a seemingly endless series of in camera discussions on the organizational issue. The Soviets accepted the prosecution arguments in toto, while the French were deeply troubled by matters of principle and the British apparently were unable to make up their minds what to do. Biddle insisted that they should pass over the general questions for the time being and decide merely how they were going to hear the prospective witnesses for the organizations. The American view finally prevailed, and on March 13 the Tribunal announced that a special commission, chaired by two of the Tribunal's legal aides, would be formed to receive testimony from members of the organizations. The defense would also have an opportunity near the end of the trial to put representational witnesses on the stand and to make a general presentation on the organizations.[74] With that, the most pressing problem had been solved, but at the end of the trial a showdown on the broader issues would be inescapable.

The defense opened its case on March 8, starting with the presentation for Reich Marshal Hermann Goering. The demeanor and bearing of Dr. Otto Stahmer, Goering's defense counsel, was indicative of the change that had come over the defense during the three months of the trial. Most of the shock and depression had disappeared, and Stahmer showed that the defense would put up a vigorous struggle. Many of the counsel were still baffled by the trial procedure and their actions sometimes appeared clumsy and unimaginative, but this may have resulted as much from twelve years of experience in Nazi courts as from the peculiarities of Nuremberg. The counsel definitely had lost most of their suspicions of the Court; although they complained of certain rulings, as lawyers always do, they seemed to regard the Tribunal as generally fair and reasonable. Three days before Stahmer began, all the defense counsel's morale had been boosted when the Tribunal chastised the occupation authorities for permitting press attacks on defense attorneys.[75] The Tribunal, additionally, lauded the services provided by the defense attorneys under what it realized were extremely trying conditions, and gave notice to the Allied military command in Germany that the defense counsel were under the Tribunal's protection, and that the Court would not tolerate any further press or public attacks upon the counsels.

The defense was seriously lamed by only one Tribunal ruling, a requirement that lists of prospective defense witnesses and documents be submitted to the Tribunal for prior approval. This procedure was authorized in the London Charter to prevent the defense from using the trial as a forum for Nazi propaganda. It also helped the prosecutors, who controlled most of the documents and the prospective defense witnesses, and thus wanted the Tribunal to screen defense requests carefully ruling out items likely to entail long, fruitless searches. The Tribunal accepted the prosecution's reasoning and an evidentiary application and screening procedure was established. Psychologically, the defense was thereby placed at a distinct disadvantage, as a humble suppliant to the Tribunal and the prosecutors. The practical obstacles facing the relatively small number of defense personnel—for example, their difficulty of movement inside Germany—were also formidable, and they were not eased by the Tribunal's caution in screening defense requests for witnesses and documents. The Court, in part, succumbed to the prosecution's obsessive fear that the defense might resort to disruptive tactics and "attacks on the prosecution" to prolong and discredit the trial. The prosecutors had held worried discussions on how to meet this threat long before the trial began, and they were ever anxious to bring this possibility to the Court's attention. Every defense application for a witness or a document had to be framed in such a way that the prosecution could not raise the possibility that it might further the cause of Nazism. The prosecutors feared propaganda so acutely that they resorted to highly questionable tactics to avert it. In December, Goering gave an interview to the press, and the Soviet prosecutor convinced his colleagues that the propaganda dangers arising from the incident were so great that each prosecutor should "discuss the matter privately" with members of the Tribunal in order to prevent similar occurrences in the future.[76]

But the prosecution's effort in this regard paled into insignificance compared with what it did concerning documents that might be damaging to its case. There is no evidence to indicate that the prosecutors tampered with the captured documents, but it is definitely clear that the prosecution feared "counter charges" from the defense if certain documents were put in evidence. Even before the trial opened, the British and Americans agreed not to use certain State Department and Foreign Office records or to allow access to British Admiralty records because of the existence of materials that "might be embarrassing to produce."[77] Some of these documents concerned Nazi-Soviet relations; others touched on points that compromised the Western Powers, such as the British preparations for landings in Norway before the German attack. Furthermore, it was also clear to members of the prosecution that many of the Allied diplomatic papers did not support the simple charges of Nazi aggression contained in the indictment. Thus, the conclusion is inescapable that the decision to base the prosecution solely on German documents was motivated, in part, by a desire to keep compromising Allied documents out of the hands of the defense.[78]

In the course of the trial, the Tribunal showed itself to be very receptive to prosecution pleas that *tu quo que* arguments (i.e., that the Allies had committed the same acts as the defendants) should be inadmissible, and that all general discussions of Allied policies and European diplomatic conditions should be avoided. But there is, again, no documentary evidence to suggest that the Tribunal knew that the prosecutors were controlling the form and types of materials presented to the Court in order to keep the defense away from exonerating or mitigating documentation. The Court seems to have been reluctant to grant defense requests for general background material on the diplomatic setting because it feared that, once this door were opened, it would be unable to close it again—although the Court, like the defense lawyers, did not know what was in the Allied archives. Already groaning under a burden of unresolved legal complications, the Tribunal had no desire to adjudicate the general history of interwar Europe and therefore every effort of the defense to bring up for consideration such matters as the Treaty of Versailles was swiftly blocked. A number of defense counsel surely misread the Court's intentions and made repeated, almost frenzied, efforts to raise these issues by arguing that fairness to the German nation, as well as to the defendants, required that the whole European background of World War II should be considered before the charge of conspiracy was resolved. Actually, the Court was trying to move away as far as possible from the general issue of conspiracy, and in its closed deliberations the majority of the Tribunal members were taking a cautious approach to all the broad allegations of the prosecution.

The defense attorneys, of course, lacked foolproof means of testing the Court; nor was there any compelling reason for them to abandon their suspicion of Allied intentions. But, for whatever reasons, they rarely caught the signs that did reveal the mood of the judges. The Court bent over backward to let the defense handle the witnesses it was granted in any way it chose, but usually the attorneys just led witnesses through long historical accounts and testimonials to the good character of the defendants. Lawrence's leniency in allowing free rein to the meandering defense aroused as much opposition from some of the members of the Tribunal as had the loose presentations of the prosecution. The Soviets formally protested the irrelevancies, while Birkett had reached such a state that he wrote in his diary:

When I consider the utter uselessness of acres of paper and thousands of words and that life is slipping away, I moan for this shocking waste of time. . . . I have now got completely dispirited and can only chafe in impotent despair.[79]

Biddle wanted to join the Soviets and stop what he called this "hog-wash,"[80] but Lawrence and Donnedieu de Vabres firmly opposed such a move. With a change thus blocked by a two–two tie, Biddle also gave up, and by the end of May resignedly noted that he, along with everyone else, was bored "to death."[81] In the last few days of the defense presentations, even Judge Lawrence succumbed, and, in the middle of an excrutiatingly repetitious presentation, he leaned over and asked Biddle in a whisper whether he recalled an "indecorous" old music-hall song with the line "You can't stop a girl from thinking."[82] Such instances of Lawrence's bonhomie probably helped prevent a revolt on the bench, but they also led the defense counsel to conclude that things were going swimmingly, and that their presentations were more effective than they were. Through ir-relevancies and repetition, the defense actually frittered away its best opportunities to impress and guide the Tribunal.

If the Soviet view had prevailed, the defense would have had little opportunity to engage in irrelevancies or anything else. During the consideration of defense witnesses, Nikitchenko repeatedly voted to deny witnesses whom the other Tribunal members were prepared to grant.[83] On the eve of the defense presentations, the senior So-viet member also bitterly opposed the practice of allowing the Nazi defendants to testify under oath, especially if they sat in the witness box, which had been used by the prosecution witnesses. This reac-tion so outraged Parker that the American alternate threatened to resign, but Biddle calmed him and the two then combined to out-vote Nikitchenko and uphold the right of defendant testimony. Lawrence then came forward with one of his patented conciliatory gestures.[84] Noting that the witness box was dangerously close to where Birkett sat at the end of the bench, Lawrence agreed to move it slightly to assure the safety of Tribunal members. The defendants were thus able to testify and Nikitchenko was able to maintain that a visible distinction had been made between the prosecution and the defense.[85]

All this had been fought out and settled before the defense testimony began, and Nikitchenko's only serious objection during the presentation itself was to Lawrence's extreme tolerance and patience. Even here, Nikitchenko was in a poor position to object too strongly, for in the last stages of the prosecution presentations some of the Soviet prosecutors had floundered helplessly and other members of the Court had wanted to intervene. Once, when Biddle had suggested that they cut short one of the Soviet prosecutors, it was Nikitchenko who urged tolerance, because they might "mix him up." [86] The Tribunal forebore, on this and other similar occasions, so that when the defense later droned on meaninglessly, Nikitchenko made but one effort to stop it. When that failed, he sank into boredom along with his colleagues.[87]

The defense attorneys were unaware of this situation, but they did sense that it was possible to raise issues that could embarrass the Soviets and, at the same time, weaken the charges against the defendants. They concentrated their initial fire on the accusation that the Nazis had murdered large numbers of Polish officers in the Katyn forest. The Soviets had specifically included this charge in the indictment and, as indicated above, had then publicly demanded that the list of massacre victims be increased tenfold. It has subsequently been quite convincingly demonstrated that the Soviets themselves had committed the massacre—perhaps through a mix-up in orders—but even at the time there were a number of obviously disquieting features in regard both to the facts and to the Soviet allegations. Nikitchenko had to labor diligently and call upon every ounce of his colleagues' goodwill in order to work out formulas that would limit the courtroom presentations on Katyn. The other Tribunal members ultimately went along and allowed the Soviets to save face with a minimum of snide remarks from the Western judges and prosecutors, but the continued defense probing on Katyn did produce inter-Allied tension and seems to have accentuated the distance between the Soviet and Western judges.[88]

The Katyn issue raised few side questions, except to show that the Nazis might not have a monopoly on atrocities, but a second target of the defense attack had more serious implications. On the eve of the Nazi invasion of Poland, the Soviet Union and Nazi Germany had signed a nonaggression pact. That the Russians had aligned themselves with Hitler in 1939 clearly undercut the prosecution's contention that Nazi aggressive plans were so definite and so obvious that the lowliest defendant could not seriously plead ignorance. But this was not the sum of the difficulty—in addition to the general pact, the Nazi-Soviet agreement had contained secret clauses in which the two partners cynically agreed to divide Poland and establish independent spheres of influence spreading over much of central and eastern Europe. Surely, if the prosecution were correct that there was collusion, or a conspiracy, in the planning of aggression against Poland in 1939, then Stalin was one of the parties to the conspiracy. The defense attorneys seized every possible opportunity to drive this point home, but what they sought above all was an occasion that would allow them to put the secret clauses of the pact into evidence. The first difficulty facing the defense was that none of the defendants had retained a copy of the secret clauses, and without the actual text much of the possible dramatic effect would be lost. At this critical juncture, aid for the defense seems to have come from a most unlikely source—a member of the prosecution who handed over a confidential copy of the secret clauses.[89] Before the trial began, both the British and the American prosecutors had copies of this document in their possession, and as early as October–November 1945 they had worriedly discussed how to minimize the embarrassment that might arise from it.[90] The identity of the individual who actually transmitted the document is still not clear, but it seems certain that the document came from the American prosecution team. The anti-Soviet sentiment among the American prosecutors had reached flood proportions long before; from Jackson on down there came an endless series of complaints and caustic remarks about the Russians. Jackson had a copy of the document in his files, but in all probability it was not passed to the defense directly on his orders.[91] Nonetheless, the justice had created the atmosphere that made the incident possible, and little or nothing was done to identify and punish whoever had actually given the secret protocol to the defense.

What to do about this document presented the Tribunal with the most difficult evidentiary problem of the trial. The Soviets adamantly opposed every defense suggestion that it be admitted in evidence, and they also tried to block all witness testimony on the matter. The Western judges were caught in a quandary: how to respect the traditional rules of evidence without precipitating a serious crisis with the Soviet judges. Finally, the Tribunal hit upon an ingenious escape route—they would allow the document in evidence if the defense attorneys could certify its authenticity by explaining how they had obtained it! [92] With a shudder, the defense realized that the document game was over—no one in the prosecution would dare to certify the document or admit how it had come into the hands of the defense. Only through the testimony of participants in the nonaggression pact negotiations, especially ex-Foreign Minister von Ribbentrop and his secretary, did the defense manage to put the gist of the secret clauses into the court record. But this contrived and indirect approach deprived the information of most of its punch.

It is probable that, though appearances were maintained, the Western Tribunal members bore some resentment against the Soviets for putting them through such an ordeal. The judges may also have surmised the role the American prosecution played in the affair, thus tainting its reputation. But, if the defense had hoped that the issue might overturn the case or produce an irreparable breach between the judges, they were disappointed. The incident demonstrated one more flaw in the prosecution's conspiracy case, but a number of judges had already indicated that they had ceased to take that case at face value. Whatever the momentary stresses and strains, the Tribunal was not destroyed by another blow at conspiracy or by an East-West split. Nothing comparable to the anti-Soviet fervor that gripped the American prosecution ever appeared on the bench. Even while the judges split over Katyn and the Nazi-Soviet Pact, they were uniting on other issues, and the divisions did not harden on geographical or ideological lines. The Court kept its eye on the practical problems, always sought to prevent the intrusion of any new issues, and for the most part retained its sense of humor. Through it all, the Western judges maintained cordial personal relations with "Nick," and neither Katyn nor any other issue seems to have seriously threatened their resolve to get along, solve the problems, and produce a creditable judgment.

The Tribunal's cheerful cooperativeness, which blunted some of the best sallies of the defense, also unintentionally produced confusion regarding the judges' attitudes toward individual defendants and their counsel. The most serious misapprehension concerned Lawrence's attitude toward Doenitz's defense attorney, Flottenrichter (Naval Judge) Otto Kranzbuehler. Sir Geoffrey was so considerate of Kranzbuehler that the navy lawyer was jokingly referred to by other defense counsel as Lawrence's "pet." [93] When Kranzbuehler applied for permission to question the American Admiral Chester Nimitz with the implied intention of justifying Germany's submarine attacks on merchant ships by citing comparable American attacks on Japanese merchantmen, the Tribunal granted the request. This seems to have been accounted for by some other defense counsel as simply an instance of Lawrence's sympathy for Kranzbuehler, but, in fact, Lawrence wanted to deny the petition, and he never wavered in his determination to convict Doenitz for his conduct of submarine warfare. Kranzbuehler's request was allowed over Soviet and British objections simply because Biddle would not give up his opinion that it should be granted and made it an issue of personal privilege. [94]

In general, the judges' feelings about the other defense counsel seem to have had no more influence on the proceedings or the Judgment than did Lawrence's alleged sympathy for Kranzbuehler. The two defense counsel who most provoked Birkett's wrath were those representing Papen and Speer. He found the former's presentations vacuous and once referred to him as "my ordeal of the last few days." [95] Then Birkett secretly chastised Speer's counsel for carrying on the same "evil tradition with unashamed and unabated zeal." [96] Yet, in the final Judgment, Speer received a mild Nuremberg penalty, twenty years' imprisonment, and Papen was acquitted. Among the defense counsel who most raised Biddle's ire were the chief counsel for Raeder and the SA's attorney, whom he respectively characterized as "impudent" and "unusually stupid." [97] But again, the final verdicts bore no relation to these opinions, for Raeder was spared the noose and the Tribunal refused to designate the SA as a criminal organization. The only case in which the personal failings of a defense lawyer may have affected a final verdict concerned the deputy defense counsel for the SS. Biddle repeatedly gave voice to his personal dislike of the man and his low estimate of his work as a lawyer. On one occasion, Biddle's notes even suggested that his estimate tallied with Goering's, for he observed that the Reich Marshal smiled all through one cross-examination, during which the unfortunate counsel had "as usual" done "abominably." [98]

There was more to all this than mere personal hostility. The lawyer in question had solicited donations from SS men who feared what might happen to them if the SS were declared a criminal organization, although such fund raising had been strictly prohibited by the Tribunal. This case of misconduct was turned over to the local Nuremberg bar for an opinion, and, when that body ruled against the attorney, Biddle delightedly noted that the Tribunal had immediately discharged him.[99] Of course, the deeds and reputation of the SS were such that it would be unreasonable to place much of the responsibility for its designation as a criminal organization on the back of its wayward deputy defense counsel. But there was at least a possibility that certain subgroups, such as units of the military (*Waffen-*) SS, which were composed of large numbers of conscripts, might have escaped condemnation. Their interests were not very clearly presented to the Tribunal in any event, but it seems from the surviving records that even the hesitant steps made on behalf of the SS were nullified by the suspect deputy counsel, who made most of the presentations in court. However, it must be reiterated that this is merely conjecture, and that this is the only instance where personal hostility might be said to coincide with a cloudy judgment. By and large, considering the reputation of most of the defendants and the weaknesses of some of the counsel, the judges showed themselves remarkably open-minded.

Generally, the defense seems to have been hurt less seriously by its own members' failings than it was dramatically aided by the failure of Jackson. The defense attorneys, as well as the Soviet and French prosecutors, had substantial difficulty with the unfamiliar procedure of cross-examination, and one would have anticipated that the advantage from this procedure would have gone to the Anglo-American prosecution. In fact, early in the trial Jackson recommended that the Soviets and the French not be allowed to do important cross-examinations, because they were likely to make "a mess of them." [100] But any continental or defense problems with the procedure were dwarfed by Jackson's catastrophic defeat in his cross-examinations, first of Goering and then of Schacht. The story of these confrontations has been told so often that little of it bears repeating. Suffice it to say that Jackson's judgment may have been clouded because he had not been named Chief Justice of the Supreme Court when Justice Harlan Stone died, and because he was involved in an unseemly public controversy with Justice Hugo Black. Jackson disregarded the early signs of Goering's toughness and in the end seriously underestimated his opponents. Both Schacht and Goering had some knowledge of the English language, while Jackson did not understand German; the defendants grasped the thrust of his questions immediately and had ample opportunity to prepare careful replies while pretending that they were waiting for the questions to be translated. The results were disastrous for Jackson. The defendants parried his thrusts, eluded his snares, and countered with lengthy replies that confused every issue. By the end of the first day's cross-examination of Goering, Jackson was beside himself and word of his distraught condition reached the Tribunal. Norman Birkett believed that part of the blame for the debacle lay with the Court itself, and he wanted to order Goering to confine his answers directly to the questions asked. Initially, Lawrence seems to have supported Birkett, but Biddle deprecated any need for the Tribunal to "protect" Jackson, and Lawrence then swung to Biddle's side and no order was issued. In Birkett's interpretation, both Parker and Biddle opposed the issuance of the order because of their antipathy toward Jackson.[101] Certainly, irritation at what the Tribunal considered Jackson's erratic behavior and high-handedness had been growing among the American judges, and perhaps with others, ever since the trial began. There may well have been a touch of malicious pleasure in the Tribunal's decision to let Jackson go it alone. In any event, after a shaky start, the justice managed to get through the second session of Goering's cross-examination, "nervous" and, as Biddle noted, "a little angry." [102] Yet, the effects of the incident did not end there. Birkett believed that Jackson's failure to break Goering, and the Tribunal's reluctance to restrain him, put the trial out of control, and he seems to have been right.[103] The subsequent loose and meandering defense presentations probably owe more to the Jackson–Goering confrontation and the Court's attitude of laissez-faire than any of the defense counsel realized.

What some of the members of the Tribunal were made to acknowledge, however, was that Jackson had been deeply humiliated by the whole experience and his fragile self-control had been shattered. Three weeks after the encounter with Goering, Jackson arranged a private meeting with Parker and Biddle and, in a "wild" and "uncontrolled mood," he poured out all his complaints about the Court and its members. He accused Lawrence of always ruling against the Americans, blamed Biddle for undermining the morale of the prosecution, and in the end threatened to resign. The American judges found themselves in the anomalous position of trying to calm and reassure him, but Biddle recognized that Jackson bore him a great deal of personal animosity. He, in turn, seems to have had a fair degree of antipathy toward Jackson, though he ended his notebook account of this strange meeting with the remark that Jackson was "very bitter. He seems to me very unfair and unhappy. I am sorry for him." [104] Birkett, too, remarked that Jackson had taken the whole cross-examination very hard and "his instinct is to run away from the scene of his failure." [105] Jackson, however, hung on until May, when he cross-examined the former economics minister and head of the Reichsbank, Hjalmar Schacht. The same difficulties that had occurred with Goering surfaced again, in muted form, and Schacht was also able to dazzle Jackson and the Court with his incomparable technical knowledge. The result, in Birkett's words, was a "failure," "a perfectly futile cross-examination"; [106] Biddle characterized it as "weak" [107] and, with no remaining trace of sympathy, added that Schacht was "much too clever for him." [108] Every vestige of Jackson's earlier domination over the Court and the trial was eliminated, and even members of the prosecution staff openly reported to Washington that he might quit and go home. [109]

Yet, even with this extreme failure by the prosecution, the defense was unable to make effective use of its five months at the rostrum. As Birkett observed, most of the testimony was not only repetitive, it was simply irrelevant to the main issues of the case. [110] The defense never focused its attack on the sensitive points, in part because it was even less united than the prosecution. The twenty-two defendants came from very diverse backgrounds and were deeply divided along occupational and class lines. Some of the defendants hated each other, as did Schacht and Goering, while the old aristocrats treated the commoners with thinly veiled condescension. The military looked down upon the civilians, and the rest of the defendants considered Streicher and Kaltenbrunner too unsavory for their company. Since the men in the dock had been selected by the prosecution to represent the diverse organizations and aspects of the Nazi system, their earlier political activities and the charges they faced varied greatly. While Kaltenbrunner was a powerful figure during the last days of the Nazi regime, Neurath was retired, and Speer was systematically disobeying Hitler's orders. Goering assumed the role at Nuremberg of defender of the regime, while Schacht, who had spent the last period of the war in a concentration camp, openly denounced it. Under the circumstances, no meaningful common defense was possible, and agreement even on the approach to such fundamental charges as the conspiratorial plan to wage aggressive war could not be established. Although all the defendants were charged under Count One as members of a general conspiracy, six of them were not charged with aggressive war planning under Count Two, including Bormann, Frank, Streicher, Kaltenbrunner, some of the most notorious of the defendants. Even among the sixteen charged with planning aggression it was still not possible to come to a common agreement. If the defense stressed that the aggressive war charges prior to the military attack on Poland should not be sustained, some of those out of important office by 1939, such as Papen and Schacht, might be saved, but the additional weight of the charges would then fall on the military leaders of 1939, such as Raeder, Keitel, and Jodl. Similarly, if the defense tried to argue that the subsequent military actions, such as those against the Soviet Union, were not separate acts of aggression but merely outgrowths of the original attack, then those deeply implicated in the later actions, such as Rosenberg, might escape, but more responsibility would fall on the heads of those initially involved in the decision to attack Poland.

Faced with the general conspiracy charge, the natural response of each defendant was to plead ignorance and dissociate himself as much as he could from the most horrifying aspects of the regime. To assert that one had opposed the extermination of the Jews, or that a fellow defendant had done so, was to admit knowledge of the mass killings and thus open oneself to liability as an accessory or as a principal in a criminal conspiracy to commit Crimes Against Humanity. The prosecution's overemphasis on common plan and Nazi unity forced the defense to exaggerate the diversity and lack of homogeneity within the Nazi system. Two great caricatures of Nazism emerged. The prosecution's picture of an enormous and unified conspiracy implemented through a welter of aggressive wars and atrocities was matched by the defense's collage of twenty-two individuals, each pleading ignorance and lack of responsibility.

The defense attorneys, however, tried to prevent the case from splintering completely because, if each defendant tried to save himself by blaming others, the general cannibalism would destroy them all. In addition, they also had to face the charges against criminal organizations which would mean an uncertain fate for hundreds of thousands of individual members of such units as the SA and SS.[111] The defense had its greatest success in establishing reasonable positions and a common front in support of the organizations. Specific arguments, such as the contention that the Cabinet was so small as to be negligible, and that the High Command and General Staff was not a group with a common identity, did help particular organizations. Only the defense attorneys for the SA, however, stressed significant issues that came close to the heart of the prosecution case. The solid argument was raised that the SA lost its significance on June 30, 1934, when Hitler wiped out its leadership in the Blood Purge, and therefore it was of no importance during the time of serious war planning. This obvious change in the nature and significance of the SA unquestionably saved it from being declared a criminal organization by the Tribunal. A comparable, if much more difficult, argument might have been made for the SS—that it, too, had changed radically in the course of the war, and that many of the (Waffen-)SS units were composed primarily of conscripts. But in addition to the vagaries of the assistant counsel for the organization, the defense was hampered by lack of relevant data, and this contention was not put forward with notable vigor.

The difficult task that the defense attorneys for the organizations faced was made virtually impossible by the determination of some of the individual defendants to try to save themselves at all costs. Only Goering and some of the generals and admirals made more than feeble efforts to shield their subordinates. None of the defendants was willing to assume the burden of general responsibility, whether for the activities of the Cabinet, the SA, the Gestapo, the SS, or the Nazi party officials. The situation confronted by the defense attorneys was shown most graphically by the case of Kaltenbrunner and the SS. Kaltenbrunner had been Himmler's deputy for two years; he was trained as a lawyer and had been through ten years of the most hideous police work. There was no reasonable basis for him to entertain a hope of acquittal, yet he spent day after day on the stand denying all knowledge and responsibility. When the trial was over and he had been sentenced to death, one of the defense attorneys went to him and asked why he had not assumed the burden for the SS atrocities and aided the Court by identifying and protecting the men within the SS who had been innocent. Kaltenbrunner's reply embodied all the egotism and cynicism of the Nazi regime. "A trial is a game," he sneered, "and everyone plays to win." [112] With such clients, no group of counsel could have carried out a defense based on principle and a sense of responsibility.

Only the defense attorneys believed that a stand should be made to protect the little man and to defend the reputation of Germany. In their frustration, they believed it was their duty to shield the name of Germany from the stain of collective guilt, [113] and they expended an enormous amount of time and energy on this mission. Under the circumstances, it was an understandable and perhaps laudable effort, but it had little to do with the case at hand. Although the French were sympathetic to the idea, the Tribunal never seriously considered a declaration of German collective guilt. But the defense attorneys were so weighed down by the general charges, the impossibility of conducting a truly united defense, and the frightful evidence before the Court that they became obsessed by the need to record the existence of another, and better, Germany.

Such concerns were so far removed from the problems the judges faced that the Court may not even have been aware of what the defense was trying to do. It did understand that neither the attorneys' references to the Germany of Goethe nor the defendants hopelessly repetitious assertions of their own innocence would help to solve the legal problems at hand. The prosecution had failed to clarify most of the basic issues in the case, and the defense presentations had likewise done little to bring the Tribunal closer to effective solutions. The old questions still remained: what was to be done on criminal organizations; had there been a broad conspiracy; what did aggressive war planning consist of? Midway through the defense presentations, the Tribunal members reluctantly and wearily came to recognize that there was no help on the horizon, and that, if the job was going to be done, they would have to do it themselves.

The public sessions of the Court were allowed to drone on, but behind the scenes the Tribunal met in nearly continuous secret session from mid-June until September. In this confidential setting, the judges pondered and discussed the vital problems of the trial, and, in the end, this is where they resolved them.

CHAPTER 5

Judgment I: Conspiracy

Conspiracy is one of those things that, the more you talk about it, the less clear it becomes.

James Rowe [1]

THE EIGHT MEN who had to resolve the legal problems of Nuremberg were not jurists of long experience or of towering stature. There was no Holmes or Coke among them, and since some top jurists of both the United States and Britain had refused to serve on the Nuremberg bench, the only Supreme Court justice at Nuremberg, Jackson, was, ironically, a prosecutor and thus in no position to advise the Tribunal. None of the members of the Court had experience in international relations, and only one, Francis Biddle, had held a cabinet-level post in government. In a letter written during the trial, Norman Birkett bemoaned the modest talents and limited experience of his colleagues; what was required, he felt, "was not only a knowledge of law but a knowledge of history, particularly German History, a knowledge of men and world affairs." [2] No one at Nuremberg had this erudite knowledge, but all the judges did have a generous measure of political and personal prejudice. Birkett stated privately that not only were the defendants on trial but a "whole nation" as well. [3] When the proceedings were over, Sir Geoffrey Lawrence frankly admitted that, in his view, one of the purposes of the trial had been "to bring home to the German people and the peoples of the world the depths of infamy to which the pursuit of total warfare had brought Germany." [4] In his own blunt way, Biddle expressed the same feeling by remarking, in his notes, that one of Himmler's particularly atrocious appeals to the SS was "very German"; [5] after the trial, he declared that "we were a jury as well as a court" and were "inevitably conditioned by conflicting currents of prejudice and policy." [6]

Along with bias, one may well charge the judges with a measure of insensitivity because of their comfortable, if not ostentatious, manner of life, amid the ruins and mass suffering of devastated Nuremberg. They each had a private residence, and through the latter part of the trial they were accompanied by their wives—a privilege denied to the defense attorneys and even to the prosecutors. [7] They also had well-stocked larders and wine cellars, and a number of judicial evenings were spent in parties gay enough to leave legal brains clouded for the following morning's trial session. [8]

Yet, there is also much to be said in defense of the Nuremberg bench. The trial sessions were long and tedious and were frequently followed by discussions in chambers that were equally as boring, if not always of such long duration. Because of the novelties in the trial situation and the lack of settled procedure, the Court was continually called upon to consider and rule on minor points that would have been routinely handled by a clerk in an English or American court. [9] Evaluation of defense applications for documents and witnesses was especially time-consuming and forced the judges to work long beyond the normal day. Overall, though some members of the bench were more self-indulgent than others, all put in very long days in court and in deliberations in chambers, and a number of them also spent considerable time studying and analyzing the case. This hard labor tended to offset some of the most dangerous aspects of their ignorance of the history of Nazi Germany and of international relations during the interwar period. One can cite countless examples of the factual errors they made, as well as numerous instances in which their views were far too simplistic. Some of these, such as Biddle's scrawled question beside Adolf Eichmann's name in an early draft of the Judgment—"Who was he?" [10]—seem shocking to us today, but were actually not so important in the context of the case that the judges had before them in 1946. In any event, it is clear that in the course of the trial the judges' dutiful performance even on such routine matters as witness and documentary applications, went a long way in providing them with an adequate working knowledge of the people and processes in Hitler's Germany. By the end of the trial, they were far more knowledgeable about what had gone on, especially during the war years, than the majority of supposed experts on Nazi Germany who did not have as much opportunity as the judges to see firsthand documentation on the operation of the Nazi system between 1939 and 1945.

Most of the Tribunal members were good enough jurists and honest enough men to be troubled by legal aspects of the case even when they were somewhat at sea regarding the historical facts. As early as December 1945, Lawrence and Biddle questioned Colonel Storey of the U.S. prosecution very sharply on a range of questions concerned with criminal organizations.[11] At the same time, Biddle received a memorandum from one of his top legal aides, Herbert Wechsler, which cast doubt on the whole of the criminal organization prosecution.[12] By January, Donnedieu de Vabres made a motion during a discussion in chambers that would have established a series of protective regulations for organization members who might be brought before an occupation court. This motion lost three to one, [13] but after the open-court discussion of criminal organizations in February and March, the Court showed increasing doubts about this aspect of the case and by May was prepared to consider severing certain subgroups, including subunits of the SS.[14] At the same time, Lawrence not only indicated that counsel for the High Command of the armed forces had demolished much of the prosecution's case, but also raised the question during an in camera session whether this particular case should not be dropped altogether.[15]

There are indications that Biddle was also having trouble on the conspiracy case long before the testimony ended. In January, he emphasized in his notes that the German absorption of Austria was not charged as an aggressive war, and that the whole Austrian issue would consequently hang on the conspiracy charge.[16] One month later, he put the British deputy prosecutor, Maxwell Fyfe, through a short but taxing series of questions intended to get the prosecution to define clearly what the elements of the conspiracy charge were and also to pinpoint just when conspiratorial planning had begun.[17] Maxwell Fyfe managed to work his way around Biddle's questions, but his answers did little to clarify the situation or allay the doubts that were rising on the bench.

By the last four months of the trial, the judges' familiarity with the facts and the issues had developed to such a point that they intervened repeatedly in the questioning of witnesses. Not only did the Court assert itself more to cut short irrelevancies, but individual judges, especially Biddle, took over much of the direct questioning. When defendant Fritz Sauckel was on the stand, the American senior judge put him through an examination which was almost as long, and was far more telling, than that which had occurred during the prosecution's cross-examination.[18] Such incidents show not only how far the prosecution had lost control of the case by the spring of 1946, but also how greatly confidence and knowledge had developed on the bench. Six months before, Francis Biddle had not known enough about Fritz Sauckel to give him even a minimally fair hearing, but by June he was able to develop a line of questioning that showed such a firm grasp of the issues involved that it clearly hurt Sauckel's defense.

The rapid increase in Biddle's knowledge and effectiveness in the course of the trial owed a great deal to the efforts of the American judicial staff. It would have been hard for Biddle and Parker to assemble a more competent group of advisers and assistants than the team of Wright, Wechsler, James Rowe, Adrian Fisher, and Robert Stewart. Wright and Wechsler had impeccable credentials as academic legal authorities, and all the members of the group except Stewart had extensive governmental experience. The five advisers also had close personal or professional ties to the judges. Stewart was an old family friend of Judge Parker, and the other four men had worked closely with Biddle. Both Wechsler and Rowe had served as assistant attorneys general under Biddle during his years in the Justice Department. There were, of course, differences and conflicts within this advisory group. Wechsler and Wright frequently did not see eye to eye, and there was a recurrent line of demarcation which pitted the "academics" (Wechsler and Wright) against the younger men (Fisher, Rowe and Stewart) who had come to Nuremberg directly from military service. The latter group was initially not very tolerant of what they considered Wechsler's and Wright's abstract and academic reservations about summary justice for the Nazi culprits. As the trial wore on, however, the harsh views of the three "military men" were somewhat tempered, and by the spring of 1946, with their moderation rising, they found themselves in control of the field,[19] since Wright had returned to the United States fairly early in the trial and Wechsler had gone back to Columbia University in April or May of 1946. Even so, Biddle still depended heavily on the advice of Wechsler and Wright after they were in the United States; he corresponded with them on crucial questions, and at least one portion of the final Judgment was written by Wechsler.

The judicial staffs from the other three countries could not match the size or quality of the one from the United States. The French and Russians had legal clerks but not advisers comparable to those brought by Biddle. The British Foreign Office legal adviser, Patrick Dean, was attached to the British prosecution team and, after the first sessions in Berlin, consulted with a British judge only once (on the criminal organization question discussed above). The British judges used a military officer, Major Airey M. Neave, to perform various duties for the Court, such as aiding the defendants to obtain counsel and hearing petitions by members of criminal organizations. Lord Justice Lawrence's marshal, or legal aide, John Phipps, was a lawyer and a close family friend, but he had completed his legal training only recently. He could not give Sir Geoffrey weighty legal advice or lend a prestigious name to his arguments, even though he was competent, hardworking, and devoted to Lawrence.

The real workhorse of the British delegation was the alternate judge, Norman Birkett; in contrast to Sir Geoffrey, who loved the courtroom but abhorred legal paperwork,[20] Birkett was an experienced and highly competent legal draftsman. Since the Americans and the French, as well as the British, were extremely wary of allowing the Soviets to speak for the Court, and thus opposed every suggestion that the four senior judges rotate responsibility for voicing the Tribunal's views, it was inevitable that Sir Geoffrey, as president of the Court, would have the responsibility for preparing the Court's written opinions. What this meant in practice was that the judges would deliberate, a decision would be made, Sir Geoffrey would be asked to prepare a document expressing the Court's opinion, and then Norman Birkett would actually draft it. Throughout the trial, Birkett managed to preserve an outward appearance that suggested he was satisfied with his role as draftsman, and, in fact, he seems to have received some pleasure from being the secret orchestrator of the Court's voice. But the diary that he kept during the trial shows that beneath his satisfied veneer lay a reservoir of bitterness because he had been passed over as senior judge and become the draftsman for those whom he felt to be less worthy.[21] He seems to have relished and nurtured a sense of being ill-used and may have taken on so many tasks of judicial drudgery with such good grace in order to reinforce his feelings of being exploited. This syndrome played havoc with his psychological well-being, but it was a marvelous boon to the Tribunal. Since Birkett wrote everything, it was possible to contain the squabbles over drafting within reasonable limits, and, by the time the trial was well advanced, Birkett had developed an invaluable ability to synthesize the major issues of the case.

In April 1946, when the Tribunal members faced the fact that they would have to resolve the major legal difficulties of the case themselves, the procedure they adopted to cope with the situation grew directly out of the method they had used to deal with every other decision the Tribunal had been called upon to make. Sir Geoffrey, as president, asked his colleagues whether the time had not come to begin work on a general opinion, or judgment, and he also apparently tentatively suggested that the task should be divided up between the four delegations. On April 12, Wechsler sent an advisory memorandum to Biddle, outlining some suggestions on such an opinion but stressing that the responsibility for actually preparing a draft "is by common consent that of the President." [22] Wechsler's view prevailed, and Sir Geoffrey was given the task of producing a draft opinion, which, as everyone associated with the Court knew, meant that it would be prepared by Birkett.

That such an assignment would fall on the shoulders of one man would seem too much of a burden even for Birkett's vocation of martyrdom, but a number of circumstances combined to lighten the load. By this time, Birkett had five months' experience preparing the Court's position papers and for the task at hand he had at his disposal full verbatim transcripts of the Court proceedings to date. In addition, each of the judges had made personal evidentiary summaries while the sessions were in process, and one may assume that at least Lawrence's summaries, as well as his own, were at Birkett's disposal. Both the American and the British staffs had also decided, during the earliest days of the trial, to prepare abstracts of the evidence to be used in readying a final opinion and judgment. Phipps for Britain and Fisher for the United States had been relieved of other duties and had spent the bulk of the trial period preparing these abstracts. [23] In May, they began separately to hammer their material into memoranda that were then fed on to Birkett. The content and scope of Phipps's memoranda cannot be determined on the basis of the available evidence. But by May, Fisher had prepared papers on "The Status of the Conspiracy by Mid-1933," "Economic Planning and Mobilization for Aggressive War," "Crimes Against Peace," "Aggressive Action Against Austria and Other Countries," "Persecution of Jews," "Slave Labor," "Concentration Camps," and "General War Crimes." [24] These memoranda clearly influenced Birkett's draft; some of Fisher's arguments and even some of his phrases and sentences were taken over directly. In the course of the first weeks of June, Stewart and Rowe joined Fisher in preparing more memoranda on general policies, specific organizations, and individual defendants. A portion of these papers may also have gone to Birkett, but most were composed after his rough draft was finished.

Birkett worked on the opinion from late April through the third week of June. In the course of his work, he showed a draft to Lawrence, Biddle, and Parker and asked for their reactions and criticisms. [25] On the basis of their suggestions, he made additional changes which culminated in the eight-page outline and sixty-four-page draft that the Tribunal began discussing in a closed session on June 27. [26] It is important to emphasize that, until the June 27 meeting, there were no indications that basic disagreement might develop on the nature and form of the opinion. The judges were agreed that they had nearly unlimited discretion on the procedure to be followed at the end of the trial. The Charter merely stated that they should "deliver judgment" and "pronounce sentence" while providing "the reasons" for their action. [27]

Despite some serious disagreements in the course of the trial, and the rising concern over specific legal issues that had led the Court to begin drafting an opinion long before the trial ended, no one on the bench seems to have felt that a serious battle might develop over the Judgment. This is probably the greatest paradox in the Tribunal's handling of the whole trial. The judges knew they were taking a major risk in starting to prepare a draft opinion before the defense had completed the presentation of its case. Birkett warned his colleagues when he distributed copies of his draft in June that the utmost secrecy had to be observed, because their consideration of an opinion at this stage of the trial would surely be "misunderstood" if it became public. [28] Even in the second week of July, while writing to Wechsler for his views on a specific legal question, Biddle stressed the great secrecy that surrounded the Court's early preparations of a judgment and urged Wechsler to keep the information strictly confidential.[29] However, in preparing the opinion, the judges did not act as if the issues involved were serious enough to warrant these risks. No effort was made to come to grips with the major points of controversy such as aggressive war, criminal organizations, or conspiracy before Birkett started drafting. It was as if the Tribunal members knew the problems were there, knew something would have to be done, but still hoped that, once the basic evidence were down on paper, answers would simply appear and it would be possible to work out compromises that avoided serious conflicts or deep divisions in the Court.

Once discussion of the Birkett draft actually began on June 27, hope for reaching smooth and easy agreement on a judgment quickly evaporated. Each judge was asked, in turn, to express his opinion of Birkett's work, and Nikitchenko, Lawrence, and Biddle gave voice to the customary mixture of praise, criticism, and practical advice. But Donnedieu de Vabres not only advanced some detailed criticisms of the draft, he also made a long and impassioned argument that the Court throw out the whole conspiracy–common plan charge.

Until Donnedieu de Vabres spoke, the topic with the best potential for dividing the Court would seem to have been that of criminal organizations or perhaps the general issue of aggressive war. But Donnedieu de Vabres drew the line on conspiracy, and Biddle quickly voiced sympathy for the position taken by the French judge.[30] The other members of the Tribunal continued to talk about the details of Birkett's draft, but it was already too late for that. Conspiracy had become the issue that would dominate the deliberations of the judges for the next two and a half months and would also shape not only the form of the Judgment but the verdicts and sentences of many of the defendants as well.

Donnedieu de Vabres put forth his argument against conspiracy in two long, deliberative sessions (June 27 and August 14) and backed up his verbal statements with two memoranda, one written soon after the June 27 meeting and the other on July 8.[31] Beginning with the obvious objection that the crime of conspiracy was unknown to both continental and international law, Donnedieu de Vabres stressed that, in the case at hand, the prosecution had even gone beyond Anglo-American practice to charge the Nazi leaders with a grand conspiracy lasting twenty-five years and covering the history of half a continent. In the French judge's view, the prosecution had failed to establish the necessary precondition for any conspiracy or common plan conviction—proof that a group of people had, at a specific time and place, agreed on definite criminal objectives and the criminal methods they intended to use to attain them. Instead, the prosecution had merely gathered up various expressions of Nazi principles, such as passages from the party program and quotations from *Mein Kampf*, contending that these were the core of a fixed criminal plan. According to the prosecution, this was sufficient to establish that anyone who joined the party had thereby knowingly entered a criminal conspiracy. Such a contention, however, was erroneous, argued Donnedieu de Vabres, because there had been no fixed Nazi plan. The Nazi advance to power in Germany and the subsequent expansion over Europe had been the result not of a clear master plan but of a series of improvisations. Furthermore, planning to achieve power in Germany and the preparations made to overthrow pacts such as the Versailles Treaty could not be considered criminal offenses, because conspiracy was not a crime against international law at the time the acts were committed. Any conviction based on grandiose conspiracy charges would be ex post facto and an affront to justice.

In addition, according to Donnedieu de Vabres, the prosecution could not even provide a clear picture of the legal charges that were supposed to make up the conspiracy. The London Charter had listed three prosecutable crimes—War Crimes, Crimes Against Humanity, and Crimes Against Peace, the last consisting, in part, of "participation in a common plan or conspiracy" to plan, prepare, initiate, or wage "a war of aggression, or a war in violation of treaties." At the end of Article VI, the mysterious short paragraph had been added that stated that all those who participated in "a common plan or conspiracy" to commit any crimes would be "responsible for all the acts performed by any persons in execution of the plan." [32] As indicated above, however, when the prosecutors drew up the indictment they did not proceed on the basis of three crimes, but of four—Crimes Against Peace (Count Two), War Crimes (Count Three), Crimes Against Humanity (Count Four), and the added crime, Count One, which charged every defendant with participation in a common plan or conspiracy to commit the other three crimes. Thus, the prosecution had taken the mysterious final paragraph from Article VI of the Charter and used it as the basis for charging participation in a grand conspiracy to commit war crimes and crimes against humanity, as

well as crimes against peace. Such a reading of the Charter was totally unwarranted in the view of Donnedieu de Vabres. He held
that the final paragraph in Article VI was aimed at complicity and
did "not provide for a specific general crime" of conspiracy.[33] Consequently, he argued, no statutory basis for prosecuting a grand conspiracy existed, and the Tribunal would have to drop the charge.

In presenting his argument, Donnedieu de Vabres was forced to
anticipate a number of legal problems and possible objections. Since
he held that conspiracy was not an international crime at the time of
the alleged offenses, the question arose whether either Crimes
Against Humanity or Crimes Against Peace had, in fact, been crimes
at the time of the events cited in the indictment. Donnedieu de
Vabres accepted the American prosecutors' argument to cope with
this difficulty, concluding that international law is not primarily statute law but grows by precedent and changes in public attitude. On
that basis, the Nazi aggressive attacks and atrocities were crimes at
the time they were committed, and the defendants knew it. But no
one then had said that conspiracy or war planning was an international crime, and for that reason the defendants could not have
known that this aspect of their behavior was criminal.

So far so good, but how could the French judge get around the
fact that both the Charter and the indictment specifically declared
that "participation in a common plan or conspiracy" to commit "a
Crime against Peace" was an international crime? Donnedieu de
Vabres tried to do so by ignoring the delicate possibility that the
Charter might have contained a legal error; instead, he stressed a
number of practical reasons why the Tribunal should not find the defendants guilty of participation in a conspiracy to commit Crimes
Against Peace. First he held that such a finding would be unnecessary, because the substantive crime of waging aggressive war could
be easily proved; since the defendants had planned, prepared, initiated, and waged the war, it was better to proceed on the basis that
"the crime absorbs the conspiracy" and convict them for what they
had done, not on what they might have conspired to do.[34] Furthermore, Donnedieu de Vabres made the surprising assertion that the
existence of an aggressive war conspiracy involving the defendants
had not been established by the prosecution evidence. In his view,
statements in which Hitler announced his willingness to "break" the
Versailles Treaty but did not explain clearly the means whereby he
would do this, could not serve as the basis for convicting other indi-

viduals of participation in a criminal plan. Only if it could be demonstrated that they knew of Hitler's intention to use illegal methods, such as aggressive attacks, could they be found guilty even as accessories. Even meetings in the late 1930s, at which the Führer told his top aides that he intended to expand eastward by force, could not be cited as instances of conspiratorial planning, in the French judge's opinion. For Donnedieu de Vabres, a conspiracy required a certain tendency toward equality among the participants, but no such condition had existed in the *Führerstaat* of Nazi Germany. In the meetings of the late 1930s, "only one voice" [35] was heard, and that was Hitler's voice. Those who listened to the voice and worked to carry out its orders became, when they carried them out, criminal accessories, according to Donnedieu de Vabres, but, he continued, they were too lowly and too passive to be called participants in a common plan or conspiracy. Summing up his position in a long statement on August 14, the French judge pleaded with his colleagues to convict for substantive crimes and, where necessary, also to punish accomplices and accessories, but to drop the conspiracy charges and thereby avoid the appearance of an ex post facto proceeding that would be so distasteful to world legal opinion.

Donnedieu de Vabres's willingness to advance this argument in the vengeful atmosphere of 1946, while France was still weak and battered, required considerable moral courage. After the trial, when he published carefully edited summaries of his presentation, he was heralded as something of a moral and legal hero by those, especially in Germany, who were most critical of the Nuremberg proceedings. But the critics of Nuremberg had to be very selective in their use of Donnedieu de Vabres's argument, for it could easily rebound against them. One major objection to the Nuremberg evidence was that the summaries of Hitler's late 1930s meetings with his military commanders and political aides did not accurately reflect the extent to which his subordinates had spoken up and given voice to their opinions and criticisms of his plans. How much merit there is to these objections is still hotly debated, but one thing is now clear: if any of the summaries used at Nuremberg would have included instances of comment or criticism by individuals who continued to serve the regime, one of Donnedieu de Vabres's most telling arguments against the general conspiracy charge would have been demolished. If any give-and-take implying relative equality between Hitler and such men as Raeder and Neurath had appeared in evidence, Donnedieu de Vabres's objections could have been easily brushed aside and the participants found guilty in an aggressive war conspiracy as defined by the Charter.

Many German observers, including some of the defense lawyers, believed that the conspiracy charge contained an implicit accusation of "collective guilt" against the German people.[36] To the degree that Donnedieu de Vabres undermined the conspiracy charge, he might have been viewed as a savior of German honor. But the disparity between the views actually held by the French judge and those of the many Germans who later applauded him shows up distinctly when one examines Donnedieu de Vabres's appraisal of who was actually responsible for the horrors of Nazism. Although he was very reticent about publicizing his views on this question after the trial, Donnedieu de Vabres had no intention of absolving Germany from guilt. During the deliberations, he repeatedly stressed to his colleagues that, in his view, the main cause of the "Hitlerian crimes" was rooted deeply in the German people, and he advanced a three-level hierarchy of responsibility and guilt for Nazism. At the top he placed, as most guilty, the German people as a whole; next came Adolf Hitler, whom he considered only moderately guilty; and finally, at the bottom and least responsible of all, were the twenty-two defendants before the Court.[37] This odd structure reflected Donnedieu de Vabres's fear that the conspiracy doctrine might provide the basis for another "stab in the back" legend as much as it reflected his anti-German prejudices. If the Tribunal laid the blame for Nazism on the heads of the handful of men before the Court and convicted them of participating in a criminal conspiracy, the broad mass of the German people might then claim that they bore no responsibility for what had happened since 1933 because everything was the result of this secret Nazi plot. After World War I, Hitler and the generals blamed Germany's defeat on a Jewish-Marxist conspiracy; after World War II, there might be danger of the German people blaming both the war and the defeat on a Nazi conspiracy. In Donnedieu de Vabres's view then, it would be wiser for the Allies to convict the twenty-two defendants of specific crimes and give them moderate sentences than to further conspiratorial rationalizations. With sentencing accomplished, it would be possible to lay the basis for future peace by making a declaration of where the guilt and responsibility really belonged—on the whole German people.[38] Thus, despite his post-trial reputation as a moderate, Donnedieu de Vabres had no desire to be soft on the Germans, and his colleagues on the Court never accused him of any such intention. The lines in the Court's debate were drawn not on the basis of pro- or anti-German sentiments, but solely on the issue of whether the grand conspiracy approach should be discarded.

In the original conspiracy discussion of June 27, only Biddle showed much sympathy for Donnedieu de Vabres's position. When Biddle, in his turn, tried to elicit some support from among the American legal aides for the idea of dropping the conspiracy charges, he received an understanding hearing only in a letter from Wechsler. Everyone else involved with the case argued adamantly that the conspiracy charges should be retained. Nikitchenko and Lawrence supported conspiracy, as did the four alternate judges and all the American legal aides remaining in Nuremberg. The judges favoring retention of conspiracy took three long in camera deliberative sessions (August 14, 15, and 19) to develop their arguments, and, in addition, produced so many memoranda that at one point Donnedieu de Vabres complained that he was suffering from wounds inflicted by the scale and intensity of the memoranda bombardment.[39]

The chief point emphasized by the advocates of conspiracy–common plan was the obvious one that the Nazi leaders had, in fact, been engaged in planning and preparing expansionist wars. Although they conceded that there might be some disagreement on when the planning began, Lawrence and Nikitchenko, as well as the alternates, argued strongly that aggressive war planning had taken place. The defenders of the conspiracy charges were less certain about whether such war planning was illegal. All agreed, however, that the war planning the Nazis had done fell within the punitive provisions of Crimes Against Peace listed in Article VI of the London Charter. But Parker, Birkett, and Falco were reluctant to consider whether conspiring or planning an aggressive war had, in fact, been a crime in international law at the time the Nazis had allegedly discussed and planned their wars in the 1920s and 1930s. Lawrence, on the other hand, was prepared to assert openly that the Tribunal had to follow the Charter wherever it led, and in one session he came close to contending that the terms of the Charter should be applied even if they produced unjust, or ex post facto, convictions. Biddle noted that this session showed the "British at their worst." [40] But both Lawrence and Biddle seem to have been left speechless by Nikitchenko's position. The Russian judge, who was obviously irritated by long discussions of principle, stressed that, in his view, the judges should act like practical men and not like a "discussion club." [41] The charge of conspiracy as a crime against international law was an innovation, Nikitchenko said, and he admitted that it would lead to ex post facto convictions. But, he queried, why were the Western judges so upset by that? He calmly noted that much of the Tribunal's actions contained innovations, such as the definition of certain crimes and the banning of the defense of superior orders, yet nobody seemed especially concerned about these. In the Soviet view, the judges were there to innovate, and they should frankly admit that they were establishing a new basis in international law. [42]

Such a position was far too daring and potentially dangerous for the Western judges, and they hurriedly moved the argument back inside the perimeters of customary legal discourse. Lawrence rejected Donnedieu de Vabres's argument that the existence of a conspiracy was inconsistent with the reality of Hitler's all-powerful dictatorship. According to Sir Geoffrey, the Führer only originated the aggressive ideas; without his aides no aggressive plans would have been developed and no such wars would have occurred. The assertion that a degree of equality between the planners was necessary to establish a conspiracy was also invalid, Lawrence contended, because it was impossible to measure equality, and the idea was not an established legal test for conspiracy. [43] Falco, the French alternate, supported Lawrence's arguments, adding that a defense appeal to the *Führerprinzip* had been barred by the provision in the Charter prohibiting a defendant from invoking superior orders as a complete defense. [44] Nikitchenko, quite understandably, did not see any inconsistency between the existence of a dictatorship and common planning for war, and, from a very different point of view, Parker also felt that they were perfectly compatible. [45] Like a voice from an earlier and more naive America, Parker argued that "aggressive war is almost always made by dictators and their henchmen," [46] and it was therefore essential that the concept of punishing an aggressive war conspiracy, which was such an effective means of striking at this evil, should not be impaired.

Over and over again, the supporters of the conspiracy charge returned to the serious consequences they believed would result if Donnedieu de Vabres's course were followed. Nikitchenko argued that without conspiracy there was no basis to convict the Propaganda Ministry official Hans Fritzsche, [47] and Biddle admitted that this was also the only charge that could net the former minister of economics and head of the Reichsbank, Schacht.[48] In mid-July, Biddle made a similar observation in a letter to Wechsler, contending that if conspiracy were dropped there would be no likely grounds for convicting Papen.[49] Taking a broader view, Volchkov, the Soviet alternate, made the point that the heinous Nazi crimes, such as the exterminations, were so complex and widespread that it would be impossible to cope with all the culprits unless some general idea such as conspiracy were employed.[50] Nikitchenko furthered Volchkov's point by observing that the very complexity of the relationships and the crimes made it unnecessary to apply the strict rules for prosecuting conspiracy that were customary in Anglo-American domestic law. The crimes were so extreme and so complicated, Nikitchenko contended, that the Court was fully justified in breaking new ground by punishing international criminal conspiracy.[51]

Parker was deeply concerned that, if the common plan–conspiracy charges relating to aggressive war were thrown out, the slow and halting progress made toward controlling war would be aborted. If war planners could not be legally punished, then, Parker felt, efforts to prevent war by such instruments as the Kellogg-Briand Pact would lose all meaning. He also registered the telling point that without conspiracy it would be difficult to justify a finding of criminality against the organizations, for such a judgment would have to rest on the contention that the organizations "constituted criminal conspiracies." [52] If the Tribunal nonetheless threw out conspiracy and still prosecuted organizations, the individual members of such groups would, in Parker's opinion, be deprived of their best legal shield. The defining rules of conspiracy, that membership had to be voluntary and the members had to know the criminal intentions of the group, were the strongest possible protection for individuals accused of being criminal organization members. Consequently, for Parker, conspiracy had to be retained in order to prosecute organizations and, at the same time, protect innocent individuals within them from unmerited punishment.[53]

Parker advanced the most complicated defense of conspiracy, but it was Birkett who delivered the most emotional and far-reaching denunciation of the ideas of Donnedieu de Vabres. The chief importance of the trial, Birkett told his colleagues on August 15, was to prove the existence of a common plan or conspiracy. If this count were lost, the heart would be torn out of the case and the value of the trial would go, too. The result would be a "national disaster," for, even if some individuals were convicted without conspiracy, the Nazi regime would be acquitted, and thus, presumably, the suffering and sacrifice that had made the Allied victory possible, would lose all meaning.[54]

Obviously, with passions so high and divisions so deep, the Court was in desperate need of a compromise formula. If the judges held strictly to the provisions of the Charter, those favoring conspiracy had the votes to win in a showdown. But the senior judges were divided, with Nikitchenko and Lawrence favoring conspiracy and Donnedieu de Vabres and Biddle inclined, at least, to limit it sharply, despite the likelihood that this would make some convictions problematical. Article IV of the Charter declared that, in the event of a two-two tie by senior judges on any question other than a verdict or sentence, the president of the Tribunal could cast the deciding vote.[55] If the conspiracy issue had been played out to the end, the grand conspiracy would ultimately have been sustained by a vote of three to two. Biddle was wise enough to see the handwriting on the wall and from the beginning of the debate indicated a willingness to compromise. Some of the judges on the other side also realized that such a victory on a fundamental question would surely be pyrrhic. Parker showed a readiness to make concessions and told his colleagues on August 19 that it was more important to reach a general understanding than for any one person's view to prevail.[56] In the course of the discussions, some others advocating retention of conspiracy also indicated that there were elements of the general charge they would be ready to limit or abandon. The three Western alternates were prepared to dump the charges alleging a composite conspiracy to commit War Crimes and Crimes Against Humanity. Parker agreed with Donnedieu de Vabres that these counts in the indictment had no statutory basis in Article VI of the Charter.[57] Falco, in turn, thought that they were legally valid but felt that since the prosecution had failed to prove them, they should be dropped.[58] In the middle of his impassioned defense of conspiracy, Birkett also acknowledged that he was prepared to "disregard" these two aspects of the grand conspiracy, although he did not make it clear whether he held them to be vulnerable on legal or evidentiary grounds.[59] With Donnedieu de Vabres, Biddle, and the three Western alternates inclined to restrict the conspiracy charge to Crimes Against Peace, it became much easier to work out a broad compromise.

The development of the points that formed the basis of the compromise may be delineated in the general argument used by some of the supporters of the grand conspiracy idea. Two of the American legal aides, Fisher and Stewart, wrote memoranda in May and June 1946—before Donnedieu de Vabres presented his arguments—discussing the conspiracy question, and both of the Americans came down in favor of holding that an aggressive war conspiracy had existed.[60] Significantly, neither took seriously the prosecution's contention that there had been conspiracies to commit War Crimes or Crimes Against Humanity. Both Stewart and Fisher assumed that the conspiracy charge would be limited to Crimes Against Peace.

In an undated memorandum, Stewart wrestled with the question of when the aggressive war conspiracy had formed and quickly rejected as "unlikely" the prosecution's contention that it should be dated from the founding of the Nazi party in the early 1920s. Stewart thought that conspiracy could "justifiably" be asserted to have begun at the time of Hitler's public announcement of rearmament (1935), or when the Nazis occupied the demilitarized zone of the Rhineland (1936). But, in any case, he was sure that "the evidence shows an agreement had been formulated" by November 5, 1937, when Hitler, in the so-called "Hossbach conference," announced to his aides that he was determined to seize Austria and Czechoslovakia by force.[61]

In numerous memoranda during May and June 1946, Fisher touched on several aspects of the aggressive war and conspiracy question. Two brief ones, on the persecution of Jews, made short work of the prosecution's assertion that the Nazis' anti-Semitic program had been carried out in order to destroy domestic opposition to their aggressive war plans. The anti-Semitic program was "a blind unreasoning hatred" that had originated "from Hitler's own disordered mind," Fisher concluded, and it had nothing to do with preparations for aggressive war.[62]

In evaluating the economic basis for the rearmament program, Fisher also found it difficult to apportion criminal responsibility, or to substantiate the existence of a conspiracy, because the prosecution's evidence had been devoted to showing "<u>how</u> Germany rearmed not <u>why</u>."[63] Generally, Fisher concluded that there was no evidence worth considering for the existence of a conspiracy during the 1920s, and January 1933, the date of Hitler's appointment as Chancellor, was also not a suitable beginning point, because the majority of the members of his first Cabinet were not members of the Nazi party. A date in mid-1933 was possible, but Fisher observed that there was "little direct contemporaneous evidence" from this period to show that the government was acting on the basis of a "single plan or conspiracy." [64] Fisher was generally inclined to leave the question open as to whether there had been aggressive war planning at any time prior to the mid-1930s. On one occasion, he, like Stewart, asserted that whether such a conspiracy existed in 1933 or 1936 was an open question, but "it is quite clear that a conspiracy was in existence on November 5, 1937," that is, at the time of the Hossbach conference. [65]

In the course of June, however, Fisher came back to write a forty-page memorandum, specifically on the subject of "Conspiracy to Wage Aggressive War," and in this paper he explored the question much more thoroughly and reached more definite conclusions. After carefully sifting the evidence again, he produced an impressive circumstantial picture of a great Nazi diplomatic, economic, and military push toward territorial expansion. Even while granting that Hitler had worked by improvisation, and acknowledging a tendency "to impute a connection which may not have existed at the time," [66] Fisher was prepared to hold that a criminal aggressive plan was in existence by late 1933, and that from that date on the government and Party leaders should have known that they were participants in a criminal enterprise. By the end of 1933 or early 1934, purges and repression had broken the opposition within Germany; the days of coalition government were over, and, in Fisher's view, those who remained surely knew that they would have to support the Nazi program, including its expansionist provisions. If this line of argument contained too many suppositions to convince everyone, Fisher developed what he thought was an even stronger argument to support the existence of an aggressive war plan in the mid-1930s. By 1936, the Nazis had torn up the clauses of the Versailles Treaty limiting armaments and had reoccupied the Rhineland. This, according to Fisher, left nothing in the treaty except its territorial provisions, and henceforth, whenever Hitler spoke of "freeing Germany from the shackles of Versailles," any reasonable person should have inferred that force would be used to seize the territories that Germany had been required to cede to its neighbors after World War I. [67] If, then,

Fisher concluded, Germany's frantic efforts to expand her military power were viewed in conjunction with her diplomatic actions, there would be an overwhelming case to prove that an aggressive war plan in fact existed by 1936.[68]

The Stewart and Fisher memoranda were read by at least Biddle and, presumably, Parker, and, although Biddle's marginal marks suggest that he was not impressed by Fisher's case for the existence of a conspiracy in late 1933, he does seem to have felt that "a good deal" could be said for the 1936 date.[69] Some of the memoranda, but not Fisher's long one of June 22 dealing directly with conspiracy, were also given to Birkett to be used by him in preparing the draft opinion. Like Stewart and Fisher before him, Birkett did not directly confront the possibility of rejecting the conspiracy charges; he simply described the diplomatic and military developments of the 1930s in a chronological sequence, thereby creating the impression that they were part of a coherent system or plan. But Birkett did combine his discussions of Counts One and Two, which implied that they could be merged, the charge of conspiracy thus limited to Crimes Against Peace and the charges relating to War Crimes and Crimes Against Humanity safely dropped. Birkett also included "Notes to the Tribunal" at select points in his manuscript, and these provide invaluable indications of the way he looked at the conspiracy problem. The crucial question facing the Tribunal, in Birkett's view, was whether it was necessary to determine when the aggressive war conspiracy began or whether it was sufficient to indicate a date when it was definitely in existence.[70] Birkett obviously favored the latter alternative, and on both occasions when he discussed this question he suggested using the same date—late 1937, after the Hossbach conference.[71] The only difficulty that Birkett thought might develop if the Tribunal followed this option concerned the Crimes Against Humanity charges. Since the Charter declared that such crimes occurred only in connection with another crime, and since Crimes Against Peace and War Crimes could not have taken place before the war, any pre-1939 Crime Against Humanity would have to be tied to conspiracy. But even this consideration did not deter Birkett from inclining toward 1937 as the defining date for conspiracy, because, as he explained in a passage concerned with the persecution of Jews, even if such a course left pre-1937 anti-Semitic actions outside the jurisdiction of the Tribunal "the Jewish Pogroms of November 1938 and the mass murders of Jews after that date form a record before which the earlier years almost pale into insignificance." [72] Thus, long before Donnedieu de Vabres raised his challenge, Birkett had taken a position that the conspiracy charge should focus on aggressive war and should be limited to the years 1937–45. He had also advised the Tribunal to base its conspiracy finding on "specific criminal planning" rather than relying on inferences drawn from "the Nazi program as a whole." [73] Quite obviously, all of these qualifications which Birkett brought forth fitted neatly into a limited interpretation of conspiracy.

When the writings of Stewart, Fisher, and Birkett are placed side by side with the views expressed by Donnedieu de Vabres, the reasons for much that happened at Nuremberg become abundantly clear. Nearly every Westerner associated with the bench failed to share the American Government's vision that a grand Nazi conspiracy had existed, and from the scattered references at hand it also appears that the Soviet judges attached little or no importance to it. Only a minority of the judges and their aides wanted to reject the whole conspiracy idea, but even most of those who wished to retain it were determined that it should be limited in time and restricted in form. Washington's hope to develop conspiracy to a degree that would condemn the whole Nazi system was never held to be a serious possibility during the Tribunal's deliberations. The crucial question was whether conspiracy was to be completely rejected or only sharply limited. Once Donnedieu de Vabres failed to win over two senior judges to his view, some modified form of conspiracy was inevitable, and the papers of Stewart, Fisher, and Birkett make it obvious what form the compromise had to take. The conspiracy would be limited to Crimes Against Peace, while the prosecution's charges of conspiracy to commit War Crimes and Crimes Against Humanity would be eliminated. In addition, a defining date for conspiracy would be established, and the early treatments of the problem indicated that the date would most likely fall between 1936 and 1939. Once a point in that period, such as the Hossbach meeting, was accepted, it was a foregone conclusion that Birkett's advice to focus on "specific criminal planning" rather than on the general Nazi program would have to be followed, for by the mid-1930s the days of Nazi program development were long past, and the operations against Austria, Czechoslovakia, and Poland were just around the corner.

Inclined toward compromise from the start, Biddle took the initiative in finding a formula that would be acceptable to all. On July 10, he wrote a long letter to Wechsler, summarizing the situation and describing Donnedieu de Vabres's criticisms of the grand conspiracy case. After underscoring that he was much influenced by Donnedieu de Vabres's argument, Biddle asked Wechsler to send his own reactions and reflections.[74] During the subsequent long month, while the Court worked on general provisions of the Judgment, Wechsler wrestled with the conspiracy problem and Biddle bided his time. By August 19, the American senior judge had apparently received Wechsler's reply for on that date he stepped into the middle of the conspiracy controversy and suggested to the other judges that the time for a compromise had come.[75] Biddle granted that some portions of the general conspiracy count would have to be saved in order to get at such defendants as Schacht, but he also contended that the counts charging conspiracy to commit War Crimes and Crimes Against Humanity should definitely be jettisoned. By stressing planning as an integral part of the waging of war, and by focusing on a series of Nazi aggressive war plans rather than on one general conspiracy, Biddle believed that it would be possible to meet the most pressing wishes of each of the judges. After a sharp discussion of this proposal, Biddle was authorized to try to prepare a compromise formula. On September 4, he brought forth the draft which Wechsler had prepared. In an introductory vote on it, Biddle, Lawrence, and Donnedieu de Vabres overrode Nikitchenko, and the charges of conspiring to commit war crimes and crimes against humanity were discarded.[76] The Biddle-Wechsler compromise was also given tentative approval by the other judges during this session, although Nikitchenko was opposed to the inclusion of any suggestion that a grand Nazi conspiracy might not have existed, while Donnedieu de Vabres felt, conversely, that the compromise formulation should include a definite statement that the Tribunal had rejected the existence of such a conspiracy. Through additional polishing in the subsequent two or three days, Biddle added enough supple phrases to enable him to ease the compromise past his French and Soviet colleagues during the second week of September.[77]

In the final form of the Judgment, the Biddle-Wechsler compromise is a short, three-page section tucked away in the middle of the document and labeled paragraph V, "The Law as to Common Plan or Conspiracy." [78] Despite its brevity, it is a section of great importance. Biddle and Wechsler initially tried to mollify Donnedieu de

Vabres and Nikitchenko by the ingenious device of retaining Counts One and Two as distinct counts, while merging the discussion of them in the Judgment. "Planning and preparation are essential to the making of war," they began, going on to argue that, since the first count charged a conspiracy–common plan while the second charged "the planning and waging of war" as a crime, the two fit perfectly together.[79] In addition, Biddle and Wechsler contended that the prosecution itself had merged the two by introducing the "same evidence" for both. This was generally correct, but only because of the prevalence of what the British prosecution characterized as American "poaching" on the British case.[80] The Americans had skimmed off the best documents and the British had been forced to do the best they could to fit their Count Two presentation into the American system. This situation provided Biddle and Wechsler with the necessary appearance of homogeneity, and they concluded it was possible to discuss the two counts together, "as they are in substance the same." [81] By approaching the problem in this way, the two Americans managed to avoid an initial discussion of whether a grand Nazi conspiracy had, in fact, ever existed. With Donnedieu de Vabres and Nikitchenko partially pacified, or at least outmaneuvered, Biddle and Wechsler went on to deal with the prosecution contention that the Nazi party had been engaged in an aggressive war conspiracy covering the twenty-six years from "1919 to the end of the war in 1945." The Charter, they conceded, did not define conspiracy, but in their view a common plan or conspiracy had to be "clearly outlined in its criminal purpose" and "not too far removed from the time of decision and action." [82] Here again, the Americans tried to thread their way between the French and Soviet positions; they asserted that it was "not necessary" to decide whether there had been a single aggressive war grand conspiracy, because "plans were made to wage wars as early as November 5, 1937" (at the time of the Hossbach conference). Yet, even while granting that militarism was "an integral part of the Nazi policy," [83] the Americans were unwilling to accept the grand conspiracy idea, and they finally had to come down more on the side of Donnedieu de Vabres than of Nikitchenko. A summary sentence hidden away in the middle of the narrative stated flatly that "the evidence establishes with certainty the existence of many separate [war] plans rather than a single conspiracy embracing them all." [84]

Thus, Donnedieu de Vabres largely won out on the main points.

The Tribunal announced that it would "disregard" the conspiracy charges related to War Crimes and Crimes Against Humanity because they were not authorized by the London Charter. In addition, what was left of conspiracy–common plan as applied to aggressive war could hardly be distinguished from the law applicable to accomplices and accessories that prevails in both Anglo-Saxon and continental countries. But Biddle and Wechsler would not accept the French judge's contention that this kind of common plan was incompatible with the *Führerprinzip* of Hitler's dictatorship. Donnedieu de Vabres's "measure of equality" between participants was not, they concluded, an appropriate test to establish the existence of a common plan. Once the "statesmen, military leaders, diplomats, and businessmen" had learned of Hitler's aims, yet continued to give him "their cooperation," they automatically became "parties to the [criminal] plan he had initiated." [85] Presumably, everyone who knew of specific aggressive war plans and continued to serve the regime would therefore be criminally liable under the formula Wechsler and Biddle developed. The sole limitation was that liability for participation in conspiracy–common plan should apply to Crimes Against Peace.

This conspiracy compromise disposed of most of the fundamental legal threats facing the Tribunal in a way that brought few criticisms from the legal fraternity. When the Judgment was read out on September 31, 1946 one of the defense attorneys noted in his diary that the Tribunal had taken the "middle way" on the conspiracy problem, and that the defense attorneys were generally satisfied with the results. [86] In subsequent legal and popular commentaries, the conspiracy provisions of the Judgment evoked little interest and even less criticism or comment. Biddle and Wechsler so successfully defused the issue that the importance of these sections of the Judgment largely escaped public notice. But the verdict on nearly every individual and organization was framed on the basis of the defining elements embodied in the conspiracy decision. Defendants were found guilty of planning or preparing aggressive wars according to how extensively they had cooperated in the development of aggressive plans that were subsequently put into effect. This meant that the plans for operations against Austria, Czechoslovakia, and Poland, as well as the various invasions of neutral countries after that, were the only "common plans" that might produce a conviction.

The solitary loophole was the phrase that held defendants liable who, after knowing of Hitler's aggressive aims, continued to give "him their cooperation." This passage provided the Tribunal with grounds to convict a man who served the regime in any significant capacity after he had learned of aggressive plans, even though he himself had not played a direct part in their preparation. Although little different from the provisions covering accessories in most legal systems, this passage could produce very debatable findings because of the complexity of the Nuremberg case. The large number of alleged crimes and the long period of criminal liability (1937–45) produced very tenuous connections between "knowledge" and subsequent "cooperation." If the judges at Nuremberg had stayed as far from this thicket as possible, their verdicts on individual defendants would have drawn less criticism. But the word "cooperation" in section V of the Judgment lies at the root of nearly every questionable Nuremberg verdict and sentence.

The conspiracy provisions of the Judgment, however, protected the defendants much more than they put them in jeopardy. Once the conspiratorial planning charge was restricted to the specific operations prepared for 1938 and subsequent years, the Court was also forced to limit sharply the scope of Crimes Against Humanity. The Charter provision requiring that the latter crimes be associated with other convictable offenses meant that nothing done before 1937 was punishable. Since the Court had no evidence before it of specific plans to enslave or murder the Czech, Austrian, or Polish populations as part of the preparations for attacks on those countries (only evidence dated after September 1, 1939, showed specific preparations for enslavement, mass murder, and so forth), no defendant was actually held liable under Count Four (Crimes Against Humanity) for an act that had been committed prior to 1939. By this combination of decisions, all defendants were released from criminal liability (in this jurisdiction) for acts committed in Germany prior to the outbreak of war as well as for diplomatic and military actions taken without knowledge of Hitler's criminal "aims." In one swoop, the Tribunal eliminated at least a third of the prosecution's evidence and saved such defendants as Schacht and Papen from the threat of severe punishment. It also marked the demise of the War Department's grand design for war crimes prosecution; not only was the general Nazi conspiracy discarded, but Bernays's basic idea of linking prewar persecutions to wartime atrocities by means of a conspiracy charge was also completely rejected by the Tribunal.

In spite of its moderation, and the good marks it has generally received from lawyers, the Court's ruling on conspiracy has not been received sympathetically by historians. Historical criticism has focused on the Tribunal's acceptance of the charge that a Nazi aggressive war plan, or a series of such plans, actually existed. Historians simply do not look at military and diplomatic developments in the same way that lawyers do, and for them the phrase "aggressive war plan" sounds as artificial and contrived as the term "legal insanity" does to many psychologists and psychiatrists. When historians look at most wars, they think of them not as events that are planned, but as things that happen. Expansion may be prepared, an attack may be organized and launched, but wars are usually spread on too big a canvas and depend on too many causes and responses by too many parties to be planned. What is true of war is doubly true of the phrase "aggressive war," for it has a slightly unpleasant odor that makes historians fear that a noxious and polemical substance may have leaked into their domain.

Consequently, no trial that uses a concept like "aggressive war" can expect very gentle treatment from historians—but the Nuremberg case has had to bear a special curse. For fifteen years, a battle has raged among diplomatic historians as to whether Hitler was an improviser or an accomplished strategist who unfolded a detailed design for eastward territorial expansion.[87] The two sides have suffered ups and downs in the course of the debate, but the general tendency has been to place more stress on linking Hitler's basic racist and anti-Soviet views to his improvisatory nature and less stress on his skills as the executor of a fixed expansionist plan. Quite obviously, the further the historical argument moves in this direction, the more phrases like "aggressive war planning" appear to be polemical and self-serving creations of the victors.

Since the Court and the historians have used much of the same evidence, the Trial's reputation and prestige have also been tarnished by the documentary soft spots that have come to light during the last thirty years. This is particularly true of the way in which the Court handled records of conferences that Hitler held with his armed forces commanders in 1939 and with the heads of the three military branches and the foreign minister in 1937. Once the Court decided to restrict the conspiracy count to planning for specific aggressive wars, the records of these conferences were central in establishing the existence of such plans and in identifying those who were parties to them. Although Donnedieu de Vabres was somewhat uneasy about placing heavy reliance on such "unofficial" documents,[88] the other judges attached great weight to the conference records. The most cursory reading of the Judgment itself, as well as preparatory memoranda and Biddle's notes, make it abundantly clear that the summaries of Hitler's conferences were fundamental to the shaping of the general Judgment and many of the individual verdicts.

During the trial, the defense emphasized that the extant records were not verbatim transcripts of these conferences but merely summaries that individual partipants had written down after the event. In at least one case, three summaries of the same conference were extant, and they did not altogether tally on specific details.[89] Nonetheless, it is easy to see why Hitler's conference records made such an impact on the Tribunal. Perhaps it is excessive to call the 1940s a humane and enlightened age, but few people then enjoyed today's commonplace privilege of listening to political leaders plan cynical and brutal measures to further their own, and their country's, interest. To sit down in 1945–46 and follow Hitler coldly weighing the best means to devour his neighbors was such a unique experience, not only for the judges but for the public at large, that a few discrepancies among the documentary accounts seemed of minor significance. No one then could point to comparable documents involving the leaders of other countries, and it seemed natural to conclude not only that the German leaders had planned aggressive wars but that their brutal cynicism was a characteristic peculiar to the Nazis.

Thirty years later, after passions have cooled and the sense of Allied moral virtue has somewhat dimmed, historians have tended to be much more critical of these materials. It has been pointed out that the picture of the "plan" that emerges from some of the records of these meetings does not always accord with Hitler's subsequent actions. In the Hossbach conference, for example, Hitler laid out a picture of eastern expansion for the army commanders and the later Nuremberg defendants, Goering, Raeder, and Neurath. During the Trial, the prosecution and the Court emphasized that, according to the only extant record of the meeting, a record that Colonel Hossbach made five days after the session had occurred, Hitler had declared that he intended to absorb Austria and destroy Czechoslovakia. But many historians now stress how the record shows Hitler telling his listeners that he intended to move first against Czechoslovakia and then against Austria, while, in fact, the sequence turned out to be reversed. In addition, none of the three situations that Hitler allegedly said were necessary for an assault on Czechoslovakia in fact existed when he moved against the Czechs in 1938 and 1939. Other historians have gone further, arguing that Hitler was not presenting serious attack plans at the Hossbach conference at all, but merely trying to intimidate the more conservative and cautious Cabinet ministers, such as Schacht and Neurath, in order to get them to force the pace of rearmament. One Swedish scholar has even asserted, on the basis of some unusual circumstances surrounding the prosecution's authentication of the Hossbach record, that the document was purposely doctored by the American prosecution in the fall of 1945 so that it would be easier to convict the defendants of conspiracy.[90]

Some of these are weighty criticisms, and few of them can be dealt with effectively. Hitler's statements on his plans for Czechoslovakia and Austria, as recorded in the Hossbach memorandum, are sufficiently imprecise so that historians may honestly question whether the Führer had made up his mind at that point; yet the account resembles the subsequent course of events closely enough so that a court could also honestly interpret it to be an announcement of a real plan. On this point we are once again in the realm of difference between lawyers and historians. In the world of law, once a criminal act has been committed, a wide range of judicial discretion is generally accepted regarding what elements must fit together in order to show that a criminal plan also existed. Historians may speculate as to why Hitler described specific expansion plans to his aides in 1937, and A. J. P. Taylor and others may be correct in their belief that he was in part merely using scare tactics.[91] But whatever questions of detail remain, Hitler did have a general intention of expanding eastward by force and ultimately he did so. It is, therefore, only fair to point out that if a defendant in any case can be shown to have been present when a plan for an act was outlined that generally resembled a criminal action that took place, talk about scare tactics would not offer much protection against conviction before any court.

Only on one of the criticisms of the Hilter conference documents is it now possible to make a categorical statement, and that concerns the accusation that the Hossbach document was falsified by the prosecution. The new evidence shows overwhelmingly that the charge is false. The circumstances surrounding the document were certainly unusual enough to arouse suspicion, for it has never been established where in the German records it was found or why it was the only major document not submitted to the Court in its original form. Unfortunately for mystery and scandal enthusiasts, however, we now have easy and harmless explanations based on records from the War Department, the State Department, and the American prosecution. On May 25, 1945, the State Department representative assigned to General Dwight Eisenhower's headquarters at SHAEF (Supreme Headquarters Allied Expeditionary Force), Ambassador Robert Murphy, dispatched a microfilm copy of the Hossbach memorandum to the State Department, together with a cover letter explaining that the document had been discovered among captured German records in the custody of the G-2 section of SHAEF.[92] Murphy described the document as "extremely interesting and of real historical importance," but officials in the State Department, not Murphy, were the ones who decided that the document should also be brought to the attention of members of Jackson's prosecution staff in Washington.[93] In June, one of Jackson's assistants made a summary of the Hossbach document that was sent to London on the 25th together with a cover letter from Colonel (later General) Telford Taylor to Jackson, stressing the importance of the Hossbach record.[94] At approximately the same time the British military authorities also became aware of the Hossbach summary, presumably from their people in SHAEF G-2, and on July 7 they started the cumbersome process necessary for the Anglo-American Joint Intelligence Committee to clear the document for transmission to the war crimes prosecutors. This proceeding never went very far because the prosecutors already had obtained the summary through State Department channels, but the incident does show that by midsummer the existence and general content of the Hossbach document were well known to important British and American officials.[95] During the summer of 1945, the prosecutors in London and Nuremberg went ahead, using the summary without troubling themselves much about the original. Then, in the first week of September, it apparently dawned on them that the Hossbach document was vital to their conspiracy case, but they did not have the original in their possession. On September 7 an urgent cable from Nuremberg reached the prosecution office in Washington, with instructions to get a photostatic copy of the Hossbach microfilm and have it authenticated because the State Department material was "better evidence of [the] original than anything found here." [96] Pursuant to these instructions, the Washington prosecutors made a photostatic copy from the microfilm, had it duly authenticated by Acting Secretary of State Dean Acheson, and on September 25, six weeks before the start of the trial, sent it to Jackson. [97]

The prosecutors clearly did not falsify the Hossbach memorandum—the item submitted at Nuremberg was identical with the document appended to Murphy's original dispatch of May 25. The possibility that the document was tampered with by Murphy or by the military authorities before it was sent to the State Department is too farfetched to warrant serious consideration. At the time there was no conceivable motive for falsification, because the Hossbach microfilm was sent to Washington fewer than three weeks after the end of the war. In the fourth week of May Jackson's prosecution staff had barely taken shape, and no one had a clear idea of what it was going to do or how it was going to do it. Whatever one may think of Murphy's capabilities and performance, he never showed a capacity for either divination or forgery. It is unfortunate that the original Hossbach record has not yet come to the surface; it may very well still lie in the National Archives, quietly entombed by the security restrictions that apply to SHAEF records. But this is not an important issue for the question at hand.

The Hossbach record was a legitimate, though not necessarily accurate, document, and the Court used it and the other records of Hitler's conferences as crucial parts of the evidentiary picture that pointed toward a series of Nazi aggressive war plans. The result may not have been good history, but it was defensible legal practice. By so doing the Court disposed of the grand conspiracy charge and opened the way for the preparation of a final judgment.

During the months from June to September, while the Court wrangled over conspiracy, it was also dealing with a series of smaller controversies ranging from how to handle the Nazi-Soviet Pact to the problem of criminal organizations. Agreements on each of these issues was achieved little by little and in the end this series of understandings was spread over the conspiracy compromise to form the final Judgment. Since we have now put the conspiratorial skeleton in place, it is time to flesh out the creature by examining the appendages that, taken together, made up the rest of its anatomy.

CHAPTER 6

Judgment II: General Provisions and Criminal Organizations

You can't punish a regiment, you can punish only a man.

Francis Biddle [1]

THE NUREMBERG COURT was a new creation, bereft of tradition and established system, but it quickly developed procedures that disposed of numerous problems in record time. Between June 27 and August 8, the Court worked on Birkett's drafts and redrafts of the introduction and the sections on aggressive war. Although these deliberations were held in secret, they took place in a relatively open atmosphere, with legal aides allowed to come and go without hindrance. On August 8, however, the Court decided to tighten further the security surrounding its deliberations and henceforth excluded everyone but the judges and two interpreters from the deliberation room. In the closed sessions that followed, the major decisions on conspiracy and criminal organizations were made, and the verdicts and sentences for the individual defendants were decided.[2]

In the deliberations both before and after the ruling of August 8, the Court's operating procedure remained approximately the same. Prior to each session, copies of the relevant portions of Birkett's draft, including translations for the French and Soviets, were circulated to the individual Tribunal members. Early on, Nikitchenko suggested that the paragraphs of the redrafted portions be numbered, and once this was done it quickened the pace of discussion considerably.[3] When the judges met, each senior and alternate member was allowed an opportunity to express his opinion on the material at hand, and after that a general discussion followed. Except on fundamental questions, such as that of conspiracy, understandings were achieved without recourse to a formal vote; if the majority of members were dissatisfied with a portion of the draft, the discussion continued until a formula was found that seemed satisfactory, and Birkett was then asked to redraft the section accordingly.

In order to operate this way, the Tribunal members must have achieved a certain measure of confidence in each other's capacity and integrity. Although conflicts and bewildering moments of non-communication abounded, there was a kernel of truth in Biddle's later comment that "over the long months of the trial" the eight judges "had become friends." [4] The Soviet judges took a consistently hard line and were very suspicious of long, theoretical arguments or decisions that seemed to challenge the Charter, but it is not possible to speak of any consistent East-West split during the final deliberations. The Soviets were on the short end of a number of three to one votes, but Nikitchenko did not lose consistently, and the senior Soviet judge had an unusual capacity to come back from defeats. He frequently made practical suggestions of great value, even on passages that had been adopted over his opposition.[5] All the judges were clearly determined to make the system work, and, even though fatigue and frayed nerves made the going difficult as the deadline for public announcement of the Judgment approached, the Tribunal members carried an unusual spirit of camaraderie right through to the end.

The Court saved itself considerable grief by a unanimous decision in early August to reject consideration of prosecution briefs that had not been presented in Court. The rejection of this petition not only protected the judges' judicial integrity, but set some limit to the body of evidence that had already reached mountainous proportions.[6] Another early decision that simplified matters was the Tribunal's acceptance of Birkett's general plan for the Judgment. This format, which was retained throughout the whole period of deliberation, used a general introduction and a historical section, followed by summaries of the Nazis' aggressive wars, war crimes, and crimes against humanity. The Court wisely decided to deal first with the practical descriptive data that were to go into the Judgment, and it reached agreement on the introductory material by the end of its second meeting on July 11.[7]

Somewhat more troublesome was the question of style, for all the Tribunal members fancied themselves to be legal literati, and Birkett's role as draftsman was not always an enviable one. Most of his colleagues felt that he was too verbose and the French and Americans repeatedly expressed the view that his prose was also too emotional and perhaps too polemical. Nikitchenko, however, usually came to Birkett's defense on this score, arguing that the Englishman's most impassioned phrases were both appropriate and necessary. In consequence, the general thrust of the redrafting was to tone down Birkett's language, but the judges expended an enormous amount of time and effort in order to achieve this result. Biddle's files are literally crammed with drafts and redrafts of portions of the Judgment, each of which has been laboriously corrected and revised by hand. Due to the impossibility of getting eight judges using three different languages to meet and reach agreement on a particular word or phrase, most of this effort was wasted. On August 8, the judges finally recognized the inevitable and decided that henceforth, after all matters of principle had been agreed to and a general style established, particular matters of expression would be left to the author. The Judgment that was ultimately made public reads, therefore, as could be expected—it is a document with content and general tone established by a committee, but with occasional personal touches written by Norman Birkett.[8]

However, no such simple formula could be found to deal with the many substantive problems facing the Tribunal; they had to be resolved one by one, and in some cases the solution to one riddle negated an answer that had earlier been agreed to for another. The historical portions summarizing the background of the Nazi movement and the history of the Third Reich were rather troublesome. The judges disagreed both on what general aspects to emphasize and which details to include. Lawrence wanted to stress the Nazi rise to power, while Biddle thought this was unimportant and the emphasis should be placed on the regime's repressive measures. Birkett accorded the Blood Purge of June 1934 considerable space, but Nikitchenko managed to have this passage shortened and more attention given to the Reichstag fire and the resulting Nazi suppression of the Communist party and the trade unions.[9] Each of these controversies took extended discussion and at least one redrafting, but when the general questions such as conspiracy were resolved and the individual verdicts determined, much of the work had to be redone. Passages from *Mein Kampf* that contained early indications of Hitler's desire for an expansionist war had received extended treatment in early drafts, but when the grand conspiracy charge was dropped these quotations had to be eliminated. Similarly, the generous descriptions initially accorded to the activities of Papen and Schacht had to be trimmed or cut once it was decided that these men should be acquitted.

Most of the controversies of this type had only marginal political overtones, but a handful of disputes arose over more serious political and ideological issues. Early in the deliberations, Nikitchenko tried to convince the other judges that the role of the industrialists and the Nazi diplomats should occupy a prominent place in the historical section. But the Western judges, led by Biddle, quickly disposed of this suggestion, arguing that Hitler had broken the independent power of both groups at an early date. On another occasion, late in the deliberations, Donnedieu de Vabres wanted to insert a section on the methods of warfare used by the partisans in order to provide a context that would better explain the Nazis' savage methods of repression. This time Nikitchenko bristled and managed to obtain enough Western support so that the French judge ultimately dropped the idea.[10]

Generally speaking, surprisingly few political issues surfaced during the discussions on the historical section and those parts of the Judgment concerned with War Crimes and Crimes Against Humanity. Birkett recommended in one of his early drafts that the discussion of war crimes should receive the heaviest emphasis because they were most on the minds of people in all countries. But his advice was not followed; as always at Nuremberg, the weight was placed on the aggressive war question, and that is where the serious controversies arose.[11]

The long section III of the Judgment devoted to aggressive war began with introductory pages on the Nazi seizure of Austria and

Czechoslovakia, together with a discussion of the aggressive war evidence, especially the records of Hitler's conferences in 1937 and 1939. Subsections then followed, devoted to consideration of the specific aggressive attacks charged in the indictment, beginning with the Nazi invasion of Poland in September 1939 and ending with the singular charge that Germany was guilty of aggression against the United States in 1941. The introductory portions underwent repeated revision during the deliberations, as the Court wrestled with the conspiracy question, and the final version was much less emotional and more descriptive than earlier drafts. Although in the course of the conspiracy controversy Donnedieu de Vabres advocated cutting back the treatment of the attacks that were made after 1939 because these were virtually inevitable once the war began, his fellow judges rejected the idea and each invasion was accorded at least one page in the Judgment's final form. Still, the question of the relative space that should be allotted to each occurrence and how each one could best be handled produced no end of discussion and revision.[12] The most troublesome problem was posed by Soviet conduct on the eve of the German invasion of Poland in 1939, for Stalin's signature on the Nazi-Soviet Pact had left Hitler free to move against Poland. Once the secret clauses of that pact appeared in evidence, even in summary form, it was difficult to avoid the conclusion that Stalin, like some of the defendants in the dock, had continued to "cooperate" with Hitler after he knew of the Nazi attack plans. If this kind of conduct would earn defendants such as Wilhelm Frick prison sentences or death, what was the Court to say about the actions of the Soviet Union? The difficulty was compounded by the fact that, when it was Russia's turn to be an invasion victim in 1941, the Germans justified their assault on the grounds that Stalin was preparing to tear up the Nazi-Soviet agreement and was about to launch his own attack on them. Thus, there appeared to be no way for the Court to deal with the alleged aggressions against Poland and the Soviet Union without touching on the Nazi-Soviet Pact.

Adrian Fisher, the American legal aide, was the first person associated with the bench who tried to solve the problem. In the memoranda he wrote prior to the preparation of the first draft of the Judgment, he skipped over the Nazi-Soviet Pact with barely a word, but when he covered the Nazi invasion of Russia in 1941 he declared flatly that there was no evidence of Soviet preparations to attack

Germany, and that all indications supported the conclusion that the Russians had scrupulously met the terms of the pact. This praise of the Russians because they had not prepared an attack on Germany and had honored a pact whose existence was not previously acknowledged added a somewhat jarring note to Fisher's narrative. But for the American to laud Stalin because of his loyalty to an agreement with Hitler in the middle of a chronicle stressing the obviousness of Nazi evil was so contradictory that it should have been taken care of very early in the deliberative process.[13] The peculiar formulation, however, had a surprisingly long life. Birkett adopted Fisher's treatment almost word for word and it lasted through the first three drafts of the Judgment. It might, in fact, have gotten through the final revision except that in the third draft a passage on the background of the Nazi attack on Poland in 1939 was included that contained a long quote from Hitler's speech to his generals on August 22, 1939. In this quote, the Führer contended that the Nazi-Soviet Pact had doomed Poland by diplomatically isolating her. In the discussion of this draft, the Soviet judges understandably strove mightily to have this portion of Hitler's remarks deleted. On August 8, both Nikitchenko and Volchkov argued that it should be cut because, in their view, it was a distortion. This first effort failed to move the other judges, but Nikitchenko pressed the attack on September 7 and finally managed to have the offending passage eliminated. In its place, Birkett added a limp sentence stating that in August 1939 Ribbentrop had been sent to Moscow to negotiate a nonaggression pact. An introductory sentence was also added to the section on the German attack on the Soviet Union in 1941 merely declaring that a Soviet-German nonaggression agreement had been signed in August 1939. The final form of the Judgment thereby dealt with the delicate issue of the Soviet signing of the pact by totally ignoring it. It similarly skimmed over the related questions of the pact's subsequent fulfillment and the consideration of the German assault as preventive war. Inadvertently, the Judgment may have given credence thereby to the defense contention that Russia was preparing to attack Germany in 1941, although this claim lacked any significant supporting evidence.[14]

The troubles over the Nazi-Soviet Pact produced some of the most disjointed passages in the Judgment and also constituted one of its shabbiest political episodes. But the treatment of the German attack on Norway did not lag far behind either in awkwardness or in political expediency. The central difficulty in holding the Germans guilty of an aggressive attack on neutral Norway was that, at the moment of the German invasion in the spring of 1940, British forces were preparing to make their own landings there. It is true that the Allied operation was on a smaller scale than the German, and it also would probably not have led to the total subjugation of the Norwegians. But that is all that can be said in defense of the Allied operation, for it was clearly a violation of Norwegian neutral rights. In the course of the trial, defense testimony established that German forces fighting in Norway during 1940 had captured Allied documents that proved beyond question that an Allied landing in Norway was being prepared prior to the German attack.[15] The prosecution tried to meet this testimony by showing, through captured German documents, that the Nazis had planned their assault independently of any firm information that the British were about to land. If the Tribunal accepted this evidence and argument as valid, and ultimately it did so, the German attack might be held to have been aggressive no matter what the British were doing or intended to do. Yet, to justify the punishment of German leaders while ignoring Allied aggressive plans on the ground that two wrongs do not make a right strains both legal propriety and common sense.

In order to evaluate the Court's handling of the Norwegian question, it is first necessary to explore whether the Tribunal members knew definitely that Allied landings in Norway were being mounted in the spring of 1940. As indicated above, the British Government knowingly withheld certain materials from the Court, and some of these concerned Norway.[16] The leaders of the British prosecution, Lord Shawcross and Maxwell Fyfe, must have known that this was done and why it was done. It is not so clear, however, whether the British judges had an accurate picture of the British Government's document policy or of what had happened in Norway. There is no currently available documentary evidence pointing either way, but it must at least be granted that, as men in British public life, the judges were in a position to hear rumors from government circles as well as from those involved in the Norwegian operation. They should have realized that there was considerable force in the claims of the German defense.

The Tribunal members from the other countries, however, had much less occasion to suspect the British Government or to accept the contentions of the defense at face value. Indeed, Biddle seems to have been favorably impressed by the evidence of German aggressiveness presented by the prosecution in December 1945, and he subsequently registered doubts about the adequacy of the defense argument for Raeder put forward on this question in July.[17] Considering the cloudy water that envelops the Norwegian affair, it seems best to conclude that at least the non-British judges had not been made privy to convincing information about what had actually happened there.

Nonetheless, enough compromising testimony had been placed in evidence to make some of those associated with the bench move warily. When Fisher prepared the initial summary on Norway, he did not approach the difficulty directly but did imply that the final German decision to invade had been triggered by the imminence of the British landings.[18] On this occasion, however, Birkett did not follow Fisher's lead, and his first two drafts of the Judgment flatly declared that the German contentions that they had acted to forestall a British invasion were "unfounded."[19] Birkett's treatment of the question was warmly seconded by Donnedieu de Vabres, who asserted that the Court should not discuss the question of Britain's aggressive "intentions" in Norway.[20] But Nikitchenko found Birkett's sharp handling of the German actions unreasonable; the attack on Norway was different from the initial wars of aggression, in Nikitchenko's view, because, once war began, military necessity took charge and the Germans were forced to try to control Europe's right flank.[21] Of course, the Soviet Union had made an assault on its own Scandinavian flank in Finland, a few months before the Germans had gone into Norway, so Nikitchenko's remarks were not free from special pleading.

It was Parker who brought forward the compromise formula on Norway that was used in the final Judgment, but this one was not very satisfactory. Parker forced the British judges to back down and a summary of the evidence showing that the British Government had definite plans for Norwegian landings was written into the Judgment. But then Parker, writing for the Tribunal, went on to nullify the main contentions of the defense by concluding that the evidence that indicated that the German leaders knew of the British preparations before they decided to strike was not convincing. In the final opinion of the Tribunal, the German attack on Norway in April 1940 was solely the product of a long period of independent planning, and the closely paralleled timing of the British and German operations was merely coincidental. Thus, the German landing was neither defensive nor retaliatory, and the Court flatly rejected the idea that attacking another country could ever be a legitimate application of the right to self-defense under international law. These arguments are not in themselves unreasonable, and by using them Parker, speaking for the Court, managed to achieve his two major objectives: he prevented Birkett from whitewashing the British role in Norway, and he retained the Norwegian affair as an instance of Nazi Germany's aggressive wars. But the legalistic tunnel vision used to reach this result must leave most members of the laity with their heads shaking in wonder.[22]

After all of the careful definitions and arguments run their course, the obvious conclusion that still lies buried in Parker's work is that both Germany and Britain were guilty of aggressive war planning against Norway. Defenders of the Nuremberg system would later struggle mightily to justify the Tribunal's use of this double standard; the Court had to deal with the case at hand, it had no jurisdiction over the British government, and so forth and so on. All this is true, but with the best will in the world there is also no gainsaying the fact that no such court can make a trial visibly fair if it is directed solely at the leaders of one country. When the trial at Nuremberg was over, Winston Churchill, one of those who had planned landings in Norway, was a recipient of the Nobel Peace Prize. Another planner of Norwegian landings, the German Admiral Raeder, was given a life sentence mainly because of his role in Norway. A third planner, Alfred Rosenberg, was hanged because of his preparations for the Norwegian campaign as well as for his later activities in occupied Russia. The Nuremberg judges tried hard to produce a fair and legally defensible judgment, and by and large they succeeded. But surely Norway was not their finest hour.

The scenario for the third Nuremberg conflict over aggressive war, the German invasion of Greece, was similar to that for Norway. The Germans had attacked Yugoslavia and Greece, simultaneously and without warning, during the first week of April 1941—but whether the assault on Greece was an instance of aggressive war was made doubtful by the fact that, at the time, British troops were already in Greece. In late 1940, Mussolini had invaded Greece and, although the Greeks did very well against the Italians, the British landed support troops during the first week of March. When the Nazis struck, Hitler justified his attack by declaring that he was simply trying to counter a British effort to build up a Balkan front against Germany similar to the one that had existed in World War I.

As he had done on Norway, Fisher made a gallant effort to skirt the central issue on Greece, but he left the impression that the German attack was a response to the British landings.[23] In his early work on the question, Birkett tried two differing approaches. His first draft mentioned that there was evidence suggesting that Hitler was trying to block the British in the Balkans, but he then ignored this point to conclude that the German action was purely aggressive. In his second draft, Birkett cut some of the material on Greece and dismissed the British presence there as a matter of no importance except as a "pretext" for German aggression.[24] When the latter draft came up for discussion by the Tribunal on July 17, Biddle recommended that the German invasion of Greece be dropped as an instance of aggressive war, but he failed to receive the full support of any of the other judges. Nikitchenko granted that the Greek case was questionable, but believed that the Germans had acted on the basis of long-term aggressive planning rather than as a response to the British landings. Parker and Lawrence were prepared to accept some rephrasing in Birkett's draft, but they were not ready to strike Greece from the list of German aggressive war actions. Biddle's opposition was silenced and in the final version the Tribunal limited itself to describing the long, involved German planning for an invasion of Greece that had been made before the British landings. As a slight sop to Biddle, it was noted that Hitler had justified his actions by pointing to the British presence in Greece. But even this gesture was quickly neutralized by a qualifying phrase that made it seem self-evident that the British were there only to aid the Greeks against the Italians, and that they had not entertained any thought of building up a Balkan front against Germany.[25] This interpretation of the causes of the Greek campaign rested on an exceedingly narrow reading of the relevant facts, but it is neither as contrived in form nor as unfair in its result as the one that had been used on Norway. The Greek and Balkan realities were, as always, very complex and the parallel between British and German actions was not as close as that which had existed in the north. Most important, no defendant went to jail or to the scaffold because of his part in planning the German attack on Greece, and that may be as moderate and humane a result as could be hoped for under the circumstances.

The last controversy over a specific aggressive war charge appears almost as a moment of comic relief when compared with the three mortal and bloodstained issues that went before. In the indictment, the prosecution charged Germany with a Crime Against Peace for inciting Japan to attack the United States and for declaring war on America the day after Pearl Harbor. When examining this charge, it is important for Americans to recall that, whatever the high motives of the government in Washington during 1941, the United States waged undeclared naval war against Germany in an effort to aid Britain. No valid parallel exists between what happened on the high seas in 1917 and in 1941; in the latter case, the United States clearly violated virtually every established rule of neutrality. During the trial, the American prosecution team struggled valiantly to find some support for the charge that Germany had been planning aggression against the United States prior to Pearl Harbor. This effort had the transparent purpose of vindicating American aid to the Allies by showing that the United States had been in danger and that Hitler had marked it out for future attack. The result of the prosecution's labors, though, was disappointing. There were a few scraps of low-level planning papers pointing to possible German acquisition of Atlantic bases for use in the event of future conflict with the United States, but these were much too trifling to support a weighty charge. [26] The prosecution did present a great deal of documentation to show that German officials worked assiduously to convince Japan that it should enter the war by attacking other countries in 1940–41. But the documents showed that, even though the German authorities from Hitler to Ribbentrop were anxious that Japan should attack first Britain and later Russia, they were very cool toward a Japanese action that might vault the United States into a general war. Since Britain and Russia were already fighting Germany at the time of these incidents, this Hitlerian sales campaign could not be considered part of aggressive war planning. When, in the fall of 1941, the Germans did indicate agreement with Japanese plans for an attack on both the British and the American possessions in the Pacific, it was clear that the Nazis did so reluctantly.

After surveying the problem in May 1946, Fisher concluded that there was "little evidence" to indicate that Germany had been planning "a direct attack on the United States." He decided that the only case that might be made under the charge rested on the blank check that Ribbentrop and Hitler had given to the Japanese in the fall and winter of 1941. [27] Birkett also seems to have had difficulty with the problem and in his first draft dealt with it by the simple expedient of omitting it altogether. In his second draft, however, perhaps out of a feeling of Allied good fellowship, he did his best to make a case. While agreeing with Fisher on the lack of evidence for direct attack planning, he contended that the Germans had discussed such a possibility as "a matter for the future," and that they had encouraged the Japanese in their attack plans. By subsequently entering the war on Japan's side, he concluded, the Nazis had "made themselves parties to the crimes in which the Japanese were engaged." [28] Though imaginative, the latter argument failed to impress Biddle, who, in the deliberative session of September 9, asked that it be cut from the final version. Biddle's request was acceded to and in consequence the section on aggression against the United States was left hanging in midair; it reviewed the main actions that the Nazi leaders took regarding the United States but failed to make any ruling on whether this constituted a case of aggressive warfare. [29]

On this anticlimactic note, the Tribunal ended its survey of the specific cases of Crimes Against Peace, but it still needed to prepare a statement on the general question of aggressive war in international law. In two of his first notes to the Tribunal, Birkett suggested to his colleagues that they be very cautious about making legal references in the body of the Judgment, but he also noted that lawyers everywhere would expect the Court to make some general declaration regarding the law of the case. [30] The three senior Tribunal members from the Western countries expressed the view during the opening deliberative session in June that a general legal statement was necessary, and, although Nikitchenko raised objections to it in early September, he later reversed himself and agreed to its inclusion. [31] Some work was done during the summer on the statement, which became the eight-page section IV of the final Judgment, but it is not altogether clear who was responsible for its final form. Biddle definitely had a hand in its preparation, and there are indications that the whole statement was primarily the product of the American judicial team. [32]

The final form of the statement contained few surprises, for it was not motivated by legal garrulousness, only by the desire to meet objections that the Court knew were sure to come. One of the most prestigious schools of legal thought at the time was legal positivism, whose most distinguished spokesman, Hans Kelsen, held that valid law rested solely on prevailing statute, procedure, and usage; to the legal positivists, the traditional references to general or universal legal principles were simply meaningless. Little imagination was necessary to determine which portions of the Nuremberg Judgment would be attacked by Kelsen and his fellow positivists, for they would inevitably zero in on the question of whether aggressive war was a crime and whether individual government leaders were criminally liable at the time the acts charged in the indictment had been committed. In short, the legal problem for the Court, as Biddle frankly told Nikitchenko in September, was to show that its proceedings were not *ex post facto*.[33]

The first line of defense taken by the Tribunal was to assert that, through the Nazis' unconditional surrender, the Allies had acquired sovereign legislative power in Germany and could do whatever they wished. The London Charter was an expression of this power, and the Court was, in turn, a legal creature of the Charter and bound by its provisions. The Tribunal implied that due to these facts it actually did not need to trouble itself about the state of pre-existing law.[34] But the Tribunal members knew that this would not meet the broader objections of the critics and they therefore based their legal justification on the assertion that aggressive warfare was in fact both illegal and punishable at the time the Nazis planned and launched their assaults. Even so, they carefully followed the advice of Donnedieu de Vabres and avoided any definition of aggression, merely averring that since in the current case both the terms "aggressive war" and war "in violation of international treaties" covered the facts, no additional statement on the question was necessary. To establish that Crimes Against Peace were, in fact, crimes, the Court used essentially the same arguments and most of the same facts that had been employed by the prosecution. Once again, it was stressed that international law is not primarily statute law but is shaped by custom and "the general principles of law," [35]—a phrase not very well suited to appease the legal positivists. Such agreements as the Locarno Pact (1925) and the Kellogg-Briand Pact (1928) had, in the Tribunal's view, made aggressive war illegal by the 1930s.

If this explanation was rather unimaginative, the Court did somewhat better with the question of whether individual violators of international law might be tried and punished. Along with the usual collection of instances where courts had tried violators of international law, as in cases of piracy, the Tribunal also pointed to what had occurred under the Hague Rules of Land Warfare (1907).

Stressing that the Hague Convention itself had not established courts or a trial method for those who violated its rules, the Tribunal noted that the signatory states had nonetheless regularly tried and punished violators of the convention in their own domestic courts. If this was valid law for the Hague Convention, the judges argued, then the same principle should hold for the Kellogg-Briand Pact and other agreements outlawing aggressive war.[36] The Tribunal neglected to mention, however, that in the case of the Hague rules, each state had added the provisions in question to its own legal code, while no such development had occurred for the Kellogg-Briand Pact.

The Tribunal's general treatment of the law on aggressive war and individual liability, as well as its argument supporting the Charter's denial of a superior orders plea as a complete defense, was neither very distinguished nor presented with notable vigor. Of the eight men on the bench, only Donnedieu de Vabres could have been considered a legal theorist, and he seems to have taken but a perfunctory interest in the preparation of this section. Biddle was more concerned about the problem, but theory was not his forte and after his argument regarding the Hague rules was accepted he also seems to have lost interest. As usual, the Tribunal members were not trying to merit a place in legal history, but merely attempting to get through the legal snares with their reputations intact. Their essay on the law was a respectable defense—not stunning, but respectable—and that was good enough for them. As Nikitchenko never tired of repeating, they were "practical men," [37] with little time for theory and a multitude of problems to worry about.

The conspiracy controversy had been their most fundamental challenge and the specific instances of aggression among the most troublesome, but the problem that never seemed to leave them alone was that of criminal organizations. Some of the Tribunal members had begun to fuss about it long before the trial opened, and all through the trial it kept coming back to present new difficulties to the Court. The Tribunal did not reach final agreement on it until just four days before the Judgment and verdicts were read out in open court. The reasons that the controversies and uncertainties over the organizations had such a long life are not difficult to see. This was the most novel of the prosecutions, with no precedents in international law and few, if any, in the domestic laws of the major states. During the trial, the Court dealt with every manifestation of the organization question either by evasion or by using a stopgap solution. Added to this near mountain of difficulties was the unfortunate fact that neither the defense nor the prosecution presentations on the organizations was very effective. Nuremberg participants almost universally agreed that, with the exception of the High Command and General Staff case, which was argued ably by Telford Taylor for the prosecution and Hans Laternser (who replaced Dr. Franz Exner) for the defense, the organizational presentations were lackluster at best.[38] Even in the High Command and General Staff case, the defense was hampered by the bizarre notions of legal process displayed by the men on trial. In mid-December, two groups of senior German officers, led by Generals Erhardt Milch, Walter Warlimont, and Walther von Brauchitsch (all defendants as members of the High Command and General Staff), made two secret petitions to the Tribunal, requesting that they be represented by an army general rather than by a court-appointed civilian attorney. The petitions, which were routinely denied by the Tribunal, were probably motivated largely by the desire of the military leaders to be represented by someone with greater technical knowledge than a civilian attorney, but the petitions were framed in such a way that the generals appeared to be asserting that they were a caste apart that should not be contaminated by contact with the judicial process governing the lives of common people.[39] Nothing could have been better designed to increase the hostility of the jurists on the bench or to help persuade them that a German High Command and General Staff had actually existed as a distinct group or organization.

Thus, everyone concerned with the criminal organization case had a burden to bear, and, when Fisher and Rowe wrote up their initial evaluations of the cases on the six organizations, they made it clear that each one had special characteristics that made a judicial ruling difficult. The case against the SA was especially doubtful because of the lack of a suitable representative defendant and because of the group's loss of power and influence after 1934. Even Colonel Storey, who presented the prosecution case against the SA, submitted an affidavit stating that "by the end of 1934, the SA had been fairly well eliminated," [40] and under questioning by Lawrence, Storey himself awkwardly groped toward the same conclusion by stating that, "as I understand, Sir, the SA reached its height of popularity in 1934 and immediately after the purge began to decline . . . after 1934 the SA started a rapid decline in its importance." [41] If the Tribunal would not sustain the existence of a conspiracy prior to 1934—which, in fact, it would not—there was then no possible ground on which to declare the SA criminal.

It is important to note how the unlikelihood of a criminality declaration against the SA signifies the Bench's distinction between organizations and individual defendants. Some of the judges did not face up to the possibility that any of the defendants might be acquitted on all counts until very late in the deliberations, and this produced no end of difficulty in dealing with the cases of people such as Schacht. But, in regard to the organizations, once the Tribunal reached its compromise agreement on conspiracy, it was fairly obvious that at least one organization, the SA, would not be declared criminal. Consequently, since the dam had been so obviously broken, it was much easier for the judges to think in terms of noncriminality findings in regard to other organizations, especially as each of them had its own mitigating quirks and peculiarities.

As Fisher pointed out to Biddle and Parker, the Reich Cabinet contained only a handful of people, forty-eight in all between 1933 and 1945, and throughout most of 1933 it included a majority of non-Nazis. If the Tribunal held that there had been a conspiracy existing after January 1933, a solid case could be made against the Cabinet, but otherwise a finding of criminality would be difficult particularly because the Cabinet did not meet after 1933.[42] Even the cases against the SS, the Gestapo-SD, and the "Leadership Corps" of the Nazi party were not open-and-shut, in Fisher's view. Although the SS was primarily a maze of voluntary subgroups, a considerable number of men had been drafted in the armed (*Waffen-*) SS in the course of World War II, and others had obviously joined as an alternative to conscription into the army. Furthermore, it could be questioned whether a majority of the men in these armed SS units actually knew of the "criminal purposes" of the organization at the time they became members. To find a group criminal under these circumstances troubled Fisher, who also pointed out that for the SS there was once again a problem of finding a representative defendant. Although Kaltenbrunner was a high SS official, he was also the main representative defendant for the Gestapo-SD and it did appear somewhat odd that one man's actions could serve as the link to declare two groups criminal.[43]

The general case against the Gestapo-SD was easier to establish, in Fisher's view, although there was the difficulty of determining which parts of Himmler's amazingly complex police empire should be included in the designation of criminality. In addition, the prosecution had concentrated so much of its attention on Gestapo actions in the occupied territories that Fisher was somewhat uncertain whether the evidence had established that a man who joined the Gestapo in wartime Germany would necessarily have known that he was entering a "criminal organization." [44]

But these doubts were relatively modest compared with the reservations Fisher raised in regard to the case against the "Leadership Corps" of the Nazi party. The prosecution had pictured the party organization as a conspiratorial hierarchy ranging from the Reichsleiter (national leaders) at the top to the Blockleiter (neighborhood officials) at the bottom. Fisher concluded, however, that the cohesiveness in this picture was greatly exaggerated, and that the two lowest levels of authorities, those on the *Zell* (ward) and *Block* (neighborhood) level, should be excluded from the Court's consideration. This would leave only the Party leaders on the *Reich* (national), *Kreis* (regional) and *Ort* (town) levels, together with their staffs, to constitute the component parts of the organization. But Fisher, who had few reservations about conspiracy aspects of other parts of the case, still was not ready to give the prosecution a clear stamp of approval, even on this restricted form of the "Leadership Corps." He advised Parker and Biddle that the evidence for common planning by this organization was so sparse and dubious that a ruling should be based solely on the overt acts of the group. Even so, there was precious little concrete evidence, and the only item Fisher thought worthy of consideration by the judges was Bormann's use of the "Leadership Corps" in 1944–45 to encourage the lynching of Allied fliers. [45]

In contrast to Fisher's doubts, Rowe showed little hesitation about the organization that he evaluated. Rowe went through the case against the High Command and General Staff in a long, forty-page memorandum and concluded that Telford Taylor had established that the organization was criminal. Although Rowe's memorandum did not fully explore two of the major arguments against such a designation regarding the High Command—that the 132 men covered by the indictment were not a coherent group, and that the development of attack plans is not an activity peculiar to the German military—he did draw attention to the small size of the group in question. Of the approximately 132 men who had occupied the relevant positions, only 118 were still alive—a sufficiently small number, so that they could be dealt with by individual trials rather than through the criminal organization procedure. Thus, even this preparatory memorandum, which made the strongest argument for designating a group criminal, had to grant the existence of circumstances that struck at the root of the whole criminal organization trial system.[46]

When the judges deliberated on the fate of the organizations in September, they had to find ways to deal both with the complications inherent in each of the groups and with general doubt about the equity of organization prosecution itself. As Biddle later pointed out, the term "collective guilt" was not then fashionable, but the dangers in the idea were clearly in the minds of the judges, especially those from France and the United States.[47] A possible way out of the problem, one that received the most attention during the trial proceedings, was for the Court to identify certain subgroups, or "classes," of membership that might be exempted from the general ruling of criminality. When the deliberations on the Judgment began, Donnedieu de Vabres still halfheartedly suggested that this was the best answer to the problem, but he received little support from the other Tribunal members.[48] It was obvious to most of the judges that large organizations such as the SS and the Gestapo were made up of so many rapidly changing subgroups that it would be impossible to make an effective general ruling on the basis of the information available to the Court. Although the American judges wanted some subgroups exempted, they recommended that instead of drawing the principal line on the basis of the internal structure of the groups, the Court should place the main emphasis on a time line designating when the organizations were criminal.[49]

The French and British soon came around to support the American point of view that a distinction based on time periods was of fundamental importance, but the Soviet judges were not convinced. The Americans neither forced an immediate vote on the issue nor specified what limiting date, or dates, they had in mind; they simply accepted the indications of Anglo-French support and bided their time.

In the course of the discussions on September 3 and September 13, Donnedieu de Vabres suggested another partial solution to the general problem, one that he had advocated since the early days of the trial. He asked the Court to establish rules on organizations to be used by the occupation courts in the four Allied zones and, if possible, to also establish fixed penalties for each category of members.[50] The Court was no more receptive to the latter suggestion than Jackson had been when he had heard the same idea from Assistant Secretary of War Peterson seven months earlier. The Soviets, during the deliberations, were also just as firmly opposed to any form of interference with what they considered the internal affairs of their zone as they had been during the hearings in February.[51] But the French, seconded by the Americans, held their ground, strongly favoring that some recommendations be made to the occupation courts. The British, though more hesitant, finally agreed that something of the sort should be done. The precise form that such recommendations should take was not agreed to until the last deliberative session on September 26, but from at least September 3 on the three Western judges favored the inclusion of some such recommendation.[52]

Whatever could be done on setting a time limit or making recommendations to the occupation courts would still touch only part of the problem. Someone had to try to get to the core of it, and this was finally done by Biddle. Ever since the discussions aboard the *Queen Elizabeth*, he had been troubled over what to do on this issue, and it must be remembered that he had much more to be concerned about than the other judges because he was one of the three U.S. Cabinet members who, back in January 1945, had signed the paper recommending to Roosevelt that a trial system based on criminal organization prosecution should be used. With characteristic frankness, Biddle later admitted that, when the time had come to make the declarations of criminality, the hesitation he had begun to feel in the mid-Atlantic could no longer be kept so "theoretical." [53] By September 1946, he had concluded that the original recommendation of January 1945 "was wrong," and that the whole approach had to be repudiated by the Court. "This group crime [is] a shocking thing," he told his fellow judges on September 3, and went on to suggest that the charges against all six organizations be thrown out.[54] Ten days later, in the second deliberative session on the organizations, he once more advocated the same course but failed to receive the support of a single one of his Tribunal colleagues.[55]

Predictably, Nikitchenko vigorously supported the idea of criminal organization prosecution—continuing his turnabout since London—and objected to every suggestion that particular subgroups be exempted from the declaration.[56] More surprising was Lawrence's contention that the criminal organization approach was basically sound, and that the judges should not be overly worried about what might happen in the courts of the occupying powers. To Lawrence's mind, the fundamental issue was merely procedural, a view that prompted Biddle to remark caustically in his notes "Gawd!" and "British fake." [57] Yet even Lawrence was prepared to admit that certain organizations posed serious problems; he was, thus, ready to exempt some organizations completely from the declaration, while sharply limiting the findings in the cases of others.[58] Donnedieu de Vabres was also willing to make extensive exclusions, and he, too, did not shrink before the prospect of finding some organizations not criminal. Pointing out that it would be possible to cite practical grounds for the most urgent qualifications and restrictions, the Frenchman thought that the Court could thereby avoid resorting to Biddle's extreme alternative of throwing out the whole case. Donnedieu de Vabres conceded that after vigorously opposing the idea of conspiracy he was being somewhat hypocritical in asserting the collective guilt of some organizations. But he found that it was simply impossible for him to vote to exempt groups such as the Gestapo and the SS. The inhabitants of every French village knew that there was a fundamental difference between the SS and units of the German Army, Donnedieu de Vabres claimed, and public opinion simply would not understand or accept the failure of the Court to declare groups like the SS to have been criminal.[59]

During this discussion, Biddle was probably on the side of the angels insofar as libertarian principles were concerned, but Donnedieu de Vabres was surely closer to the realities of the European situation in 1946. It was relatively simple for Biddle to admit a mistake and to repudiate a position taken by the U.S. Government that did not touch the marrow of American experience. But the peoples of Europe had been too physically and emotionally tortured by the Gestapo and SS system to be able to brush aside the criminal organization question once it had been raised. The passage of thirty years makes it difficult to grasp how completely the Nazi occupation system had served to degrade and humiliate the inhabitants of every country. Aside from the physical aspects of control and torture—which were grim enough, even by today's standards—it was the refusal of the Nazis to give the conquered people more than the thinnest sliver of self-respect and dignity that made the occupation such a crushing experience. The first months of liberation had not brought very rapid improvement in standards of living, but they had removed the yoke of humiliation and established the basis for a revival of popular self-respect. Donnedieu de Vabres rightly understood that, if this inter-Allied Court failed to declare the SS and the Gestapo criminal, it would not only produce political protests, but would create a psychological situation that many Europeans would find simply unbearable.

Whether Biddle ever grasped the strength of feeling behind Donnedieu de Vabres's argument is doubtful, but he was a seasoned enough politician to realize that he did not have the votes to win. If he could not throw out the whole organization case, he was ready to fall back on a second alternative that had already been prepared by Parker. The American alternate had suggested in a memorandum prepared in early August that there was a simple answer to the criminal organization problem: the Court needed only to recognize that it was analogous to a conspiracy prosecution and employ the two protections customarily applicable to defendants in such cases, voluntary participation and knowledge of criminal purposes.[60] To declare an organization criminal, Parker suggested, all the Court needed to do was define the organization as having a membership limited to those who knew the group was criminal and who had joined voluntarily. In subsequent proceedings before occupation courts, if an individual could show that he had been forced to join or had not known the nature of the organization at the time of his entry, then he would fall outside the definition of the criminal organization and would thus not be punishable. In his original formulation, Parker substantially weakened the protection that this approach might afford to individuals by suggesting that the responsibility for proof should fall on the individual defendant rather than the prosecution. But, during the Court's general discussions, Biddle persuaded Parker to drop this provision, and in his final formulation the burden of proof regarding knowledge and the voluntary nature of membership fell to the prosecution, in conformity with the traditional maxim that a person should be considered innocent until proved guilty.[61]

As Biddle once remarked about a suggestion of Birkett's, the recommendation that Parker made on criminal organizations was one of pure genius. By drawing the analogy with conspiracy, Parker based the position on an approach familiar to Anglo-American jurists and at the same time laid a basis for establishing the limitation and protections desired by Donnedieu de Vabres for subsequent proceedings. The knowledge and voluntary membership criteria also gave the Court a handy means of avoiding a decision on the tangled subgroups of the SS and the Gestapo; all that was necessary was to provide a rough definition of the general organization and leave the internal technicalities to be fought out in the occupation courts. Even more importantly, Parker's proposal offered the Tribunal an opportunity to stand up for legal and humane principles and yet quietly bury the whole system of criminal organization prosecution. As the judges surely realized, none of the occupation authorities was going to proceed very far with the task of prosecuting two million to three million cases, in each of which they would have to prove that the defendant was a voluntary and knowledgeable member of a criminal group. Parker's criminal organization proposal, though unusually clever, was typical of the solutions employed by the Nuremberg bench: without fanfare or ringing phrases, it flanked the main issues yet prevented the war criminal cases from producing grave miscarriages of justice.

During the discussion of Parker's proposal, which took place off and on through two deliberative sessions, Nikitchenko voiced some objections and other judges registered reservations here and there, but gradually it emerged that in a showdown the Parker plan would at least receive the support of the three senior Western judges and would thereby prevail. Once this had become clear and it was understood that the Americans would write up the general opinion sections on the organizations, Biddle called for a vote on the six groups. All four senior judges agreed to hold that the SS, the Gestapo-SD, and the "Leadership Corps" of the Nazi party had been criminal organizations. Then the three Western judges joined together and, by successive votes of three to one, overrode Soviet objections and ruled that the Reich Cabinet, the SA, and the High Command and General Staff should not be declared to have been criminal.[62]

The actual voting was over very quickly, but, in contrast to other episodes in the deliberations, many of the most important features of the final organization ruling were not explicit in the vote; rather, they emerged in the wording of the general opinion and in the detailed findings for each specific group. The drafting of this section of the Judgment was completed in roughly two weeks and was carried through by Biddle, Parker, and the American judicial aides. Its dominant theme was embodied in a sentence that characterized group prosecution as "a far-reaching and novel procedure" that, "unless properly safeguarded," might "produce great injustice." [63] Underscoring the analogy with conspiracy, the opinion stated that knowledge of criminal purposes and voluntary membership were the defining characteristics for determining who was liable for punishment. The Tribunal also established a defining date for the three organizations declared criminal (the SS, the Gestapo-SD, and the "Leadership Corps" of the Nazi party): no individual would be held liable because of membership prior to the outbreak of the war on September 1, 1939.

The ruling noted the actions that the Allied occupation authorities had taken in regard to criminal organizations and rather sharply criticized them. The Control Council had passed Law #10, which was supposed to regulate organization prosecution in the four zones, but, as the Tribunal indicated in its opinion, it left the occupation courts with the option of assigning any penalty up to and including death for mere membership. Subsequently, the American authorities had passed a denazification law for their zone—the law General Clay had earlier mentioned to Assistant Secretary of War Peterson—that set specific, and more moderate, penalties for various war crimes, including the "crime" of organization membership. The Tribunal opinion recommended that the provisions of Control Council Law #10 be amended to coincide with those of the American denazification law and added that no individual should be subject to prosecution under both statutes. [64]

When the opinion prepared by the Americans came up for general discussion on September 26, 1946, the Soviets bitterly objected to its main provisions. They wanted no limitations placed on the occupation courts and no recommendations made to the Control Council on how it should conduct its business. Nikitchenko was especially determined in his opposition to the defining date of 1939 and once again recommended that the Nazi prewar acts in Germany should be made punishable. All this availed him nothing, however, and the general American formulation on criminal organizations was accepted by the Tribunal in a series of routine votes of three to one. [65]

Essentially, the same result occurred regarding the wording of the Court's rulings on the specific organizations, but most of this did not require formal votes. The reasons advanced to explain why three organizations had not been declared criminal contained no surprises. The SA was not considered significant enough after the Blood Purge of 1934 to justify prosecution; in the words of the Tribunal, it had become merely a collection of "unimportant Nazi hangerson." [66] Similarly, the people who made up the Reich Cabinet were too few in number to warrant a general ruling, especially since they, too, had lost their importance as a group after the middle 1930s. The small size of the High Command and General Staff was also mentioned as a reason for not declaring it criminal, but the chief reason the Court advanced for not making such a declaration was that the phrase "High Command and General Staff" was an artificial invention of the prosecution, and that the organization, as such, "did not exist except in the charge in the indictment." [67] Whatever the conduct of the men in question, to hold them liable for membership in a nonexistent organization was too much for the Tribunal. Nonetheless, the Court took the opportunity to note that these men were "responsible in large measure for the miseries and suffering that have fallen on millions of men, women, and children" and recommended that the guilty ones should be brought to trial individually. [68]

The qualifications spelled out by the Court for the three organizations that were declared criminal were obviously more significant and, in some of the cases, more complex. For the SS, Kaltenbrunner was taken as the representative defendant, and the Court went on to build up an overwhelming argument against the organization on the basis of the Tribunal's own rules and definitions. The instances of substantive crime were legion, and once the Court accepted Himmler's boastful accounts of the effectiveness of his indoctrination program—a very questionable conclusion, by the way [69]—it was easy to maintain that the bulk of the SS members had been informed of the criminal nature of the organization. Even so, the Court made two significant qualifications in its ruling in addition to the general time restriction that made it only applicable to the wartime period. Honorary members of the SS as well as the so-called SS equestrian units were excluded, and the Court underscored that no one who had been drafted into the SS and had not committed specific crimes was legally liable. [70]

The Court's ruling on the Gestapo-SD contained fewer important limitations. Not troubled by the prospect of using the same man to represent two organizations, the Tribunal again named Kaltenbrunner as the representative defendant. The possibility that a person might have joined the Gestapo without knowing of its criminal purposes seemed so remote to the Court that it did not even discuss the question directly. It merely cited the general "wartime only" rule and the necessity of establishing knowledge of criminal purposes before any individual could be convicted. Consequently, the only limitation emphasized by the Court was the exemption of specific subgroups. Following the suggestions made by the prosecution, those Gestapo-SD employees assigned to secretarial, janitorial, and other routine duties were dropped, as were the army intelligence officers who had been transferred to the SD in 1944–45. The Court also excluded a subgroup to which it gave the unusual name of non-SS "honorary informers," by which it presumably meant those neighborhood spies who were not members of Himmler's SS order and who had provided their dishonorable services without pay.[71]

The passages of the Judgment that applied to the "Leadership Corps" of the Nazi party were both complex and indicative of the factors that led the Tribunal to declare the group criminal. In the course of the trial and during the early stages of the deliberation, a number of judges showed doubt about the slender prosecution evidence applicable to the lower party officials, the *Zellenleiter* and *Blockleiter*. Concern similar to that expressed in Fisher's May memorandum also seems to have existed on the bench, namely, that there might be little to connect any member of the "Leadership Corps" to specific wartime crimes except those of mistreatment of Allied POWs and the possible incitement to lynch downed Allied fliers. In the last stages of the trial, however, the prosecution did produce some spotty evidence showing that the party organization was used to prevent rumors about the "final solution" of the Jewish question from gaining broad currency among the German civilian population. This item, together with extensive evidence indicating the important role the "Leadership Corps" performed in operating the slave-labor program for foreign workers, seems to have been decisive; at least, it convinced the American judges to declare the group criminal.[72] But the prosecution was less successful in proving to the Court that the bulk of the Nazi party officials should be held liable. Not only did the Tribunal exclude the staffs of the lower officials from the ruling, as the prosecution had suggested in its February presentation, but it also eliminated the whole lower party hierarchy, including the *Zellen-* and *Blockleiter*. Even on the higher organizational level, only the top three ranks of officials (*Reichs-*, *Kreis-*, and *Ortsgruppenleiter*), together with their immediate section chiefs, were covered, while all other officials and subordinate staff members were excluded. When this series of exclusions was added to the general limitation that nothing done before September 1939 was punishable and knowledge and voluntary membership had to be proven in every case, it was obvious that the ruling could have few harmful consequences for the members of the "Leadership Corps." [73]

These provisions moderating and circumscribing the specific criminal organization rulings were not agreeable to the Soviets and increased their dissatisfaction with the way the whole subject had been handled. As the trial and deliberation process progressed, the Soviet judges found themselves on the short end of a number of important votes and their unhappiness with the general situation became more obvious at the end. In the initial skirmishes it was not so clear that the Russians would be frequent losers, and, even late in the trial, other judges failed in crucial confrontations, for example Donnedieu de Vabres on conspiracy and Biddle on criminal organizations. But as these two incidents show, even when the Western judges lost the battle, they were still able, through rewordings or qualification, to make their points and to win the war. When the Soviets, however, lost a crucial vote, in part because of their unfamiliarity with the Western system, there was no tomorrow and they really lost. Nikitchenko tried to put a good face on the situation, but some of the discomfort of repeated defeat surely remained. The Soviet judges strove vigorously to reach agreements that would be acceptable to the Russian Government and thus allow the four Allies to maintain a united front in public.

Repeatedly, the judges emphasized to each other the vital importance of compromise in order to avoid the unpleasant appearance that would result if a judge wrote a public dissenting opinion. On a number of occasions, an individual Tribunal member had to choke down the impulse to write such a dissent, but, up to the very end, the appearance of unanimity was maintained. Again, this was especially difficult for the Soviet Tribunal members, not only because they were the most frequent losers, but because, when a Western judge failed to win a point, it was merely a defeat for his personal interpretation, while a Russian failure may have meant that the judge had not achieved the result desired by the Soviet government. By the end of the trial, pressures on Nikitchenko had reached stifling proportions, but even after the string of defeats on the organization question he still indicated that he would not make a public dissent.[74] The Court's actions on organizations goaded the Moscow government, though, and, shamefacedly, Nikitchenko had to inform the other judges that the Soviet members would write dissenting opinions and make them public, after all.

Of the resulting six Russian dissents, only two were on organizations, while the other four were on findings for individual defendants. The Soviets decried the failure to declare the Reich Cabinet a criminal organization, because, in the Russian view, the individual Cabinet members had possessed great power, and also because it was unrealistic to judge the members of the murderous "Hitler government" by the same rules as might apply to "an ordinary rank and file Cabinet." [75] Soviet disapproval of the ruling on the High Command and General Staff was even more intense; the Russians disputed both the Tribunal's conclusion that this was not a real group and the implication that it had not functioned as a leading organ in the establishment and execution of Nazi policies. Little evidence or argument was put forth by the Soviets to support either contention in their dissenting opinions, but a large number of incidents were cited to show the aggressive desires and ruthlessness of the Nazi military leaders. Clearly, the Soviets were dissatisfied not so much with the means by which the Tribunal had reached its conclusions as with the conclusions themselves; they felt that, whatever the legal difficulties, it was politically and psychologically necessary to condemn the Reich Cabinet and the High Command as well as the SS and the Gestapo.[76]

Significantly, the Soviets did not make any public dissent regarding the limitations that were contained in the findings on the organizations that were declared to have been criminal. They also did not protest the failure of the Court to declare the SA criminal, although Nikitchenko had voted to so declare it. This suggests that the Russians were not much interested in obtaining a mandate to carry out mass punishment of organization members—a prospect that had frightened both Jackson and the American judges—and, in fact, they did not carry out any general organization persecution. What they had apparently wanted was an Allied declaration discrediting the most prominent Nazi leaders and organizations and at the same time affixing to them the sole responsibility for the war and its attendant suffering and destruction. The Russians were prepared to let the SA slip by because of its minor importance as an instrument of Nazi policy and its marginal utility as a political symbol, but they wanted every other group condemned.

If this estimate is correct, there was probably no possible formula that would have satisfied the legal doubts of the Western judges and at the same time have given the Soviets the blanket condemnation they desired. The Americans, and to a degree the French, may have been pursuing hobgoblins when they strove to eliminate from the criminal organization rulings the worst threats to the civil liberties of individual members. Mass persecutions may not have followed in any case; however, the climate was ripe for mass reprisals in both the East and the West, and, if the Tribunal's ruling had been less circumscribed, many innocent people might well have been punished along with the guilty.

Given this situation, it is difficult to fault the general organization opinion that the Court wrote or the specific organization findings. As was revealed on the conspiracy issue, the Court performed most effectively when coping with complex and practical legal problems. When it entered the realm of abstract legal theory, as it did on the general question of the criminality of aggressive war, the results were disappointing. When the issue under consideration was a specific incident with strong political overtones, such as that of Norway or the Nazi-Soviet Pact, the results were sometimes outrageously unjust. But, in the middle zone, the Tribunal successfully resolved most of the important dilemmas and established definitions and rules that made relatively fair proceedings possible for both organizations and individuals.

With this accomplished, the phase of legal problem-solving was over for the Tribunal, and it had to turn to the life and death phase of its deliberations—the determination of the fate of the twenty-two defendants of Nuremberg was now at hand.

CHAPTER 7

Individual Verdicts: Hermann Goering to Seyss-Inquart

Goering looks like the Queen in "Alice."

Francis Biddle.[1]

T HE PROCEDURES used by the Tribunal to determine verdicts and sentences were neither novel nor particularly complicated. Between September 2 and September 10, the Court held a long series of exploratory sessions in which the judges expressed their views on each defendant and cast tentative ballots on guilt or innocence. Then, immediately following the last introductory discussion on September 10, the Court moved right into its second and final series of deliberations, which lasted from September 10 to September 13. In both the first and the second phases of the discussions, all eight judges were able to express their opinions and to vote on the charges facing the defendants. But in the final sessions only the votes of the four senior Tribunal members counted in determining the actual verdicts and sentences.[2] Article IV, section (c), of the London Charter provided that all convictions and sentences "shall be imposed by affirmative votes of at least three members of the Tribunal," which seems sufficiently straightforward, but on September 9, Nikitchenko, apparently chafing under a series of defeats on preliminary votes, unleashed a sharp but short-lived controversy by arguing that this provision did not mean that a two–two tie required acquittal. Nikitchenko apparently wanted to consign such cases to a kind of judicial limbo until they were retried, but his interpretation was defeated three to one and the principle that a minimum of three affirmative votes by senior Tribunal members was necessary to convict or set sentence was thereby firmly established before the final phase of the deliberations began on September 10.[3]

The discussions over defendants did produce a number of disagreements and protracted discussions on what modes of punishment were acceptable and appropriate. The judges wrangled over whether to confiscate the defendants' property and they also debated whether to include specific provisions that stolen property should be returned to its rightful owners. Apparently as much from exhaustion as from conviction, the Tribunal finally decided to ignore the whole property question, and it is not mentioned in the Judgment or in any of the verdicts.[4] The same fate finally overtook Donnedieu de Vabres's pet scheme that the Court should choose between giving a guilty defendant "honorable" detention or "dishonorable" incarceration. Although the Frenchman brought up this idea on every possible occasion, he never succeeded in making the distinction he had in mind clear to his colleagues, nor could he persuade them that a punishment based on honor was appropriate to any of the Nazi defendants. When Donnedieu de Vabres went on to suggest that shooting be used as a more honorable form of execution than hanging, he did manage to elicit a comment from Biddle suggesting that they employ hanging as the normal method and shooting as a form of "mitigation." But even the thought of using a form of capital punishment as a kind of mitigation did not catch Nikitchenko's fancy, and he decried the waste of time taken up by a discussion of what he termed "ridiculous trifles." [5] Nikitchenko thought that hanging should be the chief form of punishment, and in this he generally had his way, for, though the Tribunal handed down some prison sentences, invariably over Russian objections, it used hanging as the only form of capital punishment.

The Russians were less successful in their suggestion that defendants be declared guilty simply on the basis of the positions or posts they had held. Robert Falco, the French alternate, supported the Soviet idea just as Professor Gros (the French alternate at the London negotiations) had done, and even Lord Justice Lawrence seems to have spoken in favor of the idea during the deliberations. Donnedieu de Vabres and Biddle, however, were firmly opposed to this approach, so much so that in the midst of the discussion Biddle blurted out that it was "preposterous" to convict a little "Jew baiter" like Streicher, simply because he was "a friend of Hitler, or a Gauleitor, or a Nazi." Lawrence took offense at Biddle's remarks and, in one of the most heated altercations of the deliberations, accused him of having bad manners. But Judge Parker finally smoothed over the situation, and the idea of convicting individuals without a demonstration of their personal guilt was quietly shelved. With this, the last big hurdle in the way of deliberation on individual verdicts had been crossed.[6]

In the initial deliberative phase, the judges began by taking up the defendants in the sequence in which their names appeared in the indictment, starting with Goering and presumably ending with Fritzsche. From the first days, however, the discussions moved in such a meandering fashion that after consideration of the first handful of defendants, individuals were discussed and tentatively voted on pretty much at random. Despite this untidy appearance, the Court did give substantial consideration to most of the individual cases, and it also eliminated one technical problem by deciding, in principle, that, if there were inconsistencies between the general sections of the indictment and the long appendix specifying the charges against individuals, the appendix should rule.[7] When the final deliberative phase came around on September 10, the judges again started to move through the defendants in the same order in which they appeared in the indictment, but because of the preliminary discussions the Tribunal members knew which cases were likely to produce the most serious disagreements. Consequently, six defendants—Schirach, Raeder, Doenitz, Papen, Schacht, and Fritzsche—were removed from the regular sequence and considered at the end. Since this final deliberation was the decisive one, the cases of the twenty-two defendants will be presented here using the same sequence of names the Court followed between September 10 and September 13.

Hermann Goering

In the absence of the dead Adolf Hitler, Reich Marshal Hermann Goering was the perfect representative defendant for the Nazi regime. He had joined Hitler's movement in the early 1920s and occupied many of the most powerful and honored positions of the party and state during the Third Reich. He had led the SA during the early days, presided over the formation of the Gestapo, headed the Four-Year Plan for rearmament, established the new German *Luftwaffe* (Air Force), and commanded it during the whole war. At every significant decision-making conference, Goering was at Hitler's elbow, and his proximity to the center of power was formalized by Hitler's decision that, in the event of his own death, Goering should succeed him as Führer. Goering's authority and influence covered military, diplomatic, and domestic political and economic questions, thus giving him a transcendent responsibility for the policies and actions of the Nazi system.

Throughout his years of glory, Goering cultivated the reputation of himself as a man more of power than of ideology, tough and practical, relishing political realism above all. When the war began to go badly for Germany and many of the other Nazi leaders reacted by striving for new levels of fanaticism, Goering responded in a manner peculiarly in tune with his sense of practical realism: he retreated to his estate at Karinhall to indulge in debauchery for as long as the good days lasted. From time to time, he roused himself to attend the Führer or perfunctorily perform his official duties, but, by and large, the years 1942–45 were an unusually long, lost weekend for Hermann Goering. In the last days of the regime, while Hitler played out his hand in a bunker in Berlin, Goering managed to reach southern Germany. From there, he made the mistake of telegraphing Hitler to ask if the time had come for him to succeed as Führer. After putting up with Goering's useless self-indulgence for three years, Hitler enthusiastically seized this opportunity to gain his revenge and promptly ordered Goering's arrest. The Reich Marshal, therefore, ended the war by suffering the triple indignity of being a prisoner of narcotics, obesity, and the Gestapo.

The six months he spent in Allied custody, from the time of Germany's capitulation until the start of the trial, helped Goering greatly. He lost weight, freed himself from his drug habit, and in countless interrogations recovered much of his old vigor and combativeness. By the third week of October, when Major Neave and Adrian Fisher officially informed him of the procedure to be used for selecting a counsel, Goering was well aware of his rights and took the occasion to point out what he thought were inequities in the London Charter.[8] A British Foreign Office representative, who was present during one of his interrogations in early November, noted that Goering showed no signs of being a "cowed and defeated enemy" but "was obviously enjoying this opportunity to air his views." In the Englishman's opinion, Goering was an "unashamedly unrepentant gangster." [9]

Even so, defendant Goering faced a nearly impossible situation. He had been on every Allied roster of major war criminals since the British prepared their first lists in April 1944, and the Four Powers had thereby been in a position to gather a very large body of evidence against him.[10] Unless the prosecution failed to prove every single part of its case or the Court decided to throw out all the charges, nothing could save Goering, because he had some measure of responsibility for virtually everything that had been done in the Third Reich. His only asset was his personal formidability, which might make the prosecutors hesitate before taking him on in an open court fight.

At least one of them, American deputy prosecutor and head of the OSS, General William Donovan, decided on the eve of the trial that a confrontation with Goering was not desirable. In response to an overture from the Reich Marshal, Donovan made a tentative agreement with Goering and his counsel in mid-November whereby Goering would answer a questionnaire made up by the prosecution, and, once the questions and answers had been agreed to by both sides, he would take the stand and give his testimony in open court. Although, in a letter written in November, Donovan stressed to Jackson that he had not negotiated or made a "bargain" with Goering, he also acknowledged that the American prosecutors had agreed that no proposal for a defendant to testify on behalf of the prosecution would be permitted unless he had made written statements that "incriminated other defendants." [11] In another message to Jackson, Donovan declared flatly that, during his interviews with Goering, the latter had "already incriminated certain of the defendants." [12] Apparently, the Donovan-Goering discussions did not progress far enough to be called plea bargaining, but they were very close to it, and Donovan attached great importance to them because he felt that "a confession from the last sane leader of the gang" might be the best "practical means of bringing home to the German people the guilt of these men." [13] Jackson, however, did not agree and vetoed Donovan's work with Goering. A sharp exchange over this and related matters resulted, and shortly after the trial began Donovan resigned and returned to the United States. [14]

With the abandonment of the Donovan plan, Goering had no choice but to assume the role of champion of the regime and use all his abilities to hold the other defendants in line in order to mount the best possible defense of the Nazi system. His performance during the cross-examination duel with Jackson was the high point of this campaign and must have given him particular satisfaction because it had been Jackson who had blocked Goering's effort to cooperate with the prosecution. The skill with which the Reich Marshal performed his role was not lost on the Court, and a number of judges noted during the trial that he showed unusual intelligence and was adept in dominating the other defendants. But when he became too crass in his efforts, as he did in trying to bully Schacht's defense witness, Hans Gisevius, he confronted a determinedly hostile group of judges, including Francis Biddle, who was very angered by the incident. [15]

Yet none of these dramatic courtroom affairs had any significant bearing on the Tribunal's verdict on Goering; in a stand-up fight he could frustrate individual prosecutors, but he could not defeat the indictment or the legal definitions and categories established by the Tribunal. He had been charged under all four counts, and, as both the summary of his case prepared by James Rowe in May and the final Judgment pointed out, he had, during his career, performed virtually every form of criminal act that the Tribunal held punishable. He had participated in the preparation of every "aggressive war plan" and in the launching of each of the actual attacks. He had helped establish and carry out the programs for looting art, plundering the economies of the occupied territories, and maltreating and killing prisoners of war. Goering even had the distinction of having signed the only extant written order that gave Heydrich responsibility for preparing the "final solution" of "the Jewish question." [16]

On September 2, the Court finished its first-phase consideration of his case in nearly record speed. Donnedieu de Vabres reserved his decision on Count One (Conspiracy), as he would do for every defendant until he was tentatively satisfied by Biddle's compromise formula completed on September 5. But this was the only qualification and otherwise the Court unanimously agreed that Goering was guilty on all four counts.[17] When his case came up in the second round, on September 10, the judges were in as complete agreement and worked just as fast. The best that any of them had to say was Donnedieu de Vabres's characterization of him as a "high-class brigand," but that was not much protection in a trial for life and death.[18] All eight judges held Goering guilty on the four counts and voted for a sentence of death. Donnedieu de Vabres wanted him shot, but the other judges favored hanging, and, by a vote of three to one, Goering was sentenced to death by hanging.[19]

Rudolf Hess

Like Goering, Hess was an early Nazi who later rose to high position in party and state. He was an even closer personal confidant of the Führer's, and, as a reward for his devotion, Hitler named him his alternate successor in the unlikely event of the demise of both Hitler and Goering. Hess did not expand his authority and gobble up offices and honors the way the Reich Marshal did. Instead, for many years he remained at his post as the Führer's deputy for party affairs, and, with Martin Bormann as his assistant, ruled over the party apparatus in Hitler's name. His fall from grace came much earlier than did Goering's. Apparently suffering from the lack of importance in his wartime role, as well as from mental instability, Hess flew to Great Britain in the spring of 1941 in an effort to dazzle the world by producing peace between Britain and Germany. Instead of praise and acclaim, however, he received four years in British captivity and a denunciation from his beloved Führer, who characterized him as a madman.

Hess's 1941 flight significantly affected his trial. Throughout the remainder of the war, the Soviet government was gripped by a suspicion that some sinister British-Nazi arrangement lurked behind the flight. A few days after Hess landed in Scotland, Germany invaded the Soviet Union, and Stalin was apparently convinced that Hess's mission was to negotiate a deal for common action against Russia. In this he was definitely right, but Stalin also seemed to believe that the subsequent British captivity of Hess was done so he would be available should they ever decide to arrange a separate peace and a common Anglo-German war against Russia. Between 1941 and 1945, Moscow used diplomatic and public pressure to hammer the British on this point, even though the London government tried repeatedly to assure the Russians that they had no dastardly intentions of using Hess to help them escape from the war or to plot anti-Soviet activities.[20] The easiest way for the British to have escaped from the difficulty would seem to have been to place Hess on trial and then to have executed him. Aside from the obvious fact that he had done nothing to violate their law, the British were reluctant to start wartime trials and executions for fear that it would set off a chain reaction leading to Nazi execution of British POWs.

So throughout the war the British held on to Hess and endured Soviet pressure and insult, but, when the time came for planning the postwar fate of major Nazi war criminals, the British were anxious to push him forward. The War Office—but not the Foreign Office—already had him on a major war criminal list in April 1944.[21] By May 1945, when General Donovan asked the British whether Hess should be designated a war criminal, officials in London showed themselves very sympathetic to the idea, and he was included in the British list of the ten top Nazi war criminals that they put together in June.[22] Although the Americans also placed him on their June 1945 list of the sixteen top criminals, Jackson indicated some reluctance to prosecute him because of his mental condition.[23] But throughout the summer and fall, the British never slackened in their zeal to prosecute Hess, regardless of Jackson's doubts, and, when Stalin implied at Potsdam that the British might be trying to hold back on Hess, Atlee appeared boundless in his eagerness to push Hess before the Court.[24] Similarly, during the Tribunal's hearing on his sanity held in late November, it was the British deputy prosecutor, Maxwell Fyfe, who advocated that Hess be tried, even if he suffered from amnesia, as long as it could be established that he understood the proceedings—a view of legal sanity so singular that Biddle wrote in his notes that it was "damned lawyer's bull at first blush."[25]

The Tribunal's willingness to make Hess stand trial regardless of his mental condition was determined, however, by more than Soviet and British pressure. In the early stages of the trial, the judges had not taken each other's measure and were reluctant to assume positions that clashed dramatically with the case prepared by the prosecution and the uncompromising mood of the general public. The reports of the investigating psychiatrists showed much hesitation and qualification, but in the end they suggested that Hess was capable of standing trial.[26] During the Court hearing regarding his sanity on November 30, the central question was whether he was malingering; Biddle's notes indicate that the judges felt he was, although they disagreed on the best procedure to follow.[27] Donnedieu de Vabres and Biddle wanted Hess to speak to the judges in hopes that they would be enabled thereby to take some measure of the situation.[28] After initially opposing this idea, the rest of the members ultimately went along, and Lawrence invited Hess to speak; his resulting "confession" indicating that he had been simulating amnesia unexpectedly solved the most pressing problem for the Tribunal. The petition by Hess's attorney requesting that his case be severed was immediately denied and Hess was ordered to stand trial with the other defendants. But this solution has left a long shadow hanging over the trial for thirty years: Hess's amnesia does not seem to have been feigned; rather, it was his "confession" that he was normal and competent that seems to have been the real fantasy.

Hess played no part in preparing his own defense; he refused to take the stand, and his attorney was forced to put forth a perfunctory case based on slender documentation and marginal witnesses. The impression that these circumstances helped to produce a miscarriage of justice is increased by the fact that the prosecution's case against Hess was not very strong. He was charged under all four counts, but as Robert Stewart pointed out in the report he prepared for Biddle and Parker in May and June 1945, there was little or no evidence to link Hess with the commission of War Crimes or Crimes Against Humanity. On the other hand, Stewart thought that there was a better case for Hess's responsibility in preparing for the invasions of Austria and Czechoslovakia; the prosecution had stressed the fifth-column activities of the party's foreign branch (*Auslandsorganisation*) in the aggression against these two countries, and Hess had held authority over the party and its subordinate organizations. This contention was accepted by Stewart, who also pointed to Hess's direct, if limited, personal involvement in the Austrian and Czech operations. Still, there were only a few vague hints that Hess had prior knowledge of these military invasion plans, and for the subsequent attacks on Poland and other countries there was virtually no direct prosecution evidence that he had played an impor-

tant role. Hess had signed the decrees by which Austria, the Sude-
tenland, and areas of Poland were made part of the Reich, but all
these actions came after the invasions. Stewart toyed with the possibility that Hess had flown to England "in connection" with the plans
to attack Russia, but concluded that, although there were many im-
probabilities in his tale, "extremely strong evidence" would have
been required to prove that the flight was part of a conspiracy, and
that kind of evidence simply did not exist at Nuremberg. Stewart's
general conclusion was that Hess should be held responsible for
Crimes Against Peace simply because his duties involved many activities related to the invasions and because he enjoyed extremely
close relations with Hitler. Without directly confronting the prosecution's contention that a high position in state and party of necessity
made a man a collaborator in a criminal enterprise, Stewart held that
Hess should be found guilty of Crimes Against Peace because it was
"unthinkable" that he did not know what was going on.[29]

In the summary of the Hess case that the Tribunal attached to its
verdict, little mark of Stewart's language is noticeable, but the argument is very similar. The Court de-emphasized the role of the *Auslandsorganisation* in Czechoslovakia and Austria (a sensible decision,
for subsequent evidence has shown that popular stories about this
group's activities were greatly exaggerated), and it followed Stewart
in holding Hess innocent on Counts Three and Four. Hess was also
found not guilty of being the agent of a conspiracy during his flight to
Scotland. The specific reasons which the Court advanced for finding
Hess guilty of Crimes Against Peace appear rather trivial: his preparatory activities in Austria and Czechoslovakia; a public speech in
which he praised Hitler and criticized Britain, France, and Poland
in 1939; and his approval of the decrees subsequently incorporating
all or part of the countries that the Nazis overran. The major consideration cited by the Tribunal was the same as that which had been
stressed by Stewart: Hess was guilty because as Hitler's "closest confidant" he "must have been informed of Hitler's aggressive
plans." [30]

What makes the Court's statement on the Hess case so distasteful
is that, after both Stewart and Biddle had questioned convicting a
man on the basis of his position without definite evidence of personal
criminality, Hess was found guilty on precisely this basis. In broad
historical terms this issue is not of much importance, for the governing system of the Third Reich bore little relation to formal legal

conspiracies. Rudolf Hess knew enough of the Nazi style, of innuendo and code words, of suggestion and implication, to understand that Germany's neighbors, and especially the *"Untermenschen"* at home and abroad, were not in for a picnic once Hitler got his hands on power. But during the Third Reich, and especially in the war years, Hitler simply did not sit around revealing his inner thoughts and specific plans to anyone. Hess was close enough to the seat of power and had been associated with the movement long enough to draw some obvious conclusions, if, in fact, he was of sane mind. That was also true of Hermann Goering, Franz von Papen, Martin Bormann, Albert Speer, and many others. Yet, in the latter cases, as well as those of the other defendants, the Court required a clear showing of personal knowledge of a criminal purpose or plan. Only Hess and perhaps Frick were found guilty of conspiracy on the basis of thin evidence and the assertion that they had a close personal relationship with the Führer. Of course, this does not mean that Hess was innocent, for, in another trial with different rules or perhaps in a different jurisdiction, he could have been convicted easily; but at Nuremberg, Hess clearly fell victim to a double standard.

The surviving records throw no light on how the Court came to this peculiar conclusion, but they do indicate the process that led to the decision to sentence him to life in prison. In the preliminary session that occurred on September 2, all the Tribunal members agreed that Hess should be found guilty on Counts One and Two but the Western judges indicated that they harbored some hesitation about convicting him on Counts Three and Four. Nikitchenko also paused over these counts but was inclined toward conviction. Only the Soviet alternate, Volchkov, argued strongly that Hess be convicted on Counts Three and Four, and he cited Hess's signature on the Nuremberg decrees (the harshly discriminatory legal code against Jews established in 1935) as evidence that Hess was guilty of the mass murder of Jews—a comment that caused Biddle to remark in his notes that the Soviets were indeed going to be "extreme." [31] When the Hess case came up for final consideration on September 10, Falco, the French alternate, opened the consideration by arguing that he was guilty on all four counts and should receive a life sentence. Donnedieu de Vabres then voted Hess guilty on Counts One and Two (Conspiracy and Crimes Against Peace) and not guilty on Counts Three and Four (War Crimes and Crimes Against Humanity), and spoke in favor of a sentence of approximately twenty years.

Parker and Biddle advocated convicting Hess on Counts One and Two, but not on Counts Three and Four, and sentencing him to life. The two Soviet members voted him guilty on all four counts and called for a death sentence. Norman Birkett was not present for the vote, presumably because of his work drafting the general opinion, but Lord Justice Lawrence held Hess guilty on all four counts and wanted him to be given a punishment of life imprisonment. Hess was therefore found guilty on Counts One and Two, but, on the basis of the rule that a two-two tie meant acquittal, he was found not guilty on Counts Three and Four, because the votes of Donnedieu de Vabres and Biddle canceled out those of Lawrence and Nikitchenko.[32]

Since the Tribunal was also deadlocked on the question of an appropriate sentence, Falco recommended that first they vote on whether to impose death, then on life imprisonment, and, finally, on a term of years, with the understanding that the first sentence to receive three votes by senior members would be final. This suggestion was adopted, and the death penalty quickly lost, with Nikitchenko outvoted three to one. After an initial two-two standoff on a life sentence, Biddle's notes indicate that Nikitchenko switched his vote and joined Biddle and Lawrence to overcome Donnedieu de Vabres and a life sentence was imposed on Hess by a three to one vote. The Soviet judge presumably realized that if he had not supported a life sentence, the two-two deadlock might have been resolved by an Anglo-American compromise agreement with Donnedieu de Vabres for a sentence of twenty to thirty years.[33]

The voting method used in the Hess case had a number of ironic and significant consequences. By advocating this procedure, the French alternate, Falco, was able to obtain the sentence on Hess that he wanted, life imprisonment, while thwarting the effort of the senior French judge to grant him a lighter sentence. Whether Falco clearly foresaw that this would be the result of his suggestion is impossible to say, but the incident should provide a note of caution to those who are eager to assert that the judges' actions simply implemented the policies of their respective Allied governments. The subsequent Soviet reaction to the life sentence that was given to Hess points even more strongly in the same direction, for this was the only individual sentence on which the Russians issued a public dissenting opinion, and we now know not only that Nikitchenko voted for life, but that his was the deciding vote. Nikitchenko apparently had found himself in a difficult and unforeseen situation without adequate instructions when he faced the two-two deadlock and he had made the best decision he could. Only later, in conjunction with the three individual acquittals and the rulings on the High Command and the Cabinet, did the Soviet government decide to issue public dissents. The Soviet statement on the Hess case would therefore appear to have been a last-minute afterthought and no weight should be attached to the argument advanced therein when trying to trace the steps that led to the verdict and sentence, except as it points to the general views held by Soviet officials. Predictably, the dissent stressed that Hess's mission to Great Britain was part of the plan to attack the Soviet Union and it also held him guilty for contributing to the development of the SS system and the harsh occupation rules in the conquered Eastern territories.[34] The dissent was another episode in the Soviet *idée fixe* that Hess had to be eliminated because he symbolized the threat of a Western coalition against the USSR.

Both the haunting Soviet fear and the Tribunal's questionable rulings on Hess have a continuing relevancy. All the other actions taken at Nuremberg are dispassionately historical and beyond the reach of living men. Most of the defendants are dead, and the handful of survivors are out of captivity. All, that is, except Rudolf Hess, who is still alone in Spandau prison, still of questionable mental competency, and still there because of dubious actions by the Tribunal and the obstinacy of the Soviet government.

Joachim von Ribbentrop

Unlike Goering and Hess, Ribbentrop was not an early member of the Nazi movement but came to Hitler during the immediate drive for power in the early 1930s. He held a series of advisory posts in the first years of the Third Reich, became ambassador to England in the mid-1930s, and occupied the position of foreign minister from 1938 until 1945. All the Allied governments considered Ribbentrop a prime prospective defendant in any proceeding against Nazi war criminals, and he was on every Western Allied war criminal planning list, beginning with the two British lists prepared in April 1944.[35] When the Americans decided that their major emphasis would fall on an aggressive war conspiracy, Ribbentrop became even more important, and, after his capture, the prosecutor's office asked the State Department to remember Ribbentrop's central position in the case and to keep his "involvement" constantly in mind when doing research and collecting documents.[36]

During the 1950s, Ribbentrop's widow tried to demonstrate that her husband's case had been highly controversial, but the available evidence shows that the Court did not share Frau Ribbentrop's view.[37] Both Fisher's preparatory memorandum and the summary in the final Judgment emphasized Ribbentrop's direct involvement in intimidating the prospective victims of German attacks and extensive evidence was cited to show that he knew of many of the attack plans. Fisher concluded that to believe Ribbentrop did not know of invasion plans would be "to strain human credulity past the breaking point."[38] Neither the Tribunal nor Fisher put much stock in the prosecution's effort to make the foreign minister responsible for the system of control and repression in the occupied territories, but they did heavily emphasize the deep and prolonged involvement of Ribbentrop and the Foreign Ministry in carrying out the deportations for the extermination of the Jews. Subsequent scholarship has muted the validity of the general war planning charge against Ribbentrop, but it has done nothing to weaken the evidence on his involvement in preparing invasions, and it has greatly increased the evidence showing the crucial role his organization played in the deportations.[39]

The only misgivings about the Ribbentrop case that members of the Tribunal seem to have voiced at the time concerned the long-winded irrelevance of his defense and the pitiable impression that he made on the Court. It was, as Norman Birkett remarked in his diary, as if "the main spring of his life [has] broken."[40] With an overwhelming body of evidence against him tailored perfectly to fit the legal categories established by the Tribunal, such as participation in specific war planning, nothing Ribbentrop or his counsel did could conceivably affect the result. In the first deliberative session on September 2, Donnedieu de Vabres made a temporary reservation on the conspiracy charge, but otherwise all the judges voted Ribbentrop guilty on the four counts.[41] On September 10, during the second session, the seven judges (Birkett was working on the opinion again) held him guilty on the four counts; Donnedieu de Vabres voted for the death penalty but did not specify the mode of execution, while the other six judges held that it should be death by hanging. The verdict of guilty on all four counts and the sentence of death by hanging was thereby reached very quickly and without a trace of serious disagreement.[42]

Field Marshal Wilhelm Keitel

Keitel was a career army officer who, prior to 1933, had not been particularly sympathetic to the Nazis and was never a member of the Nazi party. Until 1938, he was chief of staff to the minister of war, General Werner von Blomberg, and, when Hitler reorganized the military command structure in February, Keitel became chief of the OKW (The *Oberkommando der Wehrmacht*, or High Command of the armed forces). He did not have direct command functions or great personal stature among his fellow army officers, and, as the judgment correctly indicated, he was merely the head of Hitler's military staff. However, in this position Keitel participated in the general and detailed preparations for every Nazi attack and invasion, and he also signed nearly every order affecting military War Crimes or Crimes Against Humanity. The case against Keitel was so conclusive, if viewed in the terms established by the Charter and the Tribunal, that in May 1946 Rowe was able to summarize the whole case in five short pages. This memorandum, including the recommendation that the Court make a finding of guilty on all four counts because "there is nothing in mitigation," was printed almost word for word in the final Judgment.[43]

After the trial, some critics who felt it was both unprecedented and dangerous to ban the defense of superior orders tried to put forward various defenses for Keitel, and one of them went so far as to refer to him as "this eminent soldier." [44] But during the war the Allied governments had held no such estimate of him and the only major war criminal list on which he did not appear was the British War Office roster prepared in April 1944. By the summer of 1945, the British Government was as determined to try him as were the Americans,[45] and, when the trial started, it was the defense that was most troubled by the existence of Keitel. His actions had been so extreme and the evidence against him was so overwhelming that he threatened the general effort of the defense to prevent the designation of the High Command and General Staff as a criminal organization.[46]

Until the last portion of the trial, the representatives of the Court saw him as a weak, if not pathetic, instrument of crime. To Neave, in October 1945, he appeared "confused and shaken," [47] while later Biddle considered him the prototype of the criminally pliant general and Birkett thought that during the trial he had grown "older, greyer, and more grizzled." [48] In his testimony and cross-examination he frankly admitted his own weakness and went a long way toward admitting his own guilt, thereby producing one of the most honest and touching defense presentations made during the proceedings. By trial's end, as both Biddle and Birkett noted, the field marshal had managed to pull himself together, and in his final plea showed that he wanted to die like a brave man.[49]

The deliberations on his fate were the shortest of those for any of the defendants. On September 2, without any sign of discussion, all the judges agreed that he was guilty on all four counts; eight days later, the French made a reservation on the mode of execution, but all the judges held that he should be executed because of his guilt on the four counts, and all but the French wanted to hang him.[50] In a brief discussion on September 12, the French specified that they wanted him shot, not hanged, and Biddle hesitated because, although he wanted Keitel hanged, he favored using the firing squad to execute another defendant. But Nikitchenko and Lawrence held firmly for a blanket system of hanging and Biddle finally gave way and joined them. Keitel was sentenced to death by hanging.[51]

Ernst Kaltenbrunner

Even more than Ribbentrop or Keitel, Kaltenbrunner was doomed from the beginning, or before the beginning, of the trial. Whatever the Court decided on general legal questions such as conspiracy, only a miracle could have saved this hulking Austrian lawyer who served as Himmler's chief deputy from 1943 until the end of the regime. He was a long-time party member, SS man, and Nazi police official who gradually moved into the position of secret police chief and executioner after Heydrich was assassinated in 1942. As chief of the RSHA (*Reichsicherheitshauptamt,* or Central Security Office), he presided over the SD and the Gestapo, including such subsections as the one used by Adolf Eichmann to carry out the "final solution of the Jewish question." Although Kaltenbrunner went right on issuing murderous directives and execution orders until the last days of the Third Reich, he seems, like Himmler, to have been oblivious to the frightful reputation he had acquired at home and abroad. In March and April 1945, while Himmler was trying his hand at negotiation with the Allies in Sweden, Kaltenbrunner attempted to accomplish the same result in Switzerland by passing himself off as the leader of an Austrian opposition to Nazi extremism.[52] Neither Himmler nor Kaltenbrunner ever seems to have grasped why the Western Powers held that they were not suitable figures with whom to discuss anything. After wandering aimlessly until he fell into Allied hands, Himmler committed suicide, but Kaltenbrunner, though awash with self-pity and constantly proclaiming his innocence, let himself be routinely taken into custody and then submitted to incarceration and trial.

A look at the Allied preparations for war crimes trials might have enlightened Kaltenbrunner about the gravity of the situation he faced, for, since April 1944, he had been featured on every Allied list of major war criminals, and beginning in July 1945, the American prosecution staff made special efforts to prepare an overwhelming case "against RSHA, its criminal components and officials, and its head, Ernst Kaltenbrunner." [53] But Kaltenbrunner was in no mood to face the harsh realities; in prison he was overcome by periods of uncontrolled weeping, and he told the Tribunal's representative in October 1945 that he had great difficulty concentrating. In his depressed state he was unable to sleep properly and he was especially "afraid of appearing in court in shabby clothes." [54]

Then, just three days before the trial was to begin, Kaltenbrunner suffered a brain hemorrhage that hospitalized him and kept him out of the dock for the first three weeks of the proceedings. While he was gone, his fellow defendants were served a generous portion of evidence chronicling the horrors that Kaltenbrunner and his subordinates had perpetrated during the war years. It was very convenient for the other twenty defendants to plead pristine innocence and to place all the blame for these monstrosities on the absent Kaltenbrunner. When Kaltenbrunner recovered sufficiently to return to the courtroom, he received a chilly reception from the other defendants, but was the object of warm solicitude from the Allied authorities, who wanted to make certain that their representative defendant for the cases against the SS, the SD, and the Gestapo stayed alive until the end of the trial.

Somewhere in this process, Kaltenbrunner was pulled out of his worst depression by the determination to put up a vigorous struggle in his own defense. The prosecution had made use of some of his personal enemies in RSHA, such as Walter Schellenberg, as witnesses against him, and this may have helped persuade him to fight for revenge, no matter what the odds. With only minimal assistance from his lawyer, Kaltenbrunner prepared a series of defense arguments that, in their disregard of the facts, are quite remarkable. On the stand, he claimed that he had not been in charge of the Gestapo or other security police offices, because these units had been ruled directly by Himmler and the immediate chief of the Gestapo, Heinrich Mueller. He pleaded that he had not known of most of the atrocities, but that he had attempted to ameliorate bad conditions when they were brought to his attention. Faced by numerous incriminating documents bearing his name, Kaltenbrunner tried every possible stratagem to explain them away and, when all else failed, flatly denied that his signatures on the documents were genuine. The vigor of his denials struck a note of wonder in some of the observers in the courtroom, and one of the German defense attorneys subsequently referred to him matter-of-factly as "the man without a signature [*der Mann ohne Unterschrift*]." [55] Even some of the judges were impressed with his determination, and here and there he convinced Birkett and Biddle that a few details in the accusations against him were probably false.[56] Yet, no matter how devoted to the game of winning he may have been, Kaltenbrunner had no real chance of prevailing against the mountain of evidence the prosecution had amassed against him.

Like all the other defendants, he had been charged with Conspiracy under Count One, and he had also been held for War Crimes (Count Three) and Crimes Against Humanity (Count Four), but he had not been charged under Count Two, Crimes Against Peace. Fisher's preparatory memorandum on his case concluded that there was "very little evidence" linking him to war planning and therefore it would be "difficult to sustain count I." [57] But on War Crimes and Crimes Against Humanity the evidence was overwhelming and Fisher believed that Kaltenbrunner's assertions of his innocence and ignorance were both "inconceivable" and lacking in all supporting evidence.[58] When the judges began to consider the case on September 2, a surprisingly long and divisive discussion ensued. None of the judges had any hesitation about Kaltenbrunner's guilt on Counts Three and Four, but there was a sharp division on whether he should be held guilty under the conspiracy count (One). To add to the confusion, Biddle casually remarked that it might be possible to hold him under Count Two, even though he had not been specifically so charged in the indictment appendix section that treated his case. By citing sections of the general indictment that covered the role of RSHA on aggressive war, it could be asserted that an implied aggressive war charge could be made against Kaltenbrunner.[59] But having dropped this unusual interpretation into the discussion, Biddle immediately backed away from it and voted to hold Kaltenbrunner guilty only on Counts Three and Four.[60] In this vote he was joined by Falco and Donnedieu de Vabres, who also believed that Biddle's idea of a new charge under Count Two should be forgotten and that Kaltenbrunner should also be found innocent on Count One. Lawrence, Birkett, Parker, and possibly Volchkov also rejected the addition of Count Two but voted to hold Kaltenbrunner on Counts One, Three, and Four. Only Nikitchenko seized on Biddle's idea of a new charge and voted Kaltenbrunner guilty on all four counts.[61]

In the final session on September 10, Falco, Donnedieu de Vabres, and Biddle again voted to hold him only on Counts Three and Four. In this view, they were joined by Parker, who decided that Kaltenbrunner was not guilty under Count One, after all. Birkett was again absent from this session, but Lawrence held to the position that both had taken earlier, namely, that Kaltenbrunner should be convicted on Counts One as well as on Counts Three and Four. Nikitchenko, this time seconded by Volchkov, held to his opinion that a charge of Crime Against Peace (Count Two) should be added, and voted for Kaltenbrunner's guilt on the four counts. Kaltenbrunner was thereby unanimously found guilty under Counts Three and Four, not guilty on Count Two by a vote of three to one, and not guilty on Count One by reason of a two-two tie (Biddle and Donnedieu de Vabres versus Nikitchenko and Lawrence).[62]

On the issue of life or death, there was no disagreement; the judges unanimously sentenced Kaltenbrunner to death by hanging.[63]

Alfred Rosenberg

Rosenberg was a Baltic German, born a subject of the Russian tsar, who had received his higher education at the University of Moscow. His life in Russia was disrupted and then made impossible by World War I, the resulting revolution, and the chaotic conditions associated with the civil war. Fleeing to Munich, Rosenberg quickly gained entry to extreme rightist political circles and established a reputation as a conservative, anti-Communist, and anti-Semitic theorist. Of the defendants at Nuremberg, Rosenberg was the only one who claimed to be a thinker, and, like Julius Streicher, had enjoyed a modest stature among Bavarian rightists "before Hitler came." But Rosenberg had never been a very important politician, and in the early 1920s he quickly slipped into Hitler's orbit, becoming the editor of the Nazi party's main newspaper, the *Völkischer Beobachter*, and preening himself as the philosopher of the Nazi movement. He published a number of transcendently dull and pretentious theoretical works championing Nazi racist ideas, and these books were trumpeted as achievements of great wisdom by the party's propagandists and press hacks. But they never sold well until their inclusion in the list of official publications of the Third Reich and the available evidence suggests that they exerted no significant influence on the thinking of Hitler or of any other leading Nazis. Rosenberg was regarded as a dreamy, impractical, almost comic figure by the band of activists who surrounded the Führer, although Hitler himself was more indulgent of Rosenberg's foibles because he was an "old fighter." It was an open secret that Hitler did not take Rosenberg's official philosopher rule seriously, however, and that he frequently indicated to his intimates that he had never read Rosenberg's magnum opus, *Der Mythus des 20. Jahrhunderts (The Myth of the 20th Century)*.

The men who constituted the inner core of Nazi leaders during the Third Reich had many of the characteristics of a group of high school boys. They constantly circled around Hitler, showing their strength, determination, and aggressiveness in order to impress him. In a crisis, those who posed as tough, loyal henchmen and advocated the most ruthless course usually gained Hitler's favor. Gradually, those with doubts or scruples, as well as those who were not prepared to sacrifice everything in the game of extremism, slipped out of the inner circle and in the final years, with poetic justice, Hitler was left alone with the three ultimate fanatics, Goebbels, Bormann, and Himmler.

Obviously, a man such as Rosenberg, who had chosen to present himself as a thinker, suffered under serious handicaps in such a system. Predictably, he tried from time to time to join the ranks of the strutting men of action and show that he, too, could carry out the practical duties of a political leader. When Hitler was imprisoned in 1924, Rosenberg briefly directed one of the interim organizations that was established for members of the outlawed Nazi party. After Hitler became Chancellor in 1933, Rosenberg was appointed to a number of offices nominally concerned with foreign policy and the supervision of education, but, in fact, he had little real power. During the first phases of World War II, Rosenberg had a brief moment of importance by arranging the contacts between Hitler, German naval officers, and the Quisling circle, which facilitated the German invasion of Norway. In the campaign against the Low Countries and France, he was charged with the duty of gathering in the cultural loot and the *Einsatzstab* (Special Organization) *Rosenberg*, was responsible for sacking the art resources of Europe. On the eve of the attack on the Soviet Union, this philosopher who had preached the dangers of Bolshevism was charged with preparing and directing the system of civil administration to be used in the occupied Eastern territories. On paper, Hitler made Rosenberg the all-powerful tsar of the conquered Soviet peoples, but in reality he received the responsibility for directing the system while much of the power was given to a group of tough, practical men of action, such as Erich Koch and Heinrich Lohse, who served as Rosenberg's nominal deputies. At the same time, the military forces in Russia, and Himmler's SS and police apparatus as well, were almost totally outside Rosenberg's control. It was a classic instance of Hitler's system of divided and competing authority which he repeatedly used to help secure his position as supreme ruler. Rosenberg found that he could not operate successfully against his political competitors without Hitler's support, and here again he suffered from his old liability of being unable to impress the Führer as genuine, swashbuckling, and ruthless. Until the end, Rosenberg was gripped by the passion, characteristic of a boy on the fringe, to be a full-fledged member of the gang, but only very late could he sufficiently overcome his muddled reflectiveness, and perhaps his scruples, to play the game well.

Hesitant, inefficient, and ineffective, he nonetheless had presided over one of the most ruthless occupational systems ever established and at Nuremberg there seemed to be no end to his legal liability.[64]

The American prosecution spent endless hours asserting, and the defense took even more time refuting, the contention that Rosenberg's theoretical writings had been significant in the Nazi rise to power and that his work in education had played a vital role in preparing the German youth for war.[65] But the Tribunal never attached much importance to either of these accusations. In his preparatory memorandum, Robert Stewart decided that the Court should take a parenthetical remark of the American prosecutor Thomas Dodd as its central conclusion on Rosenberg's ideology by holding that "no man should be prosecuted for what he thinks." [66] Stewart gave somewhat more weight to Rosenberg's educational work than to his theorizing, but in its Judgment summary the Court merely mentioned his educational duties as well as his writings and did not hold him criminally liable for either of them.[67]

Both the British and the American prosecutors pounded at Rosenberg's role in encouraging and facilitating the German invasion of Norway, and the defense was not very effective in countering the allegation that Rosenberg was a knowing and active participant in this operation. Nonetheless, Stewart, who liked to make analogies with football, held that on questions of foreign policy Rosenberg had been on the "second string," although Stewart granted that he had always tried to "squeeze his way into the huddle with the big boys." Even on Norway, Stewart believed that Rosenberg's "glorified reports" had "probably exaggerated" his own role; it did not appear that he was part of the "inner ring" of planners. Still Stewart concluded that he was "involved neck-deep" in the affair and could therefore be found guilty under Counts One and Two.[68] The Court merely eliminated Stewart's colorful reservations about Rosenberg's importance, and in its final Judgment placed considerable emphasis on his activities in the Norwegian invasion.[69]

Yet Rosenberg's role in Norway was overshadowed by his part in planning and administering the Russian occupation, and the American and Soviet prosecutors seemed almost to be competing to see who could produce the largest number of incriminating documents on this count. The Americans had uncovered a hoard of papers that Rosenberg had tried to conceal, and from it a never-ending flow of horrifying exhibits came forth with details of the occupation system.

The Soviets, of course, were also able to produce ample indications from every side regarding the effects of the Nazi occupation system. Given the weight of the prosecution case, Rosenberg's defense effort was surprisingly strong and comprehensive. Though having to concede much regarding Rosenberg's role in planning and overall authority, the defense produced rather impressive evidence that he was not master of the whole house, that he had advocated more moderate policies, and, on occasion, had tried to soften the worst ferocities of his local leaders as well as the most extreme actions of the SS and the police. Stewart gave Rosenberg fair marks for the limitations cited by his defense but still concluded that he had a large share of responsibility for the planning and execution of the Eastern occupation policies.[70] The Tribunal's final summary reached the same conclusion. While granting that he had "upon occasion" tried to restrain his subordinates, the Tribunal emphasized how much Rosenberg had authorized and how deep was his knowledge both of the plans and of the grim reality. Whatever his reservations and ultimate hopes, the actual murderous conditions were never significantly lessened, and, as the Court emphasized, Rosenberg nonetheless "stayed in office until the end." [71]

Perhaps if he had not had to expend so much time and effort needlessly defending his role as a theoretician, Rosenberg might have produced a bit more evidence to minimize his role in Norway and to support the contention that he was a moderating force in the East. In view of Rosenberg's long career on Allied war criminal lists and the mass of prosecution evidence against him, such speculation may seem pointless, but, when we examine the records of the deliberations, it gains a new significance. Of the twelve defendants who were sentenced to hang, Rosenberg came closest to escaping the death penalty.

He had been charged under all four counts and in the initial deliberations on September 2, Lawrence, Nikitchenko, Volchkov, and Falco held that he should be convicted on all four. Donnedieu de Vabres, however, voted to convict only on Counts Three and Four, while both Parker and Biddle passed without casting a vote.[72] The second deliberative session, on September 10, revealed an even deeper division. The Russians and Lawrence held to their conclusion that he was guilty on the four counts and should be hanged. Falco still believed Rosenberg was guilty on all four but, for a long time, could not decide whether he merited hanging or life imprisonment. In the end, Falco opted for life, and in this conclusion he was joined by Parker, who noted that Rosenberg had shown humanitarianism. Donnedieu de Vabres also changed his mind and decided that Rosenberg was guilty on all four counts, but he still felt that he should be condemned to prison for life. With Donnedieu de Vabres and the two alternates advocating a life sentence, and the Russians and Lawrence calling for death, the decision rested in the hands of Francis Biddle. His inclination was to hold Rosenberg definitely guilty on Counts Three and Four, and probably guilty on Counts One and Two, and to sentence him to hang. But Biddle had doubts, and decided to reserve his opinion.[73] He slept on the question overnight, and on September 11 came back and reported, without further explanation, that he had come to agree with the "general opinion" that Rosenberg was guilty on all four points and should hang. Only Donnedieu de Vabres, among the senior Members, continued to call for life imprisonment, and Rosenberg was therefore unanimously found guilty on all four counts and then sent to the scaffold by a vote of three to one.[74]

Hans Frank

The now familiar tale of an early follower of Hitler who rose to high position, only to show flashes of weaknesses as he carried out the tasks of mass murder, is epitomized in the person of Hans Frank. A lawyer who first came in contact with the movement by serving as Hitler's attorney, Frank joined the party in the late 1920s. During the peaceful period of the Third Reich, he held a series of largely ceremonial posts in the Nazi legal system. Then, in 1939, he was sent east to be chief administrator of the "General Government," the portion of Nazi-occupied Poland that was not annexed directly to the Reich. In this vast area, Frank presided over the first of the large eastern conquests that were to be the setting for the ruthless application of the Nazi principles of racism and economic exploitation.

Early on, the Allied governments had a clear grasp of Frank's position and activities in Poland, but he only intermittently appeared on the major war criminal lists because it was assumed that he would be dealt with by the Poles.[75] The British finally put him on the list of "majors" that they prepared in mid-June and the Americans followed suit and included him in the group of sixteen that they produced soon after.[76] Once Frank was in custody and on his way to trial, he immediately began to show the emotional instability that would characterize his conduct throughout the proceedings. He turned over to the Allies the "diary" record of his brutal tenure in Poland, certainly one of the most remarkably vivid records of ruthlessness presented during the trial, but he then alternately passed through phases of repentant confession and self-justification. Since he had been charged under Count One as a member of a general conspiracy (but not under Count Two, Crimes Against Peace), the prosecutors made some half-hearted attempts to magnify his general importance in the Nazi system. Generally, however, they concentrated their efforts on heaping up evidence of his responsibility and cynical ruthlessness during the Polish years. On the stand, Frank made an emotional confession of the general guilt of the Nazi system for the extermination of the Jews, but then he attempted to show that he was not really responsible for it, or anything else, because he had not controlled the SS or the Gestapo and had tried to temper their worst excesses.

The judges were well aware of Frank's emotional oddities; Birkett noted that he spent "long hours" brooding in the dock.[77] When Birkett remarked to Biddle that Frank had been converted to Catholicism and seemed "deeply moved and perhaps sincere," the American duly recorded this in his evidentiary summary, but added that nonetheless Frank was "cruel looking." [78] Biddle had a strong personal antipathy against Frank's lawyer and he was totally unimpressed by Frank's attempts to show that he had opposed much of what had been done and on occasion had tried to quit. Once, when Frank testified that he had attempted to resign, Biddle noted "so what?" and when Frank asserted that he had protested against certain actions, Biddle carefully underlined his reaction to this in his evidentiary record: "but he went along!" [79]

The short unsigned and undated memorandum on Frank prepared by the American judicial staff concluded that there was little basis for a conviction of Frank on Count One but every reason to find him guilty on Counts Three and Four. Frank had obviously relished his hour of brutal power too much and had protested too little to give pause to the American staff. The majority of the Tribunal was also unimpressed by Frank's defense, and the wording used in the American memorandum was followed very closely in the Judgment summary.[80]

In the initial deliberative session, Falco and Nikitchenko went one better than the indictment and voted to convict Frank on all four counts, although he had not been indicted on Count Two. All the other judges present indicated that they wanted to convict him on Counts One, Three, and Four. The Russians dropped their advocacy of Count Two in the final session, while holding him guilty under the other three and voting for the death penalty. Lawrence, Falco, and the Americans decided he was only guilty on Counts Three and Four, but they likewise called for hanging.[81] Only Donnedieu de Vabres, who wanted to convict Frank on Counts Three and Four, showed himself, to use Biddle's words, to be "curiously tender" [82] and suggested that they withold the death penalty and give him life imprisonment. Once more, however, the Frenchman's reservations failed to move his colleagues, and the Court's conclusion was to find Frank guilty on Counts Three and Four and to hang him.[83]

Wilhelm Frick

The career of Wilhelm Frick was unusual because he was virtually the only prominent Nazi who had been a professional government official under the Weimar Republic and had also been an early supporter of the Nazi party. As a Bavarian state official, Frick extended valuable aid and protection to Hitler during the early and mid-1920s. In the Nazi advance to power after 1929, Frick's administrative skill and bureaucratic respectability were important in helping the Nazis consolidate their local electoral victories. When Hitler was named chancellor in 1933, he rewarded Frick by immediately designating him minister of the interior. During the first years of the Third Reich, he played a significant role because he controlled many of the police forces in Germany and because he was the chief administrative official who welded Hitler's revolutionary changes onto the old Weimar constitutional and bureaucratic system. Whether it was the abolition of the trade unions or the establishment of concentration camps, Frick was always ready with a formula that would make it legal and acceptable to the bureaucracy. Probably the most important organizational change that he helped to facilitate during the 1930s was the appointment of Heinrich Himmler as chief of all the important police forces. Frick tried to preserve appearances by asserting that Himmler would be a subordinate official in the Ministry of the Interior, but, before the year 1936 was over, Himmler and Heydrich were well on their way to creating a gigantic SS-police empire over which Frick had no control.

During the first war years, Frick continued his adaptive bureaucratic labors. He helped to provide the administrative machinery for the provinces that were annexed to the Reich as well as some administrative direction for unannexed areas, such as the General Government. By 1943, Frick's elastic skills had outlived their usefulness; the war had turned against Germany, and what Hitler needed above all was ruthless exploitation at home and in the occupied territories. Consequently, Himmler was made minister of the interior and Frick was sent off to Prague to serve as protector, after Hitler had carefully removed from his authority some of the police powers that had been held by his predecessor in that post. Frick, therefore, spent the last two years of the Third Reich in Bohemia and Moravia, repressing the Czech population and squabbling with the SS and police chief of the Protectorate, Karl Hermann Frank (not to be confused with Hans Frank, the defendant at Nuremberg).

The Allied governments fixed their eye on Frick at an early date and he was on all the Anglo-American major war criminal lists prepared in 1944 and 1945.[84] The American prosecution was especially anxious to prove a case against him because his work in bringing the Nazis to power and consolidating their hold seemed to be a perfect focal point for demonstrating the existence of a Nazi conspiracy. Consequently, most of the evidence presented against Frick centered on his activities in the years 1933–35, especially the laws that he prepared to suppress domestic opposition, persecute Jews, and restrict the Christian churches. His immediate prewar and wartime role was de-emphasized in the prosecution presentation, although there was evidence relating to his two years in Prague and also to the laws he had drafted relating to military expansion and to subsequent control of the conquered areas.

The defense tried to portray Frick as a simple bureaucrat who merely followed orders. His attorney also went to considerable lengths to play down his wartime activities but, no matter what the strategy, Frick was not a very cooperative client. He was a chilly, taciturn man who, despite having been put on the shelf during the last years of the regime, was a completely unreconstructed Nazi holding firmly to his belief in Hitler. The defense made the prudent decision that it was best not to put him on the stand, so Frick was the only defendant aside from Hess, who was only partially present, and Bormann, who was totally absent, who did not testify in his own defense.

The preparatory memorandum on Frick that was apparently prepared by Adrian Fisher included a full summary of the minister of the interior's crucial role in the early years of the regime. Yet, in recounting his importance in the system of repression, Fisher was careful to note that although Himmler's police empire was nominally under Frick's authority, in fact it was not, and, similarly, although Frick knew about the wartime euthanasia program to eliminate "useless eaters" from the asylums, Fisher acknowledged that it was controlled by Hitler, not by Frick.[85] The description in the final Judgment followed Fisher's account of Frick's early activities very closely and it also adopted his reservations about the interior minister's authority over the police and the euthanasia program.[86] Regarding Frick's later career, Fisher enumerated the major mobilization and annexation decrees that he had signed and emphasized that he played a significant role in planning the attack on Russia. Faced with the indirectness of much of the evidence, the memorandum still concluded that "it is unthinkable that a man with Frick's responsibility, influence and high position could be unaware that Hitler was preparing for and intending aggression."[87]

The appraisal was similarly uncompromising in the conclusion it drew from Frick's signing of the incorporation orders for the annexed provinces. Fisher decided that these orders fell under the "execution" aspect of the aggressive war clauses and were therefore punishable under both Counts One and Two. Regarding War Crimes and Crimes Against Humanity, although Fisher granted that Frick's powers in Prague were limited and that he did not have full authority over the police or the concentration camps, the memorandum still concluded that there was enough indirect evidence remaining to convict him on Counts Three and Four. The final recommendation of the memorandum was that Frick should be held on all four counts and, in the only suggestion regarding sentence advanced in any of the memoranda, called for him to "pay the supreme penalty."[88]

The first deliberative session on Frick, held by the Tribunal on

September 2, showed more signs of indecision than of sharp division. The judges were presumably troubled by the same factor that makes the case unsettling now: there was little direct evidence of Frick's personal involvement in the worst horrors of the wartime regime. Aside from his time in Prague—and even here there could be doubts—Frick was primarily liable as a knowing accessory, or accomplice, but rarely as a principal. Nonetheless, the British and the Russians wanted to convict him on all four counts and Parker favored holding him on all but Count Two. Falco, like Parker, favored conviction on Counts One, Two, and Four but he had doubts regarding Count Two. Donnedieu de Vabres voted Frick guilty only on Counts Three and Four, and once again Biddle passed, this time apparently without even expressing an opinion on the case.[89]

In the final deliberative session, on September 10, Falco, the Russians, and Lawrence called for Frick's conviction on all four counts and a sentence of hanging. Lawrence, in voting him guilty, made the pointed observation, rather chilling to those with Fifth Amendment sensitivities, that Frick had not taken the stand in his own defense.[90] Biddle voted to convict on Counts Two, Three, and Four, but, although he was ready to acquit him on Count One, he still wanted Frick hanged. Parker, who wanted conviction on all four counts, favored life imprisonment rather than hanging and made a remark in support of mitigation that was almost as disturbing as Lawrence's observation that Frick's silence implied guilt. Parker thought that Frick merited a show of mercy simply because "he was really but a bureaucrat." [91] Whether a similar sympathy for officialdom played a part in Donnedieu de Vabres's hesitation is not clear, but, though ready to convict on Counts Three and Four, he seems to have had doubts on One and Two and on an appropriate sentence. The French judge therefore reserved his opinion, but Lawrence, Biddle, and Nikitchenko went ahead to convict Frick on Counts Two, Three, and Four. With Biddle opposed to holding him on Count One, the British and Soviet judges did not have enough votes to convict for conspiracy, but the three did unite to sentence him to hang.[92] Two weeks later, on September 26, the judges held a brief, last-minute discussion of the Frick case on the basis of Donnedieu de Vabres's reservation, but no changes were made and Frick was convicted on Counts Two, Three, and Four and sentenced to death by hanging.[93]

Julius Streicher

In this long chronicle of guilt and mitigation, of convictions and hanging, the case of Julius Streicher occupies a special place. To those familiar with Nazi Germany in the 1930s, Streicher and his newspaper, *Der Stürmer*, may appropriately embody all the pornographic vulgarity and anti-Semitic savagery of the Third Reich. But from a historical-legal standpoint, it is difficult to quarrel with Robert Stewart's introductory remark, in a memorandum on Streicher written in the summer of 1946, that Streicher "was never in the inner ring" of Nazis, "had nothing to do with the formulation of Nazi policy," and therefore was "probably less important than most of the defendants for the purposes of this trial." [94]

Streicher was in the Nuremberg dock not because of his power but because of his notoriety. He had been one of Hitler's first political allies and was one of his devoted followers. He had run the Nuremberg *Gau* and presided over the *Stürmer* with a vigorous crudity unparalleled elsewhere even in the Nazi system. The Propaganda Ministry and other offices frequently found it desirable to distance themselves from Streicher's activities, and even though Hitler occasionally enjoyed popular vulgarities and rejoiced in Streicher, he, too, was repeatedly forced to try to discipline him. During the war Streicher was finally removed from his post as Gauleiter and general supervisor of the *Stürmer*. Yet, even in forced wartime semiretirement, he continued to write and to give the *Stürmer* the most brutal and crude anti-Semitic content and tone. Nothing softened him and at Nuremberg he still appeared to be a dirty old man—"the sort," as Rebecca West characterized him, "who gives trouble in parks." [95]

The Allies did not quickly or easily come to the conclusion that Streicher was a major war criminal. He was on neither of the long lists of possible "majors" prepared by the British in 1944. Only when they learned of the U.S. decision to prosecute conspiracy was Streicher added to the British list of ten, along with Keitel and Kaltenbrunner, in order to "cover the most obnoxious activities of the regime." [96] Although the Americans also put Streicher on their June 1945 "majors" list, it is clear that at that time neither prosecution group had given much serious thought to how the extermination system had actually operated or what Streicher's part in it might have been. Both Jackson and the British were then only hoping to find orders that would link the Nazi leadership to particular atrocities.[97] In the course of the summer of 1945, as the evidence regarding the extermination began to take shape, it was still easy for the prosecutors to overlook the weaknesses of the Streicher case because they were stressing a grand conspiracy and planned to catch him on his general activity as a Nazi and an anti-Semitic agitator. When the indictment was drafted in August and September, the gaps in the case became more obvious and Streicher was charged only under Count One and Count Four, Conspiracy and Crimes Against Humanity.

In the trial, the prosecutors wasted considerable time demonstrating that Streicher had a bad reputation and most of the evidence they presented that related to his activities in the 1930s came to nought because of the limited conspiracy formula ultimately employed by the Tribunal. The core of the case against Streicher came down to a question of whether he had advocated and encouraged extermination of the Jews while knowing, or having good reason to believe, that such extermination was the settled policy of the Nazi government. The prosecution placed in evidence a number of damning items that indicated Streicher knew what was going on in the wartime death camps, yet continued to urge extermination. The defense made no concerted effort to controvert this evidence, partly because Dr. Hans Marx, Streicher's attorney, seems to have viewed his task as hopeless, and also because Streicher held his own bizarre notions on how to conduct the defense. From the start of the trial, he constantly interfered with and disrupted the presentation of his own case.

The judges obviously viewed Streicher as an extremely distasteful creature and somewhat of a raving madman. When he was on the stand, Biddle noted that he became "terribly worked up," and, when his short final plea went off smoothly, both Parker and Biddle remarked, surprised, that he had spoken "with considerable dignity."[98] Although Stewart, in his memorandum, tried to discount the importance of Streicher's "unsavory character" because it bore "little relevance to the main charges against him," he could not totally overcome it.[99] After reviewing the evidence relating to his wartime agitation, Stewart noted that it was difficult to measure Streicher's responsibility for mass murder, "but that he bears some responsibility, there is no question."[100] Finally, after using another ghoulish football analogy that portrayed Streicher as the cheerleader for a team of exterminators, Stewart concluded that, "at the very least, he became an aider and abettor to this Nazi crime." [101]

In the deliberative session of September 2 and September 10, the Court made unusually quick work of the Streicher case. In the preliminary discussion, Falco and the Russians indicated that they wanted to convict him on Counts One and Four, while Lawrence was doubtful on Count One but apparently sure on Count Four. The rest of the judges voted to convict him solely on Count Four. As a special addition, Donnedieu de Vabres, Biddle, and the Soviets wanted to convict Streicher on Count Three (War Crimes), although he was not even indicted on this count. [102] In the final consideration, the idea of holding him for War Crimes was dropped, and only the Russians voted to convict him on Count One. All the judges, however, voted to find him guilty on Count Four and to sentence him to death by hanging. [103]

The Streicher case demonstrates the old rule that important civil liberties issues sometimes arise in conjunction with the trials of a society's most unsavory characters. In recent years, a number of lawyers and historians, most notably Klaus Kippham, have begun to question whether Streicher's execution was not a miscarriage of justice. [104] No one has come forward to defend Streicher's character or activities, or to deny that he might have been convictable on other charges and in a different jurisdiction. The central question is, did Streicher belong at Nuremberg along with twenty-one defendants who held important government and party posts, and was he fairly convicted on the basis of the system used in judging the other defendants? From the foregoing discussion, it should be obvious that Streicher was out of place at Nuremberg and his presence there was largely the result of ignorance about the extermination process on the part of the prosecutors. Furthermore, Streicher's terrible reputation obviously prejudiced the Court against him. Even after Biddle clearly stated that it was wrong to convict a man simply because he was "a little Jew baiter" or "a friend of Hitler's," it is impossible to avoid the conclusion that just these factors played a crucial role in his conviction.

More serious still, there remain grounds for questioning whether a connection existed between Streicher's wartime advocacy of extermination and the actual process of mass killing. Even if one applies the adage that shouting fire in a crowded theater is not a legitimate exercise of freedom of speech, the presumption implicit in this limitation is that there will be, or is likely to be, a direct connection between the advocacy and a public disaster. What was not demonstrated at Nuremberg, and what has not been dealt with very effectively by subsequent historical scholarship, is the question of whether there was a significant connection between wartime public declarations of anti-Semitism in the Reich and the actual killing process in the East. Shelves of books have been written on the exterminations, and these have universally stressed the precautions taken to keep the killings secret and emphasized that an amazingly small number of Germans was involved in the actual mechanical killing process. Only now is a serious debate taking shape between those who argue that ideological anti-Semitic conditioning of the killers was the essential element in the process and those who maintain that such conditioning was of secondary importance compared with other factors, including Hitler's own fanatical anti-Semitism, the sadistic personalities of those doing the killing, the authoritarian structure of the SS, and so forth.[105] On another level, there has been a great deal of speculation as to why most of the German population, but also the majority of the inhabitants of other countries, stood by while the deportation trains rolled toward Poland.

Whatever the outcome of these debates and however much we may wish to be spared the pain of yet another consideration of the holocaust, it seems unlikely that a strong and clear connecting line will be shown between the likes of Julius Streicher and the acts of Rudolf Hoess. That Streicher had a hand in creating the deportation climate would seem the most probable connecting link, but still there appears to have been a world of distance between this little man whose perverted mind embraced using the bullwhip or burning the local synagogue and the kind of efficient mass murder operation mounted by Eichmann and Heydrich in 1941.

Obviously, Streicher was convicted and hanged without a thought being given to these considerations. Thirty years later, one need not bemoan the fate of such a man, but it is still reasonable to harbor the feeling that it would have been better if the Court had taken more time and been more precise in dealing with the evidence. Jackson once warned against the trivializing of this major war criminal trial, but, even after three decades, Nuremberg seems a rather sorry symbol of the great tragedy of extermination, in part because it used Rudolf Hoess as a witness and sent Julius Streicher to the scaffold.

Walther Funk

As the Judgment deliberations progressed, the sequence in which the Tribunal considered the individual defendants seems to have become more important. A man whose actions might have warranted a death penalty if his case had been considered in the earliest deliberations may have escaped the gallows simply because in later consideration he did not look as dreadful as some of his predecessors. The classic defendant of this kind was Walther Funk, who had been connected with nearly every type of crime covered by the indictment, yet ultimately managed to avoid the death penalty. Funk's survival seems to have been materially aided by the fact that he was the tenth defendant to be considered and also because he was universally regarded as a weak man.

Funk joined the Nazi party in the early 1930s and held middle-level posts in the economics and propaganda ministries in the first years of the Third Reich. As Schacht was forced out of his important economic positions, Funk moved in to replace him, first as minister of economics in early 1938, then as president of the Reichsbank in January 1939. As minister of economics, he was much more directly under Goering's control than Schacht had ever been, and the Reichsbank also ceased to play a significant or independent role under Funk's direction. But, though Funk was far from dominant, he was nearly always present. He was there during the conferences on armament expansion in 1938–39, and he was also active in making the economic preparations for the attack on Poland. While before the actual invasion, the other Nazi leaders were careful to speak of the plans in guarded language, the naïve Funk wrote a letter to Hitler on August 25, 1939, in which he declared how proud he was to have participated in the planning for "financing the war" against Poland.[106] With Rosenberg and others, Funk also helped to develop the economic plans for exploiting the Soviet Union long before the actual invasion. Thus, Fisher's memorandum on Funk of July 11, 1946, as well as the summary of his case in the final Judgment, concluded that there was an open-and-shut case against him for helping to prepare Crimes Against Peace (Count Two).[107]

Funk's responsibility for War Crimes (Count Three) and Crimes Against Humanity (Count Four) was only slightly more problematical. Under Goering's general supervision, Funk was active in

organizing and executing the economic exploitation of the conquered territories and was present when the Reich Marshal made
such remarks as his declaration that he did not care if the defeated
"people will starve" as long as the necessary material was gained for
Germany. Although he had reservations about the slave-labor system, Funk remained on the board that supervised the program until
the end. One of the most dramatic and horrifying war crimes
charges that the prosecution made during the trial was likewise
directed at Funk: he was accused of having made a deal with the SS
to hold the loot from the exterminations in the vaults of the Reichsbank. Pictures were displayed in court showing heaps of gold fillings
in the bank's vaults, and some of Funk's Reichsbank subordinates
testified that they had been told that these SS "deposits" were from
the occupied territories, and they were not to ask questions about
them. In this testimony, Funk pleaded with the Court to believe his
contention that he had not known what was contained in the huge
SS shipments but in cross-examination of witnesses the prosecution
added to the evidence that indicated Funk had known that the shipments were "unusual" and that he had required silence about them
from his subordinates. Fisher concluded, on the basis of this evidence, that Funk knew what was going on, and that by implication
he was guilty of collusion in a Crime Against Humanity.[108] Biddle
was not quite so ready to accept this inference, and the final Judgment summary stated more cautiously that either Funk knew about
the nature of the SS shipments or he "was deliberately closing his
eyes to what was being done." [109]

Yet for all this, and even though the Allied governments had
placed Funk on a number of their early war criminal lists, it seems to
have been very difficult for anyone at Nuremberg to take this soft,
fleshy little man seriously. Among his fellow prisoners he appeared
ludicrously insignificant and when out of the dock he seemed to
come alive only when telling off-color jokes. The diary of the prison
psychologist is full of comments about visits to Funk in which he
found the former minister of economics "depressed and whimper-
ing as usual." [110] Even Goering was somewhat embarrassed by
Funk's insignificance, and on one occasion, when trying to divine
the Allies' purpose in holding the trial, the Reich Marshal asked rhetorically, "Where does little Funk fit into this?" [111]

On the bench, Biddle jotted down only one observation about
Funk. It was in the middle of Doenitz's testimony, and the Ameri-

can judge noted, "Funk has been sound asleep all morning." [112] An appearance of unimportance was Funk's trademark, and when Fisher prepared his summary on the case he decided that Funk had not been a "particularly significant figure in the Nazi regime," and that "it does not even appear that Funk was a vicious man." [113] In Fisher's view, all that could be said about Funk was that he was "a loyal Nazi" who "went along." [114] Similarly, when the Tribunal concluded its summary of Funk's case, it noted that he had never been "a dominant figure," and the Court ultimately accepted this as a mitigating factor. [115] But Fisher expressed the feeling of the Tribunal even more succinctly: Funk "cannot plead that he did not know better, he can only plead that he was a weak man." [116]

In the deliberations, Funk's implied plea that he was too weak and too insignificant to hang probably saved his life. On September 2, the two British judges and both Soviet judges, as well as Parker and Falco, held that he was guilty on all four counts. Donnedieu de Vabres rejected Count One, while holding him on the other three counts, and Biddle was only doubtful on the first count. [117] In the session on September 10, the Russians, Lawrence, Falco, and Parker voted to convict him on all four counts, and all but Parker (who advocated life imprisonment) voted to hang him. Biddle and Donnedieu de Vabres, however, held him guilty on only Counts Two, Three, and Four, and Biddle had doubts about the death penalty. [118] The French judge also hesitated with regard to sentence and finally inclined toward life imprisonment because Funk "didn't participate in aggressive war." [119] This cryptic remark seems to have stiffened Nikitchenko, whose country had suffered some of its worst disruption and looting because of the labors of this unimpressive little man. The Russian vainly protested that Funk's role and importance seemed "to have been underestimated." [120] Nevertheless, the judges still could not agree, and the sentence on Funk was reserved.

Two days later, on September 12, the Court picked up the Funk case again and, although there was apparently still some disagreement about the counts on which he should be convicted, it was finally decided to hold him only on Two, Three, and Four. In the course of the discussion, Donnedieu de Vabres and Biddle managed to woo Lawrence away from his support of the death penalty. Thus three senior votes sentenced Funk to life imprisonment. Nikitchenko voted for hanging right to the end. [121]

Fritz Sauckel

Funk's case may have been helped by comparison with men like Streicher and Kaltenbrunner, but Sauckel seems to have been hurt by comparison with a man like Funk. Fritz Sauckel was the only workingman in the dock; a sailor who had joined the Nazi party in 1923, he rose to become the Gauleiter in Thuringia and reaped the rewards of the party's victories by acquiring substantial political power in the Thuringian state government. In 1942, Hitler made him plenipotentiary for labor, which meant primarily that Sauckel spent the remainder of the war forcing workers from the occupied territories to labor in Germany. His activity did not stamp his name on the attention of the wartime Anglo-American governments, because their populations were not the ones that were being dragooned by Sauckel's agents. Consequently, he appeared only intermittently on their early war crimes lists and was passed over by both the British and the Americans when they prepared their top criminal rosters in June 1945.[122] Quite understandably, it was the French and the Soviets who designated Sauckel a major war criminal during the Four Power discussions on the defendant list which occurred in August 1945

During the trial, Sauckel's defense strove to undercut the prosecution's showing of the illegality and inhumanity of the forced labor system that had brought over five million workers into Germany, often under dreadful conditions. It was argued that Sauckel had not held absolute authority over the program, that he was not personally cruel, and that he had been motivated solely by a sense of dutiful efficiency. Biddle clearly grasped the main thrust of the defense presentation when he noted, on May 29, that "Sauckel's justification seems to be the need." [123] Fisher's July 24 memorandum on the case, which was printed virtually verbatim in the Tribunal's final summary on Sauckel, also stated that he was not "sadistic" and that it did not appear he had tried to exterminate the workers.[124] To Fisher, Sauckel's sole objective seemed to have been to maximize production while using the fewest possible resources to support the labor force.[125]

Both Fisher and the Tribunal dismissed Sauckel's claims of his marginal authority and his alleged efforts to ameliorate harsh conditions. The Judgment asserted that in the years 1942–45 Sauckel acted as if he possessed the power, and, although he knew the dreadful conditions that often prevailed, he still performed his duties in a "ruthless and efficient" manner. [126] In Fisher's view, Sauckel had not had a significant part in the preparation or waging of aggressive war, and the memorandum declared flatly that "he must therefore be acquitted" on Counts One and Two. But on Counts Three and Four Fisher concluded that there was no question that he was guilty and there was "very little to be said on the question of mitigation." [127]

The Court's action on Sauckel was so rapid that it is difficult to characterize it as a deliberation. In the initial session on September 2, the Soviets wanted to convict him on all four counts and Birkett wanted to find him guilty on Counts Three and Four, while reserving Counts One and Two. The other five judges routinely found him guilty only on Counts Three and Four. [128] On September 10, the Soviets stuck with their vote of guilty on all four counts, and Lawrence decided that Sauckel was guilty on Counts Two, Three, and Four. But the French and the Americans voted to convict him only on Counts Three and Four. He was consequently found not guilty on Counts One and Two and guilty on Counts Three and Four by a split vote, and then sentenced to hang by a unanimous vote. [129]

Despite the speed and unanimity with which Sauckel was dispatched, or perhaps because of it, a bit of uneasiness lingers regarding the case. It is noteworthy that Donnedieu de Vabres, who was reluctant to impose the death sentence on Frick and even on Rosenberg and Frank, dealt it out to Sauckel without any sign of hesitation. Apparently part of Sauckel's vulnerability arose from the fact that he had committed atrocities in the West as well as the East; he also seems to have come from the wrong class and possessed the wrong personality and style. Sauckel was clearly a commoner, so much so that one of the defense attorneys noted how embarrassed he and his colleagues were by the crude and uneducated German Sauckel used on the stand. [130] It was as if the German lawyers lost face by having the fact revealed among the learned that the Reich had entrusted power and prestige to such a lowly, uncouth creature. Sauckel was not able to give smooth or deceptive answers to his inquisitors, and, when Biddle asked him direct questions from the bench, he obediently incriminated himself. [131] His kind of weakness did not strike the Court as meritorious, but, when at the start of the trial Major Neave, on behalf of the Tribunal, made the rounds to talk to the individual defendants, Sauckel was the only one who was more worried about the condition of his family than about his own fate.[132] At the end of the trial, when he learned that he was to die, Sauckel said what nearly everyone else had noted about him: "I have never been cruel myself." Only then did he start to cry.[133]

It is difficult to see how Sauckel's knowledge or responsibility was so notably different from that of Funk's, and it is also hard to believe that Funk's power was more limited by his subordination to Goering than Sauckel's was by his dependence on Goering and Himmler. Perhaps the issue was best put in a memorandum presumably written by Fisher on the Speer case: if Armaments Minister Speer gave the labor quotas to Sauckel, and Sauckel then seized the laborers, can Sauckel be any more guilty than Speer? The question still hangs in midair; but the adaptable Funk and Speer went to jail, while Sauckel went to the gallows.

Alfred Jodl

Like Keitel, Jodl was a professional army officer with long experience in operational planning during the 1930s who had no special relationship with the Nazi movement. After a brief interval in a field command during 1938–39, he was brought back to Berlin on the eve of the Polish war and made chief of the Operations Staff of the High Command of the armed forces (OKW). In this position, he served as Keitel's immediate deputy and had general responsibility for the operational planning of the German attacks that followed the invasion of Poland. Though technically subordinate to Keitel, Jodl reported directly to Hitler on many matters, and, despite his professional military aloofness, and occasional bitter quarrels with the Führer, he had a deep attachment to Hitler and obviously believed in his genius and destiny.

Largely unknown to the general public, Jodl's name was missing from most of the early Anglo-American major war crimes lists. The British Foreign Office included him on the list prepared in April 1944, and he also found a place on a comprehensive roster of "possibles" produced by the Foreign Office in the spring of 1945.[134] But he was on neither the final British list of ten nor the American list of sixteen, both of which were prepared in June 1945; only through the demand of the French and the Soviet representatives was Jodl placed on the final defendant list of August 1945.[135] As a major defendant, however, it did not take long for him to impress the prosecutors and the Court with his intelligence and his determination to wage an energetic defense. In October 1945, when Major Neave explained to him the procedure for acquiring an attorney, Jodl indicated that he had no money, but, if his counsel was to be appointed by the Court, he did not want a Communist or a pacifist but a man with a "similar mentality" to his own. Jodl also remarked to Neave that he was aware that he confronted a mortal challenge, in part because so many of the documents were in the hands of the prosecution.[136] Rather than wait for the appointment of counsel, Jodl decided to petition immediately for certain materials, including documents relating to wartime crimes committed by the Allies. This request set off an amazing flurry of excitement among the prosecutors and, on October 30, Jackson and Maxwell Fyfe had a worried discussion on how to deal with this incident, which they held to be the beginning of the long-dreaded Nazi "attack on the prosecution." [137] The two prosecutors agreed that the best way to deal with Jodl's request and any other such "attacks" was for each prosecutor to narrow the issues in the case as much as possible so that Allied actions would not be touched upon and then to urge rejection of all defense petitions like Jodl's on the grounds that they were not relevant to the case.[138]

Throughout the trial, the prosecution seems to have retained its fear of Jodl and he was always handled very warily. The defense also had trouble with him because, along with Keitel, his past actions threatened to bring down a declaration of group criminality on the whole High Command and General Staff. Some of the counsel clearly felt that it would have been better to throw Keitel and Jodl to the wolves, perhaps by means of a personal confession, in order to try to save the larger group. This alternative was apparently never proposed directly to the two generals, and, although it is difficult to imagine how Keitel would have reacted if it had been, it seems highly unlikely that Jodl would have gone along. He had come to fight, not simply to fantasize a la Kaltenbrunner that he could save himself; he wanted an opportunity to explain and justify what he had done.

The judges were not particularly sympathetic to Jodl, who was hardly an endearing character, but the notes of Biddle and Birkett show that they accorded him considerable respect. During his testimony, Birkett observed that Jodl gave "the impression that he was much more than a mere soldier"; rather, he possessed "considerable political knowledge, much ingenuity and remarkable shrewdness." Birkett believed that Jodl "obviously" knew the strength of the prosecution's case against him but also knew "the best lines on which to answer it." [139] Biddle was similarly impressed by the general, and, when the British prosecutor "Khaki" Roberts succeeded in making Jodl angry during cross-examination, the American judge noted that he had only managed it by using "cheap questions" as part of a generally "cheap cross-examination" which Biddle had wanted the bench to stop.[140] In the comment he jotted down regarding Jodl's final plea, Biddle capsulized the judges' respect and aversion for the General in one short sentence. "I am always struck," he wrote, "by the apparently sincere and passionate idealism of so many of these defendants—but what ideals!" [141]

Faced with a mountain of signed orders covering invasion plans as well as such atrocities as the killing of captured Soviet Communist Party members (*Komissarbefehl*), Jodl took the only line of defense open to him. He emphasized that, as an operational planner, it was his job to plan operations and he had therefore only acted as higher staff officers do in other countries. In addition, he stressed that he had simply obeyed orders and parenthetically indicated that the Charter's ban on the defense of superior orders was itself an injustice. Jodl's broad defense was the same as the one that Foreign Office Secretary Baron von Weizsäcker would make famous in his later trial; the General contended that he had remained and taken part in much that was wrong in order to mitigate where he could and to avoid replacement by a fanatic who would make matters worse.

The prosecution's answer to this defense was simplicity itself. The evidence showed clearly that Jodl had done numerous things declared illegal by the London Charter, and in the view of the prosecution he had performed these acts with unwonted enthusiasm, while his attempts at amelioration were so feeble as to border on the imaginary. Clearly, in the eyes of both the prosecution and the Tribunal, Jodl was not just a military technician who had found himself in a difficult situation but a political general who had prepared the invasions and atrocities out of conviction.

Rowe wrote a five-page memorandum on the Jodl case in mid-August, and this document, with only minor stylistic changes, became the summary section of the final Judgment.[142] It raced through the attack plans and the atrocity orders, concluding that all charges had been proven. Rowe had no hesitation about holding him guilty on all four counts, including Count Four (Crimes Against Humanity), which, as distinct from Count Three (War Crimes), had actually not been covered by very strong evidence, except a late order for a scorched-earth retreat in Norway. The memorandum noted that Jodl's plea of superior orders had been banned as a full defense by the Charter, and Rowe did not believe that such a plea should even be considered in mitigation in Jodl's case.[143]

In the Tribunal's first discussion of Jodl, Donnedieu de Vabres wanted to convict him only on Counts Two and Three, while Lawrence voted him guilty on the first three counts. But the other Tribunal members called for conviction on all counts, including the thin case related to Crimes Against Humanity.[144] On September 10, during the final deliberation, the Soviets voted Jodl guilty on the four counts and called for a death sentence. Biddle and Lawrence also wanted to convict him on all four counts and to sentence him to death, but seem to have been uncertain whether hanging would be the appropriate mode of execution. Although Falco and Donnedieu de Vabres likewise voted him guilty on all counts, they were even more cautious in regard to sentence. Falco thought him less guilty than Keitel and believed that he should get life or a term in prison, while Donnedieu de Vabres called for an "honorable sentence" to a term in prison. Birkett was not present during this session, but Parker, in effect, took over the position earlier occupied by the English judge, for on this vote the American alternate decided not to convict Jodl for Crimes Against Humanity. With the French opposed to the death penalty, Biddle and Lawrence uncertain on the form of execution, and Parker apparently undecided on sentence, the judges concluded that it was best to reconsider Jodl in a later session.[145]

On September 12, a short and macabre discussion took place. The French, who realized that those favoring the death penalty could outvote them three to one, abandoned their opposition to execution and instead advocated that Jodl should at least be shot rather than hanged. Biddle supported the French and suggested that Keitel be hanged and Jodl be shot. Both of the Russian and English judges, however, held firmly to the decision to hang both of them. A new short-lived deadlock resulted, with two senior judges favoring shooting and two favoring hanging. The standoff ended when Biddle finally decided to capitulate and joined the British and Soviets to order that both Keitel and Jodl should be hanged.[146]

Arthur Seyss-Inquart

An Austrian attorney with close connections to the Nazi party, Seyss-Inquart was the most prominent Austrian figure used by Hitler and Goering to bring down the government of Kurt Schuschnigg in 1938 and thus pave the way for the union of Austria and Germany (*Anschluss*). Although Seyss-Inquart did not actually join the Nazi party until March 1938, he had long been a pan-German nationalist and had worked assiduously to promote the union. The prosecution spent much time on the case trying to demonstrate that Seyss-Inquart had been a sworn Nazi agent who by treachery undermined the Austrian Government and then handed his country over to Hitler. In a memorandum for the American judges prepared in mid-August, Fisher accepted much of the prosecution's evidence and concluded that Seyss-Inquart "should be found guilty under count I." [147] However, three weeks later, the Court truncated the grand conspiracy charge, thus largely eliminating the basis for convicting Seyss-Inquart on his pre-*Anschluss* actions.

Seyss-Inquart was therefore convicted and ultimately executed for actions other than those that had originally placed him in the dock. The British Government had not considered him a "major" war criminal and of the four extant British war crimes rosters he was included only in the appendixes of two as a "possible" defendant in a local trial due to his wartime position as chief of the occupation administration in the Netherlands.[148] The Americans were the ones who wanted him tried as a "major," because his Austrian activities seemed to fit into their format of charging a conspiracy to prepare aggressive war. They put him on their June 1945 list, from which he made his way to Nuremberg.[149]

The case against Seyss-Inquart for his post-*Anschluss* activities had an ad hoc, meandering quality, much like Seyss-Inquart's career itself. Although initially president and then Reich governor of Nazi Austria, Seyss-Inquart found himself out of a job when that land lost its separate identity and became simply the *Ostmark* of the Third Reich. In March 1939, Hitler sent him on a special mission to Bratislava to urge the Slovaks to declare their independence and thereby to facilitate the destruction of the Czechoslovak state. With this task accomplished, and Bohemia and Moravia made a Reich protectorate, Seyss-Inquart was once more a man without a mission. After the invasion of Poland in 1939, he was therefore sent to Warsaw to serve as Hans Frank's deputy in the administration of the conquered Polish provinces that made up the Government General. Then, in 1940, when the German armies overran the Netherlands, Seyss-Inquart finally found his niche; he was appointed "Reich Commissioner for the Occupied Netherlands" and was given the formidable task of simultaneously exploiting the area and wooing the Nordic Dutch into an affectionate loyalty to the Third Reich. Although the role of repressive suitor hardly fitted Seyss-Inquart's distant, almost pensive demeanor and personality, he remained in this post until the end of the Nazi regime in 1945.

When Fisher surveyed Seyss-Inquart's case in August 1946, he decided that there was not enough evidence to substantiate the charge under Count Two that Seyss-Inquart had prepared, or waged, aggressive war. Yet, three weeks later, the majority of the judges were inclined to convict him on that charge. It should be recognized that aside from his mission to Bratislava, which might conceivably have been part of a wide-ranging aggressive war plan, there was really no direct evidence linking Seyss-Inquart to the planning or waging of war. Here he seems to have fallen victim to his unenviable reputation as a plotter and to the residual desire of the judges who had wanted to convict him on his Austrian activities but had been frustrated by the conspiracy compromise.[150] On Seyss-Inquart's wartime role in Poland, and especially in the Netherlands, Fisher and the judges had no difficulty in fitting his activities to the charges. He had used all the hideous trademarks of Nazi occupation—economic exploitation, police terror, forced labor, and deportation of Jews. His only defense was the familiar one that he had really liked the Dutch and had tried to ease conditions where he could, and that he had not controlled the police or the orders from Berlin. Fisher, much of whose writing on Seyss-Inquart in Holland was printed in the Court's final Judgment, summarized the reasons for rejecting the former Reich commissioner's defense in one sentence. "It is not a defense," Fisher wrote, to assert "that Seyss-Inquart was less brutal than Himmler."[151]

In the first Court deliberation, on September 2, Biddle was

doubtful about convicting Seyss-Inquart on Counts One and Two, but the other judges believed that he should be found guilty on all four.[152] On September 10, Falco, the Soviets, and Lawrence favored convicting him on the four counts and sentencing him to hang. Parker, who wanted to find him guilty on Counts One, Three, and Four, but not guilty of Crimes Against Peace, also supported the death penalty. However, aside from the fact that both Donnedieu de Vabres and Biddle wanted to convict him on Counts Three and Four, it is not altogether clear what their position was. Apparently, the Frenchman wished to declare Seyss-Inquart not guilty on Counts One and Two, and to sentence him to life, while Biddle, after initially supporting the death sentence based only on Counts Three and Four, ultimately changed his mind and voted to convict him on Count Two as well. In any event, either the French or the American senior judge voted Seyss-Inquart guilty on Count Two; together with Lawrence's and Nikitchenko's vote this enabled the Tribunal to reach a finding of guilty on the last three counts. Biddle, Lawrence, and Nikitchenko then combined to vote a death sentence, and, although his case was briefly reconsidered on September 26, no further changes were made. Seyss-Inquart was sentenced to death by hanging.[153]

This death sentence was the last penalty that the Tribunal was able to determine with a minimum of argument and controversy. In two days, September 2 and 10, the Court had marched thirteen defendants through a double deliberative process, giving two, Hess and Funk, life sentences, while condemning the other eleven to death by hanging. Though some of the specific convictions and sentences might be argued, it is clear that the Tribunal generally acted like a court rather than a vigilante proceeding. Surely class bias, ideological blindness, and personal antipathy played a part in determining the fate of some defendants, such as Sauckel, Streicher, and Jodl, but it would be difficult to maintain that these failings were present in a noticeably greater degree at Nuremberg than in any court that regularly grinds out judgments on the ordinary people of the world. The Tribunal was very reluctant to grant unmerited mercy, except in the singular case of Funk, and because of this it is easier in the case of Rudolf Hess to ask whether his years in confinement since 1941 have not been enough. But one should pause before sneering at the Nuremberg bench, even when considering the pathetic shadow still in Spandau prison. The eight men of the Nuremberg Tribunal made their decisions at a time and in a place where one could literally touch the death factories of Auschwitz and Treblinka. They were a victorious Allied court, an instrument of rightful wrath, without time or inclination for endless review and reconsideration. That any of the defendants escaped from these proceedings with their lives seems sometimes miraculous; for the Court to have raced through thirteen defendants in two days, with only legal custom and their own good sense as protection against a perversion of justice was a most risky action. That, by and large, they succeeded in avoiding the precipice and fitted most of the right defendants with the right charges was a substantial achievement. Of course, their overall success must have been cold comfort for those who were executed on questionable readings of the evidence; it is rather like saying that the operation of due process was a success, but the patient died. Still, after thirty years, even with Siberian labor camps and My Lai massacres, it would be a perverted sense of morality that pushes the extermination camps aside to condemn the verdicts and to weep over the fact that the Tribunal tipped toward death rather than prison for the likes of Alfred Rosenberg and Julius Streicher.

CHAPTER 8

The Difficult Verdicts:
Albert Speer
to Karl Doenitz

Doenitz wants a counsel from the Navy and
says that no civilian would understand his
position. If the people he asks for cannot be
obtained he suggests an English or American
"U-Boat Admiral."

Major Airey M. Neave,
October 24, 1945 [1]

IN ADDITION to the three men who were ultimately acquitted,
the cases of six other defendants also cost the Tribunal substantial
time and travail. Four of these cases (Schirach, Bormann, Raeder,
and Doenitz) were identified as troublesome during the initial deliberations and they were taken from their regular place in the indictment sequence to be considered at the end. The other two, Speer
and Neurath, happened to come near the end of the indictment list
and therefore were taken up by the Court in the regular order. All
six cases involved controversies in determining guilt and innocence
and setting sentences, and although some of them were resolved

fairly expeditiously by the Tribunal, others, especially the Doenitz case, took as much time and attention as the cases of those who were acquitted.

Albert Speer

It is perhaps fitting that Albert Speer, whose actions and subsequent explanations have caused so much difficulty for historians, should have been the first seriously controversial case dealt with by the Court. As is now well known, Speer came from a professional middle-class family and received university training in architecture. He came into Hitler's orbit in the early 1930s, joined the Nazi party, and during the peaceful years of the Third Reich settled down as Hitler's architect and designing companion. In the early war years there was little immediate demand for his thunderously monumental building designs and Speer fell into a temporary limbo. Then, in 1942, with the death of Fritz Todt, he was put in charge of the war production and construction program and in 1943 was given special powers as armaments minister. In this latter position, he had dramatic initial success in hammering the inefficiencies of the Nazi system into a machine with which to wage total war. As defeat approached, however, his magic weakened and by the end of the regime he had shrunk to the stature of Hitler's other wrangling subordinates.

Nonetheless, his achievements and power were sufficient to bring him to the attention of the Allied governments; he was on both British major war criminal lists prepared in 1944, and the Americans included him among their sixteen "majors" in June 1945.[2] Although the indictment charged Speer under all four counts, neither the prosecution nor most of the Court ever took the charges against him on Conspiracy or Crimes Against Peace very seriously. The core of the case against Speer was his use of labor in war industry. Not only did the prosecution seek to demonstrate that he had given Sauckel labor quotas, knowing that they would have to be filled with forced foreign labor, it also sought to prove Speer's willing use of concentration camp labor and POW labor, the latter a violation of the Geneva Convention. Though Speer recommended that adequate food rations be provided to make maximum production possible, he clearly knew of the harsh conditions in which the slave-labor system operated, and continued to hand down huge labor demands. He even initiated a proposal that slackers be sent to concentration camps. By advocating that certain key plants and their employees (blocked industries) be held in the occupied territories, Speer may have exempted some foreign workers from the deportation labor program, as he contended, but the prosecution asserted that this was nonetheless a violation of the prevailing rules of war.

On the stand, Speer went a long way toward admitting his guilt in the use of slave labor, but he also stressed that his advocacy of blocked industries and his support for supplying adequate food and shelter should be points in his favor. His defense further suggested that he had tried to avoid using too much concentration camp labor, for the practical, if not very edifying, reason that he was wary of becoming too dependent on Himmler. The defense also questioned whether the prosecution had substantiated the argument that Speer's use of POW labor was a violation of the Geneva Convention.

The two summary memoranda for the Tribunal, both of which Adrian Fisher apparently wrote during the summer, rejected most of Speer's defense arguments.[3] Fisher pointed out that, despite Speer's hesitation, he had taken at least 30,000 concentration camp laborers from Himmler. And, Fisher felt, though Speer had recommended fair treatment for conscripted laborers, he "undoubtedly" had been informed about the harsh conditions that actually prevailed.[4] The memoranda further agreed with the prosecution's contention that the system of blocked industries was a violation of the Hague Rules and in any event was not an effective defense against the charge that Speer had used millions of slave laborers in Germany. Only on the POW question did Fisher accept an important argument put forward by Speer's defense: the Soviet Union had not signed the Geneva Convention, so that, technically, the Germans were within their rights when they employed Soviet POWs as laborers in war industries. In other portions of the Judgment, the Tribunal ruled that Germany was not free to do anything that it wished with Soviet prisoners, such as starving them to death, because, even though the Russians had not signed the Geneva accord, all belligerents were still protected by the "customary laws and usages of war." In its presentation against Speer, the prosecution had made a serious error and only presented raw POW labor statistics without specific evidence to indicate that large numbers of non-Soviet prisoners had been forced to work in war industries. Fisher decided, therefore, that Speer's defense was correct in asserting that, because of a failure to show that the use of non-Soviet POWs had reached substantial proportions, the Court had no choice but to exonerate Speer on the whole charge of misusing POW labor.[5]

Moving beyond the specific charges, Fisher noted that the fundamental problem presented by the Speer case was not a question of guilt or innocence, because, on the basis of the Charter and the evidence, he was clearly guilty; the problem was how to evaluate a number of factors that pointed toward mitigation.[6] There had been no showing that Speer was cruel, although his readiness to use concentration camps to enforce labor discipline gives one reason to pause. Furthermore, after the exceptionally thick layers of fantasy were peeled from his eyes and he recognized that Germany was defeated, Speer claimed that "at considerable personal risk" he had sabotaged Hitler's scorched-earth policies and told the Führer that the war was lost.[7] Speer also informed the Court, haltingly, and perhaps coyly, that in the last days he had toyed with farfetched, if not harebrained, plans to kill Hitler. But Speer's very ability to see and act in this manner also cut against the force of mitigation, for, as Fisher stressed, from the very beginning Speer had possessed the position, the intelligence, and the education to grasp the moral implications of what he was doing.[8] The key to the Speer judgment was whether the Court would hold that his professional status and education did more to incriminate him during the first 95 percent of his career than to exonerate him in the last 5 percent. Pushed along by Speer's personality and adaptability, as well as by the Court's social prejudices, the majority of the Tribunal ultimately decided that these factors were more pluses than minuses.

One can accept as genuine Speer's assertions that he experienced a sense of guilt and contrition while in Allied confinement and still assert that, as a clean-cut professional man with minimal ideological commitments, he had excellent prospects of impressing the Western members of the Tribunal with his repentance. By the time of his testimony, Biddle was convinced of Speer's sincerity and noted at one point that he looked "utterly crushed." [9] Later, during the deliberations, Judge Parker remarked that he, too, was impressed by Speer's personality and advanced this as an argument in favor of mitigation. Parker also noted that Speer seemed to be respected by Jackson, implying thereby that if Speer had merited the prosecutor's regard he must have the characteristics of a decent fellow who deserved a break.[10]

The Difficult Verdicts: Albert Speer to Karl Doenitz

The question that dances around the edge of the favorable impression Speer made on some of the judges is whether he simply collapsed and let fate and the Court work their will or whether he tried to nudge them along in a direction away from capital punishment. Speer's nearly incredible life history of adaptability and survival makes it difficult not to harbor some skepticism, especially in view of an incident that occurred on November 17, 1945, just as the trial began. In a letter of that date addressed to Jackson, Speer stated that he was in possession of certain information "as to military, technical questions" that "should not be made known to other persons." [11] From May 10 to May 25, 1945, while "still a free man," Speer maintained that he had provided the U.S. Strategic Bombing Survey with specific information regarding the effects of Allied bombing on German production facilities. In the process, "methods of bombardment showing faster results were discussed in detail," and these methods, in Speer's opinion, probably were "of importance in the fight against Japan." [12] Then, from June 1 until the end of October 1945, when Speer was in Allied custody at the "Dustbin" camp, he was present when large numbers of German scientists and engineers were interrogated by the Allied authorities regarding "new developments" in armaments; many of Speer's former co-workers also passed through the camp at this time for questioning on technical and scientific subjects. In his letter to Jackson, Speer asserted that he not only had volunteered all the information at his disposal, he had also tried to break down the scruples of those of his colleagues who were reluctant to talk to the British and the Americans. Furthermore, he claimed, since he was in the camp for so long and had participated in so many talks with his fellow workers who were undergoing questioning on technical matters, he had "unintentionally gained an insight as to what the present spheres of [Anglo-American] interest are." [13] Speer concluded his letter to Jackson by emphasizing that he had given information and pressed his comrades to do likewise out of "conviction," and that he had not done it "in order to gain personal advantages for the future." [14] Still, he would "feel miserable" and would prefer to make "any personal sacrifice" rather than to be forced to furnish this information to "third persons." [15] Put somewhat more directly, this meant that he was telling the American prosecution that he wanted to avoid questioning on the stand that would make him provide military and technical information to the Soviet Union.

Now, what is one to make of this strange missive? Surely, aside from Speer's fantasies, there was no possibility that the Anglo-American prosecution or a court presided over by a British judge was going to compel him to make available technical information that would be disadvantageous for the Western Powers. Despite his protestations that he was not trying to gain the favor of the prosecutors, is it possible that Speer did not recognize that this approach was perfectly tuned to have such an effect, especially with the rising cold war mentality of a man like Robert Jackson? Speer is probably right when he states that he underwent a postdefeat conversion, and this change was probably facilitated by a desire to transfer his anti-Soviet attitudes from the camp of the Third Reich to that of the Anglo-Americans. Nonetheless, one is forced to note that, whether consciously or unconsciously, Speer presented his repudiation of the Third Reich and his acceptance of the Anglo-American cause in ways that would make the most favorable impression on the majority of the prosecutors and judges.

During the first deliberation on the Speer case, it was not clear how many on the Court were favorably disposed toward him, for, although the Soviets wanted to convict him on all four counts, the French, British, and Americans wished to hold him only on Counts Three and Four, while Birkett and Parker reserved their opinion on Counts One and Two.[16] In the second session on September 10, again only the Russians called for conviction on the four counts, Lawrence wanted to find him guilty on Counts Two, Three, and Four, and the other judges voted to hold him only on Counts Three and Four. Lawrence spoke in favor of Speer, noting that he had taken over an existing system of slave labor—a rather peculiar justification when part of the point at issue was whether he knowingly engaged in a criminal enterprise. On the same occasion, Parker gave voice to his own defense of Speer's respectability and called for a limited sentence.

On the question of sentence, the divergent views regarding Speer came quickly to a head. Both French judges and Lawrence and Parker wanted to have him imprisoned for a limited term of years; Lawrence proposed a sentence of fifteen years and Donnedieu de Vabres voted for it. But then Biddle voted against it, recommending instead that Speer be sentenced to death, a proposal warmly seconded by Nikitchenko. The Court was thus locked in a two-two tie, and in the midst of the standoff Norman Birkett arrived and recommended that they give Speer a sentence of ten years. This seems to have been so irrelevant that it forced the Tribunal members to acknowledge that they were hopelessly deadlocked, and they voted to adjourn.[17]

Overnight, Biddle apparently softened on Speer and on the following morning advanced a compromise. The Soviets were outvoted three to one and Speer was convicted only on Counts Three and Four. Biddle then gave up his advocacy of the death penalty, and Lawrence and Donnedieu de Vabres accepted a longer term of imprisonment. Apparently, again by a vote of three to one, the Western judges agreed early on the morning of September 11 to sentence Albert Speer to twenty years in prison.[18]

Konstantin von Neurath

Of all the defendants who were ultimately convicted, Konstantin von Neurath may have presented the Tribunal with the most complex challenge. He was an aristocratic diplomat who had been included in Hitler's first Cabinet as foreign minister because Hindenberg, the ancient president of the republic, demanded that he be there as a moderating influence. From 1933 to 1938, Neurath continued to serve as foreign minister although Hindenberg had died in 1934 and the Cabinet and the country had taken on a progressively darker Nazi coloration as the years went by. Neurath was obviously somewhat nervous about the pace and recklessness of Hitler's foreign policy moves in this period, but he was a convinced German nationalist and swallowed the regime's "excesses" at home and abroad while helping to put a good face on them for foreigners. Though present during the Hossbach conference of November 1937, Neurath contended that it upset him so much that he suffered a heart attack soon after. In any event, both Neurath and Hitler agreed that the shake-up of the military command structure that the Führer pushed through in February 1938 also provided a suitable occasion for the foreign minister's resignation, with Neurath giving way to Ribbentrop. After leaving him on the shelf for a year, Hitler provided another demonstration of his gift for pushing hesitant people into compromising positions, by persuading Neurath to accept the post of protector of Bohemia and Moravia after Germany had dismembered Czechoslovakia in the spring of 1939. Neurath performed the duties of top executive officer in this area for two years, and during that time he signed repressive orders as he squabbled with Hitler and the local SS and police chiefs in his efforts to soften some particularly harsh policies. These conflicts caused Neurath to go on "sick leave" in 1941, while Karl Hermann Frank, Reinhardt Heydrich, and Kurt Daluege were sent in to clean up Czech resistance. During the years 1941–43, Neurath kept the title of protector but had no hand in the operations, and, finally, in 1943, he was allowed to retire and make room for the next official who had proven to be too timid at home, Wilhelm Frick.

The Western Allied governments were cool to the idea of trying Neurath as a major war criminal. The British put him on Foreign Office lists of "possibles" in 1944 and June 1945, and the War Office also included him in a 1944 roster appendix of men who might be tried for crimes in local areas. But neither the Americans nor the British listed him among the "majors" in June 1945, and it was the French and the Soviets who in August picked him to be a defendant at Nuremberg.[19] Since the Americans did not feel he was an especially appropriate individual through whom to show the Nazi aggressive war conspiracy, Neurath's career as foreign minister became a difficult episode for the prosecution to handle. As indicated above, one of the junior members of the American staff who worked on the Neurath case thought it was so marginal that, on October 4, six weeks before the trial began, he recommended that Neurath be dropped from the defendant list.[20] Although this suggestion was not followed, the general course of the trial failed to strengthen the case against the former foreign minister. Since he came near the end of the indictment list, his defense presentation occurred very late in the proceedings, and the relative weakness of the case against him was thereby thrown into bold relief when compared with those defendants who had been involved with actions more horrible and more easily prosecutable.

The defense made the most of Neurath's respectable reputation in diplomatic circles, his advanced age, and the fact that he had never been a convinced Nazi. His attorney, whom Birkett thought mediocre at best, did manage to suggest that Neurath had striven against extreme measures both as foreign minister and as protector of Bohemia and Moravia. Sometimes the defense assertions of Neurath's innocence bordered on the simpleminded, as when his counsel had him testify that in 1939 he had actually believed that the

Czechs wanted to be "protected" by Nazi Germany.[21] Despite such episodes, Neurath's defense did put a tolerably good face on all his activities, even the wartime repressive orders he had signed in Prague.

When the prosecution went after Neurath in cross-examination, a psychological error may have been made because the attack was pushed forward so aggressively that at least some of the defense attorneys felt that Neurath appeared like a helpless old man, tormented and badgered beyond all reason.[22] The prosecutors stressed not only that Neurath had gone along with Hitler's actions but that he had also given them a cloak of respectability that helped to lull the outside world. Much evidence was also provided on the orders that Neurath had signed in Prague; his repressive measures were spelled out in laborious detail, especially the holding of students as hostages and the execution of some of them. Although such evidence fitted the charges, it necessarily lacked dramatic effect because the Tribunal was asked to attach great weight to the fate of a handful of students while all around the courtroom there hung the shadow of the millions of victims who had elsewhere been sent to their nameless graves by more diabolical methods of extermination.

On the bench, Biddle at least had serious doubts about the prosecution effort, holding that Jackson's summary attempt to link Neurath with the anti-Semitic and religious persecution policies was "rather thin." [23] Nor did the presence of Neurath at the Hossbach conference necessarily carry decisive weight with Biddle, who noted that, "if we are certain he broke away" soon after, his presence at the conference "hardly establishes guilt." [24] The memorandum that Fisher wrote on the case in mid-August was also cautious about asserting Neurath's guilt, although it laid heavy emphasis on his activities as foreign minister in the mid-1930s and greeted many of his claims of good intentions and protestations of innocence with such comments as "very unlikely to be accurate" and "a little difficult to believe." [25] Among the incidents Neurath had been unable to explain away convincingly was the fact that, after his resignation as foreign minister, he had come back briefly to fill in for the absent Ribbentrop during the Austrian *Anschluss* crisis. He had then, as both the prosecution and Fisher stressed, worked assiduously to put a good face on the Austrian incident for foreigners, this, after he had resigned because he allegedly disagreed with Hitler's aggressive plans. Fisher concluded that Neurath's resignation did indicate that he had opposed aggression, but he also decided that Neurath definitely knew of the expansionist plans and, because of his activity at the time of the *Anschluss*, had made himself liable under Count One as a participant in a conspiracy–common plan.[26] Regarding Neurath's career as protector, Fisher, though conceding that the actions were relatively mild, noted that Neurath had ordered Jewish persecutions and the killing of nine students and, in addition, had established systems of economic repression. The memorandum's conclusion was that he should therefore also be found guilty under Counts Three and Four.[27]

Both Fisher's memorandum and the final Judgment summary wrestled briefly with a complex legal problem raised by the Neurath case. Under one view of international law, if a country has been "subjugated," then the sovereign authority over the territory may pass to the victor. In such a situation, rules like those in the Geneva Convention are no longer binding on the victorious government, which can treat the conquered population pretty much as it chooses. Of the territories Germany occupied in World War II, none occasioned a formal transfer of sovereignty except for some border provinces, and in most cases groups of officials claiming to represent the legitimate authority of the conquered lands went into exile abroad and denounced the German occupation regimes as illegitimate. One of the few possible exceptions to this pattern occurred when the Czech provinces of Bohemia and Moravia were occupied in 1939. On that occasion, the Czech president, Emil Hácha, was summoned to Berlin and there, in an atmosphere of intimidation, signed a statement agreeing to the German occupation and the establishment of the German Protectorate. Neurath's defense consequently held that this act constituted a legitimizing of subjugation; the sovereign authority over the two provinces had passed to the Reich and the German Government was free to do whatever it wished there.[28]

The Allied governments' appraisal of this contention was complicated by the fact that their own occupation of Germany rested on exactly the same general interpretation of the law. By the act of unconditional surrender in 1945, the sovereign authority over German territory and population had passed to the Allies and they were no longer restricted by limitations, such as those in the Hague rules, that governed their actions during actual hostilities.[29] There was thus the dangerous possibility that if the Nuremberg Court issued a flat repudiation of Neurath's "subjugation" defense, it would cut the legal ground from under the Allied occupation system. Fisher met this difficulty in his memorandum on Neurath by concluding that legal subjugation had not taken place in Czechoslovakia; the so-called Protectorate was, in fact, merely a military occupation; consequently, the German Government authorities were still bound by the laws and usages of war.[30]

In its final summary the Court was unwilling to use simply this clipped view of the facts; instead, it argued the issue at some length and then came to substantially the same conclusion as had Fisher. In the Tribunal's view, Hácha's consent, since it had been obtained "by duress," could not "be considered as justifying the occupation," and in any event it could be contended that the subjugation doctrine was not applicable in cases of aggression. Furthermore, there was, in the Tribunal's view, a contradiction in the German position. In March 1939, Hitler had declared that Bohemia and Moravia had become part of the territory of the German Reich, but he also established the protectorate, which implied to the Tribunal that "Bohemia and Moravia had retained their sovereignty," subject only to the limitation expressed by Germany's role as a protector. What existed in Bohemia and Moravia after March 1939, then, was a military occupation and, even though Czechoslovakia was not a party to the Hague Convention (Czechoslovakia had not existed in 1907), the Tribunal decided that the German occupation system, including Neurath's powers, were subject to its limitations because the convention "was declaratory of existing international law." [31] By this circuitous route the Tribunal managed to leave the principles of the subjugation doctrine unimpaired and also make Neurath's actions liable to punishment under the rules established at The Hague and in London.

The first vote on Neurath revealed that the Soviets, the British, and Falco favored convicting him on all four counts, while Donnedieu de Vabres wanted to hold him only on Counts Two and Three. Both of the Americans, however, were unusually hesitant; Biddle thought that conviction should come on Count One and "perhaps" others, while Parker apparently was so doubtful that he did not express an opinion at all.[32] In the final session, on September 11, the Russians and the British still supported conviction on the four counts and Donnedieu de Vabres decided that Neurath should be held on Count One as well as Counts Two and Three. The

American hesitation had given way to a decision by both Parker and Biddle, which was also shared by Falco, that Neurath should be found guilty only on Counts Three and Four. When the discussion turned to the fixing of a sentence, the appearance of symmetry vanished, for the judges who had lined up together on the individual counts had very different ideas regarding punishment. Of those who wanted to convict him on all four counts, the Soviets voted for death, as usual, while Lawrence spoke in favor of a life sentence. Birkett, after initially hesitating, suggested fifteen years' imprisonment and Donnedieu de Vabres also wanted to sentence him to fifteen years on the basis of a conviction on the last three counts. Those who voted for conviction on Counts Three and Four only were also seriously divided on sentence. Falco did not specify exactly what it should be but thought it needed to be a "rather heavy penalty." [33] Biddle, on the other hand, advocated a sentence of fifteen years and Parker wanted it to be only five. Parker seems to have felt that, since Neurath was removed by Hitler at the same time as Generals Fritsch and Blomberg, who had also been at the Hossbach conference, it would not be fair to put heavy emphasis on the Foreign Minister's presence at the November 1937 meeting.[34] Since Blomberg was not on trial—Fritsch had been killed early in the war—only Neurath would be punished for having stayed on three months after the Hossbach meeting. Of course, Parker's argument failed to touch the chief accusation made by the prosecution—that Neurath, unlike the others, had returned to serve the regime by holding positions from 1938 to 1941.[35]

The votes on conviction and sentence for Neurath left the Court facing a complicated situation. The former foreign minister was unanimously convicted on Count Three and was also found guilty on Count Two, with Biddle dissenting, and on Count Four, with Donnedieu de Vabres dissenting. Count One was left in a two-two stand-off, with Nikitchenko and Lawrence voting yes and Biddle and Donnedieu de Vabres voting no. There was also a deadlock on sentence, with Biddle and Donnedieu de Vabres holding out for fifteen years, Lawrence for life, and Nikitchenko for the death penalty. Obviously, a compromise was necessary, and this time it was Nikitchenko who lost in a short round of horse trading. Either Biddle or Donnedieu de Vabres, or perhaps both, agreed to convict Neurath on Count One if Lawrence would go for a sentence of fifteen years. The British judge accepted the swap. Neurath was convicted on all four counts and sentenced to fifteen years, with the Soviets probably voting no right to the end.[36]

As with the Hess case, appearances surrounding the verdict and sentence for Neurath were deceptive. When the Tribunal's decision was announced, some observers found its action puzzling. Neurath's conviction on all four counts appeared unduly harsh, but, on the other hand, except for his advanced age, the sentence of fifteen years seemed relatively merciful. What no one could have suspected until now is that Neurath received the light fifteen-year sentence only because Justice Lawrence agreed to accept it in exchange for a blanket conviction on all four counts.[37]

Martin Bormann

In light of the continuing thirty-year speculation, in the press and among the public, about Bormann's fate, his career and the Allied handling of his case have a special interest. Until 1941, Bormann was merely Hess's deputy, and, although he had a reputation in party circles as a rough, if not ruthless, man, he was little known to the general public even in Germany. With Hess's flight to Britain, however, Bormann assumed control of the Nazi party Chancellery and in April 1943 became, in effect, Hitler's secretary and immediate paladin. Though not universally known even then, Bormann did attain a measure of notoriety by war's end, and the Anglo-American authorities had a quite accurate picture of his role and influence. The British included him on both of their lists of major war criminals, and by the summer of 1945 the American prosecution had developed adequate biographical material on him.[38] The obvious difficulty in declaring him a defendant was that he was not in Allied custody. Even though stories began to circulate very quickly indicating that he might—but also might not—have been killed while attempting to flee from Berlin, the Americans and the British, with hundreds of major prisoners and a multitude of documents in their possession, never seriously considered mounting a prosecution against the shadowy Bormann. But, in the August 1945 sessions on the indictment, the French, who had no prisoners of note in their custody, and the Soviets, who had only a handful, demanded that Bormann be indicted because he had been so extremely important and might yet surface alive. The British and the Americans were still

cool to the idea, but the French and Soviet negotiators were ada-
mant, and, under the provisions of Article XIV of the Charter, if two
chief prosecutors desired the inclusion of a particular individual, he
was automatically added to the defendant list.[39]

When the Tribunal first convened in mid-October 1945, none of
the judges, including Nikitchenko, was enthusiastic about the prospect of trying Bormann in absentia. On October 17, Biddle declared
flatly that he opposed an absentia trial and on the same day the prosecutors admitted that the information available suggested that he
was dead.[40] The prosecutors ultimately persuaded the Tribunal to
do nothing on the Bormann question for the time being, and wait
until the trial began to decide whether to separate his case.[41] The
documentation for the Tribunal's handling of the affair in mid-
November is so spotty that definite conclusions are not possible, but
the Court seems to have been so weighted down with the beginning
of formal proceedings and so rent by the struggle over Krupp that
the judges sought to take the easiest available road on Bormann.
Consequently, they did nothing; his case was not separated, and
since he had not been found his retention on the list of defendants
meant that he could be tried only in absentia as authorized by Article XII of the Charter.[42]

The record of the proceedings relating to Bormann create the impression that there was little more here than a parody of a fair trial.
As Dr. Friedrich Bergold, the defense attorney who was assigned to
represent Bormann, rightly complained, without a defendant present
to give leads regarding his career and his case, it was virtually impossible to obtain material for a defense. All Bergold could do was try to
controvert the evidence presented by the prosecution and attempt
to use other defendants' material that might favor his absent client.
Of course, no one was prepared to exert himself very much for a
man who might not exist, and there were few, even in the Third
Reich, ready to extend warm feelings or help to Martin Bormann.
Instead of aiding Bormann's defense, most of the other accused
found him an ideal figure on whom to deposit all the responsibility
they could possibly brush off themselves. By the end of the trial, the
prosecution and the various defendants had produced such a towering picture of Bormann's malevolent influence and power that his
image threatened to overshadow that of Hitler himself.

In its summary of the case, the Tribunal paid its respects to
Bergold's troubles, noting that he had "labored under difficulties,"
but it added that, in the light of the signed Bormann documents

placed in evidence by the prosecution, it was difficult to see how the defense could have done much "even were the defendant present." [43] The Court indicated that the evidence against Bormann on Counts Three and Four was overwhelming, owing to his important role in subjugating the occupied territories, persecuting Jews, and maltreating slave laborers and prisoners of war. Subsequent research by historians has rounded out this picture considerably, but it has done little to lessen the impression that in the last two to three years of the war Bormann was the Führer's most powerful, and probably most ruthless, deputy. Thus, the questions that linger regarding the Bormann case concern legal issues rather than the facts relating to War Crimes and Crimes Against Humanity.

In the initial deliberative session, on September 2, seven of the judges apparently advocated convicting Bormann on Counts One, Three, and Four (he was not specifically charged with Crimes Against Peace). Only Biddle dissented from this view and suggested that the Court simply declare that he was dead, while rendering no verdict on his guilt or innocence. The Russians opposed Biddle's recommendation because they felt that, without conclusive evidence that he was dead, it would be imprudent of the Court not to convict him. Birkett suggested finding him guilty on the three counts because he was "evading justice," and Parker wanted to go beyond everybody in being doubly sure by both convicting him and stating that he was dead. In the midst of this discussion, with the great majority of the judges inclined to convict Bormann on the three counts, Nikitchenko raised an additional problem regarding the case; the Russian thought the general passages of the indictment implied that Bormann was also involved in Crimes Against Peace. The Soviets apparently wanted the Court to rule that the failure to charge him under Count Three was a misprint and to go ahead and convict him on all four counts. [44]

On September 11, Nikitchenko's theory of the four counts was quietly allowed to die, and, although Biddle again recommended that the Court simply declare him dead and make no other finding, this idea also perished without the support of any of the other judges. Lawrence, Falco, and Nikitchenko voted Bormann guilty on the three counts, and all three judges apparently favored the death penalty. The Russians adopted Birkett's earlier argument and suggested that the Tribunal state that, although Bormann was apparently dead, the evidence was not conclusive, and he was therefore convicted and sentenced because he was evading justice.

Donnedieu de Vabres, Parker, Birkett, and, ultimately, Biddle spoke in favor of convicting Bormann only on Counts Three and Four, while sentencing him to hang. Parker wanted the Tribunal to declare that they thought Bormann was dead, but Birkett spoke against this idea and Biddle, like Nikitchenko, recommended that they include an explanation in the final opinion, stating that they thought he was evading justice.[45]

Out of this muddle of sentiments and justifications came the showdown vote: Bormann, in absentia, was convicted unanimously under Counts Three and Four while spared under Count One by a two-two tie (Lawrence and Nikitchenko for conviction, Biddle and Donnedieu de Vabres against). Then by a unanimous vote, Bormann was sentenced to death by hanging.[46]

Overall, this case was one of the most casual and haphazard of the Court's performances. It was also one of the most disturbing instances of the Tribunal's inclination to get around problems rather than to confront them. The absentia trial issue was not faced squarely during the early stages of the proceedings, and for ten months the Bormann case was allowed to meander along while the Court routinely denied motions requesting separation and did its best to avoid recognizing that this was hardly an instance of due process. Perhaps fittingly, neither the deliberations nor the explanatory opinion on Bormann appears to have been carried through with clarity or vigor. In justifying its actions, the Tribunal merely noted that the evidence for Bormann's death was "not conclusive," that it had the power to try him in absentia under the London Charter, and that the evidence available to the Court pointed toward conviction and the death penalty. The only palliative it offered to those with reservations about trying and sentencing any person to death in absentia was to note that if Bormann turned up alive, the Control Council for Germany could "alter or reduce sentence, if deemed proper."[47] This was not much to give in exchange for the loss of one of the fundamental rights guaranteed by Western law.

Baldur von Schirach

Schirach joined the Nazi party as a student during the mid-1920s and gradually picked up posts in the Nazi student and youth organizations. In 1931 he was made youth leader for the party and, after

Hitler came to power in 1933, became "Leader of Youth" for the German Reich. His position required him to perform two main tasks: to undermine and finally eliminate all independent youth groups, and to gather the overwhelming majority of young Germans into the Hitler Youth and related organizations, where they would receive massive doses of Nazi ideological indoctrination. When the war came, the importance of youth work declined, and Schirach also had increasing personal and professional difficulties with the leaders of the party hierarchy. In consequence he gave up active control of the youth movement and assumed the position of Gauleiter in Vienna. Schirach stayed at this post until just before the total Nazi collapse in Austria, and during his nearly five years in Vienna he did the things that all the local chiefs performed in wartime Nazi Germany, from deportation of Jews to administration of the slave-labor program.

Officials of the British Government kept their eye on Schirach for a long time, and by 1944 he had already been placed on both the Foreign Office and War Office lists of major war criminals.[48] In June 1945, however, when the British prosecution team boiled down the lists to a group of ten "majors," Schirach was not included, nor was he on the American roster of sixteen prepared in the fourth week of June.[49] When the British, however, saw the American list, they suggested that it might be advisable to drop Admiral Doenitz as a defendant and put on Schirach instead. No serious discussion of this proposal seems to have occurred, though, because throughout the rest of June and July all the prosecutors were immersed in the Four Power negotiations on the Charter. When attention returned to a defendant list during the August discussions on the indictment, it turned out that the French and the Soviets wanted Schirach added to the American list of sixteen; since the British were already sympathetic to the idea, this was easily accomplished.[50]

In the indictment, Schirach was charged under Count One (Conspiracy) as well as Four (Crimes Against Humanity). The prosecution made a vigorous effort to link him to Hitler's general plans by stressing the great importance the Führer attached to the indoctrination of youth and by showing that the military and ideological training that Schirach had provided in the Hitler Youth fitted in with the Nazi "blueprint" for aggression. Some prosecution attention was also given to alleged participation of the Hitler Youth in the wartime atrocities, but the really significant evidence presented against

Schirach on Count Four had nothing to do with the Hitler Youth, but came from the years when Schirach was Gauleiter of Vienna. He was routinely responsible for the implementation of the forced-labor system in his *Gau*, so the prosecution's accusations in this regard were easily made, and easily proven. The accusations against Schirach in regard to Jewish deportations, had a special vividness, however, because of three pieces of prosecution evidence. When Schirach took over as Gauleiter, the first frightful stage in the deportations had already been completed and only 60,000 Jews were left from this once flourishing community. In October 1940, Schirach asked Hans Frank to take the remaining group of Viennese Jews into the Government General, and two months later Schirach was informed by Berlin that his request had been granted and the Jews would be deported. The crucial issue raised for Schirach's defense by this ghastly affair was the extent of his knowledge of what was happening to the Jews who were being deported to Poland. If he knew, or had good reason to suspect, what was happening, namely, that they were destined for the death factories, then his role in the deportations was patently culpable. The prosecution produced two pieces of evidence to show that Schirach had acted knowingly and out of conviction. During the last phase of the deportations from Vienna, Schirach's office was on the circulation list for the reports made by the *Einsatzgruppen* ("Special Unit") murder squads in Russia. These reports, which contained detailed tabulations of the slaughter, including the "liquidation" of thousands of Jews, were made after Schirach's initial deportation request. Yet the deportation trains that he had asked for continued to roll until the fall of 1942, and during most of this period the *Einsatzgruppen* murder reports were piling up in Schirach's office. When the deportation trains finally stopped because no more Jews remained alive, Schirach made an extremely compromising public speech, in which he boasted that his act of deporting "tens of thousands of Jews into the ghetto of the East" was a contribution "to European culture."

Somehow Schirach's defense not only had to demonstrate that the defendant's actions as chief of the Hitler Youth were well intentioned and based on good character, but it also had to refute the obvious connection that seemed to exist between Schirach's anti-Semitic teachings in the 1930s and the Viennese death trains of the 1940s. The task was made more difficult by Schirach's own muddled views and his rather unstable personality. Like Hans Frank, Schirach was subject to moods of melancholy self-incrimination, and he did make declarations on the stand that almost reached the point of repentant confessions. But, as soon as he worked his way down to the specifics of his past behavior, only long meandering statements of self-justification emerged.

It is difficult not to agree with Schirach's former wife that he was essentially a weak man for whom the pose, rather than the purpose, was the important thing.[51] His life and attitude seem to have been unusually episodical and he may well have been the perfect member of what Donnodieu de Vabres once suggested might be called the "chameleon conspiracy"—a criminal plan with constantly changing objectives, in which the members took on different shades of criminal coloration from the leader, Adolf Hitler.[52]

In any event, Schirach's testimony did not do much to help his case—"hogwash," Biddle called it—and his self-styled image as the virtuous young idealist who had been led astray was little more effective.[53] Biddle characterized him as a "typical" YMCA boy when he was on the stand, and that was obviously not intended as a compliment.[54] His defense did manage to undercut the prosecution charges that the Hitler Youth had been engaged in serious military training, but nothing was done to lessen Schirach's image as the Nazi ideological mentor for German youth. Regarding the Vienna phase of his career, the defense could do little but assert that his most incriminating remarks had not been intended the way they sounded and to contend that he was such an inefficient administrator that he had not known what was going on in his office and therefore had neither read the *Einsatzgruppen* reports nor even heard the name of his subordinate official who was directly in charge of them.

The summary of the case, presumably written by Fisher, as well as the Tribunal's deliberations, suggest that Schirach's defense presentation was not the decisive factor that saved him from the gallows. His actions did not look quite as bad as those of some of his fellow defendants, and he benefited from the comparison. The prosecution's case against him had also been presented rather haphazardly and his own disjointed career did not fit neatly into the definitions of crime used by the Tribunal. His escape from severe punishment seems to have been due chiefly to this gradual accretion of extenuating muddle.

The Tribunal's preparatory memorandum began by discussing Schirach's activities in the Hitler Youth and immediately dismissed from consideration the organization's military training as marginal and insignificant. Ideological and emotional preparation for war was the central issue, and, as the memorandum acknowledged immediately, it raised "a very difficult question" indeed.[55] There was no evidence that Schirach had received information on any specific aggressive plans and he obviously had virtually no influence on the shaping of broad Nazi policies. His crucial function was to develop a war enthusiasm among youth, and the memorandum concluded that this was "a key part in Hitler's aggressive plans." Even if Schirach "did not know of the specific plans for aggressive war," the memorandum continued, "he must have realized that he was preparing them to fight." [56] The writer of the memorandum, therefore, hesitantly decided that "he would appear thus to be guilty under count I," but then went on to assert that Schirach would also "appear to be guilty" to an equal degree under Count Two (for preparing wars of aggression), whereas the prosecution had not even charged him under that count.[57]

The nub of all this caution and wavering on Count One was that the prosecution's presentation had failed to link Schirach's agitation specifically to aggressive war but had tied it to war in general. Since international law considered defensive war a legitimate activity, it was difficult to feel completely at ease with a flat statement that Schirach's indoctrination for war was necessarily criminal. Yet, this was a rational legal consideration, while underneath it all those associated with the bench evidently had a strong visceral feeling that the Nazis had always intended forceful expansion and that Schirach had scrambled the minds of his young charges with enthusiasm for war and conquest. As the memorandum writer stated, with evident emotion, the mental condition of the youth "for the next 25 years" would be the chief obstacle to the solution of the "German problem" and for this "Schirach was responsible." [58] Like many summary statements and prophesies this one was not very accurate, but it does reveal the fundamental Allied concern in the case. If the judges could have found a satisfactory means, they would have been delighted to convict Schirach for his work with the Hitler Youth. The grounds for such a conviction, however, were just too dubious, and it was only with Schirach's sojourn in Vienna that the Tribunal had any prospect of finding him guilty. So the Court concentrated on the Viennese war crimes aspects.

The memorandum on Schirach stressed that as Gauleiter he was evidently guilty of participation in the slave labor system and also concluded that he was culpable because of his role in the anti-Jewish measures, especially deportation to the death camps and use of Jews for slave labor late in the war. As for Schirach's claim that he did not know of the exterminations, the memorandum writer observed that "he must have realized" what was going on, and, if by some miracle he had not, it was only because he was "purposely closing his eyes." [59] The memorandum concluded anticlimactically that Schirach "would thus appear" to be guilty under Count Four for his activities as a Gauleiter. [60]

One of the reasons that the memorandum's conclusions on the case were so hesitant was that here again the Court was face to face with the problem of surrender and subjugation. The *Anschluss,* which had made Austria part of Germany, had been recognized "as a fact" by the United States as well as the other powers, and it was difficult at this late date to assert that it was a military occupation and not an instance of subjugation. But simply to accept this would raise the same danger as in the Neurath case, and Schirach might emerge with a covering defense regarding Crimes Against Humanity. The only way out suggested by the author of the memorandum was to emphasize that the German expansion into Austria was part of a broad aggressive war conspiracy. If the Tribunal asserted this with sufficient firmness it would then be possible to connect other acts to it and thus permit conviction on Count Four. If the *Anschluss* were held to be part of a conspiracy, then Schirach's actions on slave labor and Jewish deportations could be deemed to have been carried out "in connection" with it. [61]

All this involved much straining and groping, but the Tribunal accepted it as the only available means to get at Schirach, and the argument put forth in the memorandum was taken over almost word for word in the final opinion. Emotionally, the Court was tipped very strongly against Schirach, but with its limiting definition of conspiracy, the defendant was virtually unconvictable on Count One, and without some way around the subjugation problem he would have gotten off on Count Four as well. In an emotional sense the Court had to accept the line between Crimes Against Humanity and a declaration that the *Anschluss* was part of an aggressive war conspiracy, but it left obvious untidiness in the verdicts. Schirach's conviction was linked to a declaration on subjugation completely different from the one that had been used for Neurath. Furthermore, although the Tribunal held that the *Anschluss* was part of an aggressive war conspiracy in Schirach's case, the two defendants in the dock most intimately connected with the *Anschluss* were not declared liable for their direct participation in that affair. Seyss-Inquart, found guilty and executed for his activities in the Netherlands, had his Austrian role passed over almost in silence by the Tribunal. And more significantly, in the case of the German ambassador in Vienna Franz von Papen, the Court held that there was "no evidence that he was a party to the plans under which the occupation of Austria was a step in the direction of further aggressive action," and he was acquitted. But because Gauleiter Schirach carried out his atrocities in Vienna, rather than in some other city, he was convictable simply because this territory had come to Germany by means of a conspiratorial plan, of whose existence even two of the most important participants in the action were unaware. A thin line of argument, indeed, and not a very convincing one.

Given the complexities of the case and the shakiness of the available arguments, it is understandable that the Court's deliberation on Schirach was divisive and protracted. The Tribunal did not initially discuss him until September 9, a week after most of the other defendants, because of their work on the conspiracy question.[62] The French and the Americans advocated convicting him on Count Four but not on Count One; Lawrence and the Soviets, however, wanted to hold him on both counts, and Nikitchenko pointed to his statements on the deportations as the crucial link between Crimes Against Humanity and Conspiracy. Two days later, on September 11, after a long, heated, and indecisive discussion regarding Doenitz, the Court took up the Schirach case for final decision.[63] The Soviets and the British again advocated convicting him on Counts One and Four. Although Birkett thought that Schirach's training of youth for the SS and his boastful speech on the deportations incriminated him deeply, he still wanted to sentence him to only twenty years in prison. The Soviet judges and Lawrence took a far graver view of the case and voted for the death penalty; Lawrence made the surprisingly ethnocentric supporting argument that Schirach had revealed the degree of his criminality when he had advocated retaliatory bombing of an English town at the time of Reinhardt Heydrich's assassination. Falco, who had been forced to cope with far more graduates of Schirach's educational system than had Sir Geoffrey, changed his mind in the two days since the first deliberation and this time spoke in favor of holding the former youth leader on both Counts One and Four. Noting that Schirach had written a letter to Streicher approving of his approach to "the Jewish question," Falco also drew attention to Schirach's deportation statements, the availability of the *Einsatzgruppen* reports, and Schirach's astounding explanation to the Court that he had advocated deportation because he thought it would be "better for the Jews." [64] The conclusion was obvious, according to the French judge: Schirach should be sentenced to life imprisonment or, perhaps, death. Donnedieu de Vabres, as usual, was more doubtful than his junior colleague and noted that in 1946, when everyone could see the logical consequences of Hitler's policies, things looked different. He thought that it would be fairer to put oneself in Schirach's position "at the time," thus seeing that criminal intent was not so clear. [65] Better to play it safe, Donnedieu de Vabres concluded, and convict Schirach only on Count Four with a sentence of somewhere between twenty years and life. Like the senior French judge, Parker seems to have wanted only to hold Schirach on Count Four, and Biddle, too, was more doubtful about the case than most of the other judges. The senior American Tribunal member apparently did not express an opinion regarding sentence during the first round of discussion, but he stated that Schirach's work with the youth movement should be disregarded, while his involvement as a Gauleiter was serious enough to find him guilty on Count Four. [66]

The result of the voting was to convict Schirach unanimously on Count Four, and to acquit him on Count One because of a two-two tie (Lawrence and Nikitchenko for conviction, Donnedieu de Vabres and Biddle against). What happened in regard to sentence, however, is not quite so clear. Biddle and Donnedieu de Vabres apparently picked up Birkett's idea that Schirach be given twenty years' imprisonment, and, with the Court then deadlocked between two for death (Nikitchenko and Lawrence) and two for twenty years (Donnedieu de Vabres and Biddle), the latter pair seem to have ultimately persuaded Sir Geoffrey to give way. With a combination of the three Western judges, then, Schirach was given a twenty-year sentence. [67]

There are a few loose ends on the Schirach case that deserve a moment's consideration before turning to the possibly more significant, and certainly more controversial, cases of the German admirals. Schirach was placed on trial as a major war criminal with an eye to his youth work, but then through a tortured argument on subjugation he was convicted for his activities as a Gauleiter. His actions in Vienna were surely loathsome, but they did not differ significantly from those of the other Gauleiter in Greater Germany. One could argue that, although Schirach was more vocal than many, he was also less personally cruel and brutal than a large number of the local Nazi satraps. Furthermore, no one at the trial, including the prosecutors, ever suggested that Schirach stand as a good representative for the Gauleiter subgroup of the Nazi party's "Leadership Corps," a group the Court was asked to declare criminal. The conclusion is inescapable that, although Schirach may not have been a nice man, he was not a *major* war criminal. On the basis of the legal categories established by the Tribunal and the political system of the Third Reich, it was simply a matter of chance that he, rather than hundreds of others, was the one selected to go to jail for twenty years.

In his subsequent efforts to grapple with what had happened to him and why, Schirach managed only to underscore how weak and confused he really was. The crucial accusation that troubled him was that he had urged the deportation of the Jews when he knew that it meant extermination. It turns out that his former wife had possessed the courage to protest to Hitler personally about the deportations, while Schirach himself had not.[68] In his memoirs, appropriately titled "I Believed in Hitler" (*Ich glaubte an Hitler*), Schirach went over the whole ground again and managed to confess that he had learned of the death camps, but maintained that he had done so only after the deportations from Vienna were long over.[69] He recounted how he had sat in a Gauleiter meeting and listened horror-struck while Himmler described the extermination of the Jews; he even quoted extensive passages from Himmler's address. But he then went on to date Himmler's speech in the spring of 1944 when, in fact, it had been given on October 6, 1943.[70] Even when the trial was over and after he had served his sentence, Schirach could still not bring himself to face the question of knowledge and responsibility without, perhaps unconsciously, playing with the data in order to lessen the period of his knowledge and, hence, of his guilt. To the very end he remained a dazed fellow traveler, perhaps the archetype of his breed.

Erich Raeder

The Tribunal's handling of the case against Erich Raeder appears to have been another instance where the judges felt serious difficulties were involved but, instead of patiently unraveling them, chose simply to cut their way through. Erich Raeder was the commanding admiral of the German fleet and chief of the Naval High Command from 1928 until his retirement in 1943, midway through the war. His case was intertwined with that of his fellow admiral, Karl Doenitz, who initially commanded the German U-boat arm and then succeeded Raeder as commander in chief of the navy. But the routes by which the two admirals became defendants at Nuremberg were totally different. From an early date the Americans wanted to try Doenitz, while Raeder only became a major war criminal because he happened to be in the wrong part of Germany at war's end. Although the Western Powers were fully informed about the main phases of his career, Raeder was not included on either of the two British lists of major war criminals compiled in 1944 and was also omitted from the British and American lists of "majors" drawn up in June 1945.[71] He even escaped the first approved listing for the indictment that was completed in mid-August; but then, on August 27–28, as already related, the Soviets insisted that two of their prisoners be included, and with French concurrence Hans Fritzsche and Raeder were added to the defendant list.[72]

Since Raeder was charged under the first three counts of the indictment, but not accused of Crimes Against Humanity, the prosecution understandably concentrated its attack on proving that he had participated in aggressive war planning. Extensive evidence was submitted to show that Raeder had authorized wholesale violations of the naval armaments clauses of the Versailles Treaty, in some cases even before Hitler became chancellor. But the prosecution had difficulty demonstrating that these actions were directed toward aggressive purposes, especially as the Anglo-German Naval Agreement of 1935 made clear that the British Government had been prepared to accept some German naval expansion, even in violation of the Versailles Treaty, as long as it remained within agreed limits. The prosecution was more successful in documenting Raeder's participation in the invasion planning of 1938–39, for he and Goering were the only defendants who had been present at the Hossbach meeting and had continued to hold their offices. In addition, Raeder, like Goering, had attended all the major attack planning sessions held in May and August 1939. The navy commander in chief had also been active in developing, or had at least been informed about, the subsequent assaults on Norway and Denmark, the Low Countries, Greece, and the Soviet Union. The significance of the navy in the last three of these operations was limited, and the prosecution conceded that Raeder had opposed the attack on Russia but it stressed that his opposition was due to an appraisal of the military risks rather than to moral or legal scruples. On the other hand, Raeder had ceaselessly urged the German Government in 1940–41 to press the Japanese to expand the war by attacking Britain in Asia, and the prosecution also made out a strong case that the German Navy had played the decisive role in the invasion of Norway in the spring of 1940.

Compared with the broad case that the prosecution developed for Conspiracy and Crimes Against Peace, the War Crimes charge against Raeder focused only on a handful of incidents. In the first days of the war, a British passenger liner, the *Athenia*, had been sunk and the London government accused the Germans of having dispatched it by a stealthy and unprovoked submarine attack. The Germans, in return, accused Winston Churchill of having sunk the ship himself in order to create a juicy incident to facilitate anti-German propaganda. At war's end, the captured German naval records showed that a German U-boat had, in fact, sunk the *Athenia*, and that the Berlin government had gone to great lengths to cover up the facts while attempting to put the blame on the British. The prosecution endeavored to make something of a *cause célèbre* out of this incident, but the defense presentation, and even some of the prosecution materials, showed that the ship had been sunk by a trigger-happy U-boat skipper who had disobeyed orders. The German campaign to blame the British was irresponsible, but it had started at a time when the German naval authorities had believed that their forces were not responsible. If the navy command were guilty of anything, it was that it reacted too rapidly and, once the error had been discovered, did not admit its mistake and disavow the propaganda campaign against the British. Obviously, these were errors rather than crimes, and the *Athenia* affair, which initially appeared so ominous for Raeder's case, ultimately played no direct role in the Tribunal's ruling.

On the other hand, the Germans use of unrestricted submarine warfare was, in the words of the Court, the "most serious" charge against Raeder as well as Doenitz, for the commander in chief bore the ultimate responsibility for the combat methods employed by the navy. Raeder's defense seems not to have clearly grasped the vital significance of the issue, but from the beginning Doenitz understood that it was a matter of life or death for him and centered his whole defense on meeting this charge. In the end, he was successful, and, as the Court's ruling made clear, he saved not only himself but Raeder as well. The Tribunal's opinion held merely that Raeder was not liable under this charge and for an explanation of its reasons referred the reader to the explanation on the Doenitz case.[73] Since the issue was decided outside the parameters of Raeder's defense, we will follow the lead of the Court and consider it as part of the Doenitz case, noting merely that on this charge Raeder was found not guilty.

After the collapse of the charges related to U-boat warfare and the *Athenia*, the whole war crimes case against Raeder devolved by default into consideration of his transmission of the so-called commando order, which Hitler had secretly issued in 1942. By the terms of this order, military and security police authorities were specifically required not to treat captured commandos or members of similar formations as prisoners of war, but to liquidate (that is, execute) them without trial, even if they were captured in uniform. The circulation of this order played a part in the convictions of Jodl, Keitel, and Goering, as well as Raeder, but in the other three cases there were additional atrocities that pointed toward conviction, while, for Raeder, his guilt or innocence on war crimes rested solely on this issue. The prosecution easily demonstrated that Raeder had passed on the order, and the navy commander in chief himself admitted that he had not protested its issuance. Evidence of a number of incidents in which the navy had captured commandos and turned them over to the SD for killing were cited by the prosecution, and in one case it was shown that the navy itself had carried out the execution. Even more damning was a comment written on a naval war staff document that noted that, although these actions were taken in pursuance of a Führer order, the execution of military personnel captured in uniform was "something new in international law"— which strongly suggested that the Naval High Command knowingly participated in criminal acts.[74]

If the commando order is considered solely within these limits, then it is rather easy to assert its criminality and, if the plea of superior orders is barred, then Raeder is guilty, at least as an accessory. But there are additional considerations related to the question that may make such a conclusion more debatable. A military order that passes beyond the "laws and customs of war" must not necessarily be considered illegal if it can be shown that it was a reasonable and necessary reprisal for an act, or series of acts, committed by the enemy. The secret execution of uniformed POWs would seem to leave no room for such a justification, but the circumstances surrounding the issuance of the commando order indicate that it was not merely an act of arbitrary savagery on the part of Hitler. A general factor underlying the question that was apparently not clearly grasped by the Tribunal was that, though in the East the Nazis practiced wholesale extermination of POWs for ideological as well as for practical reasons, in the West the German Government's POW policy approximated the one customarily used by Western Powers. There were, of course, incidents of maltreatment of such POWs, and the policies of using prisoners in war industries, as well as the failure to provide adequate rations, fell outside some provisions of the Geneva Convention. But the German Government's policy was to try to stay within hailing distance of the Geneva Convention in Western Europe. In part, this position was facilitated by racist feelings of kinship with the Western peoples, in contrast to the hatred directed at the Eastern *Untermenschen*, but it also rested on a shrewd estimate of political realities. Like the Western leaders, Hitler knew that nobody would win a battle of reprisals against POWs, and he may have realized that such a contest would be especially dangerous for him. To adopt public policies that invited Allied reprisals against German POWs would strain civilian patience to, and perhaps beyond, its limit. The government obviously had enough difficulty trying to justify its harsh Eastern policies in the face of worried inquiries from German civilians concerned over their kin who were captured or missing in the East. By portraying the Soviets as beasts who could not be mollified in any case, it was possible to keep this civilian pressure at bay, but the same trick simply could not be turned in the West in 1942. If German POWs began to be killed or maltreated in reaction to policies that the Nazi government could control, a public outcry might result. Certainly Hitler, of all people, did not want to provide a handle that might shake the civilian population out of its lethargic obedience and lead to questions about the conduct of the war. It was therefore definitely in his interest to do nothing that would produce a conflict over treatment of POWs in the West.

Some of the Allies' actions, however, especially the methods used by the British commandos, put heavy pressure on Hitler's unsteady self-control. The commandos on occasion not only used "gangster" weapons, such as the famous knuckle-dusters, but also had operational procedures for shackling prisoners and, under certain very restricted conditions, were authorized to kill POWs. Apparently, it was the German capture of commando directives authorizing such actions, as well as the seizure of actual shackles, that drove Hitler into the rage that resulted in the commando order. The German military leaders seem to have brought this evidence of commando excesses to his attention in order to impress on him the severity of the tasks they faced, but, in fact, they overplayed their hand. Either because of fear of reprisal or simply as a terror tactic, the Führer opted not to make a public warning on commando operations, but instead demanded, and ultimately obtained, the issuance of the secret extermination order.

Considering the touchiness of the Nuremberg Court about any defense effort to justify German actions by quid pro quo arguments, it would probably have been wisest for the defense to marshal as much information as possible on the background of the commando order and use it in a plea for mitigation. But the disunity of the defense, and the differing responsibility of those defendants who had prepared the order (Keitel and Jodl) as against those who had merely transmitted it (Raeder and Doenitz), meant that the available defense arguments and evidence were frittered away piecemeal. The Court never obtained a clear picture of the circumstances surrounding the issuance of the order or of general German POW policy and, consequently, when Raeder's case came up for consideration, the commando order continued to loom as the one firm point for his conviction on Count Three.

Rowe's short memorandum on the case asserted bluntly that Raeder was guilty on Count Three "because of the Commando order," and this conclusion was duplicated in the Court's final Judgment.[75] The memorandum was more cautious about Raeder's liability under Counts One and Two, conceding to his defense that violations of the Versailles Treaty were not necessarily steps toward aggressive war. Raeder had some grounds, the memorandum also acknowledged, to discount the Führer's bellicosity in 1938–39 because of the unpreparedness of the navy and Hitler's assurances that he did not want war with England. Rowe also granted that the navy's role in the war against Poland had been minor, and he indicated that Raeder might well be right when he justified the preparations for the actions against Greece as countermeasures directed against the British, who had already landed there. Regarding the attack on the Soviet Union, Rowe noted that, although Raeder had spoken against the operation, he had also authorized advanced submarine attacks against Soviet shipping, even before the invasion began.[76] The core of the case against Raeder under Counts One and Two, however, was the German invasion of Norway; here, although he mentioned Raeder's assertions that the assault had been intended to head off the British, Rowe attached no significant weight to it and concluded that Raeder should be found guilty on Counts One and Two "primarily because of Norway."[77]

The case against Raeder was certainly not overwhelming and one may have the uneasy feeling that personality played a part in determining the outcome. Raeder himself was a rough blend of feistiness and pedantry. He sharply challenged every prosecution assertion, big and small, and seems thereby to have earned himself few good marks from the Tribunal.[78] But if Raeder was not an endearing character, he shone brightly when compared with his chief defense counsel, who managed simultaneously to irritate Birkett with his boring repetitiveness and to anger Biddle because he continuously performed like "an impudent fellow."[79] It is instructive to read the diary of one of Raeder's assistant counsel in conjunction with Biddle's evidentiary summary, for the comparison shows how greatly the defense misjudged its abrasive ways and also failed to focus on some of the issues that would be crucial when the Court began deliberation.[80] On the other hand, it is necessary to note that the defense presentation on Norway, stressing the British preparations for a landing, was handled quite skillfully, yet failed to make a corresponding impression in Biddle's notes. From the materials available, it seems that, when Raeder's case went into the deliberative chamber, it had to paddle itself upstream as best it could because the Court extended little understanding or sympathy to the defendant.

The first deliberation on Raeder was very short, coming as it did on the heels of a long and exhaustive session devoted to the Doenitz case. In the initial voting, Donnedieu de Vabres favored convicting Raeder on Counts Two and Three while Biddle called for a finding of guilty on Counts One and Two and, "perhaps," Three. The rest of the judges wanted to find the admiral guilty on all three counts. Apparently, the only comments made during the voting were Donnedieu de Vabres's observation that his guilt was greater than that of Doenitz, and a short exchange between the American judges on an appropriate penalty, with Parker opposed to the death penalty and Biddle inclined to have Raeder shot.[81]

On September 11, the final deposition of the case took place as another brief interlude in the midst of larger controversies. This time Raeder was squeezed in between Schirach and Doenitz. During the deliberations Donnedieu de Vabres remarked on the similarity with the Doenitz case and Falco mentioned Raeder's transmission of the commando order, but no other comments are recorded. All the judges present had come around to the view that the admiral should be convicted on the three counts. The Soviets called for the death penalty, Lawrence and Biddle wanted life imprisonment, and Donnedieu de Vabres suggested twenty years; the Tribunal was thus deadlocked in exactly the same way as it had been in the Hess case, and, although the details of what happened this time are not clear, either Nikitchenko went down to a life sentence or Donnedieu de Vabres went up to it. In any event, the Hess pattern was followed quite closely; Raeder was unanimously convicted on all three counts and then was sentenced to life imprisonment.[82]

Karl Doenitz

Both in the amount of time and attention the Court gave to the case and in the depth of disagreements that resulted, the proceedings against Doenitz completely overshadowed those against the other eighteen defendants who were convicted. Doenitz came up for consideration by the Court on four different occasions, and the preparatory discussion of his case on September 9 took up the better part of a complete day's session. At first glance it may seem surprising that a career naval officer should have produced so much division, but Doenitz's career had been unusual, and his case had also evolved in peculiar ways. In 1935 he had been made commander of the newly unveiled submarine program and he retained direct command of

U-boat operation until 1943, when he replaced Raeder as commander in chief of the navy. Then, in the last days of the regime, just before his suicide, Hitler passed over his old party comrades to name Doenitz as his successor. Thus, Doenitz was not only the representative of submarine warfare and later of German naval operations; for twenty days he had been head of state and was the second and last head of the Third Reich.

Doenitz's appearance in Nuremberg as a defendant, however, came about only through a number of peculiar twists and turns. He was not placed on the British war criminals lists of 1944, and it was Jackson who first mentioned him to the British as a prospective defendant in May 1945.[83] But the British did not include him in their roster of ten "majors" prepared in June, although his name did appear as a remote possibility on a Foreign Office war criminals roster prepared in the same month.[84] The Americans were determined to get Doenitz and he was among the sixteen majors identified by Bernays and his staff in London.[85] Still, the British were not ready to follow the American lead and, as already mentioned, they came back with a counterproposal that Doenitz be held back as a possible defendant while Schirach was added to round out the main list of sixteen.[86] The matter officially rested there until the formal Four Power discussions on the defendant list took place in mid-August. In the interim, both the British and the Americans had strengthened their respective positions. The U.S. prosecutors had obtained extensive documentation on the German U-boat program, including what they felt was strong evidence for the existence of a formal system of killing survivors of torpedoed ships. Armed with this material, the American officials were more convinced than ever that Doenitz should be made a defendant.[87] But British officials from both the Foreign Office and the Lord Chancellor's Office who reviewed the Doenitz case in August, concluded just as strongly that he should not be prosecuted. At the core of the British hesitation was the view of the Admiralty that the German Navy had, by and large, fought a clean war, and that Doenitz should be left alone.[88] What the Admiralty did not say was that the Western Allies were at least as responsible as Doenitz for any violations of international law that had occurred on the high seas. The British authorities simply did not want the navy's linen to be washed in public, and even after Doenitz was made a defendant the Admiralty notified the British prosecutors that it retained an "interest" in the case and wanted to be kept informed.[89]

The British representatives fought hard during the Four Power talks to prevent Doenitz from being made a defendant, but they were overcome by the determination of the Americans, who easily obtained support from the French and Soviet negotiators. Once in Nuremberg, Doenitz showed not only that he was going to battle the prosecution every step of the way, but that he had immediately grasped the main issues in his case and was prepared to meet them carefully and intelligently. By the time Major Neave visited him on behalf of the Court in October, in order to discuss the system of attorney selection, Doenitz had already requested that he be represented by a leading German naval lawyer, Dr. Otto Kranzbuehler.[90] As the epigraph at the head of this chapter indicates, he had also decided that his best line of defense was to stress the parallel between German and Allied submarine warfare. In addition, Doenitz asked Neave how he should go about obtaining documents for his case, and he also informed him that henceforth in interrogations by the prosecution he thought that he would only "put the points which he intended to use in his defense," at least until "his counsel arrived."[91]

Obviously, if Doenitz had been left to his own devices he would have been among the more formidable defendants, but his attorney, Otto Kranzbuehler, was also exceptionally able and had such good rapport with his client that Doenitz was helped immeasurably thereby. It was Kranzbuehler who hit on the brilliant idea of turning the customary law argument back against the prosecution, by contending that since elements of the international law regarding submarines were unclear the Allied naval chiefs should be questioned in order to establish what were the prevailing usages and customs. Of course, Kranzbuehler and Doenitz knew that, if the British and American naval authorities answered honestly, they would have to admit that they had used submarine policies at least as harsh as those the Germans had employed. When Kranzbuehler's petition was presented to the Court, the judges also had a fair inkling of what was involved, and Nikitchenko recommended that they flatly reject it.[92] The French and the English wavered, but Biddle stated firmly that he thought the petition was legitimate, and, since it was a question that touched upon the conduct of the U.S. Government, he invoked personal privilege, asking his colleagues to yield to him. Partly as a matter of courtesy, Lawrence did so, the French and Soviet judges then followed suit, and the Doenitz petition was unanimously approved.[93] This incident was not only Francis Biddle's shining hour, it was also the decisive turn in the Doenitz case, because henceforth it was impossible for the Court to avoid comparing Allied and German submarine policies.

Yet, as should occur in the trial of an admiral, the court proceedings were not all smooth sailing for Doenitz. He was not an endearing or lovable soul, just a tough U-boat commander who looked and acted the part. The very vigor of his defense reinforced the image of him as a man dedicated and combative to the point of fanaticism and probably beyond it. No warm or sympathetic notes about him appear in the records of Birkett or Biddle. The most personal remark made by the British alternate was a comment on one occasion that Doenitz appeared to be teetering on the edge of despair.[94] Although Biddle was struck by how "stirred" Doenitz became in asserting that survivors of sinkings had not been killed, it is obvious that he did not understand or sympathize with parts of the admiral's testimony.[95] Only during Raeder's appearance on the stand did Biddle permit himself a personal comment on Doenitz, and that was to observe that "the other Grand Admiral is sound asleep!"[96]

The Doenitz case was briefed by both Sir Geoffrey's marshal, John Phipps, and the American legal aide, James Rowe; the latter produced a memorandum that was unusually comprehensive and detailed.[97] Rather than following the volleys in the case made by the prosecution and defense, the main issues will be examined here through the points in the Rowe memorandum. The views put forth in the memorandum seem to have closely paralleled Biddle's own at a time when the attitudes of the American judge were decisive. Rowe, who, it is important to note, was an officer in the U.S. Navy during the war and was therefore familiar with naval law, had to begin by dealing with the questions of conspiracy and the planning and waging of aggressive war, since Doenitz was charged under Counts One and Two as well as Count Three (War Crimes).

Concerning Doenitz's tenure as chief of U-boats up to 1943, Rowe decided that he was not instrumental in planning aggressive attacks, but in a marginal comment Biddle observed that Doenitz had prepared a memorandum in 1939 on the desirability of obtaining U-boat bases in Norway.[98] Rowe's discussion of Doenitz's activities after

January 1943 called forth no comparable comments from Biddle. The crucial question was whether Doenitz had made himself guilty by assuming the naval command of an aggressive war, and Rowe was inclined to agree with the defense's contention that, by the time he took over, the war had become a defensive, rather than an offensive, conflict for Germany, and Doenitz should therefore be found innocent. Rowe also dismissed all the evidence indicating that Doenitz was an enthusiastic Nazi, evidence that was plentiful then and is more extensive now. The American legal aide decided that this material was not relevant to Doenitz's selection as Hitler's successor and should therefore play no part in the verdict.[99] Even though Doenitz admitted on the stand that he had purposely prolonged the war in an effort to give more Germans an opportunity to escape from the advancing Russian Army, Rowe believed that this "should make no real difference" in determining his guilt on Counts One and Two. Generally, the memorandum concluded that Doenitz's last-minute appointment as head of state "would seem to be irrelevant to his guilt or innocence and should therefore not be considered." Similarly, although the question of whether he had waged aggressive war was debatable, Rowe was inclined to decide it in Doenitz's favor and therefore recommended that "in the opinion of this writer Doenitz should be found Not Guilty under counts one and two." [100]

Troublesome as these issues were, they appeared to be trifles when compared with various aspects of the war crimes case covered by Count Three. The general issue was the conduct of submarine warfare, but this question was so complicated that Rowe had to move through it very deliberately. Doenitz denied that he had any knowledge of a general decision by the German Government to plan or wage submarine warfare in violation of international law, and, as Rowe noted, the prosecution had failed to "shake him in his denial." [101] Therefore, each particular aspect of Germany's conduct of submarine warfare had to be examined separately. The first question was whether the German decision to attack enemy merchant ships without warning was an unwarranted violation of the naval understandings of 1930 and 1936, as alleged by the prosecution. The defense contended that the British had armed merchant ships, used convoys, and, in fact, by means of a radio warning system, had turned their merchantmen into belligerent vessels. German unrestricted U-boat warfare against enemy merchant vessels was a necessary reprisal, the defense argued, because once merchant vessels were armed it would have been suicidal for the U-boats to try to obey the rules of international law and stop such ships for search prior to attack. Rowe clearly agreed that the defense arguments had demolished this aspect of the prosecution's case. The refusal to stop and warn an armed merchantman was "common practice" for all navies, he noted, including the submarine services of Russia, Britain, and the United States. Furthermore, Rowe declared, the legal view that once a merchant ship was armed it forfeited its immunity, which had been advanced by the defense, was also "shared by most international law experts." [102] With the facts and the law on its side, the defense was right that these attacks could be considered legitimate retaliation and Doenitz should not be punished for them.

The general charge that German submarines had attacked neutral—in contrast to belligerent—merchant vessels, had two aspects. The Germans had used a blanket system of sinking all vessels that traveled darkened at night, and they had also declared certain sea zones closed and then sunk any vessel that penetrated into the forbidden areas. Regarding the first part of the problem, attacks on darkened vessels, Rowe noted that the prosecution seemed to think that when the Germans argued that blackouts made ships inherently suspicious, their statements were somehow disingenuous. But Churchill had admitted that the British Navy proceeded on the same assumption, and Rowe added that "it was of course the American practice." [103] So this aspect of the neutral sinkings problem was disposed of in Doenitz's favor, leaving only the more complicated question of restrictive zones. Such zones had been used by both sides during World War I, but the interwar naval agreements had not specifically mentioned them as legitimate exceptions to the general limitations established for submarine warfare. On its face, this omission seemed to mean that proclaiming a zone did not free the belligerent from the restrictions imposed by international agreements. At Nuremberg, such an interpretation would have meant that the Germans had not had the right to attack neutrals anywhere, without warning. The defense, however, put a very different construction on the question, contending that the powers deliberately had not banned these attacks in the interwar agreements because each government wanted to reserve to itself the decision whether it should use such zones. This explanation, while good history, was uncertain law; because a statute does not deal with a specific possible exception to a general prohibition, it does not necessarily mean that it has condoned it. Yet once again, Rowe was surprisingly tolerant of the position taken by the defense and concluded that the failure of the agreements to mention zones was, in fact, deliberate, and that Doenitz's interpretation of the law was "rather sound." [104]

The shadow that hung over this whole discussion of neutral rights, zones, and submarine attacks was the conduct of the U.S. Government in the Atlantic in the two years prior to Pearl Harbor. It was not Berlin but Washington that had first resorted to zones. Initially, the United States had prohibited its vessels from entering European belligerent waters and it also inspired the inter-American governments in October 1939 to declare certain Western Hemisphere waters "sea safety zones" that had to be kept free of military or naval action. When the Germans came to establish their "unrestricted attack" zones, they merely reversed the American system and stated that entry into certain waters, particularly those around the British isles and in the North Sea, would expose all vessels to attack without warning. The subsequent American actions, whereby the United States extended military aid to Britain, undertook convoy patrol, and ultimately issued "sink on sight" orders against German submarines throughout much of the North Atlantic, were complete contradictions to existing international practice and the customary status of a neutral. So completely did the U.S. Government violate international law that these acts were considered by many circles at home, as well as by the Berlin government, to have been intentionally provocative. On the stand, Doenitz made no bones about his feelings in the matter; he had wanted to launch reprisal attacks against the Americans, but the Führer had forbidden such action because, though seething, Hitler was determined to avoid war with the United States for as long as possible.

In this setting, Rowe's acceptance of the defense arguments on zones becomes more understandable. As with virtually every other aspect of the submarine case, the American legal aide measured Doenitz's actions by the standard of American practice, and on the zone question, the admiral certainly was no more guilty than the American leaders. Rowe also decided that Doenitz had seriously tried to prevent the sinking of neutral vessels, including those of the United States, outside of the prescribed zones. Doenitz maintained that when such sinking incidents had occurred they were simply mistakes, and Rowe commented that in light of the large number of Allied sinking errors, the facts "would seem to bear him out." [105]

Thus, Doenitz was given a clean bill of health on his handling of attacks on neutrals, and Rowe even went out of his way to give him the benefit of the doubt on the one narrow aspect of the question where he was most vulnerable. In January 1940 he had issued an order authorizing unlimited secret attacks on all vessels along enemy coasts where it could be pretended that they had hit mines. In Court, Doenitz was somewhat embarrassed by this order and claimed that it had been intended only to confuse British intelligence. The other possible interpretation was that there was doubt in the mind of the U-boat command about the legality of their zone attack system and they were trying to disguise what they were doing. But Rowe refused to follow this trail of argument that had been laid down by the prosecution and decided that the order referred only to a counterintelligence maneuver and did not indicate that Doenitz was acting in bad faith when he established the zone system.[106]

An equally serious, and emotionally more volatile, question was that of killing, and failing to rescue, passengers and crews from ships sunk by U-boats. The London agreement and other naval warfare codes required submarines to make adequate arrangements for rescue of all crews and passengers of ships that were attacked. The prosecution held that Doenitz had followed a general policy of nonrescue from the beginning of the war, and that he had never attempted to live up to the terms of the London agreement. The general defense argument was that the German U-boat service had tried to abide by the agreement, but had been forced away from it step by step due to circumstances and to techniques of the British, such as arming merchantmen, that made it impossible for the U-boats to use halt-search-and-rescue procedures.

The prosecution submitted two pieces of evidence to support its broad contention that Doenitz's nonrescue policy was planned from the opening of hostilities. The first of these was a statement made by Hitler to the Japanese ambassador, Hiroshi Oshima, that U-boats did not rescue as a matter of fixed policy. The second was a specific order issued by Doenitz early in the war forbidding U-boats to pick up survivors. The defense replied that Hitler's statement to Oshima was merely an instance of the Führer's tendency to show off with tough talk in front of foreigners, and that the statement bore no relation to what was actually being done on the high seas. Regarding the second and more formidable piece of evidence, Doenitz's early no-rescue order to U-boat commanders, the defense said that this was not a general order but merely a response to special circumstances existing in 1939–40. It had been issued at a time when the handful of U-boats available were operating next to enemy shores and rescue attempts under such conditions would have been suicidal. Doenitz pointed to evidence indicating that later, when the battle moved out to the open seas, this order had been rescinded. Rowe traced the defense argument approvingly and accepted its main contention that the nonrescue policy had been applicable only in special circumstances. In Rowe's view, the prosecution had failed once again to prove that the U-boat command had operated on the basis of broad criminal policies.[107]

Even so, Doenitz was far from home free because other sensitive orders had been issued regarding survivors in subsequent stages of the six-year naval war. In 1942, the U-boats were directed to pick up captains and engineers from sunken ships, and the prosecution contended that, if the Germans were capable of rescuing these people, then the decision to leave other survivors was simple murder. The defense, however, produced a strong counterargument to this accusation: the order in question had resulted in the rescue of only a handful of captains and engineers over a three-year period and so the basic defense contention that there was not sufficient room aboard submarines to rescue the bulk of the survivors could not be gainsaid.

The most trenchant challenge to this defense position was not the captain and engineer order, but a second Doenitz directive on survivors, also issued in 1942. This so-called *Laconia* order demanded, in strict terms, that the submarine commanders act in a hard and determined manner, never imperiling their ships by attempting to rescue survivors. The tone of the order was extremely harsh, and the prosecution used it to assert that here was the real Karl Doenitz, a fanatical, ruthless instrument of the Nazi cause who relished the opportunity to draw a line between "us" and "them" and mercilessly to condemn the sinking victims to death. The prosecution produced as a witness the officer in charge of briefing U-boat crews before they set sail; he asserted that he had understood the *Laconia* order to mean that survivors should be killed, and he had instructed departing crews to that effect. A junior watch officer also affirmed, in an affidavit, that he had once received the impression from Doenitz himself that the *Laconia* order was intended to encourage, or at least to authorize, the murder of survivors. Finally, one fully documented incident occurred, the "Eck case," in which a U-boat had systematically moved through a sea of survivors and deliberately killed them by small arms fire.

On the stand, Doenitz flatly denied that the *Laconia* order authorized the killing of survivors and he also put the responsibility for his rigid nonrescue policies squarely on the shoulders of the Allied authorities who had made use of uncontrolled air attacks on U-boats. Going back to the *Laconia* incident itself, the defense pointed out that when this British vessel had been sunk, the U-boat commander discovered that it had Italian POWs aboard, and he therefore made special efforts for rescue. Not only did he notify all naval commands of the location of the sinking, and provide what aid he could, but he also called in other U-boats to assist him in towing toward shore lifeboats filled with survivors. Instead of summoning Allied rescue operations, however, his messages brought forth Liberator bombers, which ignored the victims in the water and began to bomb the U-boats that had gathered to assist in the rescue operations. It was this incident, Doenitz contended, that had snapped his last reserve and made him order his captains not to jeopardize precious submarines and crews by such humane, but foolhardy, rescue attempts. He admitted that from this point on he was ready to fight without quarter, but this meant only that survivors would not be helped, not that they would be systematically killed. The U-boat briefing officer was wrong when he concluded that this was a kill order, Doenitz maintained, and his defense attorney gathered affidavits from virtually all the surviving U-boat captains, stating that they had not understood the order to mean that they should kill survivors. The junior watch officer whose affidavit had asserted that the Doenitz order implied survivors should be killed changed his testimony on the stand, and Rowe concluded that his original statement would therefore have to be disregarded.[108]

Since Doenitz was eager not only to save himself but to defend the honor of the navy's U-boat arm, it is not surprising that the submarine captains should rally around his flag. The efficiency of Doenitz's defense, and the unanimity with which members of the U-boat service supported whatever the admiral said does make such unanimity hard to accept. But there are also two other strong pieces of evidence supporting the contention that Doenitz did not establish a policy that survivors should be killed. In 1942, the German Foreign Ministry reported that 80 percent of the crews of torpedoed enemy merchant vessels were getting home safely and implied that the U-boat arm should develop some more effective way of eliminating them. But Doenitz ignored the Foreign Ministry approach and refused to order the killing of Allied crews—a decision that, coming as it did at a time when Hitler's aides were competing to see who could come up with the worst atrocities, took both principle and courage. Even more supportive of Doenitz's defense position was the conduct of U-boat Captain Heinz Eck, who was tried by the Allies in a separate proceeding for the massacre of the survivors of a sinking. The only possible defense open to Eck was to claim that he was obeying orders, and there are suggestions that the prosecution may have tried to lead him into this position. But Eck refused to invoke a superior orders defense and asserted that he had made the decision to kill on his own initiative, in order to avoid detection. Although it meant that he would be executed, Eck clung tenaciously to his assertion that he had not acted on the basis of higher orders. This was either an instance of incomparable devotion to a lost cause or telling evidence that Doenitz had, in fact, not directed his captains to kill survivors.

The presentation made by Doenitz's defense convinced Rowe, and he concluded his discussion of the survivor issue by stating that the prosecution's contention that the admiral had issued a kill order simply had "not been maintained." [109] But Rowe went further in upholding the line put forward by the defense, noting that it had met every specification on the case set down by the prosecution and had discussed the international legal issues, which the prosecution had not done. On these grounds alone, Rowe implied, there was good reason to find Doenitz not guilty, but beyond them loomed the even more basic issue of Allied submarine policy. Admiral Chester Nimitz of the United States and British Admiralty officials all admitted, in affidavits, that their navies had waged unrestricted submarine warfare, sinking without warning and refusing to pick up survivors, except under special circumstances. Nimitz also stated flatly that the United States had followed these policies from the first day of the Pacific war, in December 1941. Of course, as Rowe conceded, the prosecution might technically be right that the parallel with the Allied conduct of submarine warfare would not be relevant for determining German guilt or innocence. The two Allied affidavits had been authorized only to help clarify the actual state of maritime law and practice related to submarines. Still, Rowe observed, there was the undeniable fact that the United States had waged submarine warfare "in a particularly ruthless way" that went beyond the worst violations of international law charged against the Germans. To convict Doenitz under such circumstances, Rowe concluded, would inevitably remain "offensive to the Anglo-American concept of justice," and he should therefore be acquitted on all charges related to submarine warfare.[110]

The remaining aspects of the Count Three charges against Doenitz seemed comparatively minor once Rowe had resolved the submarine questions in the defendant's favor. Regarding the commando order, Doenitz admitted that he knew of it, but since it did not apply to submarine warfare he contended that he had not passed it on to his subordinates. He also asserted that, though commander in chief of the navy from 1943 on, he was unfamiliar with a general navy memorandum on the question and was uninformed of the one commando execution incident that had been cited by the prosecution. Rowe concluded that because Doenitz's responsibility was sufficiently unclear, and the circumstances surrounding the one navy-related execution so cloudy, the admiral should not be held accountable for the commando order.[111]

The only vulnerability that Doenitz had on the matter of slave labor fell in the period January–June 1943, because after the latter date, Albert Speer was made responsible for naval construction. During the six months when he was navy commander in chief and did bear the responsibility, Doenitz had once suggested that 12,000 concentration camp laborers be used for merchant ship construction, but beyond this there was no prosecution evidence. Late in the war Doenitz had made a compromising suggestion regarding one of Hitler's more foolhardy ideas. When the Führer suggested that Germany denounce the Geneva Convention (by this time German popular resentment against Allied bombing had put public opinion on his side regarding harsh measures for Allied fliers), Doenitz recommended that it would be better to take "the measures considered necessary" but not to denounce the Convention publicly. At Nuremberg, Doenitz maintained that the "measures" he had in mind were not violations of the Convention, but only innocuous actions regarding POWs. This statement led Rowe to remark that Doenitz was "probably lying," [112] but in any event the Convention had not been denounced and there were no indications that last-minute systematic violations of it had been carried out.

Throughout, Rowe treated the nonsubmarine-related charges under Count Three as if they were of minor importance—"trifling," Biddle would later call them. But it must be noted that Rowe made no effort to plumb the depths of the prosecution's contention that Doenitz's Nazi fanaticism was at the bottom of the harsh naval policies. Furthermore, some incidents were not considered, such as Doenitz's alleged praise of an officer for directing that a German Communist be killed while they were both prisoners in Allied hands. Still, Rowe's thirty-page treatment of the case was exceptionally thorough and deliberate, and his conclusions were also unusually straightforward—Doenitz should be found not guilty on all three counts. [113]

When the Doenitz case moved off the preparatory memorandum and into the deliberation room on September 9, exhaustive consideration continued, but most of the straightforward conclusions vanished. Only Nikitchenko and Volchkov were prepared to reject flatly all contentions of the defense and convict the admiral on the three counts. The Russians held that the zone system violated international law, and if the Court acquitted Doenitz it would amount to declaring that his system of waging submarine warfare was "legal and proper." [114] The two French judges groped wildly in search for a way to reconcile a conviction of Doenitz with the checkered evidence and the uncertainty surrounding the law. Falco wanted to convict him only on Counts Two and Three—on Count Two because of the invasion of Norway and Count Three, in part because of submarine warfare but chiefly because of Doenitz's other actions related to war crimes. While granting that the Nimitz affidavit had "simplified" the legal problems, Falco still thought the *Laconia* order was criminally ambiguous, and that Doenitz was also guilty because of his attempts to blame sinkings in certain waters on mines. But Doenitz's chief guilt, in Falco's view, arose from his handling of the commando order, his suggestion that concentration camp labor be used for ship construction, and his having attended, and drafted the minutes of, a meeting with Hitler in which reprisals against Danish saboteurs were discussed. The French alternate was apparently also considering holding Doenitz criminally liable for his praise of the officer who had authorized the killing of a Communist while in a POW camp. [115] Donnedieu de Vabres was his usual doubting self, believing that Doenitz should not be convicted on Counts One and Two because he was a "subordinate officer" at the time of the attack on Norway. On submarine warfare he cited the numerous factors in Doenitz's favor, concluding that although his directives were equivocal, there was no specific order to kill survivors. The French senior judge granted that Nimitz's affidavit had helped Doenitz, even though the Americans had justified their action as retaliation for the Japanese attack on Pearl Harbor. He also wondered aloud whether submarine warfare did not stand outside international law, and whether the British blockade had not also been a violation of international agreement. On all counts, then, there was much to be said in Doenitz's favor, but this still did not deter Donnedieu de Vabres from reaching the surprising conclusion that the admiral should be convicted on Count Three and given "a very mild sentence." [116]

Parker's approach to the Doenitz problem was unusually historical. He maintained that the United States had entered World War I in order to insist on "the international law of warning." The interwar treaties had not changed the legal obligations relating to submarines, and armed merchantmen had not specifically been given the status of naval vessels. Doenitz had indiscriminately sunk both ships in certain zones and ships running without lights; he had thereby violated the law, and the Tribunal, Parker stressed, had no right "to disregard the law." Though the United States might have used similar policies, it was Doenitz's submarines that had "destroyed the Treaty of London," Parker argued, thus making the treaty "hard for other nations to consider." [117] This conclusion ignored the fact that Japan subsequently followed the treaty rules rather closely while the United States and Britain did not. Yet such considerations did not deter the American alternate, who held that because the prime responsibility belonged to Doenitz, he should be convicted on Count Three. Parker also favored finding him guilty on Count Two, apparently because he was too enthusiastic about "waging" wars that the Tribunal considered aggressive. The usually calm and deliberate Parker appears to have been thoroughly aroused by the harshness of Doenitz, and Biddle was probably right when he later mused that Parker simply could not get beyond the chilling picture of the "ruthless machine gunning of sailors clinging to the wreck of their torpedoed ship, adrift in the vast waste" of the sea. [118]

Lawrence, however, believed that Parker had given an accurate summary of the law, and he shared the American alternate's attitude toward Doenitz and his actions. Characterizing Doenitz's system of indiscriminatory sinking of ships within certain zones as a "murderous declaration," Lawrence asked rhetorically what justification there was for torpedoing dimmed vessels. Admiral Nimitz also might have sunk without warning, Sir Geoffrey acknowledged, but he brushed aside the Allied actions as reprisals and laid the prime responsibility at Doenitz's door. Lawrence was ready to give Doenitz the benefit of the doubt on the survivor question, admitting that there may not have been an order to kill; but everything else, he contended, from the handling of the commando order to the incident with the Communist in the POW camp, showed the real nature of the man, "typically National Socialist—harsh and inhumane." [119] Therefore Doenitz had to be convicted on Count Three, and Lawrence also concluded that since the admiral had gone on "waging an aggressive war" he should also be found guilty on Count Two.

In the middle of this discussion, Francis Biddle launched into what must be considered the most sensational piece of advocacy that occurred during the deliberations. Arguing that armed merchantmen were "war vessels," he noted "how silly" it would be for the Court to penalize Doenitz for not giving warning and picking up survivors when doing so would have made submarine warfare impossible. This was especially true, Biddle contended, because at that time Britain was arming merchantmen and the Allied naval authorities were issuing submarine orders identical with those used by Doenitz. Biddle called for the admiral's complete acquittal and he concluded his presentation with a statement that probably left his colleagues somewhat shocked and breathless. "Germany," he said, "waged a much cleaner [naval] war than we did." [120]

Following this acrimonious discussion of September 9, it was obvious that no easy agreement would be possible. Nevertheless, on the next day, the Court tried again, but after an indecisive skirmish it was decided that the case would have to be "left over." [121] On the 11th, with Birkett present, the Court finally settled down to hammer out a verdict and sentence. Biddle again argued strongly that Doenitz should not be convicted for his conduct of submarine warfare, but he failed to move any of his colleagues, who were determined to find the German guilty on Counts Two and Three. Regarding sentence, the basic position was established by Robert Falco who suggested that Doenitz be give ten years' imprisonment because his guilt was "much less" than Raeder's. [122] The other judges then took positions on various sides of the ten-year proposal.

Parker supported it, holding that Doenitz's sentence should not be more severe than Raeder's (only the death penalty would have been), and, although he felt that ten years was on the low side, it would be acceptable to him. Lawrence also spoke in favor of ten years and repeated his earlier contentions regarding Doenitz's ruthlessness and the need to condemn the zoning system. The determination of the British judges to convict, which was so completely at variance with the stand on Doenitz taken earlier by the Admiralty, showed up even more clearly in the suggestion of Norman Birkett that Doenitz be sentenced to twenty years because a ten-year term would be "inadequate." [123] The Soviets, who at first suggested darkly that a "most severe sentence must be accorded to the least guilty," [124] also acknowledged that they would accept a lesser penalty for Doenitz than the one that had been given to Raeder. Toward the end of the discussion, Nikitchenko quietly agreed to go a step further and accepted a sentence of ten years. Donnedieu de Vabres, almost invariably on the low side of every controversy on penalties, was close to the majority position this time and suggested a sentence of five to ten years. [125]

Only Biddle failed to go along with the idea of convicting on Counts Two and Three, and he also did not agree to a ten-year sentence. In the course of the discussion, he seems to have threatened his colleagues that, if they insisted on convicting Doenitz on submarine warfare charges, he would file a public dissent. [126] The two American judges were deeply divided, with Parker nearly as determined to convict as Biddle was to acquit. The American alternate avowed that he still could not believe that the U.S. Government had conducted the same kind of "damnable warfare" as had Doenitz. [127] It was essential, in Parker's view, that the Tribunal condemn the German policy of sinking neutral ships, but he did agree, albeit reluctantly, that it would be acceptable to avoid a declaration regarding attacks on armed vessels. This concession went part of the way toward meeting Biddle's insistence that Doenitz not be condemned for his conduct of submarine warfare, and Parker also suggested that Biddle join with him and write the opinion of the Doenitz case. The latter suggestion apparently laid the basis for the most surprising, if not shocking, compromise developed during the deliberations: the other judges agreed that, if Biddle would abandon his idea of a public dissent, they would let him write the final opinion in the case! [128] Biddle accepted the arrangement and the interminable wrangling on the Doenitz case finally ended with the admiral convicted on Counts Two and Three and sentenced to ten years in prison. [129]

For two weeks, Biddle worked on the Court's final statement on Doenitz; it was apparently approved by the Tribunal on September 26 with "almost" no changes. This summary has often been discussed and analyzed and there is little reason to repeat the exercise. The argument is long, disjointed, and not very consistent. The reason for this is now clear—it is the opinion of a dissenting judge trying to make the majority position seem as close as possible to his own. In the summary, Doenitz was found guilty of waging aggressive war on the vague grounds that he was of unusual "importance to the German war effort." [130] Regarding submarine warfare, the opinion refused to hold him for his attacks on armed merchant ships but did condemn him for the zone system, which it held was a violation of the London naval agreement. It also censored him especially for the ambiguity of his policies and orders regarding survivors. Parker thereby had his way. The attacks on armed merchant ships were passed over and the attacks on neutrals were condemned. But then Biddle added the most sensational sentence in the Judgment, stating that, in view of the fact that the British and the Americans had also used unrestricted submarine warfare, the sentence against Doenitz had not been "assessed on the ground of his breaches of the international law of submarine warfare." [131] The opinion thus implied that he had been convicted for the "trifles" that were then chronicled: his handling of the commando order, his suggestion that concentration camp labor be used for naval construction, and his cryptic recommendation in 1945 that "measures" be taken that were outside the Geneva Convention. Biddle did his best to dress these up and make them sound as serious as possible, but, compared with the actions cited for other convicted defendants, they appear petty and consciously exaggerated. The opinion was, after all, merely a piece of window dressing; the majority of the Court had convicted Doenitz because of submarine warfare but had agreed to say that he had been convicted on other grounds. Little wonder that the explanation is not very convincing!

It is difficult to say much that is ennobling or edifying about the Court's actions in the Doenitz case. The justifiable limit toward compromise and pragmatism may have been passed. Since the Soviets were eager to hang everyone, the limited Judgment on Doenitz was produced by the resolve of the British judges to convict, and by Donnedieu de Vabres's willingness to line up with the British rather than the Americans. For his part, Biddle thought that the important issue was not Doenitz's guilt or innocence but the need to explain the grounds for conviction in such a way that the Anglo-American judges would not appear to have been guilty of hypocrisy. This Biddle accomplished, although he was subsequently troubled by the thought that he had been inconsistent. While he had struggled to clear the record in the Doenitz case, he had not been shy at other points in the trial about convicting Germans for the kind of aggressive war planning that the Soviets had simultaneously executed against Finland and Poland.[132] Even in his later pensive mood Biddle was not prepared to add the British operation in Norway to the list of possible points of inconsistency. Still, whatever reservations one must hold about the whole affair, Biddle did take a step that helped to prevent possibly greater evils. Because of the Doenitz decision, the Court failed to make its Judgment a clear declaration that victors should totally ignore their own conduct while applying "justice" to a defeated enemy. However inconsistent the Court may have been, the opinion in the Doenitz case produced a pause in our Orwellian rush toward ever more total war and vengeful peace.

As always in trials pivoting on weighty issues, the fate of the defendant tends to get lost. Admiral Doenitz believed that he fell victim to a double standard, and that the Court's explanation was so much self-justifying double-talk. Yet it is now clear that it was Biddle's advocacy, and the resultant protracted controversy, that gradually wore down the other judges and inclined them to accept a relatively mild sentence as part of a general compromise. This sentence gave Doenitz a measure of what he wanted: his primary aim had been to vindicate the U-boat arm and he had done it well enough so that he received a moderate sentence.

Conversely, it is just this result that makes it difficult to move away from the Doenitz case with a light heart. Even today, when reading the remarks that the admiral made in late 1943 lauding Himmler for his ruthlessness, it is difficult not to go back and vote with Lawrence that he should have been held guilty because the harsh U-boat system resulted from the ferocity of Doenitz's Nazi enthusiasms.[133] Furthermore, to most Anglo-Americans, Doenitz remains the practitioner of a most horrible and terror-laden form of warfare—silent and heartless destruction at sea. That many Germans have an equally vivid sense of horror regarding the death at the bottom of the sea that overcame the vast majority of those in the U-boat service has never made a serious impact on the feelings of people in the United States and Britain. Thus, there was little chance that the Court's ruling, or any other possible verdict, could have been both rationally and emotionally satisfying. Even when the Tribunal's imprecision and inconsistency are revealed in all their nakedness, as in this case, the question still looms whether it would really have been better to have hanged Doenitz for doing what Nimitz did or, conversely, to have acquitted him and put an international stamp of approval on unrestricted submarine warfare. Truth may well have lain with one or both of the alternatives advocated by Parker and Biddle, but the judges finally recognized that for them prudence and safety lay somewhere in between. When they chose this middle way, they may have inadvertently voted for what was the safest and most prudent course for the rest of us as well.

CHAPTER 9

The Acquittals: Schacht, Papen, Fritzsche

THERE IS a sense of relief when one has passed through the nineteen convictions and can turn to the three cases where no one went to prison or to the scaffold. Whether the defendant is Joachim von Ribbentrop or Fritz Sauckel, and no matter what the deeds or the evidence, a chill hangs over an account that points to death by hanging. Of course, judges, especially when pressed against the horror of deeds and the mood of times, are not supposed to be deterred by such feelings, and, with the exception of Donnedieu de Vabres's unaccountable flashes of "tenderness," there are no indications that the Nuremberg bench was seriously troubled by imposing either prison or the rope. The greater calmness that we bring to acquittals rather than convictions would seem to be a product of our distance from the postwar responsibility that the judges assumed. Those who actually had to make such decisions may well have been more troubled by the complications that led to acquittal than by the simplicities that pointed toward conviction.

As with the defendants who were convicted, the Court took up the cases of the three acquitted men independently from each other, but there was much more conscious, and perhaps unconscious, interconnection between these three cases. At the start of the trial, none of the judges was inclined to vote for any acquittals; they seem initially to have assumed that evidence would be presented to incriminate all twenty-two defendants. Only gradually and fitfully did individual judges recognize that the case against a specific defendant was weak on this count or that, and acquittals on these charges would have to follow. From this position, individual Tribunal members moved even more haltingly to the conclusion that a particular defendant might have to be acquitted altogether. Generally, the two defendants who were most responsible for this evolutionary process were former ambassador to Austria Franz von Papen and an upper-middle-level official of the Propaganda Ministry, Hans Fritzsche, whose presence in the dock became increasingly inexplicable not only to Hermann Goering but to the men of the Court. The Tribunal obviously worried and fussed with the Fritzsche and Papen cases all through the deliberations, and, when both American judges voted to find them not guilty in the initial discussions, the acquittal of at least one defendant became a serious possibility. Therefore, although much of the discussion of the Schacht case came first, the judges were constantly looking over their shoulders at defendants number twenty and twenty-four, mentally comparing notes and trying to decide whether the guilt of other men was really much greater than that of these two men who were likely to escape punishment. Although the cases of the three acquitted men will be discussed here in the same order as they were considered by the Court, the interconnections should be kept in mind.

Hjalmar Schacht

With the possible exception of Hermann Goering, Schacht was the most complicated and formidable of the defendants. Like the Reich Marshal, he was also viewed with extreme hatred and distrust by much of the press and public. Part American in origin—the indictment demurely did not list his double middle name of "Horace Greeley"—Schacht had spent most of his life in international financial and political circles. Well known in the major capitals of the world and universally recognized as a financial expert, Schacht also had a less enviable reputation as a German apologist and political opportunist. He had emerged from the disillusionment of World War I as a democrat, but soon began a gradual movement toward the political right. In 1923 he attained worldwide fame, and to some appeared to be a financial wizard, as a result of his crucial role in ending Germany's runaway inflation. By the eve of the Nazi assault on power in the early 1930s, Schacht had migrated to the Nationalist party, so it was relatively easy for him to develop a working relationship with Hitler. Schacht helped introduce Hitler to German business circles, to make him *salonfähig,* and this effort received considerable critical attention, and probably some exaggeration, from the liberal and left-wing newspapers in Germany and abroad. To his reputation as a financial wizard was thereby added the picture of a capitalistic political manipulator who had pulled the strings that brought Hitler and the German capitalists together. Viewed from this perspective, Hitler's appointment of Schacht first as president of Germany's central bank, the Reichsbank, two months after the Nazi seizure of power, and then as minister of economics and plenipotentiary of war economy within the next two years, seemed merely a partial payment for services rendered. Nor did Schacht's performance in these posts disappoint either his supporters or his critics. By a series of unorthodox financial expedients ranging from peculiar instruments of credit called Mefo Bills to blocked accounts, Schacht managed to supply greatly increased monetary resources to the Nazi government. Since that government's most obvious use of the money was for rearmament, a third level of imagery was added to Schacht's name: that of the ultimate merchant of death who had used his cleverness and chicanery to provide the means for Hitler's Germany to attain overwhelming power.

Then, beginning in 1937, Schacht and his public image began to run into trouble. He lost a battle with Goering over control of the economic machinery for mobilization, and thereafter, step by step, he came into a sharp confrontation with Hitler. In 1937, Schacht resigned his positions as economics minister and plenipotentiary for war economy and then was dismissed as president of the Reichsbank in 1939. Finally, in 1943, he lost his last official post, that of minister without portfolio, and was thrown into the eminent prisoner section of Dachau concentration camp in the late summer of 1944. At war's end, Schacht was eager to present himself as just another victim of Hitlerian repressive measures. Despite his espousal of the cause of the German resistance, however, public opinion in Britain and the United States, to the degree that it remembered Schacht at all, was much more inclined to regard him as the manipulator who had brought Hitler to power and financed German rearmament. As Felix Frankfurter wrote to Jackson soon after the latter accepted the post of American chief prosecutor, Schacht was his "pet villain of the Nazi regime," and he hoped that an opportunity could be found to put him in the dock.[2]

However, those who bore the responsibility for choosing the major defendants moved much more hesitantly on Schacht. In 1944, the British War Office included him on a list of possible major war criminals, but the Foreign Office, which prepared a similar list at the same time, did not.[3] A year later, when the time had come for the British and Americans to agree on a list of "majors," Jackson mentioned Schacht as a possible defendant in the first exploratory talks in May.[4] But the British Foreign Office was still doubtful about him, and this uncertainty was heightened by fear that the Americans were about to launch a broad attack on the prewar and wartime German industrial leaders. Although Schacht received oblique references in a list of "possibles" completed in mid-June, his name was accompanied by a number of worried comments by Foreign Office officials urging that he be omitted, and that if an economics figure had to be included to appease the Americans, it should be Sauckel or Funk rather than Schacht.[5] The formal British list of ten "majors" did not include Schacht's name, so it was left to the Americans to try to put him in the dock and they thus placed him on their list of sixteen in June.[6]

The British, however, as with Doenitz, were not ready to acquiesce quietly in Schacht's inclusion, and in mid-August the Lord Chancellor's office made a "thorough appraisal" of the situation, concluding that the former economics minister would be very difficult to convict and should not be indicted.[7] In the discussions on the defendant list that took place in mid-August, the British presumably raised some of these objections but found them quickly swept aside by the other Three Powers. That the Soviets would want Schacht included was a foregone conclusion, but one of the surprising features of the early stages of the trial preparations was the intensity of French hostility to the German industrial leaders. At this point, the French were more extreme than either the Americans or the Russians.[8] So Schacht was routinely included in the defendant list despite British doubts and objections.

At Nuremberg, where the task was not indicting but convicting, Schacht showed that the British worries had not been misplaced. When Major Neave made the rounds of the defendants on behalf of the Court, Schacht indicated that he was in no mood to let matters take their course; he knew how the game was played, and he informed Neave that he wanted a good lawyer and he wanted him fast. Of the attorneys on the Court's list, Schacht thought Dr. Rudolf Dix would be acceptable and Dix was, in fact, assigned to him.[9] Soon after this was done, Schacht also made it clear that he would not cooperate in any overall defense plan to justify the regime or exonerate all the men in the dock.[10] He was out to save himself, and, like Goering, he decided that the first thing to try was a direct approach to the prosecution. On November 14, 1945, Schacht wrote to the American assistant prosecutor, General William Donovan, stressing that he welcomed the establishment of the Nuremberg Court because it would reveal Hitler's crimes to the whole world. Stretching the truth considerably, Schacht went on to assert that he had submitted himself "voluntarily to this court" because of his conviction that "the trial will prove that I am in no way guilty of any crime or immorality." [11] After an amazing sentence eulogizing Donovan by enumerating his "high standing," "experience," "wisdom," and "well known international reputation," Schacht finally got down to business and asked whether Donovan would be willing to "look into a brief summary of the underlying reasons and conditions of the dreadful Nazi-regime, as I have experienced them." Schacht concluded his letter with more praise of Donovan, stating that he would "prefer to submit such [a] summary to a man of your judgment and capacity than to any of the lawyers or defense counsels which may appear before courts." [12]

Donovan understandably took this to be an overture from a man willing to cooperate with the prosecution, and on the same day that the letter arrived he wrote to Jackson, outlining his appraisal of the Schacht situation. Donovan reminded Jackson that there had been previous indications that Schacht wanted to make a contact, and that Donovan had informed the justice of these. The time had come, in Donovan's view, to decide how the Schacht case stacked up and what was to be done about the approaches from him. Donovan noted that, because of Schacht's role in rearmament and "what he should have known of Hitler's character," the prosecution might "have enough to hold him for aggressive war." The General admitted that "there is a strong argument in this," but that there were also considerations on the other side, some of which were well known, others of which were quite delicate, if not sensational.[13] Schacht contended that he had tried to distract Hitler from aggressive war by suggesting colonial acquisitions, and when that had failed he had tried to cut off the money. In consequence, he was thrown out of office and had then worked with the resistance until sent to a Gestapo prison and a concentration camp. But Schacht also asserted that, beginning in 1940, he had been in contact with, and had performed services for, the Allies. He contended that Roosevelt had sent him a secret message indicating that "he would be needed after the war," which, although Donovan did not say so, was probably just a bit of embroidery on the well-known Schacht–Sumner Welles talks in 1940. The item, therefore, was not so startling.[14] But Donovan also admitted that his own organization, the OSS, had indirectly obtained information from Schacht during the war. Hans Gisevius, who was deeply involved in the anti-Hitler plots of the German resistance, was also in touch with the OSS, and he had used Schacht as a source for some information that was passed on to Allied authorities.[15] But even this was merely incidental to Donovan's real bombshell. In 1940–41, the first secretary of the U.S. Embassy in Berlin, Donald Heath, was a contact through whom Schacht communicated with the Department of State. As described in Donovan's letter to Jackson, Heath reported, among other things, "that our advance notice of the attack on Russia was given to Heath through Schacht." [16] If true, this was a revelation of the first order and might well give the prosecution reason to pause before launching into a knockdown struggle with Schacht in open court. Donovan drew the obvious conclusion and suggested that:

consideration be given to the possibility of giving him [Schacht] the opportunity to fight his way out by actual testimony dealing with the facts. He could strengthen our case considerably and without promises he could be given the chance in the direct case to state his position.[17]

This suggestion did not quite amount to a recommendation that Schacht be turned around and made into a prosecution witness, but it came very close to it. Donovan was too experienced a lawyer and had spent too much time as head of the OSS to be led in blind, however. Ten days later, in a memorandum discussing the general use of witnesses, Donovan remarked that he had informed Schacht's counsel that he would not see his client until Schacht "made clear exactly what he was prepared to do." [18] But neither Schacht nor Donovan had an opportunity to explore this question further, because two days later, on November 26, Jackson sent a long, burning message to Donovan, in which all the disagreement and hostility between the two men finally flashed into the open. As has long been known, the argument centered on Jackson's belief that the case should rest almost exclusively on documents, while Donovan wished to make greater use of witnesses. But the cutting edge of the conflict was Donovan's effort to turn Goering and Schacht around to benefit the prosecution. As Jackson stated bluntly, "We do not see alike about the defendants such as Schacht. I do not think he will help us convict anyone we do not already have convicted on the documents." [19] Jackson also refused to countenance any arrangement whereby the prosecution would "negotiate" or "bargain" with any defendant to give him "advantage" for his testimony. After reviewing the various aspects of their conflict, Jackson concluded, "Frankly, Bill, your views and mine appear to be so far apart that I do not consider it possible to assign to you examination or cross-examination of witnesses." [20]

The next day, Donovan sent back a stinging reply that chronicled his version of the whole sorry episode. In addition to citing his criticisms of Jackson's general direction of the prosecution, many of which were tellingly accurate, Donovan also took pains to clear himself from the insinuation that he had intended to "negotiate and bargain" with Schacht or Goering. He stressed that he had already told Jackson, and Schacht's lawyer as well, that there could be no discussion until Schacht laid out what he was prepared to do. Donovan characterized Jackson's other fears and suspicions as "tilting at windmills" and, with obvious relief, ended his letter by reaffirming that he was quitting the case and leaving Nuremberg in the immediate future. [21]

With Donovan's departure, all contact between Schacht and the prosecution seems to have broken off, and in the months of heady confidence that characterized the start of the trial Jackson and his staff appear to have been untroubled by the questions that Donovan had raised about the case. But after the cross-examination debacle with Goering, the prosecution began to take the Schacht problem much more seriously. Elaborate arrangements were made to amass every conceivable piece of evidence against Schacht, and Jackson's assistants prepared long lists of points that might prove damaging to the defense.[22] Jackson was clearly worried, however, and on March 29 he made arrangements to see Donald Heath, the man in the U.S. Embassy who had purportedly received the reports from Schacht regarding Hitler's decision to attack the Soviet Union in 1941. The information that Jackson obtained from this discussion was probably even more damaging to his case than he had feared. Heath reported that when Welles was in Berlin in 1940, an arrangement had been made for Schacht to transmit "information" through Heath to the State Department. From that point through the next year and a quarter, Heath and Schacht met "on the average about once a month." Heath also stated that he had concluded that, "at least from 1939 on, Schacht was avowedly anti-Nazi." Although much of the information that Schacht gave to Heath took the form of "generalities," in the spring of 1940 he had advised that the time was ripe to restrain Italy, and he had also provided a broad hint in the week before the invasion of the Low Countries that an assault was in the offing.[23] On Russia, Schacht had been especially clear and precise. As Heath told Jackson:

on or about 6 June 1941, approximately two weeks before the invasion of Russia, Schacht told Mr. Heath that Hitler was determined to invade Russia on or about 20 June. [The invasion occurred on June 22.] Schacht stated that Mr. Heath could take this as established fact; it was not open to surmise. Mr. Heath immediately contacted the State Department with this information, and the State Department thereafter used the information in the manner they deemed most expedient.[24]

It is no wonder that, with the Goering defeat in his mind and this information in his hand, Jackson went into the cross-examination of Schacht without overweening confidence. Actually, Heath's account of Schacht's message on the Nazi decision to invade Russia sounded as if the incident had more historical importance than it actually seems to have had. At the time of his last talk with Schacht, Heath was in the process of being transferred to a new post in Latin America, and, unless he transmitted the information to the State Department independently through special channels, the report that reached Washington was a watered-down account sent on June 8 by a Heath associate. Though starting his message with the statement that he had "received rather impressive testimony that within a fortnight Germany will invade Russia," Brewster H. Morris, the third secretary of the Embassy, did not mention Schacht as the source of the information. What was worse, he added his own speculation about how difficult it was to divine Hitler's intentions and further observed that the "tremendous preparations on the Russian border" might yet be a "form of final pressure on Russia or a mask for action in some other area." [25] By all indications, Morris's qualifications and observations took the sting out of Schacht's message, and the Washington authorities never saw its significance or passed it on to the Soviet Union. It is perhaps the culminating instance, though heretofore unknown, of the thesis advanced by Barton Whaley that the Germans were able to achieve surprise in their attack not because of effective secrecy, but because so many pieces of conflicting information were available that the intelligence systems of their opponents were glutted and thus unable to filter out a clear picture of the situation. [26]

Jackson, however, did not know that Schacht's message had led nowhere, and it probably would not have made much difference if he had known it. His task was to portray Schacht as a devoted and dangerous Nazi, while knowing full well that Schacht had also been an Allied intelligence source. Of course, he may have surmised that Schacht would be reluctant to announce in open court that he had provided the Allies military intelligence information that might have cost thousands of German lives. Nonetheless, the danger existed that, if Schacht were driven to desperation, he might be forced to do just that in an effort to save himself. The cross-examination exchange between Jackson and Schacht was therefore a restrained and limited skirmish that neither side had an interest in pushing to extremes. Such a situation obviously works to the advantage of the defense, and since Jackson was trying to prove the most nebulous of phenomena, Schacht's knowledge of aggressive war intentions at a time that he was master of economic details, the result was a foregone conclusion.

Birkett, Biddle, and presumably the rest of the Tribunal members as well, had no illusions about who had emerged victorious from this genteel exchange. Schacht not only avoided being cornered, he gave such a convincing demonstration of his intelligence and ability that he acquired a new respect in the eyes of some of the judges. By the time of his final plea in August, both Biddle and Birkett were obviously impressed with him and Biddle remarked in his notes that Schacht was "proud and very moved" when he addressed the Court.[27] On the eve of the deliberations regarding his case, no one associated with the bench seems to have had any uncertainty about what the central issues really were. Adrian Fisher had prepared the basic American memorandum on Schacht during the second week of July, and, although he took a good deal of care and thirty-five pages to brief the case, he dismissed all questions of War Crimes and Crimes Against Humanity from the very beginning. Schacht had been charged only on Counts One and Two, but in the course of the trial the prosecution had intimated that he might be held liable for persecution of Jews and related matters. Fisher decided that, no matter how the Court interpreted conspiracy, Schacht could not be held accountable for war crimes because he had been "consistent in opposing atrocities." [28]

The heart of the case, according to Fisher, was "the part he [Schacht] played in preparation for war," specifically, whether he had aided German rearmament either because he favored aggressive war or because he knew of the aggressive war plans.[29] Fisher acknowledged that, although the signs indicating that he favored aggression were sparse and dubious, there were better grounds to hold that he had known that the military forces he was helping to build were to be used "to back up a program of territorial expansion, by threat, if possible, but by force if need be." Schacht's intelligence, as well as the large number of specific indications he had received from Goering and others, "must have made him aware," in Fisher's opinion, "of Germany's aggressive intentions." [30] Furthermore, Schacht's statements relating to the time he broke with Hitler were not altogether clear or convincing. Not only did his resignations and dismissals stagger down over a six-year period from 1937 to 1943, but he gave assistance to the regime at the same time that he was working against it. Most incriminating were the occasions when Schacht lavished public praise on Hitler following the *Anschluss* and the fall of France, because these occurred at times when Schacht claimed that he had broken with the Führer out of opposition to aggressive war. Fisher concluded that, though Schacht was a key figure in rearmament, there had been no showing that he favored aggressive war, and it was most likely that he opposed it. His real guilt, Fisher held, was that after 1936, when he was losing control, he failed "to withdraw," and it "would appear," therefore, that he was a participant in a common plan to wage aggressive war up through 1938 and should be found guilty under Count One. On the other hand, the fact that he did "withdraw" prior to the attack on Poland led Fisher to recommend that the Court find him not guilty of being an accessory under the planning and waging war provisions of Count Two (Crimes Against Peace).[31]

Most of Fisher's analysis did not call forth especially sharp rejoinders from Biddle's pen, but the cautious suggestion that Schacht be found innocent under Count Two definitely did. Although Biddle had progressed a long way in his respect for Schacht, he was not one of those, like the British legal adviser, John Phipps, who believed from the beginning of the trial that Schacht would be acquitted.[32] Biddle moved down through Fisher's memorandum marking a margin and adding an underline here and there, but, when he reached the concluding suggestion that Schacht be cleared under Count Two, he marked the margin heavily, added a large question mark, and wrote, "Why? If he prepared an aggressive war, and it broke out, is he not guilty as an accessory or did he withdraw?"[33]

This vigorous but somewhat cryptic comment may serve as an appropriate introduction to the deliberations on Schacht. After taking the lead in the battle to acquit in the Doenitz case, Biddle, who leaned toward conviction on Schacht, stepped back and let Parker set the tone of the discussion this time. In a thoughtful argument, and apparently also in a memorandum, Parker underscored the central issue: Was Schacht a knowledgeable participant in an aggressive war conspiracy or was he not? All other considerations were irrelevant in Parker's opinion, and there was no middle ground for the Court. Either Schacht was not in the conspiracy and his work on rearmament had no criminal intent, in which case he had to be acquitted; or he was a participant, should be convicted, and then "get the works." Having posed these extreme alternatives, Parker urged his fellow judges to favor acquittal, because, to his mind, the evidence pointed to the conclusion that Schacht was not in a "concrete, definite conspiracy," and did not "have in mind" that "this armament" should be used for aggressive war.[34] Birkett agreed with Parker that the Court had either to acquit or severely punish, but he wanted to look at other factors while trying to determine Schacht's real attitude. The British alternate was troubled by Schacht's public praise of Hitler after he nominally had broken with him, but he also put weight on the large amount of evidence in Schacht's favor, and the fact that he had ultimately joined the resistance. Birkett wanted time to review the evidence, but his inclination in the first deliberation was to grant that a reasonable doubt existed and the Court should therefore acquit. [35]

Lawrence also favored acquittal but was much more firmly convinced of Schacht's innocence. He advanced the unusual argument that, although Schacht had not been present at the Hossbach conference, the existence of that meeting indicated that there had not been a general recognition of Hitler's aggressive war plans by the German leaders prior to November 1937. Everyone who attended the conference was "amazed" by Hitler's plan to attack Austria and Czechoslovakia, according to Lawrence, and he concluded that if the aggressive war plans had, in fact, been made previously there would have been no reason to hold the Hossbach meeting. The subsequent removal of Generals Fritsch and Blomberg had opened Schacht's eyes, and from then on, Lawrence was satisfied, Schacht had worked diligently and consistently to oppose Hitler. [36]

Sir Geoffrey actually held that, unlike the other defendants, Schacht was not a ruffian but a banker, and therefore should be given special consideration because he was a "man of character." [37] Lawrence's blending of attack plans and general war conspiracy was difficult for some of his fellow judges to accept, but his defense of Schacht's class and character left Biddle, and presumably the Soviets, in openmouthed amazement.

Despite this howler, Nikitchenko conceded that he was troubled by the Schacht case and by Parker's arguments. It was with some evident reluctance that Nikitchenko affirmed his inclination to uphold the conspiracy charge and convict Schacht on Counts One and Two. His junior colleague Volchkov, however, had no hesitation about conviction, and Biddle observed that he seemed to have "prepared a whole book on Schacht." [38] Biddle himself was very hesitant, and, though inclined, with Birkett, to convict Schacht on Count Two, he wanted to study the testimony and examine the exhibits before reaching a final decision.

With Lawrence set for acquittal and Nikitchenko and Biddle leaning toward a finding of guilty, the position of the French judges was of crucial importance. Again, Donnedieu de Vabres led with his heart; he was therefore unable to accept Parker's extreme dichotomy. He did not want to acquit any of the defendants because the breadth of the Nazi "crimes" was so enormous that the individual defendants, "irrespective of their personal fault," could not be given a stamp of approval by the Tribunal.[39] Schacht had contributed to rearmament and, Donnedieu de Vabres pointed out, "everyone knew" that when Schacht took office an offensive policy was probable. Even though he had seen at an early date that Hitler "was condemned to failure," Schacht still publicly shook hands with him after the fall of France. So a basis of guilt did exist, but it was not excessive; in any event, the French judge observed, "the law is new" and should be applied with prudence and caution. Rather than acquit, it would be better to convict defendants like Papen and Schacht, and then give them light sentences on moral grounds. Donnedieu de Vabres remarked, in conclusion, that he would be "shocked" if Schacht were acquitted and Keitel hanged.[40]

Falco took a much more analytical approach to the case and was obviously inclined to be much harder on Schacht. In his view, although Schacht had wanted to rearm slowly and avoid war, he, like the other defendants, "thought Hitler would achieve his aims without war." "No one had the firm will for aggressive war," Falco observed, but they "believed in [securing] the aims of Germany by all means, including aggressive war." Falco thought Schacht's good intentions were a slender reed, for he was ambitious, and, even though the *Anschluss* had made Hitler's aggressive plans self-evident, Schacht still "congratulated him." The former economics minister's participation in the anti-Hitler plots carried little weight with Falco, who was definitely inclined to convict and seemed to feel that Schacht should get more than a token sentence.[41]

This long initial discussion made the Tribunal members aware of the depth of the divisions and the size of the barriers standing in the way of a quick decision on Schacht. They started to use a short interval in the session of September 10 to work on his verdict, but then quickly decided that this would not suffice and the case was "left over." [42] Two days later, they set aside most of their session for the difficult cases, and here the judges set to work hammering out a Schacht verdict. Parker again argued in favor of acquittal, as did Birkett, who reiterated the contention advanced earlier by Parker that the Tribunal had no choice except to impose a severe sentence or to acquit. The French judges, however, still did not accept this either-or alternative, and both Falco and Donnedieu de Vabres decided that Schacht should be convicted on Counts One and Two and given a token penalty of five years' imprisonment. Falco again wanted to root this conclusion in the evidence of Schacht's knowledge, or presumed knowledge, of aggressive war plans, and the French alternate implied that even after Schacht had left office he still knew about, or had some responsibility for, the attack plans implemented against countries such as Poland. Schacht should be given a light sentence, Falco concluded, but merely as an act of mitigation. Donnedieu de Vabres not only echoed Falco's conclusions but justified his position by adopting Falco's picture of Schacht as an opportunist. He saw Schacht not so much as a man who had lost place because of principle, but as someone who was simply consumed by jealousy of Goering. Schacht, he said, was shrewd enough to realize that Hitler would fail and therefore had pulled back; if, by some miracle, Hitler had pulled it off, Donnedieu de Vabres went on, "Schacht would not have had regrets." [43]

In the middle of this discussion Biddle rather unobtrusively slipped in the conclusion that he had reached after restudying the case. He had decided to reverse position and to convict, as Fisher had suggested in his memorandum on Count One (General Conspiracy) but not for specific war planning under Count Two. Regarding a sentence for Schacht, Biddle had finally opted for life imprisonment, a much harsher penalty than seemed to have been implied by his initial hesitation. Apparently he had taken seriously Parker's analysis and conclusion that there was no middle ground between the extreme alternatives; having decided that Schacht was guilty of participation in a broad common plan for aggressive war, he was prepared to see him heavily punished. [44] Although Nikitchenko had not yet voiced his final opinion on the case, he seems to have been delighted by Biddle's strong stand, and at recess he approached the American to inquire how far he thought they would have "to go down" on the penalty in order to pick up the necessary third vote. Biddle recommended that the two of them "suggest a stiff term" of years as a compromise proposal "and see what happens." [45]

Before Nikitchenko had a chance to give his summary of the case and his reasons why a severe penalty was appropriate, Donnedieu de Vabres broke in again to say that his opinion was changing and that he would be willing to go up to ten years. [46] After discussing the evidence, Nikitchenko predictably called for conviction on Counts One and Two and a sentence of life imprisonment, although he may also have indicated a willingness to consider a lighter sentence. Volchkov echoed his senior colleague, but then added the surprising suggestion that the Court should consider Schacht's advanced age "when applying sentence." [47]

Lawrence, whose commitment to acquittal was unshaken by the positions advanced by the other senior judges, made a strong argument based on the realities of international power politics. The fact of rearmament was not enough to convict, Lawrence insisted, because there had been alternative possible uses for the arms other than simply launching an aggressive war. "It is power that counts at international negotiations," he noted, adding that this might not be a "strictly moral consideration" or "utopian," but still it remains "the truth." Schacht may have wanted only to strengthen his country's hand at the bargaining table; Germany had a feeling of being aggrieved, "probably mistaken[ly]," Lawrence admitted, but it was there nonetheless. At that time, the Englishman added with a gentle thrust at his American colleagues, the view that an injustice had been done to Germany was held in many circles outside the Reich, including the United States. Under these circumstances it would not be just to convict Schacht without clear proof that he intended aggression, and no argument that he was negligent in gauging Hitler's moods would suffice. Proof of participation in a conspiracy required that intent be established, and, in Lawrence's view, it had not been. [48]

This presentation set Donnedieu de Vabres to pondering again, and he apparently backed away from his suggestion that the Court sentence Schacht to ten years. In order to pick up his vote, Nikitchenko and Biddle were forced to go down to an eight-year prison term based on conviction on the Conspiracy Count only. A peculiar twist was added to this verdict as well, because the Court specified that the sentence would take account of the time Schacht had already served. Not only was the year he had been in Allied custody to count in his favor, but he was also to receive credit against his sentence for the ten months that he had previously spent in the custody of the SS and the Gestapo. If the sentence had stood, Schacht would have had to serve fewer than six years. [49]

But no sooner had the Court reached this decision than forces were put into motion to undermine it. The rest of the afternoon session of September 12 was spent in deciding the Papen and Fritzsche cases, both of which ended in acquittal. On the first of these, Donnedieu de Vabres voted in favor of conviction and a minor sentence, but, after Papen was acquitted by the votes of the other judges, he decided to free Fritzsche as well. On the following morning, September 13, prior to a session that was supposed to be concerned with criminal organizations, Lawrence took Biddle aside and told him that Donnedieu de Vabres had changed his mind with regard to Schacht and wanted the case reopened so that he could vote for acquittal.[50] Biddle, realizing that the case was thereby lost, wondered in his notes what the British had done to Donnedieu de Vabres, and, despite British and French protestations of innocence, Biddle never gave up his belief that Lawrence had persuaded the Frenchman to shift position. When the session opened and Donnedieu de Vabres was given an opportunity to speak, he provided a fairly reasonable explanation for his actions. When he voted to convict Schacht, the French judge stated, he had assumed that they were going to declare all the defendants guilty (this was at least an exaggeration because the preliminary discussions had shown that both Papen and Fritzsche were likely to be acquitted). Since they had freed Papen and Fritzsche, Donnedieu de Vabres continued, he was forced to recognize that he actually thought Schacht less guilty than Papen; so, in fairness, the former had to be acquitted, too. This way a "unity of judgment" would be established and the three least guilty would receive the same treatment. To this reasonable contention and to his acknowledgment that he had been impressed by the opinions of his colleagues, Donnedieu de Vabres added two more bizarre explanations. He now asserted that it was not appropriate to give Schacht a sentence of six to eight years because the Tribunal was not established to "pronounce light sentences." This was the same argument that Parker, Lawrence, and Birkett had advanced, and which Donnedieu de Vabres had rejected, in the earlier discussions. Similarly the French judge on this occasion adopted the mitigation formula that Volchkov had put forward earlier, and explained that he simply could not "bear the responsibility of a sentence imposed on an old man."[51] At the time of his acquittal, Schacht was sixty-nine, while Neurath, who was unanimously convicted, was seventy-three.

After Donnedieu de Vabres had given his explanation, an acrimonious, almost raucous, discussion ensued, lasting over an hour. Parker and Lawrence rushed to Donnedieu de Vabres's defense and, amid effusive backslaps and statements that they were proud to be associated with such a courageous man, they assured him that he had expressed a "correct legal" opinion. Biddle, on the other hand, accused him of being "sentimental" and of using "his tender heart, not his mind." The American also found it "shocking" to state that Schacht's fate had been determined by that of other defendants. Nikitchenko was even more outspoken in his criticism, asserting that Donnedieu de Vabres was acting unjustly and that he had not considered the evidence. The Russian judge was so upset that he stated he might dissent and cite as grounds the method that Donnedieu de Vabres had used to arrive "at such a conclusion." [52]

With this comment, the discussion moved to a yet higher pitch of controversy and moralizing. Although Nikitchenko continued to avow that he was considering issuing dissents in this and other cases, and might even attack the system by which a two-two tie vote yielded an acquittal, it was his threat to dissent publicly against the process used by Donnedieu de Vabres to justify his change of mind that brought down the wrath of the other judges. The French judge protested against any such action because he felt that he had acted frankly, and without hypocrisy, and that he deserved professional silence in return. He was warmly seconded by Birkett, who stated flatly that no dissent should include a criticism of another judge. It was Biddle, however, who managed to reach the final crescendo in the discussion. Even though he himself later hesitated over the possibility of dissenting on the Schacht case, during this session he vigorously urged the Soviets not to dissent and managed to extract a promise from Nikitchenko that he would do nothing until he had read the Judgment summaries, then in preparation, on all the individuals. Biddle waxed eloquent on the importance of keeping the judges' deliberation confidential and urged his colleagues to remember that these discussions were private, not for publication, and the judges "should never refer . . . to anything except what is found in the record or judgment—never to what took place in secret sessions." [53] Despite these pious remarks, Biddle went right on keeping a record of the secret deliberative sessions and later published accounts of the Schacht case and others.

Although Biddle's statements and subsequent behavior must fill one with wonder, they did not alter the results in the case: Schacht was acquitted on both counts—and we are left with the question of the defensibility of this decision. Nothing that can be said about the case will completely erase the impression that it was analogous to the Keystone Kops in court. Yet, somehow, the Tribunal seems to have ended up at a spot that had the fewest pernicious overtones for the future. The American prosecutors' original decision to take Schacht out of a concentration camp and place him on trial had been a major psychological blunder, which was compounded by the weakness of the prosecution's case against him. Compared with the mass murderers and brutal governors of the conquered territories who were in the dock, Schacht looked both genteel and relatively innocent. His acquittal was therefore a direct result of the American decision to emphasize the prewar actions of the regime and to try to strike at them by means of a grand conspiracy charge. By 1946 there appeared to be a world of difference between denouncing the Treaty of Versailles and operating an Auschwitz extermination camp. Historians, even today, would be hard pressed to demonstrate that there were firm causal connections between the major phases and significant events of the Third Reich. Certainly, the prosecution evidence purporting to show that everything that happened between 1933 and 1945 was somehow part of a common plan was ludicrously weak, and, as the Soviet dissent inadvertently revealed, the portion of the case intended to prove that Schacht was privy to a plan for military expansion was not much stronger. There was no solid direct evidence; all the Soviets could point to was the fact that he was a classic evil capitalist, with sinister overtones clinging to his name and reputation. He was smart, cynical, opportunistic; from the circumstances, he should have been aware of what was going on in Nazi Germany. But what went on at Nuremberg was supposed to be a trial, not an exercise in judgment by public opinion. It seems safe to say that, on a comparable conspiracy charge with similar evidence, such a case would not even reach a courtroom in the United States today.

Whether Schacht was acquitted or received six years of imprisonment probably did not make much practical difference—perhaps not even to Schacht, who had some difficult times with the German authorities after he was allowed to leave the Nuremberg Court. A conviction certainly would have been more popular with press and public at the time, but what would have been the view of observers, granted even a few years to calm their emotions and sharpen their vision? It could only have been seen as one more step on the road to mass fanaticism and blind vengeance. As it is, we live in a world where it was actually possible for Hjalmar Horace Greeley Schacht to be acquitted by an enemy court, and that may not be a bad omen for the capability of members of the human race to survive.

Franz von Papen

Although it is difficult to believe, Franz von Papen had a worse reputation, especially in the United States, than did Schacht. Not that anyone thought of him as a typical Nazi leader, for he was much too aristocratic and debonair to be confused with the masses of the Brown Shirts. Like Schacht, Papen was known as an intriguer and opportunist, a gifted diplomat who used the most devious means to further his own interests and those of the extreme German nationalists. During World War I he had been the German military attaché in Washington, where the press and public soon identified him with German sabotage and espionage, and the U.S. Government then declared him persona non grata. He surfaced into public view again in the early 1930s, leading conservative and reactionary factions in the Byzantine intrigue that accompanied the death of the Weimar Republic. By ingratiating himself with the old president, Field Marshal Paul von Hindenburg, Papen managed to play a leading role in his country's affairs for two or three years. He was chancellor for a time in 1932, and, though supported by the president, he had no more than a sliver of popular support in the Reichstag. After his fall from the chancellorship, Papen played a significant role in the political machinations of late 1932 and the first month of 1933, which culminated in Hitler's designation as chancellor. As part of the package that brought Hitler to power, Papen was named vice-chancellor, and he remained at this post, signing loathsome laws and making the requisite idolatrous speeches about the Führer, until midsummer of 1934.

For all his cynical slipperiness, Papen was not a Nazi but one of the nationalistic aristocrats who thought they could control the Nazis and feather their own nests in the bargain. When it became clear even to Papen that no one was going to manipulate Hitler through backroom intrigue, the vice-chancellor seems to have taken alarm. He thereupon made a public speech at Marburg, in June 1934, denouncing the excesses of the regime. But with his usual cloudy perception regarding the forces of mass brutality, Papen managed to time his protest so that it occurred just two weeks before Himmler and Goering carried out the Blood Purge of June 30, 1934. On this occasion, not only was the leadership of the SA wiped out, but the SS and the Gestapo also settled many other old and new scores. Papen, clutching his dignity as vice-chancellor, was forced to cower in house arrest while the Nazi executioners liquidated his aides and assistants, carefully making certain that they wiped out those who had played a part in preparing the Marburg protest speech.

Hitler finally intervened, picked Papen up and, after dusting him off, put him back in his seat as vice chancellor. Papen now decided that discretion was his better part, and resigned this position to assume the post of ambassador to Austria. He was in Vienna nearly four years, working assiduously to promote an *Anschluss* until his recall on the very eve of the "March of Flowers" in 1938, when the German Army absorbed its Austrian neighbor. A year later, Papen was designated ambassador to Turkey and spent the war years, until August 1944, struggling to keep Turkey neutral, while surrounded by the inevitable rumors that he had transformed the German Embassy into a massive sabotage and espionage center.

Papen was one of the first prominent personages of the Third Reich to fall into Allied hands, having been gathered up from his retirement haven in western Germany in the course of the Anglo-American advance of April 1945. In his initial interrogations, Papen played cat-and-mouse with the possibility that he might be able to help in arranging a German surrender, but he was always careful to stress that he would do nothing until his "status" was clarified and he had learned whether he would be held as a war criminal.[54] It was much too late for Papen's intrigues, however, and the American military showed no interest in playing his game. Formal capitulation of the Nazi system had minor interest for them by mid-April 1945, because the regime was shattered in any case.[55] But Papen was right in being troubled about his fate as a war criminal for at that time it was far from settled. The British War Office had included him on its war criminals list of April 1944, but the Foreign Office had not followed suit.[56] A month after Papen's capture, General Donovan offered his name as a possible defendant during the first Anglo-American exploratory talks, but no one seemed to be very enthusiastic about the idea.[57] Although the men preparing the general Foreign Office war criminals list of June 1945 recognized that there would "probably be a good deal of pressure" exerted on them to include Papen, they decided that his long and spotty career would make him very difficult to convict. Consequently, he was not included in the British list of ten "majors," nor was he on the American roster of sixteen, both of which were completed in late June.[58] Once again, it was the French and the Soviets who put Papen in the dock, adding him to the defendants' roster in the course of the Four Power discussions of August 1945.

Once his designation as a major war criminal was settled, Papen, who was an old hand at escaping from tight spots, set to work trying to clear himself. In October, while talking to Major Neave, he showed no signs of being intimidated and requested an opportunity to talk to Schacht, because he rightly concluded that the former economics minister might know more about how to obtain a really good lawyer than any of the run-of-the-mill Nazis in the dock. Papen also wanted specific information on how to obtain witnesses and defense documents, and he even requested secretarial assistance.[59]

In the first weeks of the trial, the effectiveness of this practical approach to his case was overshadowed by the torrent of accusations and embarrassing incidents that rained down upon him. In demonstrating the existence of a Nazi conspiracy, Papen was one of the American prosecutors' favorite targets. At point after point in their presentation on the initial Nazi advance, Papen would pop up, suave, unscrupulous, and seemingly always ready to shoulder unsavory responsibilities. As the case rolled on, however, and passed the *Anschluss*, Papen's name dropped out of consideration, and, by the time the chief focal points of aggressive war and mass atrocities had been reached, his name had slipped completely in the background. Throughout the rest of the proceedings, Papen tried to appear as inconspicuous as possible, but his anonymity was constantly threatened by the personality of his lawyer. His attorney, Egon Kubuschok, had apparently not come on Schacht's recommendation, but Papen was nonetheless highly pleased with him; the Court, however, found him to be an insufferable nuisance and bore. In the course of the trial, Birkett achieved some of his most masterful strokes in scribbled abuse of Papen's counsel.[60]

On June 19, Biddle jotted down comments that epitomized some of the favorable and unfavorable symbols that clung to Papen's name. First, the Philadelphia aristocrat noted approvingly that he had heard that Papen "was once the leading gentleman rider and steeple chaser of Germany." [61] On the heels of this correct bit of information, he also observed that "Papen looks like a fox"—a doubly withering characterization for an upper-class political horseman.[62] Papen was nonetheless helped by his civilized manner and Biddle characterized his final plea as "excellent." The fact that he had possessed the courage to utter a public protest at Marburg seems to have aided him even more, for Biddle described it as "Very important" and was careful to underline this comment.[63]

During the Tribunal's discussion of the general conspiracy question, the possibility that a limited definition might allow Papen to escape troubled Biddle, and, when Fisher prepared the initial memorandum on the vice-chancellor, he struggled with the same difficulty.[64] Papen was charged only on Counts One and Two, and the legal threads that linked his actions to the criminal sanctions of the Charter were thin, indeed. Fisher concluded that there was no case connecting him to war crimes or atrocities, no matter what definition of conspiracy the Court finally employed, and there were nothing but trifles to tie him to Crimes Against Peace as covered under Count Two. From the beginning of his inquiry, then, Fisher assumed that the whole case against Papen hung on the possibility that he had participated in a conspiracy while engaging in political manipulations during 1932–34, or later while serving as ambassador in Vienna. On the first question, Fisher emphasized the important role that Papen had played in the Nazi attainment of power and also noted that he had every reason to comprehend what the Nazis "stood for." [65] Still, Fisher was surprisingly understanding of the situation in which Papen had found himself in the early 1930s, noting that "drastic measures were necessary" and concluding that "the only alternative" to some kind of Nationalist-Nazi coalition was "military rule." [66] Fisher therefore did not give him especially bad marks for helping to bring Hitler to power. By balancing off the Marburg speech against his expressions of sycophantic praise for Hitler after the Blood Purge, Fisher also gave Papen an even split on his public appearances in 1933–34. Although the memorandum did not address itself directly to the question, it left the impression that Papen's early activities should not be held to have been part of a conspiracy, regardless of the definition ultimately established by the Tribunal.[67]

Fisher treated Papen's years in Vienna much more comprehensively, because he felt that the final disposition of the case would depend "almost entirely" on the finding that the Tribunal made regarding Austria. The central issue was still a simple one, since, with no evidence of Papen's knowledge that *Anschluss* was merely a step in a bigger aggressive war plan, his guilt or innocence hung on whether he understood that *Anschluss* would be achieved by aggressive means if other methods failed. Fisher tracked Papen's four-year career step by step and generally rejected his protestations of pristine innocence. The ambassador had been in close touch with the Austrian Nazis and was carrying on multiple intrigues, Fisher concluded, but "there is little pointing to force." [68] Papen and nearly every other prominent German supported an *Anschluss;* the ambassador, however, had taken the additional step of trying to bring it about. It was the situation in which this activity occurred, though, that was crucial: Hitler periodically threatened the Austrians by rattling the saber, and Fisher stressed that Papen, of all people, should have known that when Hitler threatened, things were going to happen. The American legal aide therefore concluded that, even without specific evidence showing that Papen approved of the use of force, he had peacefully "hijacked" Austria, while implicitly understanding that force might be used. That, in Fisher's view, was enough; he had participated in Hitler's operations "with knowledge of what they involved" and therefore appeared to be guilty under Count One. [69]

The obvious hesitancy about Papen manifest in this memorandum surfaced even more visibly in the Court's first deliberative session on September 6. The three Anglo-American judges (Birkett was absent again, presumably working on the opinion) all came out in favor of acquittal. Biddle called for a verdict of not guilty on both counts because the annexation of Austria was not a war, much less an aggressive one, and because the limited definition of conspiracy adopted by the Tribunal was restricted to specific war planning, and in Biddle's view there was thus no way to get Papen on Count One. Parker agreed with his senior colleague and noted that there was nothing in Papen's ambassadorship in Turkey to hold him on, and, even though he had used "fraud and trickery" in Vienna, that was not illegal, because he had not used force or threatened to use it. The Tribunal did not have the job, in Parker's opinion, to punish him for being persona non grata in the United States and the American alternate even went so far as to defend Papen's embarrassing availability by noting that it was the "duty of a man to serve" his government. [70] Lawrence echoed Parker's assertion that Papen was not guilty of any crime during his time in Ankara and he was also ready to declare him free of criminal responsibility for his Viennese years. Although Lawrence had a feeling that the *Anschluss* and the subsequent wars were "strategically connected," he emphasized that Papen had actually been dismissed just before the *Anschluss* and therefore had nothing to do with the actual forced union of the two countries. The argument was rather strained, but Lawrence seems to have believed it and he voted for acquittal on both counts.[71]

The French judges, in this first session, were much less sympathetic to Papen than the English or the Americans. Although both Falco and Donnedieu de Vabres called for his acquittal on Count One, they wanted him convicted on Count Two. While conceding that the question was "delicate" and Papen's responsibility "small," Falco wanted to find him guilty because he had helped bring Hitler to power and had been "associated" with the *Anschluss*, the "first aggressive act committed by Hitler." To reach this conclusion, Falco had to perform argumentative gymnastics, substituting "aggressive act" for aggressive war, and also advocating that Papen be punished for assisting Hitler in 1933, although this preceded by at least four years any of the crimes that the Court had agreed to hold punishable. At the end of his statement, Falco tried to make his ideas more palatable by stressing that Papen should receive only a moderate sentence.[72] What Falco stated obliquely, Donnedieu de Vabres put forward frankly and without blushing. Whatever the specifics of the evidence or the definitions of the crimes, the French senior judge contended that the Court was there to "apply morals," and, since Papen was a "corrupting creature" who had spread his "immorality" and "trickery" from the United States to Vienna, he had to be convicted. He had pushed the Nazi cause forward through his deceptive diplomacy, and at crucial points he was even more guilty than Schacht; he had played a more significant part than Schacht in bringing Hitler to power, and in the late 1930s, when Schacht dropped out, Papen continued to move from one post to another. Even though he had rejected the general idea of conspiracy, Donnedieu de Vabres was eager to get Papen as an accomplice in the preparation of aggressive wars, and he ended his presentation by asking his fellow judges rhetorically, "What are we here for if we are not to put morals into international law?"[73]

On the following day, when the first-phase discussion was resumed, Nikitchenko picked up and repeated the French arguments, although the Soviet judge put his main emphasis on Papen's actions in the early 1930s. It was the Nazi seizure of power "with a view to aggressive war" that was the central crime, according to Nikitchenko, and Papen bore heavy responsibility for allowing it to happen. Although Volchkov supported his colleague, those advocating conviction had become less substantive and increasingly propagandistic.[74] Neither the Russians nor the French were able to present any evidentiary argument to counter the reasoning that Biddle and Lawrence had advanced in favor of acquittal, and, if something radical did not occur to change the situation, a finding of not guilty on Papen through a two-two tie was inevitable.

On September 12, the Court held its final deliberation on Papen, and all the participants resumed their initial parts and played them out to the end. Consequently, there was no possible result other than a finding of not guilty, with Biddle and Lawrence for acquittal and Donnedieu de Vabres and Nikitchenko for conviction. The discussion that took place in this session is therefore of interest primarily because of what it reveals about the attitudes of the individual judges. Falco supported a conviction and a sentence of five years on the ground that Papen's case was the same as Schacht's. Although he did not completely withdraw from the government, as Schacht had done, Papen did not "altogether go along with Hitler" either, and therefore he deserved a mild sentence. Donnedieu de Vabres invoked an unusual cluster of inaccuracies and irrelevancies to conclude that Papen should be punished only lightly. In support of his view that Papen was more guilty than Schacht, he cited some harsh comments made by a Spanish journalist while Papen was in Ankara, but then went on to present an amazingly jumbled account of Papen's career and the Court's stand on conspiracy, culminating in the erroneous assertion that Papen had spent several years in a concentration camp.[75] In the course of this discussion, Donnedieu de Vabres remarked that Schacht had been found guilty only as a matter of record—"a matter of curiosity," as he cryptically termed it—and this comment, together with other scraps of information that appeared here and there, suggests that the French judge's mind was fixed primarily on the Schacht case, and that he was reconsidering his vote in support of that conviction.[76] In any event, Donnedieu de Vabres concluded his comments on Papen with an impassioned plea that the judges should avoid a life sentence because the "world would be appalled" by such an act.[77] Since there seemed only a remote chance that Papen would even be convicted, it is difficult to take any of this presentation very seriously.

Parker seized the opportunity provided by Donnedieu de Vabres's remarks to point out that the reference to Papen's alleged misconduct in Turkey showed how dangerous was a loose definition of conspiracy, because the prosecution had specifically declared that there was no case against Papen relative to his ambassadorship in Ankara. Beyond this, both Biddle and Parker merely repeated the points they had advanced before and they were now joined by Birkett, who also asserted that, though the *Anschluss* was an aggressive act, it was not a war. Without evidence that Papen had desired to use force, Birkett, Parker, and Biddle concluded that there was nothing to do but swallow one's dislike of him and vote for acquittal.[78]

The Soviets deplored the direction that the discussion and probable vote were taking and observed that when the Court had limited conspiracy the result seemed to mean that the whole conspiracy charge had been eliminated.[79] In a last bid to salvage something, the Soviets stated that they were ready to give up the "supreme penalty," for once, and suggested that Papen be given a sentence of ten years.[80] But there was no gainsaying acquittal, and although he admitted that he disliked Papen even more than Schacht, because at least at some point Schacht had severed all connection with the regime, Lawrence still voted to find Papen not guilty. Again citing the lack of evidence connecting Papen with a plan to use force in Austria, Lawrence added the perceptive observation that the actual *Anschluss* had not been carried through as the final step in a carefully laid plan but had been done "in a fit of fury by Hitler." Lawrence lectured his colleagues on the broader issues and urged them to welcome the opportunity to acquit Papen because it would show that "we aren't victorious powers breaking every cause." Sir Geoffrey went on to assert that, once they had convicted Schacht and acquitted Papen, it would be a good idea to go ahead and free Fritzsche as well.[81]

Before following the Tribunal and watching them do just that, it is necessary to observe that the Papen verdict is probably the most impressive application of the law that was made by the Tribunal. All the judges bore him some degree of ill will. But from the first exchange of views, in fact from the time of the general conspiracy decision, it was nearly a foregone conclusion that he would be set free. The Court set the rules and applied them, even though the judges would have been happy to find any pretext to convict. Although the Soviet dissenting opinion predictably stressed Papen's role in the Nazi seizure of power and the "aggression" in Austria, the only serious criticism that can be raised against the verdict is that of a moralist such as Donnedieu de Vabres. Sauckel was hanged and Papen went free; it is the old story that the violent street criminal is condemned while the supple white-collar manipulator escapes punishment. A pang of regret must remain, but it is difficult to fault the Nuremberg Court for doing the same thing that elsewhere is accepted as justice and due process.

Hans Fritzsche

Of the twenty-two defendants, the one who fitted least snugly into the category of major war criminal was Hans Fritzsche. Starting in 1932 he had been a radio news announcer, probably the best known in Germany, and, although after Hitler came to power he moved over to Goebbels's Propaganda Ministry, he never occupied a high-level policy-making position. He did, however, hold a number of posts in the radio broadcasting hierarchy, culminating in his appointment as head of the Radio Division of the Propaganda Ministry in November 1942. In the course of the years, Fritzsche also developed a close enough relationship with Goebbels so that he was one of the few employees who dared openly to criticize the actions of the propaganda chief. But Fritzsche was only a trusted subordinate, and not even the top one, for Fritzsche was immediately under Otto Dietrich, the Reich press chief, who, in turn, was Goebbels's deputy. So Fritzsche was a third-level propaganda official and radio announcer, nothing more. He never played an important role in the Nazi party and he asserted on the stand, apparently correctly, that he had never spoken with Hitler in his life.

He was not included on any of the Western Allied war criminals lists prepared prior to midsummer 1945, and, in the Anglo-American discussions that took place in June, no one mentioned his name as a possible defendant. He was also not on the comprehensive list of German officials prepared by the Foreign Office in mid-June. Furthermore, when in August the American prosecutors put together a complete roster of the hundred top Nazis, including every person who might conceivably be designated a defendant, the name of the dead Goebbels was there, as was that of Otto Dietrich, but Fritzsche's name was not.[82] He was the only defendant who simply appeared at Nuremberg, like a jinni, without any preparatory work on his case being done by the Western Powers.

The reason he was ultimately included arose directly from the Soviets' desire to have some of their captives in the dock. One can imagine the consternation in the Anglo-American camp when the Soviets came up with the names of Raeder and Fritzsche. Raeder was easy to accept, for everyone was familiar with him; but, with the possible exception of a few German refugees among the advisory staff who may have remembered him as a kind of Nazi Walter Cronkite, no one had ever heard of Hans Fritzsche. Apparently as a matter of courtesy and as a gesture in inter-Allied cooperation, the Western representatives ultimately went along, however, and on August 27–28 Fritzsche was designated a defendant. Over the next two to three months the prosecutors had to work feverishly trying to build up a case from scratch. In the process they made a terrible discovery that gave the whole proceeding a special tone of unreality— Fritzsche's two supreme masters, Hitler and Goebbels, were dead, but his immediate supervisor in the Propaganda Ministry was not. The Reich press chief, Otto Dietrich, the man in the hierarchy who stood between Goebbels and Fritzsche, was alive and well in the custody of the Western Powers. Consequently, the prosecutors went to trial attempting to prove to the Tribunal that Fritzsche should be punished as a major war criminal for carrying out the orders of a man who was not even being prosecuted.

Under these circumstances, the best that can be said about the prosecutors' effort was that they made a valiant try. Fritzsche was charged under Counts One, Three, and Four, and the case summary, presumably prepared by Fisher in mid-summer 1946, disposed of the first count in half a dozen sentences. Since Fritzsche had apparently never spoken to the Führer, and within the Propaganda Ministry, aside from a few quibbles on detail, had merely followed the orders of Goebbels and Dietrich, "it would be absurd to find that he conspired to wage war with Hitler," and therefore he "should be found not guilty under count one."[83] Fisher was a bit more uncertain about whether some of Fritzsche's radio broadcasts amounted to incitement to commit war crimes and crimes against humanity. On one occasion during the war, he had spoken of the "unpleasant fate" that was overcoming the Jews, and in at least one speech he had called for all Germans to come forth and help destroy Soviet barbarism. But aside from the fact that such statements were made by every propagandist and newspaperman in wartime Germany, thereby undercutting Fritzsche's prosecution as a major war criminal, Fisher further concluded that the broadcasts were no basis for conviction. There was no showing that he knew that atrocities were being committed or planned, and, more important, Fisher noted, the content of his broadcasts fell "far short of incitement." [84] Fritzsche, who as a long-time colleague of the acid-tongued Goebbels had his share of malicious and sarcastic humor, would have been pleased by Fisher's final observation that the Nazi radio commentator's remarks "were no stronger than [the] statements of American war correspondents in Washington during the war." [85] Consequently, the only course open to the Tribunal, in Fisher's view, was to acquit Fritzsche on all three counts.

The lineup of the judges in the initial deliberative session of September 10 was only slightly different from the one in the Papen case. Again, both French judges wanted to convict, not apparently on Count One, but on Counts Three and Four. Falco believed that Fritzsche should be held guilty because he "went along" on aggressive war—he was actually not charged under Count Two—and as an accomplice on War Crimes and Crimes Against Humanity. Donnedieu de Vabres granted that Fritzsche had been "relatively moderate," that he was "the least guilty of all," and that he had even reacted against the regime's "excesses," but the Frenchman still felt that he should be convicted because of the importance of propaganda and the extreme language that Fritzsche had allegedly used. [86] The Soviets were in a difficult spot, but they also pressed for conviction. Nikitchenko launched into a long explanation on the evils of political propaganda, which must have amused his fellow judges, and concluded that the Nazi crimes could not have occurred without the work of men such as Fritzsche. "His propaganda led to atrocities," Nikitchenko stated flatly, and he called for Fritzsche's conviction on all three counts. Volchkov seconded Nikitchenko and managed to say that "we, of course, must not try journalists for what they write," but the Court should nonetheless convict Fritzsche because he was a propaganda official and because of his "false idea[s]" on racial superiority and related questions. Fritzsche's "libelous" and "slanderous" campaign against the Russian people had obviously stuck in Volchkov's craw; he argued that because of the theory of racial superiority over ten million people had been exterminated.[87] Here again, it is relevant to note that the Soviets' hardline position did not result merely from the fact that Fritzsche had been their prisoner or because of their impatience with Western notions of civil rights and due process. The Soviets had borne the brunt of the Nazi onslaught and the campaign of mass murder. It was all very well for the Western judges to talk about proper procedure and the need to give men such as Fritzsche a fair trial, but none of their countries, not even France, had experienced the full ruthlessness of the death squads, extermination camps, and mass exploitation. Under these circumstances, what is remarkable is not that the Soviets kept pushing for conviction, but that they continued to be so polite and cooperative in the face of what must have appeared to them as mere Western quibbling that consistently missed the main points.

Again, it was Parker who put the case for acquittal, and he did it with enthusiasm: Fritzsche was a "small man," Parker remarked, "Hitler wouldn't have wasted five minutes with him." The only reason that Parker could imagine as to why he was in the dock was that Goebbels was dead and a "vicarious sacrifice" was wanted. Fritzsche had "never incited any crime. A man shouldn't be convicted for what he says or writes unless it is an incitement to crime," Parker emphasized and, with his eloquence and enthusiasm rising, added that "freedom of speech is of [the] greatest importance to liberty." [88] Biddle "vigorously" supported Parker's position, and apparently the force of the American presentation left its mark on both the French and the British. Lawrence frankly admitted that he had been impressed by the arguments for acquittal and wanted time to reconsider his feeling that Fritzsche should be convicted on Count One. But Lawrence was not concerned regarding the other two counts and felt that Fritzsche should be found guilty for War Crimes and Crimes Against Humanity because he "must have had knowledge" of what was going on in Germany and elsewhere even as he continued to propagandize and urge the population to fight "to the bitter end." [89]

On September 11, the Court again tried to complete action on the Fritzsche case and again a standoff occurred between those stressing freedom of speech and the judges who urged that Fritzsche be convicted for incitement. Leading off for the latter group, Falco argued that there was no question at all of freedom of speech but only a case of propaganda supporting a political system and a war that the Tribunal was declaring criminal. For that reason, he felt, Fritzsche should be found guilty and given a nominal sentence of two to five years. Birkett concurred, calling for conviction on all three counts because Fritzsche had been "justifying crime." Volchkov warned that acquitting Fritzsche "would create the wrong impression among the German people" about freedom of speech, but he did grant that a short sentence would be sufficient. Nikitchenko, however, did not think a term of two years would be long enough, and suggested at least ten. The senior Russian judge also contended that the Americans had the freedom of speech argument backward; Fritzsche had helped suppress freedom of speech and therefore deserved to be convicted. Again, coming from a senior Soviet judge, this was a rather unusual contention, but it is also true that Fritzsche himself would more easily have understood and shared the approach of Nikitchenko than the libertarian outlook of Biddle and Parker. [90]

The Americans were not deterred by any of these considerations, however. They continued to call for acquittal, and Parker observed that convicting Hans Fritzsche as a major war criminal would be like using a cannon to shoot a sparrow. In this second discussion, the force of the American argument began to tell, and Donnedieu de Vabres announced that he had changed his mind and favored acquittal because there was no reason to convict in order to impose just a minute sentence. Lawrence had not yet come to acquittal, but he was wavering. The senior British judge stressed that he thought it was an important case, but that he had trouble acquitting a propagandist working for war. "Did he not know the wars were illegal?" Lawrence asked rhetorically. "Was that not an incitement to crime?" [91]

On the threshold of the Court's third discussion on Fritzsche, which took place on September 12, Donnedieu de Vabres approached Biddle to say that he was wavering again and thought he would most likely vote against acquittal. Falco and Nikitchenko were still the strong advocates of conviction and Parker and Biddle the champions of acquittal. The former two stressed that, since the Tribunal was going to find the Nazi government criminal, Fritzsche was therefore guilty of furthering its criminal purposes and actions.

But Biddle continued to emphasize that there was no proven connection between Fritzsche's propaganda and the atrocities—a point that might also have been considered in the case of Julius Streicher. Parker supported acquittal by using an instance of a genre of prediction that kept cropping up in nearly every deliberative controversy: "the world won't understand," Parker prophesied, if Fritzsche were to be convicted.[92] Lawrence mentioned that some of Fritzsche's testimony was incorrect, but apparently did not specify what the errors were, and, in the end, he did not express a strong opinion either way on the central question of guilt.[93] Donnedieu de Vabres also "wobble[d] round a good deal," to use Biddle's phrase, and ultimately he asked that the decisive consideration be put off until they had finished the Papen case. He would "never convict Fritzsche," Donnedieu de Vabres avowed, "if Papen is acquitted."[94]

So, once again, the treatment of the last three defendants became intertwined. The Fritzsche decision was delayed, and only after Papen was acquitted did the fourth and final deliberation on Fritzsche occur on the afternoon of September 12. This time it went very quickly. The three senior Western judges immediately declared for acquittal, and Fritzsche was freed.[95] The rest of the session was spent quibbling over the reasons that Lawrence and Donnedieu de Vabres had shifted ground as well as over the appropriate form to be used if a judge decided to dissent. Lawrence tried to justify his change of position by stating that "it would be unfortunate to acquit only Papen," and Nikitchenko immediately jumped on the inference that Fritzsche was not being freed on his own merits. Birkett tried to rescue Lawrence by asserting that the cases were not tied together, but that the political effect of two acquittals would be salutary.[96] Nikitchenko, however, was not mollified and stated that he wished to file a dissent in the case. When Nikitchenko further explained what he had in mind, it became clear that he did not want to make a public dissent but to have his protest sent to the Control Council for Germany when the main verdict was dispatched. This was the normal Soviet practice, Nikitchenko informed the other judges, and he thought that the Control Council might recommend a retrial of those who had been acquitted.[97] Nikitchenko, seconded by Donnedieu de Vabres, firmly opposed the use of a public dissenting opinion and the Soviet judge contended that they had "no right to dissent publicly as part of the judgment." This position, in turn, was flatly rejected by Parker and Biddle, who strongly protested against the French and Soviet view and affirmed that every judge had the right to dissent publicly if he wished.[98]

It is probably merciful that we can terminate the discussion of the Fritzsche case, and of all the cases, at this point, for subsequently Nikitchenko filed a public dissent on Fritzsche as well as on other cases, and his action was then deplored by his colleagues, including Francis Biddle. Perhaps the whole proceeding had been too long and the cases too involved and diverse for the judges to retain the appearance of consistency from first day to last. By the end they seem to have been operating largely by attrition and reflex action, and the Soviet dissent, when it came, merely advanced the obvious contention that Nazi propaganda was especially dreadful, and that the Tribunal had underestimated the importance and criminality of Fritzsche's activities.

Only Hermann Goering was able to give a meaningful final twist to the Fritzsche case and to the trial. When the verdicts were announced the Reich Marshal went out of his way to snub Papen and Schacht contemptuously, but then he deliberately crossed the room in order to say smilingly:

Herr Fritzsche, you really did not belong to our set [*Sie haben eigentlich nicht zu unserer Gesellschaft gehört*] and I am sincerely happy that you were acquitted.[99]

So, in Goering's view, the Tribunal was right in holding that Fritzsche did not belong in Nuremberg. But even on the way to his own death Goering also implied that the prosecution was correct on another contention: that he himself was one of a distinct group of Nazi leaders who had merited trial.

CHAPTER 10

Conclusion

Bomber Harris [of the RAF] must have got
more victims on his conscience than any individual German General or Air Marshal.

A. W. Harrison, British Foreign Office
June, 1945 [1]

WHEN THE JUDGMENT was read in open court on
September 30 and October 1, the Tribunal's work was done, and the
judges hastened to bid each other farewell and to go their separate
ways. Goering cheated the gallows by suicide, and three of the military officers tried unsuccessfully to find more honorable punish-
ments, Raeder asking for execution rather than life imprisonment
and Jodl and Keitel requesting to be shot instead of hanged. These
petitions, however, had passed beyond the Tribunal, and it was up
to the occupation authorities to determine what should happen to
those who appealed their sentences.

The period in which a line divided judicial process and executive
action had passed, and, in dealing with these petitions and others,
the U.S. Government made the suprising decision to let the opinions of the chief prosecutor, Justice Jackson, determine the general
appeals policy. The yearlong trial had not mellowed Jackson, and,
two weeks before the Court's verdicts were made public, he provided the War Department with confidential guidelines on how the
appeals should be handled. Jackson asserted that at the time the

London Charter provisions were drafted, allowing appeal to the Control Council for reduction of sentence, it was felt that there might develop some "policy reasons for clemency" or a defendant "might be spared because of past or future usefulness to the Allies." But "clemency is a matter of grace, not of right," Jackson noted, and, since none of the defendants had "rendered any service whatever to the prosecution," there were no grounds for clemency.[2] In any event, he felt that the Allied governments should avoid instituting an elaborate appeal procedure. The Control Council should simply take note of the verdicts and of any "grounds for grace" [3] that might be applicable (although Jackson implied strongly that the existence of such grounds was virtually impossible) and then either confirm or reduce the sentences. Assistant Secretary of War Peterson accepted Jackson's guidelines without change and on September 17 they were sent to the Office of Military Government in Germany. Consequently, no review of the Nuremberg cases took place, and no reduction of sentences was allowed. After information about the date and circumstances of their execution had been kept from them for two weeks, the remaining condemned men were marched into the prison yard one by one in the early hours of October 15, and there they were hanged.

The Nuremberg trial process thus ended with the Allied military authorities firmly in control, and no considerations were allowed to affect the implementation of the Tribunal's verdict except those that the military considered practical and useful. On October 6, nine days before the executions, the War Department sent the Military Government officials a series of guidelines to be used in explaining to the German people what the verdict meant. In clipped military language, the directive stated that the information to be released would have four main objectives: to stress that the trial was legal, that it had not been an ex post facto proceeding, that more trials would follow, and that the evidence "presented by the prosecution is a record of [the] Nazi regime." [4] In developing propaganda materials the army authorities were told to stress, among other things, that the verdict was not an act of vengeance but the "result of [an] impartial legal trial," and the information officers were also instructed to use the trial evidence to "counter martyrdom" and to "expose Nazi war guilt, [as well as the] background and causes of World War II." [5] So the official lesson that the Americans trumpeted to the world was that the Allied Powers had acted virtuously and that Nuremberg had discredited the Third Reich. This message quickly flooded the media in occupied Germany and was reinforced by the opinion of the majority of the defense counsel, who seem to have felt that the trial was relatively fair and the verdict reasonable and moderate. "Except for the members of criminal organizations," Carl Haensel, associate counsel for the SA, rather inaccurately exulted, "all other Germans have been cleared of criminal responsibility." [6] Most of his Nuremberg colleagues apparently agreed with Haensel and echoed his sentiments and conclusions. [7]

Determining what the German people as a whole thought about all this is a very different matter, however. The best indications seem to be that most of them acted like spectators, paying only fleeting attention to the trial when it was in process and, aside from grumbling at the verdicts of some individual defendants, trying to forget it as soon as possible when it had run its course. As Martin Broszat and others have recently suggested, the exterminations, the mass destruction, and the lost war associated with the last years of the Nazi regime had already discredited the Third Reich in the eyes of most of the German people. [8] The Nuremberg trial appeared to be merely a ritual performance intended not for their edification, but for the gratification of the victors. Caught in the grip of disaster and faced with the overwhelming tasks of reconstruction, the Germans of 1946 and 1947 had little energy or inclination to ponder the propriety or significance of a major war crimes trial. Consequently, in retrospect, it is difficult to see where the trial had any significant effect on the general development of postwar Germany.

Placed in a broader perspective, the question arises whether the whole Nuremberg enterprise was so flawed that it produced no positive result at all. Was it, as some have recently contended, merely victor's justice, without worthwhile lesson or moral for our time? Surely much of Allied war crimes policy as well as large portions of the basic American trial plan appear to be mistakes piled on folly. The actions of the negotiators and the prosecutors are also replete with blindness, miscalculation and a suicidal passion for complexity. Perhaps more basically, the whole notion of Allied action to bring justice to a war-torn world ran headlong against the main thrust of the war itself. Total war, as we can now see more clearly, has a momentum of its own and what may appear as an atrocity by one side at the beginning of hostilities looks like civilized reticence when viewed from the crescendo of carnage that develops by the end. We need not labor the point that the Nazi-Soviet Pact and the Katyn forest massacre, not to speak of Dresden and Hiroshima, went a long way toward forfeiting the claim to righteousness on which the Allies based this trial of their enemies. But the kind of war that the Allies fought in Germany, especially during its last stages, was something more than total war run amuck. The Allied governments made a conscious decision to wage war in a way that would prove to the German people that they had lost a world war. In exchange for the German bombing of British cities, Winston Churchill promised that "we will mete out to the Germans the measure and more than the measure they have meted out to us." [9] For three years, the RAF and the AAF were as good as Churchill's word and the saturation bombing drove home the lesson of defeat to the German people. Similarly, in 1945, the victorious Allied armies were guided by the "tough mood" of Franklin Roosevelt and the other leaders and they went about establishing an occupation system that would further underscore this message.

It is not the purpose of the present account to dispute the wisdom of the course the Allies chose. Harsh it surely was, and also lacking in moral force, but it can be argued that it may also have been successful, for there has been a notable lack of "stab in the back" legends in post–World War II Germany. What should be clear by now, however, is that the Allies could not emphasize the fact of defeat by harsh military and occupation measures and at the same time, expect much credence to be given to their contention that they came as the pure of heart ready to punish evil and establish justice. One may perhaps burn out wickedness, or possibly expose it by due process, but it is difficult to put much faith in those who try to play Solomon when they burn down the city first and then set up court in the ruins. There is a breathtaking moment in the summer of 1945 when Colonel Bernays, the author of the American trial plan, walked through the streets of devastated Nuremberg as part of his job of appraising the suitability of the Palace of Justice for the trial. In a letter to his wife, he chatted about his work and then gave a long and sensitive description of the mass destruction in the city and the helpless confusion and suffering of the German civilians. One waits almost breathlessly for Bernays to ask himself whether the Allies had not lost the right to sit in judgment because of the fact that they had used such patently inhuman methods of warfare. But the mood of the times created a moral tunnel vision that was too strong, and Bernays moved past a description of the rubble of Nuremberg and concluded that it would be an ideal place for a war criminal trial.[10]

So the Allies lost the moral triumph over Nazism with a double-edged quid pro quo of saturation bombing and a trial. Nevertheless, the decision to have a judicial proceeding was a boon both to contemporaries and to posterity. One can make a strong case that Nuremberg produced both substantial long- and short-term benefits. Considering the atmosphere of the time, the deliberations associated with the trial may well have forestalled a bloodbath. The summer of 1945 was not a time for calm consideration by much of the European population, and only the prospect that the Great Powers would take care of the major task through legal process served as a barrier to direct action. As it was, numerous summary proceedings took place in the areas formerly held by Germany and in the Allied zones of occupation. Such incidents as the notorious Dachau trials did little to enhance a sense of justice or due process, but the one lesson seemingly revealed by all these proceedings, as well as by the secondary Nuremberg trials, was that the longer the court action was delayed, the better chance the defendant had of receiving a fair trial.[11] Consequently, the International Military Tribunal may have made a major contribution to justice simply by delaying many of the trials for twelve or fifteen months, thus allowing time for passions to cool.

As it was, the Allied governments and the prosecutors prevented an anarchic bloodbath, though had they been able to work their will, Nuremberg might well have been a trial pro forma. The top leaders would have been quickly condemned and the declarations of criminality against the six organizations would have been confirmed, establishing a procedure whereby hundreds of thousands of people might have been punished. This precedent of wartime losers being punished through mass purge trials would surely have become a major obstacle to ending wars once they broke out. To the numerous factors already making total war largely uncontrollable would have been added the personal threat to every losing leader of having to pay for failure with his life. If it is in the interest of the people of the twentieth century to limit and control war, then it cannot also be in their interest to place belligerent leaders in a situation where the only alternatives for them are victory or death. Implicit in the original Nuremberg trial plan was the threat that this invitation to war unending would become an integral part of our way of life.

It should ever live to the glory of the Nuremberg judges that they took a major step toward dissipating this danger. By advancing a conservative and cautious interpretation of the law of the London Charter, the Court sharply limited the utility of such concepts as "aggressive war" and "crimes against humanity" in any future victors' trials. Of even greater importance was the Tribunal's achievement in virtually eliminating the collective guilt features by emasculating the conspiracy–common plan charge and the system for prosecuting members of organizations. Only a handful of individuals were convicted solely on the ground of criminal organization membership in the twelve subsequent Nuremberg trials, and even the denazification proceedings merely made a perfunctory pass at group prosecution.[12] Faced with the Tribunal's Judgment, the occupation authorities and Assistant Secretary of War Peterson lost their stomach for action against the organizations.

This limiting and mitigating influence of the Nuremberg bench was largely the result of the judges' desire to perform like a real court. That same inclination was what caused them to act so deliberately that the proceedings were protracted, giving most Germans a grace period that saved them from threats of bloodbaths. In the Court's final Judgment, they threw in enough quid pro quo, as in the Doenitz case, and enough mercy, as in the Schacht case, to make the results very mixed and the moral unclear. Consequently, future governments faced with a similar postwar situation will find such an enterprise hardly worth the effort. Who in subsequent years will want to set up this kind of elaborate system in order to collect a dozen death sentences that could have been obtained with far less effort and expense by using some form of court-martial or occupation court? The Nuremberg proceeding was, as Judge Parker said of the Fritzsche case, like using a cannon to shoot a sparrow.

One moral seems clear: a victors' trial, if it involves enough due process to impress contemporaries, is simply not an efficient way to purge the leaders or cleanse the institutions of a defeated country. Judges, in their whimsical way, do not follow the dictates of sound occupation policy; they write inconsistent verdicts and somehow manage to allow persons like Franz von Papen to go free. They do not want to appear vindictive or murderously efficient; they want to be responsible and fair-minded. If the Nuremberg situation is any bellwether, the elevation of the judicial process to the level of international politics does nothing to increase its consistency or efficiency. Judges cannot transcend the views of their own time and society, nor do they abandon the prejudices that they use in their daily lives at home. The Nuremberg Tribunal developed a formula for dealing with aggressive war that seemed reasonable and useful, but when the Court came to apply it in particular situations, such as the German occupation of Norway, the limited data available and the national prejudices of the judges combined to produce an unfair result. In regard to social prejudices the Nuremberg verdicts followed the same pattern as the one that prevails in Western domestic courts—those defendants who came from a milieu closely approximating that of the judges were the ones who received the most sympathetic treatment. The United States Supreme Court recently struck down an established system of capital punishment because of prejudice in the trial system and because judges could not rise above the limits of their class and station. So, after all procedural hurdles are crossed, the statistical results seem to remain the same—respectable malefactors receive a slap on the wrist, while most death sentences are handed out to the poor and to members of ethnic minorities. As indicated above, something similar happened at Nuremberg. Streicher and Sauckel were hanged, Neurath and Speer were given mild sentences, and Schacht and Papen were acquitted. These results were due in large measure to the merits of the individual cases, but it can also be seriously argued that if injustice were done, it owed less to the evils of victors' justice than to the effects of everyday social prejudice.

By being normally unpredictable and biased, the Nuremberg bench graphically demonstrated that such war crimes tribunals have little of value to offer in dealing with transitions from war to peace. The Nuremberg Court performed its real service by remedying the most dangerous defects of Allied war crimes policy. But even though this was a self-liquidating achievement that, one hopes, will not have to be performed again, the Court did it so skillfully that most of the public is unaware that it was done at all. What has chiefly remained in the public mind about Nuremberg and the Nazi regime is not the cautious and qualified conclusions of the Judgment, but the sweeping and often inaccurate charges made by the prosecution. The old words and phrases, "conspiracy," "aggressive war," and "crimes against humanity," retain so much of their life that historians must strain every nerve to avoid using them as interpretative straitjackets, even today.

It is in part because of the overwhelming public relations

triumph of the prosecution that the moderating role of the Court is difficult for some people to accept. This view rebukes the Nuremberg judges for not finding a way to sustain the prosecution. But the Court was simply unable to deal with the problems at hand and at the same time make a great leap forward in international law and the cause of peace. The Court did not yield to the temptation to create a dramatic, but ephemeral, advance; it chose instead to produce a clear, though modest, contribution to a safer future. If we are not emotionally satisfied by such a result, it may be that we are still trapped by the sonorous phrase and the grandiose gesture. Perhaps, then, this would be a good occasion to be grateful for what the Court did achieve, while reflecting with Robinson Jeffers that

> Justice and Mercy
> Are human dreams, they do not concern the birds nor
> the fish nor eternal God.

APPENDIX I

DEFENDANTS	COUNTS				VERDICT				SENTENCE
	ONE	TWO	THREE	FOUR	ONE	TWO	THREE	FOUR	
Goering	X	X	X	X	G	G	G	G	Hanging
Hess	X	X	X	X	G	G	NG	NG	Life
Ribbentrop	X	X	X	X	G	G	G	G	Hanging
Keitel	X	X	X	X	G	G	G	G	Hanging
Kaltenbrunner	X		X	X	NG		G	G	Hanging
Rosenberg	X	X	X	X	G	G	G	G	Hanging
Frank	X		X	X	NG		G	G	Hanging
Frick	X	X	X	X	NG	G	G	G	Hanging
Streicher	X			X	NG			G	Hanging
Funk	X	X	X	X	NG	G	G	G	Life
Sauckel	X	X	X	X	NG	NG	G	G	Hanging
Jodl	X	X	X	X	G	G	G	G	Hanging
Seyss-Inquart	X	X	X	X	NG	G	G	G	Hanging
Speer	X	X	X	X	NG	NG	G	G	20 Years
Neurath	X	X	X	X	G	G	G	G	15 Years
Bormann (absentia)	X		X	X	NG		G	G	Hanging
Schirach	X			X	NG			G	20 Years
Raeder	X	X	X		G	G	G		Life
Doenitz	X	X	X		NG	G	G		10 Years
Schacht	X	X			NG	NG			
Papen	X	X			NG	NG			
Fritzsche	X		X	X	NG		NG	NG	
TOTALS	22	16	18	18	8	12	16	16	Guilty
					14	4	2	2	Not Guilty

APPENDIX II

A Partial List of Members of the Prosecution and
Judicial Teams

Alderman, Sidney S.	American Prosecution Team
Bernays, Murray C.	American Prosecution Team
Biddle, Francis	Senior American Tribunal Member
Birkett, Justice Norman	Alternate British Tribunal Member
Champetier de Ribes, Auguste	French Prosecution Team
de Menthon, François	French Prosecution Team
Donnedieu de Vabres, Professor H.	Senior French Tribunal Member
Donovan, General William	American Prosecution Team
Dean, Sir Patrick	Legal Adviser to the British Foreign Office and the War Crimes Executive
Dodd, Thomas	American Prosecution Team
Falco, Judge R.	Alternate French Tribunal Member
Fisher, Adrian S.	American Judicial Aide
Jackson, Justice Robert H.	American Prosecution Team
Lawrence, Lord Justice Geoffrey	Senior British Tribunal Member
Maxwell Fyfe, Sir David	British Prosecution Team
Neave, Major Airey M. S.	British Judicial Aide
Nikitchenko, Major General I. T.	Senior Soviet Tribunal Member
Parker, Judge John J.	Alternate American Tribunal Member
Phipps, John	British Judicial Aide
Rowe, James H.	American Judicial Aide
Rudenko, General R. A.	Soviet Prosecution Team
Shawcross, Sir Hartley	British Prosecution Team
Stewart, Robert	American Judicial Aide
Storey, Colonel Robert G.	American Prosecution Team
Taylor, Brigadier General Telford	American Prosecution Team
Volchkov, Lieutenant Colonel A. F.	Alternate Soviet Tribunal Member
Wechsler, Herbert	American Judicial Aide
Wright, Quincy	American Judicial Aide

NOTES

GUIDE TO FREQUENTLY CITED SOURCES

Alderman—Sidney S. Alderman, "Negotiating the Nuremberg Trial Agreements," pp. 49–98 in Dennett, Raymond and Johnson, Joseph F. (eds.), *Negotiating with the Russians* (n.p.: 1951).

Assistant Secretary—Assistant Secretary of War, RG 107, "War Crimes," 000.5. Modern Military Branch, National Archives of the United States.

Bernays—The Murray C. Bernays Collection, The University of Wyoming.

Biddle—Francis Biddle, *In Brief Authority* (New York: 1962).

CAB 21—War Cabinet Committee on War Crimes, CAB 21. Public Records Office, London.

CAB 122—General War Cabinet Material, CAB 122, Public Records Office, London.

Chief of Counsel—United States Chief of Counsel for the Prosecution of Axis Criminality, Record Group (RG) 238, Modern Military Branch, National Archives of the United States, Washington, D.C.

F.B. Papers—The Francis Biddle Papers, Syracuse University, Syracuse, New York.

FO—Foreign Office, FO series, 38999–51038. Public Records Office, London.

Birkett—H. Montgomery Hyde, *Norman Birkett* (London: 1964).

IMT—*Trial of the Major War Criminals Before the International Military Tribunal*, 42 vols. (Nuremberg: 1947).

Jackson—Robert H. Jackson, *Report of Robert H. Jackson, United States Representative to the International Conference on Military Trials, London, 1945* (Washington, D.C.: 1949).

LCO—Lord Chancellor's Office 2/2980–2982, 1944–45. Public Records Office, London.

Opinion and Judgment—*Nazi Conspiracy and Aggression: Opinion and Judgment* (Washington, D.C.: 1947).

Rosenman—Papers of Samuel I. Rosenman, Harry S. Truman Library, Independence, Missouri.

State Department I—State Department of the United States, 740.00116 EW. "Prosecution," Diplomatic Branch, National Archives of the United States.

State Department II—State Department of the United States, 740.00116 EW. "Illegal and Inhumane Warfare," Diplomatic Branch, National Archives of the United States.

Preface

1. Robert Jackson to President Truman and attachments, December 1, 1945. 740.00116 EW Prosecution/12-1045. Diplomatic Branch, National Archives of the United States (hereinafter cited as *State Department I*).

2. The ultimate expression of this tendency was Telford Taylor's *Nuremberg and Vietnam: An American Tragedy* (New York, 1970).

3. A. J. P. Taylor, *The Origins of the Second World War* (New York, 1961), presents the start of the new era.

4. The 1974 meeting of the American Historical Association had a program on Nuremberg. Earlier, Eugene Davidson (*The Trial of the Germans*, New York: 1966) drew attention to the trials, but his book was a chronicle of Nazism using the defendants as illustrative examples.

5. Albert Speer, *Spandau: The Secret Diaries* (New York, 1976).

Chapter 1

1. "Memorandum for the General Secretary," October 20, 1945, Lord Chancellor's Office (hereinafter cited as *LCO*) 2/2982/x/j.7320, Public Records Office, London.

2. Interview with Dean Adrian Fisher, Washington, D.C., May 1, 1975.

3. Interview with Herbert Wechsler, New York, May 8, 1975. Interview with John Phipps, London, March 21, 1975.

4. Interview with John Phipps, London, March 21, 1975. Interview with Sir Patrick Dean, London, April 2, 1975. Interview with Dean Adrian Fisher, Washington, D.C., May 1, 1975.

5. Interview with John Phipps, London, March 21, 1975. "Notes on Conference," October 13, 1945, Box 1, Francis Biddle Papers, Syracuse University, Syracuse, New York, (hereinafter cited as *F. B. Papers*). Note by Scott Fox, October 2, 1945, Foreign Office (hereinafter cited as *FO*) 371/50989/U7875, Public Records Office, London. "Memorandum of Points for Consideration by British Judges in Berlin," October 10, 1945, LCO 2/2982/x/j.7320, *LCO*. Francis Biddle, *In Brief Authority* (New York: 1962), p. 385 (hereinafter cited as *Biddle*).

6. "Notes on Conference," October 13, 1945, Box 1, *F. B. Papers*.

7. H. Montgomery Hyde, *Norman Birkett* (London: 1964), (hereinafter cited as *Birkett*), pp. 494–95. Interview with John Phipps, London, March 21, 1975.

8. *Jackson to Horsky*, U.S. Chief of Counsel for the Prosecution of Axis Criminality, February 26, 1946, Record Group (RG) 238, Box 198, Modern Military Branch, National Archives, Washington, D.C. (hereinafter cited as *Chief of Counsel*).

9. "Notes of Evidence," April 26, 1946, vol. 4, Box 4, *F. B. Papers*.

10. *Blake to Biddle*—Press Summaries, State Department of the United States 740.00116 EW Prosecution Diplomatic Branch, National Archives, (hereinafter cited as *State Department I*) passim.

11. Note by Scott Fox, October 2, 1945, FO 371/50989/U7875, *FO*.

12. *P. Dean to Scott Fox*, December 6, 1945, FO 371/5100/U9758, *FO*.

13. Interview with John Phipps, London, March 21, 1975. Interview with Dean Adrian Fisher, Washington, D.C., May 1, 1975.

14. "Notes on Judgment," September 3, 1946, p. 26, Box 14, Folder 3, *F. B. Papers*.

15. Ibid., September 12, 1946, p. 54.

16. Carl Haensel, *Das Gericht vertagt sich* (Hamburg, 1950), p. 201.

17. The indictment appears in volume I of *Trial of the Major War Criminals Before the International Military Tribunal*, 42 vols. (Nuremberg: 1947) (hereinafter cited as *IMT*). Throughout this book all references to the final opinion and Judgment come from *Nazi Conspiracy and Aggression: Opinion and Judgment* (Washington, D.C.: 1947) (hereinafter cited as *Opinion and Judgment*).

18. Most of the legal issues are surveyed in August von Knieriem, *The Nuremberg Trials* (Chicago: 1959), and Robert K. Woetzel, *The Nuremberg Trials in International Law* (London and New York: 1962).

19. Vol. 1, p. 42, *IMT*.

20. Ibid., p. 29.

21. Ibid., p. 241.

22. "Notes on Judgment," August 15, 1946, p. 18, Box 14, Folder 3, *F. B. Papers*.

Chapter 2

1. *The Morgenthau Diary (Germany)*, vol. II, (Washington, D.C.: 1967), p. 1505.

2. "The Diaries of Henry L. Stimson," August 25, September 7, September 25, October 13, 1944 (and following). Roll 9, Yale University.

3. The French were particularly insistent; see, for example, Duff Cooper to the Foreign Office, August 16, 1944, #1470, FO 371/38999/U10825, *FO*.

4. The British and American records are replete with such references. A general statement on the question by the American Jewish Conference was sent from the State Department to the War Department on September 8, 1944. See appendix documents, Stimson to Hull, October 27, 1944, in *Assistant Secretary of War*, RG 107, War Crimes, 000.5, Modern Military Branch, National Archives of the United States (hereinafter cited as *Assistant Secretary*).

5. Again there are countless indications of this attitude in the respective British and American files. A general Foreign Office file includes a generous sampling, including the U.S. War Department's nonsegregation order to Eisenhower, issued on January 1, 1944. FO 371/38990, *FO*.

6. Aside from the documentary collection known as the "Morgenthau Diary" in the Franklin D. Roosevelt Library at Hyde Park, plus the various published offshoots of this collection, the best source for examining Morgenthau's development on this question is Henry L. Feingold, *The Politics of Rescue* (New Brunswick, New Jersey: 1970).

7. Morgenthau, and nearly every other high-ranking U.S. Government official involved in the question, has recounted the events in some form of memoir. Lieutenant Colonel Bernard Bernstein seems to have been the one who gave the directive to Morgenthau *Morgenthau Diary (Germany)*, vol. I, pp. 450, 462.

8. *Morgenthau Diary (Germany)*, vol. I, p. 447.

9. "Memorandum of Conversation with the President," November 15, 1944, Edward Stettinius Papers, Box 724, The University of Virginia.

10. *FDR to the Secretary of War*, August 26, 1944. *Morgenthau Diary (Germany)*, vol. I, p. 443.

11. The materials may be compared in the published version, *Morgenthau Diary (Germany)*, vol. I, pp. 442 f., or in the original at Hyde Park. "Morgenthau Diary," Book 765, Franklin D. Roosevelt Library, Hyde Park. It should be noted that the President did have a copy of the handbook with his own initials and dated August 25, 1944 (see Presidential Secretary's File, Box 104, Franklin D. Roosevelt Library, Hyde Park).

12. The committee idea apparently originated with Morgenthau and then was championed by Stimson. *Morgenthau Diary (Germany)* vol. I, p. 447.

13. "Post-Surrender Memorandum," September 4, 1944, and Treasury Conference Minutes, September 4, 1944, *Morgenthau Diary (Germany)* vol. I, pp. 495, 503–09.

14. Ibid., pp. 507–09.

15. *Stimson to Henry Morgenthau*, September 5, 1944 in "The Papers of Henry L. Stimson," Roll #110, Yale University (hereinafter cited as "Papers of Stimson").

16. *Stimson to the President*, September 9, 1944, *Foreign Relations of the United States: The Conference at Quebec, 1944* (Washington, D.C.: 1972), p. 125.

17. Ibid., p. 123.

18. Stimson-McCloy Conversation, ibid., p. 76.

19. Ibid., p. 77.

20. *Stimson to Henry Morgenthau*, September 5, 1944. "Papers of Stimson."

21. One anonymous War Department official had fun at their expense, writing a two-page memorandum to Stimson on September 19, outlining various fanciful ways to wreck the German economy, (see "Memorandum to the Secretary of War," September 19, 1944, Papers of Stimson.)

22. Box 314, passim, War Department G-1, RG 165, War Crimes, 000.5, Federal Records Center, Suitland, Md.

23. *Bernays to R. A. Winnacker*, August 18, 1949 in the Murray C. Bernays Collection, Box 1, University of Wyoming (hereinafter cited as *Bernays*).

24. The transmission cover letter by Bernays is in Trial and Punishment File 1, Box 4, *Bernays*. The memorandum appears at various points in the federal records and in Bernays's

papers. They are perhaps most readily accessible in McCloy to Stimson, October 27, 1944, (January 1943–December 1944 File) Box 15, *Assistant Secretary.*

25. *McCloy to Stimson,* October 27, 1944 (attachment), (January 1943–December 1944 File) Box 15, *Assistant Secretary.*

26. Transmission letter by Bernays, Trial and Punishment File 1, Box 4, *Bernays.* Bernays also prepared a chronology of the developments up through late December 1944, War Department G-1, RG 165, War Crimes, 000.5, Box 313, Federal Records Center, Suitland, Md.

27. Minute by the secretary of state, W.P. (42) 264, June 22, 1942, CAB 21, War Cabinet Committee on War Crimes, File no. 1509 Public Records Office, London (hereinafter cited as *CAB 21*).

28. *Clark Kerr to FO,* #339, November 25, 1942, *CAB 21.*

29. There were Cabinet discussions on November 10, 1943, and February 15, 1944, FO Minute, February 15, 1944, FO 371/38991/2223, *FO.* On the Cairo Meeting, see FO Minute, February 22, 1944, FO 371/38992/2822, *FO.*

30. PID list, April 10, 1944; FO list April 27, 1944, FO 371/38993/4791, *FO.*

31. Minute by the Secretary, May 26, 1944, FO 371/38994/7250, *FO.*

32. War Cabinet Minutes (44) 83, June 28, 1944, /7970, *CAB 21.*

33. *Prime Minister to General Ismay,* August 25, 1944, /7970, *CAB 21.*

34. War Cabinet Meeting, September 4, 1944, /7970, *CAB 21.*

35. Memorandum to P. J. Dixon, September 18, 1944, /7970, *CAB 21.*

36. Minute by Allen, October 3, 1944, FO 371/39004/13753, *FO.*

37. Prime Minister to the Lord Chancellor, September 27, 1944, /7970, *CAB 21.*

38. War Cabinet Conclusions, October 4, 1944, /7970, *CAB 21.*

39. Morgenthau's reaction shows especially clearly in the records of the Treasury conferences. *Morgenthau Diary (Germany)* vol. I, pp. 627 f. FDR's official complaint about the leak went to the State Department at the end of September. (See *The President to Secretary Hull,* September 29, 1944, Presidential Secretary's File, Box 44, Franklin D. Roosevelt Library, Hyde Park.)

40. November 4, 1944, "Diaries of Stimson."

41. October 27, 1944 conversation with Ambassador Winant, "Diaries of Stimson." An interesting discussion of FDR's "loss" of memory is in Donald R. McCoy (ed.), *Conference of Scholars on the Administration of Occupied Areas, 1943–1955,* (The Harry S. Truman Library, Independence, Mo.: 1970), p. 20.

42. *Stimson to Hull,* October 27, 1944, State Department of the United States 740.00116 EW/10-2744 Illegal and Inhumane Warfare, Diplomatic Branch, National Archives of the United States (hereinafter cited as *State Department II*).

43. *Stettinius to Pell,* November 25, 1944, #9920, 11-244, *State Department II.*

44. *Stimson to Hull,* November 27, 1944, 11-2744 *State Department II.*

45. *Chanler to Bernays,* December 20, 1944, Working File, Box 16, *Assistant Secretary.*

46. *Wechsler to Biddle,* December 29, 1944, Justice Department Files on War Criminal Prosecution.

47. "Memorandum Regarding Punishment of Criminals," January 5, 1945, Justice Department Files on War Criminal Prosecution. Interview with Herbert Wechsler, New York, May 8, 1975.

48. *FDR to Stettinius,* January 3, 1945, Stettinius Papers, Box 232.

49. *Biddle,* p. 470.

50. "Memorandum for the President," January 22, 1945, *Foreign Relations of the United States: Conferences at Malta and Yalta, 1945* (Washington, D.C.: 1955), pp. 402–11.

51. Ibid., pp. 405 f.

52. An effort was made in early March to obtain FDR's formal approval, but it failed. Dunn-McCloy exchange, 3-645 *State Department II.* Joseph E. Davies was FDR's first choice to ne-

gotiate the question with the British, but he became ill. Rosenman, who had been involved in earlier stages of the war criminal policy discussion, was notified of his task by cable on March 24, 1945. (see *Grew to Rosenman, #2294/3-2445 State Department II.*)

53. *Churchill to FDR*, October 22, 1944, *Foreign Relations of the United States: Conferences at Malta and Yalta, 1945* (Washington, D.C.: 1955), p. 400. *Churchill to Eden*, October 24, 1944, FO 371/39005/14953, *FO.*

54. The crucial man was the State Department legal adviser, Green Haywood Hackworth, who was cool toward the trial idea.

55. *Halifax to FO*, October 19, 1944, FO 371/39005/14328, *FO. Halifax to FO*, January 3, 1945, General War Cabinet Material CAB 122/1353/8032, Public Records Office, London (hereinafter cited as *CAB 122*).

56. "Notes of the Anglo-American meeting of April 10, 1945," Papers of Samuel I. Rosenman, Harry S. Truman Library, Independence Mo. (hereinafter cited as *Rosenman*), Box 7, War Crimes File.

57. "War Criminals Memorandum," April 9, 1945, WP (45) 225, CAB 66, vol. 64, Public Records Office, London.

58. War Cabinet Minutes, April 12, 1945, CAB 65 (45), vol. 50, Public Records Office, London.

59. Ibid., p. 264

60. *Stettinius to Rosenman*, April 11, 1945, #5747, Box 15, Alphabetical file, *Assistant Secretary.*

61. *Stimson to Weir, etc.*, April 17, 1945, #WAR 67164, Box 7, War Crimes File, *Rosenman.*

62. "Memorandum on Grew-Truman conversation," April 27, 1945, /4-1045, *State Department II.*

63. *Jackson to President Truman*, April 29, 1945 in Eugene C. Gerhart, *America's Advocate: Robert H. Jackson* (Indianapolis and New York: 1958), pp. 308–10.

64. "Memorandum," April 30, 1945, *For Presentation at San Francisco*, Document 5, Report of Robert H. Jackson, United States Representative to the *International Conference on Military Trials*, (Washington, D.C.: 1949) (hereinafter cited as *Jackson*), pp. 28–38. A note on Bernays's copy says that it was approved on May 1, 1945 by Cutter, Wechsler, Jackson, and Bernays himself. Trial and Punishment File 2, Box 4, *Bernays.*

65. "Notes of Meeting of April 16, 1945," LCO 2/2981/x/j.7320, *LCO.*

66. *Halifax to FO*, April 24, 1945. /1353/8032, *CAB 122.*

67. War Criminal Memorandum, W.P. (45) 281, May 3, 1945. CAB 66, vol. 65, Public Records Office, London.

68. W.M. (45) 57th Conclusions, May 3, 1945, CAB 65, vol. 50, Public Records Office, London.

69. *Rosenman to HST*, May 3, 1945, S.F. file, Box 15, *Assistant Secretary.*

70. Ibid.

71. Draft Executive Agreement, May 8, 1945, p. 3, War Crimes File, Box 7, *Rosenman.*

72. Draft Executive Agreement, May 16, 1945, S.F. file, Box 15, *Assistant Secretary.*

73. *Rosenman to Golinsky, etc.*, May 10, 1945, War Crimes File, Box 7, *Rosenman.*

74. Minutes of Meeting, May 22, 1945, "May through file," Box 16, *Assistant Secretary.*

75. Jackson's announcement of his core staff, May 16, 1945, RG 107, War Crimes, 000.5, Secretary of War, Modern Military Branch, National Archives of the United States.

76. *Grew to U.S. embassies*, May 18, 1945, /5-1545, *State Department II.* Note of May 29th, May–July 14, 1945, Container 17, Joseph E. Davies Papers, Library of Congress. "Memorandum by P. Dean," May 28, 1945, FO 371/51024/4355, *FO.*

77. FO Minute, May 5, 1945, FO 371/51009/3462, *FO.*

78. FO Minutes, May 14 and May 24–26, 1945, FO 371/50976/4004 and FO 371/51024/4356, *FO.*

79. "Memorandum by the Attorney General," W.P. (45) 313, May 18, 1945, CAB 66, vol. 65, Public Records Office, London.

80. Minute by P. Dean, May 28, 1945, FO 371/51024/4355, *FO.* CM Minutes, CM (1) May 30, 1945, CAB 65, vol. 53, Public Records Office, London.

81. Minutes of Meeting of May 29, 1945, p. 2. LCO /x/j.7320, *LCO.*

82. Ibid.

83. *Caffery to State Department,* June 19, 1945, #A-792, 6-1945, *State Department II.*

84. "Memorandum of Third Conversation in the Kremlin," *Foreign Relations of the United States: Conference of Berlin (Potsdam), 1945,* (Washington, D.C.: 1960), p. 48.

85. Notes of Novikov-Stettinius meeting, June 14, 1945, /6-1645, *State Department I.*

86. Ibid.

87. Copy of the U.S. plan dated June 19, 1945, registered July 3, 1945. FO 371/51028/5157, *FO.*

88. *Fite to Rosenman,* and enclosure, June 16, 1945, War Crimes File, Box 7, *Rosenman.*

Chapter 3

1. Robert H. Jackson, "The Rule of Law Among Nations," *American Bar Association Journal,* XXXI, (June 1945): p. 293.

2. *HST to General Booth,* May 25, 1945, Official File, File 325, Box 1007, Papers of Harry S. Truman, Harry S. Truman Library, Independence, Missouri.

3. The Papers of James B. Donovan (Hoover Institution, Stanford University) and the Murray C. Bernays Papers contain the best collections of participant letters currently available.

4. Gerhart, *America's Advocate,* p. 322.

5. *Jackson to Rosenman,* June 25, 1945 #36997 (filed under June 28, 1945) War Crimes File, Box 7, *Rosenman.*

6. Minutes of Meeting of the British War Crimes Executive, June 15, 1945, LCO 2/2980/x/j.7320, *LCO.*

7. Minutes of Meeting, British Executive, June 14, 1945, LCO 2/2980/x/j.7320, *LCO.*

8. Minutes of Meeting, British Executive, June 5, 1945, LCO2/2980/x/j.7320, *LCO.*

9. Note of a conversation with General Donovan, June 9, 1945, LCO 2/2980/x/j.7320, *LCO.*

10. Minutes of Meeting, British Executive, June 5, 1945, LCO 2/2980/x/j.7320, *LCO.*

11. *Dean to Maxwell Fyfe,* June 19, 1945, LCO 2/2980/x/j.7320, *LCO.* Minutes of Meeting, British Executive, June 15, 1945, LCO 2/2980/x/j.7320, *LCO.*

12. War Criminals list, June 19, 1945, FO 371/51027/4958, *FO.*

13. *Dean to Maxwell Fyfe,* June 19, 1945, LCO 2/2980/x/j.7320, *LCO.*

14. Minutes of the second Anglo-American Meeting, June 21, 1945, LCO 2/2980/x/j.7320, *LCO.*

15. Minutes of Scott Fox, June 21, 1945, FO 371/51026/4849, *FO.*

16. Minutes of the second Anglo-American Meeting, June 21, 1945, LCO 2/2980/x/j.7320, *LCO.*

17. Minutes of the first Four Power meeting, morning session, June 26, 1945, Trial and Punishment File 4, Box 4, *Bernays.* It should be noted that these are not the minutes published in *Jackson* (Document XIII, p. 71), which cover only the afternoon session. The minutes in *Jackson* were apparently made by the justice's secretary, Mrs. Elsie Douglas. There are, in addition, at least three more sets for various sessions. Minutes kept by Bernays and Robert Jackson's son are in *Bernays.* The British Treasury reporter also kept minutes. (See, for example, FO 371/51032/5931, *FO.*)

18. Minutes of Session of June 26, 1945, Document 13, *Jackson,* pp. 71 f.

19. American Draft Revision June 14, 1945, Document 9, *Jackson,* p. 58.

20. The Morning session of June 29 is a typical example, Document 17, *Jackson*, pp. 97 f.

21. *Jackson to McCloy*, June 30, 1945, #38334, "May through file," Box 16, *Assistant Secretary*.

22. *Bernays to Cutter.* July 9, 1945. "May thru file," Box 16, *Assistant Secretary.*

23. *Jackson to Rosenman*, June 26, 1945 (filed under June 28), #36997, War Crimes File, Box 7, *Rosenman.*

24. *Jackson to Rosenman*, June 27, 1945 (filed under June 29), #37207, War Crimes File, Box 7, *Rosenman.*

25. *Jackson to Secretary of State*, July 4, 1945, *Foreign Relations of the United States: 1945*, vol. 3, (Washington, D.C.: 1968), p. 1167.

26. *Jackson to Rosenman*, July 12, 1945, War Crimes File, Box 7, *Rosenman.*

27. *Jackson to McCloy*, July 18, 1945, May thru file, Box 16, *Assistant Secretary.*

28. *Jackson to Taylor*, July 19, 1945 #UK 4500/, RG 153, JAG, File No. 103-1A-Bk. 1, Box 1603, Federal Records Center, Suitland, Md.

29. *Jackson to Secretary of State*, July 19, 1945, #7285, 7-1945 *State Department II.*

30. *Jackson to Secretary of State*, July 20, 1945 #7341, 7-2045 *State Department II.*

31. Sidney S. Alderman, "Negotiating the Nuremberg Trial Agreements, 1945," in Raymond Dennett and Joseph E. Johnson (eds.), *Negotiating with the Russians* (n.p.: 1951) [hereinafter cited as *Alderman*], p. 78.

32. *Jackson to McCloy*, July 18, 1945, May thru file, Box 16, *Assistant Secretary.*

33. *Jackson to Secretary of State*, July 6, 1945, #6814, 7-645, *State Department II.*

34. Minutes of Scott Fox, July 20, 1945, FO 371/50983/5801, *FO.*

35. "Memorandum for Justice Jackson," July 14, 1945, Trial and Punishment file 1, Box 4, *Bernays*. Alternate Executive Agreement, n. d., Box 222, *Chief of Counsel.*

36. *Jackson to McCloy*, July 18, 1945, May thru file, Box 16, *Assistant Secretary*. Bernays to his wife, July 21, 1945, Personal Letter file, Box #4, *Bernays.*

37. "Memorandum by Judge Rosenman," August 1, 1945, *Foreign Relations of the United States: Conference of Berlin (Potsdam), 1945*, vol. 2 (Washington, D.C.: 1960), p. 987; *J. Donovan to Jackson*, July 23, 1945, Trial and Punishment file 6, Box 4, *Bernays.*

38. Conversation of U.S. Officials at Potsdam, July 26, 1945, *Foreign Relations of the United States; Conference of Berlin (Potsdam), 1945*, vol. 2 (Washington, D.C.: 1960), pp. 423–424.

39. Ibid., p. 424.

40. *Clyde to Scott Fox*, July 28, 1945, FO 371/51031/5860, FO. *Lord Chancellor to Prime Minister*, July 31, 1945, #317, FO 371/51031/5838, *FO.*

41. *PM to Lord Chancellor*, August 1, 1945 #332, FO 371/51031/5882, *FO;* Minutes of August 2, 1945, FO 371/51031/5877, *FO.*

42. *Clyde to Scott Fox*, July 28, 1945, FO 371/51031/5860, *FO.*

43. "Notes of the Eleventh Plenary Meeting, July 31, 1945," *Foreign Relations of the United States: Conference of Berlin (Potsdam), 1945*, vol. 2 (Washington, D.C.: 1960), p. 526.

44. Ibid.

45. FO Summary of the Twelfth Plenary Session, August 1, 1945, FO 371/51032/5974, *FO.*

46. *Rosenman to Secretary of State*, August 1, 1945, *Foreign Relations of The United States: Conference of Berlin (Potsdam), 1945*, vol. 2, (Washington, D.C.: 1960), p. 987.

47. Minutes of Conference Session of August 2, 1945, Document 59, *Jackson*, pp. 399–419.

48. Document 60, *Jackson*, pp. 420–21.

49. *Davies to Rosenman*, January 13, 1945, War Crimes File, Box 7, *Rosenman*. Jacob Robinson, "The International Military Tribunal and the Holocaust: Some Legal Reflections," *Israel Law Review*, VII, no. 1 (January 1972): 3.

50. *Alderman to Nikitchenko, Gros, and Roberts*, August 31, 1945, LCO 2/2980/x/j.7320, *LCO.*

51. Document 6o, Articles 18 and 19, pp. 426–27, *Jackson.* For the prosecution's sensitivity on these issues, see Minutes of the Chief Prosecutors Meeting, October 30, 1945, FO 371/50992/8801, *FO.*

52. Document 4, Article 11, p. 24, and Document 6o, Article 9, p. 424, *Jackson.*

53. "Memorandum by P. Dean," June 19, 1945, LCO 2/2980/x/j.7320, *LCO.*

54. *Alderman,* pp. 82–83. London Committee #1 Documents, June 23, 1945, Trial and Punishment file #4, Box #4, *Bernays.*

55. "Memorandum on Keitel, Doenitz, et al.," August 15, 1945, LCO 2/2980/x/j.7320, *LCO.*

56. "Dean Memorandum," June 19, 1945; British Draft, July 13, 1945, Trial and Punishment file 6, Box 4, *Bernays.*

57. *Taylor to Jackson,* June 25 and July 13, 1945, War Department, RG 165, G-1, War Crimes, 000.5, Box 313, Federal Records Center, Suitland, Md.

58. *Bernays to Donovan,* July 2, 1945, Preparation of Evidence file 2, Box 2, *Bernays.*

59. "Memorandum for all Legal Personnel," filed under July 25, 1945 (dated July 20), Preparation of Evidence file 3, Box 2, *Bernays.*

6o. *Jackson to Taylor,* July 19, 1945, #UK 45807, War Department, RG 153, JAG, War Crimes, 000.5, file no. 103-1A-Bk-1, Box 1603, Federal Records Center, Suitland, Md.

61. Horsky's draft, August 4, 1945, Secret Evidence file 1, Box 3, *Bernays. Bernays to Jackson,* transmitting two indictment drafts, August 8, 1945, Secret Evidence file 2, Box 3, *Bernays.*

62. Notes on Meeting of four prosecution teams, August 9, 1945, Secret Evidence file 3, Box 3, *Bernays.*

63. *Alderman,* p. 86. *Clyde to Shawcross,* August 11, 1945, FO 371/510331/6290, *FO. Jackson to staff,* August 14, 1945, Secret Evidence file 3, Box 3, *Bernays.*

64. *Jackson to staff,* August 14, 1945, Secret Evidence file 3, Box 3, *Bernays.*

65. *Jackson to HST,* October 12, 1945 (filed under October 16th), 10-1645, *State Department I.*

66. *Alderman,* pp. 84 f.

67. *Jackson to Wendelin,* August 28, 1945, #8770, 8-2845, *State Department II.*

68. *Jackson to Byrnes,* August 24, 1945, #8919, 8-2745, *State Department II.*

69. *Byrnes to Jackson,* August 25, 1945, #7289, 8-2745, *State Department II.*

70. *Jackson to Byrnes,* August 27, 1945, #8722, 8-2745, *State Department II.*

71. *Alderman,* p. 85.

72. Progress Report #5, East-West Committee, September 4, 1945, FO 371/51036/6892, *FO.* Notes of Meeting of Heads of Delegations, September 13, 1945, *FO.*

73. *Alderman,* p. 90.

74. Progress Report #6, Sub-Committee 2 and 3, East-West Committee, September 20, 1945, FO 371/51037/7448, *FO.*

75. *Storey to Jackson,* September 19, 1945, Box 208, *Chief of Counsel.*

76. *Alderman,* p. 91.

77. Ibid.

78. *Alderman,* pp. 91–92. *Dean to the Attorney General,* September 27, 1945, FO 371/50988/7678, *FO.*

79. *Alderman,* p. 92.

80. *Alderman,* pp. 92–93.

81. Extract from War Cabinet Conclusions 38 (45), October 9, 1945, FO 371/50989/8048, *FO.*

82. *Alderman,* pp. 93–94.

83. *Monigan to Amen,* October 4, 1945, Box 180, *Chief of Counsel.*

84. Troutbeck minute on Dean's Trials of Major War Criminals minute, June 29, 1945, FO 371/51029/5253, *FO.*

Notes

85. "Memorandum," August 2, 1945, FO 371/50985/6534, *FO.*

86. *Stimson to Jackson,* June 25, 1945, Secretary of War, RG 107, War Crimes, 000.5, Modern Military Branch, National Archives of the United States.

Chapter 4

1. *HST to Francis Biddle,* November 12, 1946, Document 251, *Public Papers of the Presidents: Harry S. Truman,* (Washington, D.C.: 1962), p. 481.

2. *Phillimore to Maxwell Fyfe,* September 26, 1945, FO 371/51038/7765, *FO.*

3. "Notes on Conference," October 3, 1945, Box 1, *FB Papers.* "Memorandum to Biddle and Parker," October 5, 1945, Folder 1 "Memoranda" Box 14, *F. B. Papers.*

4. Ibid,

5. Interview with John Phipps, March 21, 1975, London. Minutes of Dean, November 8, 1945, FO 371/50994/8993, *FO.*

6. *Jackson to HST,* October 12, 1945, /10-1645, *State Department I.*

7. "Notes on Conference," October 15, 1945, Box 1, *F. B. Papers.*

8. Ibid., October 13, 1945.

9. Minutes of Meeting of the Chief Prosecutors, August 31, 1945, FO 371/51036/6830, *FO. William Jackson to the Secretary of State,* October 1, 1945, /10-145, *State Department I.* Notes on Meeting of October 29, 1945, Box 1, *F. B. Papers.*

10. Minutes, Conference of October 21, 1945, Box 1, *F. B. Papers.*

11. Notes on Meeting of November 13, 1945, pp. 8–11, Box 2, *F. B. Papers.*

12. "Notes on Conference," November 6, 1945, Box 2, *F. B. Papers.*

13. J. R. Rees (ed.), *The Case of Rudolf Hess* (New York; 1948). "Notes of Evidence," vol. 1, pp. 80 f. Box 3, *F. B. Papers.*

14. *Dean to Scott Fox,* November 20, 1945, and Minutes of Chief Prosecutors Meeting, November 19, 19, 1945, FO 371/50996/8093, *FO.*

15. November 14, 1945, vol. 2, p. 10, *IMT.*

16. Ibid., p. 15.

17. Ibid., p. 8.

18. *Biddle,* p. 401; "Notes on Conference," November 16, 17, Box 1; Minutes, November 13, 15, 16, 1945, Box 2, *F. B. Papers.*

19. November 21, 1945, Volume 2, pp. 154–155, *IMT.*

20. Ibid., p. 155.

21. Minutes of Meeting of British War Crimes Executive, November 7, 1945, FO 371/50995/9198, *FO.*

22. A British appraisal of the individual defense attorneys is in a summary dated November 27, 1945, FO 371/50998/9481, *FO.*

23. Two of the best windows on the minds of the defense are Viktor Freiherr von der Lippe, *Nürnberger Tagebuchnotizen* (Frankfurt am Main: 1951), and Gustav Steinbauer, *Ich war Verteidiger in Nürnberg,* (Klagenfurt: 1950).

24. Report no. 3 of British War Crimes Executive, November 25, 1945, FO 371/51001/9763, *FO.*

25. Information considered common knowledge or beyond controversy: such as the texts of treaties, was exempted from the rule. See "Notes of Evidence," Nov. 26, 1945, vol. 1, Box 3, p. 43. Exec. Session minutes, Nov. 24 and Nov. 28, 1945, Box 2, *F. B. Papers.*

26. *Dean to FO,* November 24, 1945, FO 371/50996/9309, *FO.*

27. November 29, 1945 vol. 2, p. 406, *IMT.*

28. "Notes of Evidence," vol. I, p. 176, Box 3, *F. B. Papers.*

29. *Birkett,* p. 502. "Notes of Evidence," vol. I, p. 176, Box 3, *F. B. Papers.*

30. von der Lippe, *Nürnberger Tagebuchnotizen* p. 73. Translation is mine.

31. December 10, 1945, vol. 3, p. 341, *IMT*.
32. "Notes of Evidence," January 18 and 30, 1946, vol. 2, pp. 4, 49, Box 3, *F. B. Papers*.
33. *Birkett,*p. 506.
34. January 30, 1945, vol. 6, p. 341. *IMT*.
35. *Birkett*, pp. 505 f. "Notes of Evidence," February 12 f., pp. 93 f., vol. 2, Box 3, *F. B. Papers*.
36. "Note on Interview with Justice Jackson, by P. Dean," October 24, 1945, FO 371/50992/8625, *FO*.
37. *Scott Fox to P. Dean*, November 4, 1945, FO 371/50994/9004 and Minutes of the Prosecutors Meeting, November 16, 1945, FO 371/50998/9491, *FO*.
38. "Notes of Evidence," June 4, 1946, vol. 4, Box 4, *F. B. Papers*.
39. A large number of such references are cited below in chapters 7, 8, and 9.
40. See, for example, Biddle's comments on the testimony of Franz Blaha, a former concentration camp inmate. "Notes of Evidence" January 11, 1946, vol. I, Box 3, p. 275, *F. B. Papers*.
41. Even one of the defense attorneys subsequently referred to the decision as "incomprehensible" ("*unbegreiflich.*") [See Steinbauer, *Ich war Verteidiger*, p. 44.]
42. *Birkett*, p. 505. "Notes of Evidence," vol. 2, pp. 29 and 34, Box 3, *F. B. Papers*.
43. *Dean to Scott Fox*, November 26, 1945, FO 371/50996/9388 FO. *Jackson to Byrnes*, November 30, 1945, #1739, /11-3045, *State Department II*.
44. *Dean to Scott Fox*, December 6, 1945, FO 371/51001/9758, *FO*.
45. "Notes of Evidence," December 12, 1945, vol. I, p. 147, Box 3, *F. B. Papers*.
46. "Executive Session Minutes," January 5 and 12, 1946, Box 2, *F. B. Papers*.
47. January 14, 1946, vol. 5, pp. 228–29, *IMT*.
48. *Morgan to Jackson*, February 6, 1946, Box 40, *Chief of Counsel*. This document contains the general views of Assistant Secretary of War Peterson. *Chief of Counsel*, Box 198, is replete with recommendations from the prosecution staffs of the United States and the other Allies.
49. "Memorandum on announcement of the Tribunal of January 14, 1946," by Maxwell Fyfe, January 22, 1946, Box 198, *Chief of Counsel*.
50. *Jackson to Lieutenant Jackson*, February 6, 1946, Box 198, *Chief of Counsel*.
51. Only a cabled summary of Peterson's letter reached Jackson in time. Both the letter and the summary are in Box 14, *Assistant Secretary*.
52. *Jackson to Morgan, for Peterson*, February 26, 1946, Box 198, *Chief of Counsel*.
53. Ibid.
54. Ibid.
55. *Clay to Hilldring*, February 18, 1946, RG 218, U.S. Joint Chiefs of Staff, War Crimes, 000.5, Box 2, Modern Military Branch, The National Archives of the United States.
56. Clay to Peterson, April 8, 1946, Box 14, *Assistant Secretary*. The fact that these and related materials are not included in the important and recently published volumes of General Clay's papers (Jean Edward Smith (ed.), *The Papers of General Lucius D. Clay*, 2 vols. [Bloomington and London; 1974]) should serve as a reminder that no printed collection can hope to provide all the vital materials related to a person who held a really significant position.
57. "Memorandum to Justice Jackson et al.," February 20, 1946, Box 198, *Chief of Counsel*.
58. *Jackson to Morgan et al.*, February 26, 1946, Box 198, *Chief of Counsel*.
59. February 28, vol. 8, pp. 367–68, *IMT*.
60. Ibid., p. 369.
61. Ibid., p. 371.
62. "Notes of Evidence," February 28, 1946, vol. 2, Box 3, pp. 149–50, *F. B. Papers*.
63. March 1, vol. 8, p. 438, *IMT*.
64. Ibid., pp. 453–55.
65. Ibid., pp. 443–44.
66. Ibid., p. 441.

67. Ibid., p. 447.
68. Ibid.
69. Ibid., p. 458.
70. Ibid.
71. Ibid., pp. 464, 465.
72. March 2, vol. 8, p. 482, *IMT.*
73. "Notes of Evidence," March 2, 1945, vol. 2, p. 163, Box 3, *F. B. Papers.*
74. Ibid., March 12, 1946, vol. 3, pp. 26–27, Box 3.
75. March 5, 1946, vol. 8, pp. 532–33, *IMT.*
76. Minutes of the Chief Prosecutors Meeting, December 12, 1945, FO 371/51008/10518, *FO.*
77. Note on an interview with Justice Jackson, October 24, 1945, FO 371/50992/8625, *FO.*
78. "Memorandum by E. L. Woodward," August 2, 1945, FO 371/50985/6534, *FO. Waldcock to Barnes,* September 14, 1945, FO 371/51037/7180, *FO.* P. Dean note on interview with Justice Jackson, October 24, 1945, FO 371/50992/8625, *FO.* Notes of the Meeting of the Chief Prosecutors, October 30, 1945, FO 371/50992/8801, *FO.*
79. *Birkett,* p. 518. *Nikitchenko to the other Tribunal Members,* May 27, 1946, "Memoranda" Folder 1, Box 14, *F. B. Papers.*
80. "Notes of Evidence," May 23, 1946, vol. 4, p. 259, Box 4, *F. B. Papers.*
81. Ibid., May 27, 1946, vol. 4, p. 277, Box 4.
82. Ibid., August 12, 1946, vol. 7, p. 73, Box 5.
83. See, for example, Executive Session Minutes, December 15, 1945, Box 2, *F. B. Papers.*
84. "Notes of Evidence," February 20, 1946, vol. 2, p. 125, Box 3, *F. B. Papers.* Interview with John Phipps, March 21, 1975, London.
85. Interview with John Phipps, March 21, 1975, London.
86. "Notes of Evidence," February 12, 1946, vol. 2, p. 93, Box 3, *F. B. Papers.*
87. *Nikitchenko to the other Tribunal Members,* May 27, 1946, "Memoranda," Folder 1, Box 14, *F. B. Papers.*
88. For the Soviet prosecutor's position, see the Memorandum of May 22, 1946, Box 180, *Chief of Counsel.* For the Tribunal's decision, see Notes of IMT meeting, April 6, 1945, Box 2, *F. B. Papers.*
89. G. M. Gilbert, *Nuremberg Diary* (New York: 1947), pp. 223 f. Carl Haensel, *Das Gericht vertagt sich* (Hamburg: 1950), pp. 86 f.
90. See, for example, FO Minutes, August 18–19, 1945, FO 371/51033/6379, *FO.* Summary of Meeting of the Chief Prosecutors, October 30, 1945, FO 371/50992/8801, *FO.*
91. The copy of the Secret Protocol is in Box 222, *Chief of Counsel.*
92. Haensel, *Das Gericht,* pp. 86 f.
93. Kranzbuehler was subsequently one of the sharpest critics of the trial among the defense attorneys. Otto Kranzbuehler, "Nuremberg Eighteen Years Afterwards," *De Paul Law Review,* XIV, no. 2 (Spring–Summer, 1965), 333–47.
94. *Biddle,* p. 452.
95. Birkett, p. 519.
96. Ibid., p. 520.
97. "Notes of Evidence," July 3, 1946, vol. 5, Box 4; August 22, 1946, vol. 7, Box 5, *F. B. Papers.*
98. "Notes of Evidence," February 4, 1946, vol. 2, Box 3, *F. B. Papers.*
99. Executive Session Minutes, June 24, July 17, and August 27, 1946, Box 2, *F. B. Papers.*
100. *Dean to Scott Fox,* November 26, 1945, FO 371/50996/9388, *FO.*
101. *Birkett,* p. 512.
102. "Notes of Evidence," March 20, 1946, vol. 3, Box 3, *F. B. Papers.*
103. *Birkett,* p. 512.
104. "Notes of Evidence," April 9, 1946, vol. 3, Box 3, *F. B. Papers.*

105. *Birkett*, p. 513.
106. Ibid., p. 517.
107. "Notes of Evidence," May 2, 1946, vol. 4, Box 4, *F. B. Papers.*
108. Ibid., May 3, 1946.
109. *Taylor to Peterson*, May 22, 1946, Box 14, *Assistant Secretary.*
110. *Birkett*, p. 518 f.
111. von der Lippe, *Nürnberger Tagebuchnotizen*, p. 102.
112. Haensel, *Das Gericht*, p. 167.
113. Due to the "war guilt" controversies surrounding the Treaty of Versailles, the Germans had a long history of concern about collective guilt.

Chapter 5

1. Interview with James Rowe, Washington, D.C., May 22, 1975.
2. *Birkett*, p. 515.
3. Ibid., p. 503.
4. Lord Justice Lawrence, "The Nuremberg Trial," *International Affairs*, vol. XXIII, no. 2, (April 1947): 153.
5. "Notes of Evidence," July 27, 1946, vol. 6, Box 4, *F. B. Papers.*
6. *Biddle*, p. 473.
7. Jackson's angry explosion of April 9 was prompted partly by resentment about the special facilities that had been provided for the judges. "Notes of Evidence," April 9, 1946, vol. 3, Box 3, *F. B. Papers.*
8. *Birkett*, pp. 497 f. *Biddle to Wechsler*, July 10, 1946, Correspondence file, Box 1, *F. B. Papers.*
9. Interview with John Phipps, London, March 21, 1975.
10. "Suggested Framework of Judgment," p. 61, Folder 2, Box 14, *F. B. Papers.*
11. December 17–18, 1945, vol. 4, pp. 52 f., *IMT.*
12. *Wechsler to Biddle*, "Memorandum on the Charge Against Organizations," December 5, 1945, The Papers of Herbert Wechsler.
13. Minutes of Executive Session, January 12, 1946, Box 2, *F. B. Papers.*
14. Ibid., May 13, 1946.
15. Ibid.
16. "Notes of Evidence," January 23, 1946, vol. 2, Box 3, *F. B. Papers.*
17. February 25, 1946, vol. 8, pp. 216–23, *IMT.*
18. May 31, 1946, vol. 15, pp. 185 f., *IMT.*
19. Interview with Dean Adrian Fisher, Washington, D.C., May 1, 1975.
20. Ibid. Interview with John Phipps, London, March 21, 1975.
21. *Birkett*, pp. 494 f.
22. "The Form of the Judgment and Opinion (Comment on the President's Memorandum)," April 12, 1946, Papers, of Wechsler.
23. Interviews with John Phipps, London, March 21, 1975, and Dean Adrian Fisher, May 1, 1975.
24. "Memoranda," Boxes 5, 6, and 14, *F. B. Papers.*
25. "Notes on Judgment," p. 1, Folder 3, Box 14, *F. B. Papers.*
26. Ibid. "Suggested Framework of Judgment," Folder 2, Box 14, *F. B. Papers.*
27. Articles XXIV and XXVI, the London Charter, Document 60, p. 428, *Jackson.*
28. "Suggested Framework of Judgment," p. 64, Folder 2, Box 14, *F. B. Papers.*
29. *Francis Biddle to Herbert Wechsler*, July 10, 1946, Correspondence file, Box 1, *F. B. Papers.*
30. "Notes on Judgment," June 27, 1946, pp. 2 f., Folder 3, Box 14, *F. B. Papers. Biddle to Wechsler*, July 10, 1946, Correspondence file, Box 1, *F. B. Papers.*

31. "Notes on Judgment," June 27 and August 14, 1946, pp. 1–3, 13–15, Folder 3, Box 14, *F. B. Papers.* "Draft of Views on Count 1, the Common Plan or Conspiracy," Folder 4, Box 14, *F. B. Papers. "Note à l'occasion du plaidoyer du Professor Jahrreiss,"* (Original French memorandum) Folder 1, Box 14, *F. B. Papers.*

32. *Jackson,* p. 423.

33. "Draft of Views on Count 1, etc.," p. 1, Folder 4, Box 14, *F. B. Papers.*

34. "Notes on Judgment," June 27, 1946, p. 3, Folder 3, Box 14, *F. B. Papers.*

35. "Draft of Views on Count 1, etc.," p. 4, Folder 4, Box 14, *F. B. Papers.*

36. See, for example, von der Lippe, *Nürnberger Tagebuchnotizen,* and Steinbauer, *Ich war Verteidiger* passim.

37. *"Note à l'occasion du plaidoyer,"* p. 10, Folder 1, Box 14, *F. B. Papers.*

38. Ibid., "Notes on Judgment," June 27, 1946, p. 3, Folder 3, Box 14, *F. B. Papers.*

39. Interview with James Rowe, Washington, D.C. May 22, 1945. *Biddle to Wechsler,* July 10, 1946, Correspondence file, Box 1, *F. B. Papers.* "Notes on Judgment," August 14, 1946, p. 13, Folder 3, Box 14, *F. B. Papers.*

40. "Notes on Judgment," August 14, 1946, p. 16, Folder 3, Box 14, *F. B. Papers.*

41. Ibid., August 15, 1946, p. 17.

42. Ibid., pp. 17–18.

43. Justice Lawrence's memorandum on conspiracy (n.d.), Box 15, *F. B. Papers.*

44. "Notes on Judgment," August 14, 1946, p. 12, Folder 3, Box 14, *F. B. Papers.*

45. Ibid., August 15, 1946, p. 17. "Parker Memorandum," "The Common Plan or Conspiracy," August 13, 1946, Box 15, *F. B. Papers.*

46. Parker Memorandum, August 13, 1946, Box 15, *F. B. Papers.*

47. "Notes on Judgment," August 15, 1946, p. 17, Folder 3, Box 14, *F. B. Papers.*

48. Ibid., August 19, 1946, p. 19.

49. *Biddle to Wechsler,* July 10, 1946, Correspondence File, Box 1, *F. B. Papers.*

50. "Notes on Judgment," August 14, 1946, p. 18, Folder 3, Box 14, *F. B. Papers.*

51. "Memorandum of the Soviet IMT Member," July 17, 1946, Folder 1, Box 14, *F. B. Papers.*

52. Parker Memorandum, August 13, 1946, Box 15, *F. B. Papers.*

53. Ibid.

54. "Notes on Judgment," August 15, 1946, p. 18, Folder 3, Box 14, *F. B. Papers.*

55. The London Charter, Article IV (c), Document 60, p. 422, *Jackson.*

56. "Notes on Judgment," August 19, 1946, Folder 3, Box 14, *F. B. Papers.*

57. Parker Memorandum, August 13, 1946, Box 15, *F. B. Papers.*

58. "Notes on Judgment," August 14, 1946, p. 13, Folder 3, Box 14, *F. B. Papers.*

59. Ibid., August 15, 1946, p. 18.

60. Fisher Memorandum, "Conspiracy to Wage Aggressive War," June 22, 1946, Box 5, *F. B. Papers.* Stewart Memorandum, "General Conspiracy" (undated but filed with Fisher's May–June memorandums), Box 6, *F. B. Papers.*

61. "General Conspiracy" Memorandum, pp. 66–67, Box 6, *F. B. Papers.* Notes on Hitler's November 1937 meeting with the Foreign Minister and his service chiefs were kept by Colonel Friedrich Hossbach. For a discussion of the conference and the documentary problems see pp. 139 f.

62. "Persecution of Jews" Memorandum, May 24, 1946, and "Persecution of Jews" as a subsection of "Crimes Against Peace" Memorandum, May 11, 1946, Box 6, *F. B. Papers.*

63. Fisher Memorandum, "Economic Planning and Mobilization for Aggressive War," May 24, 1946(?), p. 103, Box 6, *F. B. Papers.*

64. "Status of the Conspiracy by Mid-1933, etc.," p. 85, Box 6, *F. B. Papers.*

65. "Crimes Against Peace," May 11, 1946, p. 219, Box 6, *F. B. Papers.*

66. "Conspiracy to Wage Aggressive War," June 22, 1946, p. 165, Box 5, *F. B. Papers.*

67. Ibid., p. 168.

68. Ibid., pp. 168–70.

69. Ibid., p. 170.

70. "Suggested Framework of the Judgment of the Tribunal," p. 24, Folder 2, Box 14, *F. B. Papers*.

71. Ibid., pp. 24 and 64.

72. Ibid., p. 62.

73. Ibid., p. 25.

74. *Biddle to Wechsler*, July 10, 1946, Correspondence file, Box 1, *F. B. Papers*.

75. *Biddle*, p. 468. Interview with Wechsler, New York, May 8, 1975. "Notes on Judgment," August 19, 1946, pp. 19–20, Folder 3, Box 14, *F. B. Papers*.

76. "Notes on Judgment," September 4, 1946, p. 30, Folder 3, Box 14, *F. B. Papers*.

77. Biddle's notes do not indicate clearly when final approval was achieved, but in the course of the second week of September, Donnedieu de Vabres overcame his reservations to convict on Count One, which suggests that it probably took place in that time period.

78. *Opinion and Judgment*, pp. 54–56.

79. Ibid., p. 54.

80. Ibid., p. 54. *Dean to the Foreign Office*, November 24, 1945, FO 371/50996/9309, *FO*.

81. *Opinion and Judgment*, p. 54.

82. Ibid.

83. Ibid., p. 55.

84. Ibid.

85. Ibid., pp. 55–56.

86. von der Lippe, *Nürnberger Tagebuchnotizen*, pp. 504, 510, 511.

87. The classic belligerents were probably Alan Bullock in *Hitler; A Study in Tyranny* (London: 1952), and A. J. P. Taylor in *The Origins of the Second World War* (New York: 1961).

88. "Notes on Judgment," July 17, 1946, p. 5, Folder 3, Box 14, *F. B. Papers*.

89. The conference of August 22, 1939. The Tribunal made some allowance in the Judgment for differences in two of the versions, and one, L-3, was not formally submitted in evidence. *Opinion and Judgment*, p. 18.

90. Henrikson Göran, "Das Nürnberger Dokument 386-PS (das 'Hossbach Protokoll')," Lund Studies in International History (2), *Probleme deutscher Zeitgeschichte* (Lund University: 1970).

91. See A. J. P. Taylor, *The Origins of the Second World War*, passim.

92. *Murphy to the Secretary of State*, May 25, 1945, #415, 840.414/5-2545 (United States Political Adviser for Germany), Diplomatic Branch, National Archives of the United States.

93. Ibid., Note on the summary, June 25, 1945, 6-2545, *State Department I*.

94. *Taylor to Jackson*, June 25, 1945, #72234, RG 165, G-1 Personnel, War Crimes, 000.5, Box 313, Federal Records Center, Suitland, Md.

95. Memo of the Joint Intelligence Committee, 301/M, July 7, 1945, RG 218, Combined Chiefs of Staff, War Crimes, 000.5, Box 3, Modern Military Branch, National Archives of the United States.

96. *Griggs to Wenderlin*, September 7, 1945,/9-1145, *State Department I*.

97. The Nuremberg Staff Analysis for the Document 386-PS states the authentication and source of the document correctly. See Nuremberg Staff Analysis files, Modern Military Branch, National Archives of the United States.

Chapter 6

1. *Biddle*, p. 470.

2. "Notes on Judgment," August 8, 1946, p. 10, Folder 3, Box 14, *F. B. Papers*.

3. Ibid., June 27, 1946, p. 2.

4. *Biddle*, p. 466.

Notes

5. See, for example, "Notes on Judgment," September 13, 1946, p. 61, Folder 3, Box 14, *F. B. Papers.*

6. Ibid., August 8, 1946, p. 10.

7. Ibid., July 11, 1946, p. 4. A note on the introductory draft portion says that it was approved on July 10, but this may be a typing error. See Draft, Folder 6, Box 15, *F. B. Papers.*

8. "Notes on Judgment," August 8, 1946, p. 10, Folder 3, Box 14, *F. B. Papers.*

9. Ibid., July 11, 1946, p. 4, and July 20, 1946, pp. 8, 9. Subsequent historical scholarship has cleared the Nazis of responsibility for starting the fire.

10. Ibid., July 11, 1946, p. 4, and September 4, 1946, p. 31.

11. "Suggested Framework of the Judgment of the Tribunal," p. 64, Folder 2, Box 14, *F. B. Papers.*

12. "Notes on Judgment," August 8, p. 10, Folder 3, Box 14, *F. B. Papers.*

13. "Crimes Against Peace," May 11, 1946, pp. 227–28 and 232–33, Box 6, *F. B. Papers.*

14. "Suggested Framework of Judgment," p. 34, pp. 42–43, Folder 2, Box 14; Draft A, pp. 25–30, 42, 43, Folder 5, Box 14; Draft B, pp. 24, 42, 43, Folder 6, Box 14; "Notes on Judgment," August 8, 1946, pp. 10, 11, September 7, 1946, p. 37, Folder 3, Box 14, *F. B. Papers. Opinion and Judgment,* pp. 31, 43–45.

15. See, for example, Raeder testimony, May 17, 1946, Vol. 14, pp. 85–100, *IMT.*

16. On October 24, 1945, Patrick Dean told Justice Jackson that the British Government did not want documents used that disclosed "British military plans (e.g., the invasion of Norway)," *Dean to FO,* October 24, 1945, FO 371/509992/8625, *FO.*

17. "Notes of Evidence," December 7, 1945, vol. 1, p. 126, Box 3. "Notes of Evidence," July 17, 1946, vol. 6, p. 97, Box 4, *F. B. Papers.*

18. "Economic Planning and Mobilization for Aggressive War" (Norway and Denmark), p. 152, Box 6, *F. B. Papers.*

19. "Suggested Framework of the Judgment of the Tribunal," pp. 36–39, Folder 2, Box 14; "Draft A," pp. 31–36, Folder 5, Box 14, *F. B. Papers.*

20. "Notes on Judgment," July 17, 1946, p. 5, Folder 3, Box 14, *F. B. Papers.*

21. Ibid.

22. "Notes on Judgment," August 8, 1946, p. 10, Folder 3, Box 14, *F. B. Papers.* There are two unidentified pages of redrafts on Norway in folder 7, Box 14, *F. B. Papers. Opinion and Judgment,* pp. 34–38.

23. "Economic Planning and Mobilization for Aggressive War" (Greece and Yugoslavia), pp. 163–65, Box 6, *F. B. Papers.*

24. "Suggested Framework of the Judgment," pp. 40–42, Folder 2, Box 14; Draft A, p. 42, Folder 5, Box 15, *F. B. Papers.*

25. "Notes on Judgment," July 17, 1946, pp. 5–7, Folder 3, Box 14, *F. B. Papers. Opinion and Judgment,* pp. 40–43. Probably the most blatant act of Allied "aggression" during World War II was the occupation of Iran, ostensibly to forestall a German invasion, but this incident was not mentioned at Nuremberg.

26. December 10, 1945, vol. 3, pp. 388–90, *IMT.*

27. "Economic Planning and Mobilization for Aggressive War," pp. 181–84, Box 6, *F. B. Papers.*

28. Draft A, p. 48, Folder 5, Box 14, *F. B. Papers.*

29. "Notes on Judgment," September 9, 1946, p. 38, Folder 3, Box 14, *F. B. Papers. Opinion and Judgment,* pp. 45–46.

30. "Suggested Framework of the Judgment of the Tribunal," p. 8, Folder 2, Box 14, *F. B. Papers.*

31. "Notes on Judgment," June 27, 1946, pp. 1–2, September 2, 1946, p. 21, Folder 3, Box 14, *F. B. Papers.*

32. *Biddle to Wechsler,* July 10, 1946, Correspondence file, Box 1, *F. B. Papers.* Interview with James Rowe, Washington, D.C., May 22, 1975.

33. "Notes on Judgment," September 2, 1946, p. 21, Folder 3, Box 14, *F. B. Papers*. Kelsen and his followers subsequently lavished criticism on the trial; see, for example, Hans Kelsen, "Will the Judgment in the Nuremberg Trial Constitute a Precedent in International Law?" *International Law Quarterly*, I, no. 2 (Summer 1947): 153–71.

34. Section IB (E), The Law of the Charter, *Opinion and Judgment*, pp. 48–49.

35. Section IV (E), *Opinion and Judgment*, p. 51.

36. Ibid., pp. 50–51.

37. "Notes on Judgment," August 15, 1946, p. 17, Folder 3, Box 14, *F. B. Papers*.

38. For a defense appreciation of Taylor, see von der Lippe, *Nürnberger Tagebuchnotizen* p. 86. For Biddle's praise of Lastner, see "Notes of Evidence," August 21, 1946, vol. 7, p. 97, Box 5, *F. B. Papers*. It should be recognized that both General William Donovan and the British Government opposed prosecution of the General Staff. Cabinet Conclusions 38 (45), October 9, 1945 (in FO 371/50989/8048, *FO*). Donovan to Jackson, November 27, 1945 (attached to *Jackson to HST*, December 1, 1945,/12-1045 *State Department I*).

39. Executive Session Minutes, December 20, 1945 and January 14, 1946, Box 2, *F. B. Papers*.

40. December 19, 1945, vol. 4, p. 138, *IMT*.

41. Ibid.

42. Organization Memos, Reich Cabinet, p. 36, Box 5, *F. B. Papers*.

43. Organization Memos, SS, Box 5, *F. B. Papers*.

44. Organization Memos, Gestapo/SD, pp. 88–89, Box 5, *F. B. Papers*.

45. Organization Memos, "Leadership Corps" of the Nazi party, Box 5, *F. B. Papers*.

46. Organization Memos, General Staff and High Command, Box 5, *F. B. Papers*.

47. *Biddle*, p. 469.

48. "Notes on Judgment," September 13, 1946, p. 59, Folder 3, Box 14, *F. B. Papers*.

49. Ibid., p. 61.

50. Ibid., September 3, 1946, p. 26, September 13, 1946, p. 59.

51. Ibid., September 3, 1946, p. 26.

52. Ibid., pp. 26–28.

53. *Biddle*, p. 470.

54. "Notes on Judgment," September 3, 1946, p. 28, Folder 3, Box 14, *F. B. Papers*.

55. Ibid., September 13, 1946, p. 63.

56. Ibid., p. 61.

57. Ibid., p. 62.

58. Ibid.

59. Ibid., p. 63. (Although the speaker's identity is not specified for this paragraph, it must have been Donnedieu de Vabres).

60. "Law as to the Accused Organizations," August 9, 1946, Box 15, *F. B. Papers*.

61. "Notes on Judgment," September 13, 1946, p. 60, Folder 3, Box 14, *F. B. Papers*.

62. Ibid., p. 63.

63. *Opinion and Judgment*, p. 85.

64. Ibid., pp. 85–86.

65. "Notes on Judgment," September 26, 1946, p. 66, Folder 3, Box 14, *F. B. Papers*.

66. *Opinion and Judgment*, p. 104.

67. Ibid., p. 107.

68. Ibid.

69. See Bradley F. Smith and Agnes F. Peterson (eds.), *Himmler Geheimreden* (Frankfurt am Main: 1974).

70. *Opinion and Judgment*, pp. 97–102.

71. Ibid., pp. 91–97.

72. "Notes of Evidence," August 29, 1946, vol. 7, Box 5, *F. B. Papers*.

73. *Opinion and Judgment*, pp. 87–91.

74. "Notes on Judgment," passim.
75. Ibid., pp. 180–83.
76. Ibid., pp. 183–88.

Chapter 7

1. "Notes of Evidence," November 22, 1945, p. 26, vol. 1, Box 3, *F. B. Papers*.
2. "Notes on Judgment," Folder 3, Box 14, *F. B. Papers*.
3. Ibid., September 9, 1946, pp. 38 and 43.
4. Ibid., September 2, 1946, p. 21, and September 10, 1946, p. 46.
5. Ibid., September 10, 1946, pp. 45, 46.
6. Ibid., September 2, 1946, p. 24.
7. Ibid., September 4, 1946, p. 30.
8. "Memorandum for the General Secretary," October 20, 1945, p. 1, LCO 2/2982/x/j. 7320, *LCO*.
9. *Scott Fox to Dean*, November 4, 1945, FO 371/50994/9004, *FO*.
10. PID list, April 10, 1944 and FO list April 27, 1944, FO 371/38993/4791, *FO*. British list, June 19, 1945, LCO 2/2980/x/j. 7320, *LCO*. American list, June 23, 1945, Trial and Punishment File, 4, Box 4, *Bernays*.
11. *Donovan to Jackson*, November 27, 1945, (Enclosure in *Jackson to HST*, December 1, 1945), 12-1045, *State Department II*.
12. Ibid., *Donovan to Jackson*, November 24, 1945.
13. Ibid., *Donovan to Jackson*, November 27, 1945.
14. Ibid., *Jackson to HST*, December 1, 1945.
15. "Notes of Evidence," April 24, 1946, vol. 4, pp. 29–30, Box 4, *F. B. Papers*.
16. One of Justice Jackson's most serious failures was his inability to clearly establish Goering's responsibility for this order, due to quibbling over translation of the word "*Endlösung.*" March 20, 1946, Vol. 9, p. 518–20, *IMT*.
17. "Notes on Judgment," September 2, 1946, p. 21, *F. B. Papers*.
18. Ibid., September 10, 1946, p. 45.
19. Ibid., p. 47.
20. See, for example, *Clark Kerr to FO*, October 16, 1942, #252, /1509, *CAB 21*.
21. PID and FO Lists, April 10 and April 27, 1944, FO 371/38993/4791, *FO*.
22. Note on conversation with General Donovan, June 9, 1945, LCO 2/2980/x/j.7320, *LCO. Dean to Maxwell Fyfe*, June 19, 1945, LCO 2/2980/x/j.7320, *LCO*.
23. Minutes of Meeting of June 21, 1945, LCO 2/2980/x/j.7320, *LCO*. American List, June 23, 1945, Trial and Punishment file 4, Box 4, *Bernays*.
24. The British Records of the eleventh and twelfth Plenary Sessions (July 31–August 1, 1945), FO 371/51032/5974, *FO*.
25. "Notes of Evidence," November 30, 1945, vol. I, p. 80, Box 3, *F. B. Papers*.
26. J. R. Rees (ed.), *The Case of Rudolf Hess* (New York: 1948).
27. "Notes of Evidence," November 30, 1945, vol. 1, p. 80, Box 3, *F. B. Papers*.
28. Ibid.
29. Memorandum on Hess, Box 5, p. 37, *F. B. Papers*.
30. *Opinion and Judgment*, p. 112.
31. "Notes on Judgment," September 2, 1946, p. 21, Folder 3, Box 14, *F. B. Papers*.
32. Ibid., September 10, 1946, p. 47.
33. Ibid.
34. *Opinion and Judgment*, pp. 178–80.
35. PID and FO lists, April 10 and April 27, 1944, FO 371/38993/4791, *FO*.
36. *Kaplan to Wendelin*, June 16, 1945, 6-1645, *State Department I*.

37. Joachim von Ribbentrop, *The Ribbentrop Memoirs* (London: 1954), Introduction.
38. Defendant Memorandum (Ribbentrop), p. 69, Box 5, *F. B. Papers.*
39. See, especially, Raul Hilberg, *The Destruction of the European Jews* (Chicago, 1961).
40. *Birkett*, p. 519.
41. "Notes on Judgment," September 2, 1946, p. 21, Folder 3, Box 14, *F. B. Papers.*
42. Ibid., September 10, 1946, p. 47.
43. Defendant Memorandum (Keitel), especially p. 96, Box 5, *F. B. Papers. Opinion and Judgment*, p. 116–19.
44. F. J. P. Veale, *Advance to Barbarism* (Appleton, Wisconsin, 1953), p. 2.
45. "Memorandum on Keitel, etc.," August 15, 1945, LCO 2/2980/x/j.7320, *LCO.*
46. von der Lippe, *Nürnberger Tagebuchnotizen*, p. 131.
47. Memorandum to the General Secretary, October 20, 1945, p. 2, LCO 2/2982/x/j./7320, *LCO.*
48. *Birkett*, p. 518.
49. Ibid., p. 21. "Notes of Evidence," August 31, 1946, vol. 3, p. 162, Box 5, *F. B. Papers.*
50. "Notes on Judgment," September 2, 1946, p. 22, September 10, 1946, p. 47, Folder 3, Box 14, *F. B. Papers.*
51. Ibid., September 12, 1946, p. 57.
52. See, for example, the OSS report to the Joint Chiefs of Staff, March 27, 1945, "Approaches from Austrian and Bavarian Nazis," CCS, 387, Germany 9.21.44 Sec. 1–4, Modern Military Branch, National Archives of the United States.
53. *Bernays to Harris*, July 17, 1945, Preparation of Evidence File 3, Box 2, *Bernays.*
54. Memorandum for the General Secretary, October 2, 1945, pp. 3–4, LCO 2/2982/x/j. 7320, *LCO.*
55. Haensel, *Das Gericht vertagt*, p. 158.
56. *Birkett*, p. 514. "Notes of Evidence," April 11, 1946, p. 246, Box 3, *F. B. Papers.*
57. Defendant Memorandum (Kaltenbrunner), p. 99, Box 5, *F. B. Papers.*
58. Ibid., pp. 101, 102.
59. "Notes on Judgment," September 2, 1946, pp. 22–23, Folder 3, Box 14, *F. B. Papers.*
60. Ibid.
61. Ibid.
62. "Notes on Judgment," September 10, 1946, p. 47, Folder 3, Box 14, *F. B. Papers.*
63. Ibid.
64. For Rosenberg's late flowering as a relatively efficient Nazi leader, see Reinhard Bollmus, *Das Amt Rosenberg und seine Gegner* (Stuttgart: 1970).
65. January 9, 1946, vol. 5, pp. 41 f., and April 14, 1946, vol. 11, pp. 444 f., *IMT.*
66. Defendant Memorandum (Rosenberg), p. 114, Box 5, *F. B. Papers.*
67. *Opinion and Judgment*, p. 121.
68. Defendant Memorandum (Rosenberg), p. 120–21, Box 5, *F. B. Papers.*
69. *Opinion and Judgment*, p. 122.
70. Defendant Memorandum (Rosenberg), pp. 130–32, *F. B. Papers.*
71. *Opinion and Judgment*, p. 123.
72. "Notes on Judgment," September 2, 1946, p. 22, Folder 3, Box 14, *F. B. Papers.*
73. Ibid., September 10, 1946, p. 48.
74. Ibid., September 11, p. 51.
75. Scott Fox list, June 19, 1945, paragraph 20, FO 371/51027/4958, *FO.*
76. *Dean to Maxwell Fyfe*, June 19, 1945, LCO 2/2980/x/j.7320, *LCO.* June 23, 1945, list, Trial and Punishment file 4, Box 4, *Bernays.*
77. *Birkett*, p. 519.
78. "Notes of Evidence," April 18, 1946, vol. 4, Box 4, *F. B. Papers.*
79. Ibid., July 11, 1946, vol. 6, p. 47.
80. Defendant Memorandum (Frank), pp. 138–42, Box 5, *F. B. Papers.*

81. "Notes on Judgment," September 2, 1946, p. 22, and September 10, p. 48, Folder 3, Box 14, *F. B. Papers.*

82. Ibid., September 10, p. 48.

83. Ibid.

84. PID and FO lists, April 10 and April 27, 1944, FO 371/38993/4791, *FO. Dean to Maxwell Fyfe,* June 19, 1945, LCO 2/2980/x/j.7320, *LCO.* June 23, 1945 list, Trial and Punishment File 4, Box 4, *Bernays.*

85. Defendant Memorandum (Frick), pp. 157, 158, 165–67, Box 5, *F. B. Papers.*

86. *Opinion and Judgment,* pp. 126–29.

87. Defendant Memorandum (Frick), p. 145, Box 5, *F. B. Papers.*

88. Ibid., p. 147.

89. "Notes on Judgment," September 2, 1946, p. 22, Folder 3, Box 14, *F. B. Papers.*

90. Ibid., September 10, 1946, p. 48.

91. Ibid.

92. Ibid.

93. Ibid., September 26, 1946, p. 67.

94. Defendant Memorandum (Streicher), pp. 169, 170, Box 5, *F. B. Papers.*

95. Most of her sharp and often cutting comments on the trial may be found in Rebecca West, *A Train of Powder* (New York: 1955), pp. 3-72.

96. *Dean to Maxwell Fyfe,* June 19, 1945, LCO 2/2980/x/j.7320, *LCO.*

97. *Jackson to McCloy,* June 30, 1945, #38334, May thru file, Box 16, *Assistant Secretary.* British War Crimes Executive Minutes, June 14, 1945, LCO 2/2980/x/j. 7320, *LCO.*

98. "Notes of Evidence," April 26, 1946, vol. 4, p. 56, Box 4 and August 31, 1946, vol. 7, p. 163, Box 5, *F. B. Papers.*

99. Defendant Memorandum (Streicher), p. 178, Box 5, *F. B. Papers.*

100. Ibid.

101. Ibid., p. 179.

102. "Notes on Judgment," September 2, 1946, p. 23, and September 10, 1946, p. 49, Folder 3, Box 14, *F. B. Papers.*

103. Ibid., September 10, 1946, p. 49.

104. Kipphan read a paper entitled "Trial of Julius Streicher: Justice Denied?" at the American Historical Association Meeting in Chicago, 1974.

105. Although this debate has not yet appeared in print very clearly, Eric Goldhagen is an exponent of the former position, while Rudolf Binion may fairly represent the latter.

106. Defendant Memorandum (Funk), p. 187, Box 5, *F. B. Papers.*

107. Ibid., p. 195. *Opinion and Judgment,* pp. 131–32.

108. Defendant Memorandum (Funk), p. 194, Box 5, *F. B. Papers.*

109. Ibid (margin note). *Opinion and Judgment,* p. 133.

110. G. M. Gilbert, *Nuremberg Diary* (New York, 1947), p. 74.

111. Ibid., p. 238.

112. "Notes of Evidence," May 9, 1946, p. 142, vol. 4, Box 4, *F. B. Papers.*

113. Defendant Memorandum (Funk), p. 197, Box 5, *F. B. Papers.*

114. Ibid.

115. *Opinion and Judgment,* pp. 133, 134.

116. Defendant Memorandum (Funk), p. 198, Box 5, *F. B. Papers.*

117. "Notes on Judgment," September 2, 1946, p. 24, Folder 3, Box 14, *F. B. Papers.*

118. Ibid., September 10, 1946, p. 49.

119. Ibid.

120. Ibid.

121. Ibid. September 12, 1946, p. 57.

122. Some officials from the British Foreign Office did see Sauckel as a potential defendant to appease the American desire to prosecute leaders of the German economy. See, for ex-

ample, the FO comments on the second meeting of the British War Crimes Executive, June 21, 1945 (comment dated June 30, 1945), FO 371/51028/5043, *FO*.

123. "Notes of Evidence," May 29, 1946, p. 5, vol. 4, Box 4, *F. B. Papers*.

124. Defendant Memorandum (Sauckel), p. 299, Box 5, *F. B. Papers*.

125. Ibid.

126. Ibid., pp. 296–98. *Opinion and Judgment,* pp. 147–48.

127. Defendant Memorandum (Sauckel), pp. 296, 299, Box 5, *F. B. Papers*.

128. "Notes on Judgment," September 2, 1946, p. 24, Folder 3, Box 14, *F. B. Papers*.

129. Ibid., September 10, 1946, p. 49.

130. von der Lippe, *Nürnberger Tagebuchnotizen,* p. 296.

131. May 31, 1946, vol. 15, pp. 201–5, *IMT*.

132. "Memorandum for the General Secretary," October 20, 1945, p. 12, LCO 2/2982/x/j.7320, *LCO*.

133. Gilbert, *Nuremberg Diary,* p. 433.

134. FO list, April 27, 1944, FO 371/38993/4791, *FO,* and FO list June 19, 1945, FO 371/51027/4958, *FO*.

135. Alderman, p. 87.

136. "Memorandum for the General Secretary," October 20, 1945, p. 10, LCO 2/2982/x/j.7320, *LCO*.

137. Minutes of the Meeting of the Chief Prosecutors, October 30, 1945, FO 371/50992/8801, FO.

138. Ibid.

139. *Birkett,* p. 518.

140. "Notes of Evidence," June 6, 1946, p. 80, vol. 4, Box 4, *F. B. Papers*.

141. Ibid., August 31, 1946, p. 167, vol. 7, Box 5, *F. B. Papers*.

142. Defendant Memorandum (Jodl), Box 5, *F. B. Papers*.

143. Ibid., p. 304.

144. "Notes on Judgment," September 2, 1946, p. 23, Folder 3, Box 14, *F. B. Papers*.

145. Ibid., September 10, 1946, p. 49.

146. Ibid., September 12, 1946, p. 57.

147. Defendant Memorandum (Seyss-Inquart), Box 5, p. 325, *F. B. Papers*.

148. PID list, April 10, 1944 FO 371/38993/4791, *FO*. FO list June 19, 1945, FO 371/51027/4958, *FO*.

149. June 23, 1945 list, Trial and Punishment file 4, Box 4, *Bernays*.

150. Defendant Memorandum (Seyss-Inquart), p. 325, Box 5, *F. B. Papers*.

151. Ibid., p. 328.

152. "Notes on Judgment," September 2, 1946, p. 23, Folder 3, Box 14, *F. B. Papers*.

153. Ibid., September 10, 1946, p. 50.

Chapter 8

1. Memorandum for the General Secretary, October 20, 1945, p. 12, LCO 2/2982/x/j. 7320, *LCO*.

2. PID list, April 10, 1944, FO list, April 27, 1944, FO 371/38993/4791, *FO*. June 23, 1945 list, Trial and Punishment file 4, Box 4, *Bernays*.

3. Defendant Memorandum (Speer), Box 5, *F. B. Papers*.

4. Ibid., p. 345.

5. Ibid., pp. 342, 343.

6. Ibid., p. 332.

7. Ibid.

8. Ibid., p. 331.

9. "Notes of Evidence," June 19, 1946, p. 191, vol. 4, Box 4, *F. B. Papers.*

10. "Notes on Judgment," September 10, 1946, p. 50, Folder 3, Box 14, *F. B. Papers.*

11. Speer to Jackson, November 17, 1945, Box 184, *Chief of Counsel.*

12. Ibid.

13. Ibid.

14. Ibid.

15. Ibid.

16. "Notes on Judgment," September 2, 1946, p. 25, Folder 3, Box 14, *F. B. Papers.*

17. Ibid., September 10, 1946, p. 50.

18. Ibid., September 11, 1946, p. 51.

19. *Dean to Maxwell Fyfe,* June 19, 1946, LCO 2/2980/x/j.7320, *LCO.* June 23, 1945 list, Trial and Punishment file 4, Box 4, *Bernays; Alderman,* p. 87.

20. *Monigan to Amen,* October 4, 1945, Box 180, *Chief of Counsel.*

21. *Birkett,* p. 520. Defendant Memorandum (Neurath), p. 358, Box 5, *F. B. Papers.*

22. von der Lippe, *Nürnberger Tagebuchnotizen,* p. 340.

23. "Notes of Evidence," July 26, 1946, p. 193, vol. 6, Box 4, *F. B. Papers.*

24. Ibid., July 23, 1946, p. 160, vol. 6.

25. Defendant Memorandum (Neurath), Box 5, p. 358, *F. B. Papers.*

26. Ibid., p. 365.

27. Ibid., p. 366.

28. Ibid.

29. See especially the Chanler-Jessup exchanges on the legal implications of unconditional surrender, January–July 1945, Charles Fahy Papers, RG 59, Box 31, Franklin D. Roosevelt Library, Hyde Park.

30. Defendant Memorandum (Neurath), p. 366, Box 5, *F. B. Papers.*

31. *Opinion and Judgment,* p. 160.

32. "Notes on Judgment," September 2, 1946, p. 25, Folder 3, Box 14, *F. B. Papers.*

33. Ibid., September 11, 1946, p. 51.

34. Ibid. One is made a bit uneasy by the fact that Biddle spelled the general's name "Fritzsche"—could he have confused him with the Propaganda Ministry official who was a defendant?

35. Ibid.

36. Ibid.

37. Ibid. von der Lippe, *Nürnberger Tagebuchnotizen,* p. 521.

38. PID list, April 10, 1944; FO list, April 27, 1944, FO 371/38993/4791, *FO.* List of August 15, 1945, *Bernays to Jackson,* Secret Evidence file, Box 3, *Bernays.*

39. *Alderman,* p. 87.

40. Notes on Organizational sessions, October 16/17, 1946, Box 1, *F. B. Papers.*

41. Ibid.

42. "Notes on Conference," November 16, 1945, Box 1, *F. B. Papers.*

43. *Opinion and Judgment,* p. 166. There is no defendant memorandum for Bormann in the Biddle papers.

44. "Notes on Judgment," September 2, 1946, p. 23, Folder 3, Box 14, *F. B. Papers.*

45. Ibid., September 11, 1946, p. 51.

46. Ibid.

47. *Opinion and Judgment,* p. 166.

48. PID list, April 10, 1944 and FO list April 27, 1944, FO 371/38993/4791, *FO.*

49. *Dean to Maxwell Fyfe,* June 19, 1945, LCO 2/2980/x/j./7320, *LCO,* and June 23, 1945 list, Trial and Punishment file 4, Box 4, *Bernays.*

50. June 23, 1945 list, (enclosure,) Trial and Punishment file 4, Box 4, *Bernays. Alderman,* p. 87.

51. Henriette von Schirach, *Der Preis der Herrlichkeit* (Wiesbaden: 1956).

52. "Notes on Judgment," August 14, 1946, p. 113, Folder 3, Box 14, *F. B. Papers*.
53. "Notes of Evidence," May 23, 1946, p. 259, Vol. 4, Box 4, *F. B. Papers*.
54. Ibid. (Biddle, in error, wrote "WMCA boy.")
55. Defendant Memorandum (Schirach), p. 278, Box 5, *F. B. Papers*.
56. Ibid., p. 279.
57. Ibid., pp. 279–80.
58. Ibid., p. 280.
59. Ibid., p. 293.
60. Ibid., pp. 393, 394.
61. Ibid., pp. 282–84.
62. "Notes on Judgment," September 9, 1946, p. 42, Folder 3, Box 14, *F. B. Papers*.
63. Ibid., September 11, 1946, pp. 51–52.
64. Ibid.
65. Ibid., p. 52.
66. Ibid.
67. Ibid.
68. Baldur von Schirach, *Ich glaubte an Hitler* (Hamburg: 1967), pp. 292, 293.
69. Ibid., pp. 296 f.
70. Ibid. Smith and Peterson (eds.), *Himmler Geheimreden*, pp. 162–182.
71. PID list, April 10, 1944, and FO list April 27, 1944, FO 371/38993/4791, *FO. Dean to Maxwell Fyfe*, June 19, 1945, LCO 2/2980/x/j.7320,*LCO.* June 23, 1945 list, Trial and Punishment file 4, Box 4, *Bernays.*
72. *Alderman*, p. 87.
73. *Opinion and Judgment*, p. 143.
74. Ibid., p. 144.
75. Defendant Memorandum (Raeder), p. 269, Box 5, *F. B. Papers. Opinion and Judgment*, p. 144.
76. Ibid., p. 267.
77. Ibid., p. 269.
78. See, for example, "Notes of Evidence," May 16, 1946, vol. 4, Box 4, *F. B. Papers*.
79. *Birkett*, p. 518. "Notes of Evidence," July 3, 1946, vol. 5, Box 4, *F. B. Papers*.
80. Compare the mid-1946 sections of "Notes of Evidence" (vol. 4, Box 4, *F. B. Collection*) with the same period in von der Lippe, *Nürnberger Tagebuchnotizen*.
81. "Notes on Judgment," September 9, 1946, p. 41, Folder 3, Box 14, *F. B. Papers*.
82. Ibid., September 11, 1946, p. 52.
83. Minutes of the Meeting of May 29, 1945, LCO 2/2980/x/j.7320, *LCO*.
84. *Dean to Maxwell Fyfe*, June 19, 1945, LCO 2/2980/x/j.7320, *LCO;* June 19, 1945, FO list, FO 371/51027/4958, *FO*.
85. List of June 23, 1945, Trial and Punishment File 4, Box 4, *Bernays*.
86. Ibid.
87. *Bracken to Jackson*, July 28, 1945, Preparation of Evidence File 3, Box 2, *Bernays*.
88. "Memorandum on Keitel, Doenitz, et al.," August 15, 1945, LCO 2/2980/x/j.7320, *LCO*. August 15, 1945 minutes, FO 371/50986/6718, *FO*.
89. *Waldcock of the Admiralty to Lord Shawcross*, November 1, 1945, FO 371/50992/8833, *FO*.
90. "Memorandum for the General Secretary," October 20, 1945, pp. 12, 13, LCO 2/2982/x/j.7320, *LCO*.
91. Ibid.
92. *Biddle*, p. 452, Interview with James Rowe, Washington, D.C., May 22, 1975.
93. Ibid.
94. *Birkett*, p. 519.
95. "Notes of Evidence," May 10, 1946, vol. 4, p. 164, Box 4, *F. B. Papers*.

96. Ibid., May 16, p. 209.

97. *Biddle*, p. 454. Defendant Memorandum (Doenitz), Box 5, *F. B. Papers.*

98. Defendant Memorandum (Doenitz), p. 32, Box 5, *F. B. Papers.*

99. Ibid., p. 239.

100. Ibid.

101. Ibid., pp. 241, 242.

102. Ibid., p. 242.

103. Ibid., p. 245.

104. Ibid., p. 246.

105. Ibid., p. 247.

106. Ibid., p. 251.

107. Ibid., pp. 249–52.

108. Ibid., pp. 256, 257.

109. Ibid., pp. 257–59.

110. Ibid., pp. 258, 260

111. Ibid., pp. 260, 263.

112. Ibid., pp. 261, 262.

113. Ibid., p. 263.

114. "Notes on Judgment," September 9, 1946, p. 41, Folder 3, Box 14, *F. B. Papers.*

115. Ibid., pp. 38, 39.

116. Ibid., p. 39.

117. Ibid., p. 40.

118. Ibid. *Biddle*, p. 454.

119. "Notes on Judgment," September 9, 1945, p. 41, Folder 3, Box 14, *F. B. Papers.*

120. Ibid., p. 140.

121. Ibid., September 10, 1946, p. 47.

122. Ibid., September 11, 1946, p. 52.

123. Ibid.

124. Ibid.

125. Ibid.

126. *Biddle*, pp. 454, 455. Interview with Adrian Fisher, Washington, D.C., May 1, 1975. Interview with James Rowe, Washington, D.C., May 22, 1975.

127. "Notes on Judgment," September 11, 1946, p. 53, Folder 3, Box 14, *F. B. Papers.*

128. Ibid., p. 53. *Biddle*, p. 455.

129. "Notes on Judgment," September 11, 1946, p. 53, Folder 3, Box 14, *F. B. Papers.*

130. *Opinion and Judgment*, p. 138.

131. Ibid., p. 140.

132. *Biddle*, pp. 455, 456.

133. For Himmler's speech and Doenitz's comments, see Micro copy T-175, RFSS, Roll 91, Frames 3282–3330, Modern Military Branch, National Archives of the United States.

Chapter 9

1. Gilbert, *Nuremberg Diary*, p. 238.

2. *Frankfurter to Jackson*, May 10, 1945, Papers of Felix Frankfurter, Folder 001371, Box 69, Manuscript Division, Library of Congress.

3. PID list, April 10, 1944 and FO list, April 27, 1944, FO 371/38993/4791, *FO.*

4. Minutes of Meeting of May 29, 1945, LCO 2/2980/x/j./7320, *LCO.*

5. Minutes of Meeting of British War Crimes Executive, June 21, 1945, FO 371/51028/5043, *FO.*

6. June 23, 1945 list, Trial and Punishment file 4, Box 4, *Bernays.*

7. "Memorandum on Keitel, Doenitz, Schacht, et al.," August 15, 1945, LCO 2/2980/x/j.7320, *LCO.*

8. Two Foreign Office minutes from the fall of 1945 provide clear indications of the French attitude: Scott Fox minute, October 24, 1945, FO 371/50992/8620, *FO;* and Dean to Scott Fox plus attachments, November 20, 1945, FO 371/50996/9353, *FO. Alderman,* p. 87.

9. "Memorandum for the General Secretary," October 20, 1945, p. 11, LCO 2/2982/x/j./7320, *LCO.*

10. Steinbauer, *Ich war Verteidiger,* p. 40.

11. Enclosure in *Jackson to HST,* December 1, 1945, /12-1045, *State Department I.*

12. Ibid.

13. Ibid. (*Donovan to Jackson,* November 14, 1945).

14. Ibid.

15. Ibid.

16. Ibid.

17. Ibid.

18. Ibid. (*Donovan to Jackson,* November 24, 1945).

19. Ibid. (*Jackson to Donovan,* November 26, 1945).

20. Ibid.

21. Ibid. (*Donovan to Jackson,* November 27, 1945).

22. A large file of this material is in Box 196, *Chief of Counsel.*

23. *Murphy to State Department and Enclosure,* April 9, 1946, /4-946, *State Department I.*

24. Ibid.

25. *Morris to Secretary of State,* June 8, 1941, 740.0011 European War 1939/11763, Diplomatic Branch, National Archives of the United States.

26. Barton Whaley, *Codeword Barbarossa* (Cambridge, Mass.: 1973).

27. *Birkett,* pp. 516–17. "Notes of Evidence," August 31, 1946, p. 164, vol. 7, Box 5, *F. B. Papers.*

28. Defendant Memorandum (Schacht), p. 200, Box 5, *F. B. Papers.*

29. Ibid.

30. Ibid., p. 225.

31. Ibid., p. 233.

32. Interview with John Phipps, London, March 21, 1975.

33. Defendant Memorandum (Schacht), p. 233, Box 5, *F. B. Papers.*

34. "Notes on Judgment," September 6, 1946, p. 32, Folder 3, Box 14, *F. B. Papers.*

35. Ibid.

36. Ibid., pp. 32, 33.

37. Ibid., p. 33.

38. Ibid., p. 34.

39. Ibid., p. 32.

40. Ibid.

41. Ibid., p. 33.

42. "Notes on Judgment," September 10, 1946, p. 49, Folder 3, Box 14, *F. B. Papers.*

43. Ibid., September 12, 1946, p. 54.

44. Ibid.

45. Ibid., p. 55.

46. Ibid.

47. Ibid.

48. Ibid.

49. Ibid.

50. Ibid., September 13, 1946, p. 58.

51. Ibid.

52. Ibid.

Notes

53. Ibid., pp. 58, 59. Biddle discusses the case in his memoirs; see *Biddle,* p. 475.
54. Interrogation of Franz von Papen, April 16, 1945, Box 110, Dwight D. Eisenhower *Papers,* 1916–52, Dwight D. Eisenhower Library, Abilene, Kansas.
55. Although the issue of a redoubt or of possible *Werwolf* resistance agitated some Allied government authorities, the highest-level American Army view was that there would be a collapse, with only isolated pockets of resistance. See *General Marshall to the President,* April 2, 1945, "Probable Developments in the German Reich," Naval Aides Germany file, Map Room, Box 167, Franklin D. Roosevelt Library, Hyde Park.
56. PID list, April 10, 1944, FO 371/38993/4791, *FO.*
57. Minutes of Meeting of May 29, 1945, LCO 2/2980/x/j./7320, *LCO.*
58. FO list of June 19, 1945, paragraph 19, FO 371/51027/4958, *FO.*
59. "Memorandum for the General Secretary," October 20, 1945, pp. 8–9, LCO 2/2982/x/j.7320, *LCO.*
60. *Birkett,* pp. 519–20.
61. "Notes of Evidence," June 19, 1946, p. 186, vol. 5, Box 4, *F. B. Papers.*
62. Ibid., p. 187.
63. Ibid., June 19, 1946, p. 165.
64. Defendant Memorandum (Papen), Box 5, *F. B. Papers.*
65. Ibid., pp. 308, 309.
66. Ibid., p. 309.
67. Ibid., pp. 309, 310.
68. Ibid., p. 315.
69. Ibid., p. 323.
70. "Notes on Judgment," September 6, 1946, p. 35, Folder 3, Box 14, *F. B. Papers.*
71. Ibid., p. 36.
72. Ibid., pp. 34, 35.
73. Ibid., p. 35.
74. Ibid., September 7, 1946, p. 37.
75. Ibid., September 12, 1946, pp. 55, 56.
76. Ibid., p. 56.
77. Ibid.
78. Ibid.
79. Ibid.
80. Ibid.
81. Ibid., pp. 56, 57.
82. *Bernays to Jackson,* and enclosure, August 15, 1945, Secret Evidence file 3, Box 3, *Bernays.* The only other name of note missing from the list was Eichmann's.
83. Defendant Memorandum (Fritzsche), p. 369, Box 5, *F. B. Papers.*
84. Ibid., p. 370.
85. Ibid.
86. "Notes on Judgment," September 10, 1946, p. 44, Folder 3, Box 14, *F. B. Papers.*
87. Ibid., p. 45.
88. Ibid., p. 44.
89. Ibid., p. 45.
90. Ibid., September 11, 1946, p. 53.
91. Ibid.
92. Ibid., September 12, 1946, p. 54.
93. Ibid.
94. Ibid.
95. Ibid.
96. Ibid.
97. Ibid.

98. Ibid.
99. Steinbauer, *Ich war Verteidiger,* p. 22.

Chapter 10

1. June 19, 1945, list and minute, FO 371/51027/4958, *FO.*
2. Adjutant General War Department (AGWAR), to United States Forces, European Theater (USFET), September 26, 1946, #WX 80525, RG 260, Office of Military Government, U.S., "War Crimes," 000.5, Box 946, Federal Records Center, Suitland, Md.
3. Ibid.
4. AGWAR to Office, Military Government, United States (OMGUS), October 6, 1946, #W82421, RG 260, OMGUS, War Crimes, 000.5, Box 946, Federal Records Center, Suitland, Md.
5. Ibid.
6. Haensel, *Das Gericht vertagt,* p. 239.
7. See, for example, Steinbauer, *Ich war Verteidiger,* p. 43, and von der Lippe, *Nürnberger Tagebuchnotizen,* p. 510.
8. Both Broszat and Hans Mommsen advanced this position at a recent conference on the Nuremberg trial, held by the National Archives, "The Nuernberg War Crimes Trials Today: History, Law, Morality," March 13, 14, 1975 (unpublished).
9. Speech to the London County Council, July 14, 1941.
10. Bernays to his wife, July 22, 1945, Personal letter file, Box 4, *Bernays.* Similar, though often undated, letters are in the James Donovan collection at the Hoover Institution.
11. John Mendelsohn, "Trial by Document: The Problem of Due Process for War Criminals at Nuernberg," *Prologue,* VII 7, no. 4 (Winter 1975): pp. 227–34.
12. *Trials of War Criminals Before the Nuernberg Military Tribunals,* Nuremberg, 1949, 15 vols.

BIBLIOGRAPHICAL ESSAY

Since this volume touches on issues related to Allied wartime policy and the general history of Nazi Germany, as well as to the Nuremberg trial, it is impossible to provide a comprehensive bibliography. Each of these subjects has an enormous literature and a combination of the three would equal a small library. Consequently, the following bibliography is restricted to those materials which have been cited or quoted in the text.

Those seeking more extensive bibliographical references to the trial may well find the best source to be William J. Bosch, *Judgment on Nuremberg* (Chapel Hill, North Carolina: 1970). A single comprehensive bibliography on Nazism is more difficult to find, but Joachim Fest's *Hitler* (New York: 1974) lists most recent works. Allied wartime policy has been the object of feverish historical research and controversy in recent years, but there are few volumes of general synthesis. Perhaps the best course to follow is to use the bibliography provided by John W. Wheeler Bennett and Anthony Nicholson in *The Semblance of Peace* (New York: 1974), for traditional works. Current revisionist controversies can be traced in the various historical journals.

UNPUBLISHED MATERIALS

Depositories

Dwight D. Eisenhower Library, Abilene, Kansas.
"Interrogation of Franz von Papen, April 16, 1945." Box 110, Dwight D. Eisenhower Papers, 1916–52.

Federal Records Center, Suitland, Maryland.
War Department, G-1, RG 165. War Crimes, 000.5.
War Department, JAG, RG 153. War Crimes, 000.5.
War Department, OMGUS, RG 260. War Crimes, 000.5.

The Hoover Institution, Stanford University, Stanford, California.
James B. Donovan Collection.

The Justice Department, Washington, D.C.
Files on the background of War Criminal trials.

The Library of Congress, Washington, D.C.
Papers of Joseph E. Davies.
Papers of Felix Frankfurter.

The National Archives of the United States, Washington, D.C.
  Diplomatic Branch
    State Department of the United States, 740.00116. "EW Prosecution."
    State Department of the United States, 740.00116. "EW Illegal and Inhumane Warfare."
    State Department of the United States, 740.0011EW. "1939 European war."
    State Department of the United States, 840.414. "U.S. Political Adviser for Germany."
  Modern Military Branch
    Assistant Secretary of War, RG 107. War Crimes, 000.5.
    Secretary of War, RG 107. War Crimes, 000.5.
    United States Joint Chiefs of Staff, RG 218. War Crimes, 000.5.

Combined Chiefs of Staff, RG 218. War Crimes, 000.5.
United States Chief of Counsel for the Prosecution of Axis Criminality, RG 238.
Combined Chiefs of Staff, 387. "Germany," 9–21–44 f.
Microcopy T–175, RFSS, Roll 91.

Public Records Office, London.
Lord Chancellor's Office, 2/2980–2982, 1944–1945.
Foreign Office, FO Series, 38999–51038.
CAB 21, War Cabinet Committee on War Crimes.
CAB 122, General War Cabinet Material.
CAB 65, War Cabinet Minutes.
CAB 66, War Cabinet Memoranda.

Franklin D. Roosevelt Library, Hyde Park, New York.
Henry Morgenthau, Jr., Diary.
Presidential Secretary's File.
Charles Fahy Papers, RG 59.
Naval Aides Files—"Germany, Map Room."

Syracuse University, Syracuse, New York.
The Francis Biddle Papers.

Harry S. Truman Library, Independence, Missouri.
Papers of Samuel I. Rosenman.
Papers of Harry S. Truman, Official File.

The University of Virginia, Charlottesville, Virginia.
The Papers of Edward Stettinius.

The Papers of Herbert Wechsler (in Wechsler's possession).

The University of Wyoming, Laramie, Wyoming.
Murray C. Bernays Collection.

Yale University, New Haven, Connecticut.
The Diaries of Henry L. Stimson.
The Papers of Henry L. Stimson.

Interviews

Sir Patrick Dean, London, April 2, 1975.
Dean Adrian Fisher, Washington, May 1, 1975.
John Phipps, London, March 21, 1975.
James Rowe, Washington, May 22, 1975.
Herbert Wechsler, New York, May 8, 1975.

Published Documents

Foreign Relations of the United States: The Conference at Quebec,1944 (Washington, D.C.: 1972).
Foreign Relations of the United States: 1945, vol. 3 (Washington, D.C.: 1968).

Bibliographical Essay

Foreign Relations of the United States: Conferences at Malta and Yalta, 1945 (Washington, D.C.: 1955).

Foreign Relations of the United States: The Conference of Berlin (Potsdam), 1945 (Washington, D.C.: 1960).

Jackson, Robert H., *Report of Robert H. Jackson, United States Representative to the International Conference on Military Trials, London, 1945* (Washington, D.C.: 1949).

The Morgenthau Diaries (Germany), 2 vols. (Washington, D.C.: 1967).

Nazi Conspiracy and Aggression: Opinion and Judgment (Washington, D.C.: 1947).

Public Papers of the Presidents: Harry S. Truman (Washington, D.C.: 1962).

Smith, Bradley F., and Peterson, Agnes F. (eds.), *Himmler Geheimreden*, (Frankfurt am Main: 1974).

Smith, Jean Edward (ed.), *The Papers of General Lucius D. Clay*, 2 vols. (Bloomington, Ind., and London: 1967).

Trial of the Major War Criminals before the International Military Tribunal, 42 vols. (Nuremberg: 1947).

Trials of War Criminals Before the Nuremberg Military Tribunals 15 vols. (Nuremberg: 1949).

Books

Biddle, Francis, *In Brief Authority* (New York: 1962).

Bollmus, Reinhard, *Das Amt Rosenberg und seine Gegner* (Stuttgart: 1970).

Bosch, William J., *Judgment on Nuremberg* (Chapel Hill, N.C.: 1970).

Bullock, Alan, *Hitler: A Study in Tyranny* (London: 1952).

Davidson, Eugene, *The Trial of the Germans* (New York: 1966).

Dennett, Raymond, and Johnson, Joseph E. (eds.), *Negotiating with the Russians* (contains Sidney S. Alderman, "Negotiating the Nuremberg Trial Agreements, 1945") (n.p.: 1951).

Feingold, Henry L. *The Politics of Rescue* (New Brunswick, New Jersey: 1970).

Fest, Joachim, *Hitler* (New York: 1974).

Gerhart, Eugene C., *America's Advocate: Robert H. Jackson* (Indianapolis and New York: 1958).

Gilbert, G. M., *Nuremberg Diary* (New York: 1947).

Haensel, Carl, *Das Gericht vertagt sich* (Hamburg: 1950).

Harris, Whitney R., *Tyranny on Trial* (Dallas, 1954).

Hilberg, Raul, *The Destruction of the European Jews* (Chicago: 1961).

Hyde, H. Montgomery, *Norman Birkett* (London: 1964).

Knieriem, August von, *The Nuremberg Trials* (Chicago: 1959).

Lippe, Viktor Freiherr von der, *Nürnberger Tagebuchnotizen* (Frankfurt am Main: 1951).

Mc Coy, Donald R., and Zobrist, Benedict K. (eds.), *Conference of Scholars on the Administration of Occupied Areas, 1943–1955*, April 10–11, 1970, at the Harry S. Truman Library (Independence, Mo.: 1970).

Rees, J. R. (ed.), *The Case of Rudolf Hess* (New York: 1948).

Ribbentrop, Joachim von, *The Ribbentrop Memoirs* (London: 1954).

Schirach, Baldur von, *Ich glaubte an Hitler* (Hamburg: 1967).

Schirach, Henriette von, *Der Preis der Herrlichkeit* (Wiesbaden: 1956).

Speer, Albert, *Spandau: The Secret Diaries* (New York: 1976).

Steinbauer, Gustav, *Ich war Verteidiger in Nürnberg* (Klagenfurt: 1950).

Taylor, A. J. P. *The Origins of the Second World War* (New York: 1961).

Taylor, Telford, *Nuremberg and Vietnam: An American Tragedy* (New York: 1970).

Veale, F. J. P., *Advance to Barbarism* (Appleton, Wisconsin: 1953).

West, Rebecca, *A Train of Powder* (New York: 1955).

Whaley, Barton, *Codeword Barbarossa* (Cambridge, Massachusetts: 1973).

Wheeler Bennett, John W., and Nichols, Anthony, *The Semblance of Peace* (New York: 1974).

Woetzel, Robert K., *The Nuremberg Trials in International Law* (London and New York: 1962).

Articles

Göran, Henrikson, "Das Nürnberger Dokument 386-PS (das "Hossbach-Protokoll)," *Lund Studies in International History* (2), *Probleme deutscher Zeitgeschichte* (Lund University: 1970).

Jackson, Robert H., "The Rule of Law Among Nations," *American Bar Association Journal*, XXXI: (June, 1945) 290–94.

Kelsen, Hans, "Will the Judgment in the Nuremberg Trial Constitute a Precedent in International Law?" *The International Law Quarterly*, I, no. 2: (Summer, 1947) 153–71.

Kranzbuehler, Otto, "Nuremberg Eighteen Years Afterwards," *De Paul Law Review*, XIV, no. 2: (Summer–Spring, 1965) 333–47.

Lawrence, Lord Justice, "The Nuremberg Trial," *International Affairs*, XXIII, no. 2: (April, 1947) 153–54.

Mendelsohn, John, "Trial by Document: The Problem of Due Process for War Criminals at Nuernberg," *Prologue*, VII, no. 4: (Winter, 1975) 227–34.

Robinson, Jacob, "The International Military Tribunal and the Holocaust: Some Legal Reflections," *Israel Law Review*, VII, no. 1: (Winter, 1972), pp. 1–13.

INDEX

Index